Cognitive Aging and the Federal Circuit Courts

Cognitive Aging and the Federal Circuit Courts

How Senescence Influences the Law and Judges

RYAN C. BLACK
Michigan State University

RYAN J. OWENS
Florida State University

PATRICK C. WOHLFARTH
University of Maryland, College Park

OXFORD
UNIVERSITY PRESS

OXFORD
UNIVERSITY PRESS

Oxford University Press is a department of the University of Oxford. It furthers the University's objective of excellence in research, scholarship, and education by publishing worldwide. Oxford is a registered trade mark of Oxford University Press in the UK and in certain other countries.

Published in the United States of America by Oxford University Press
198 Madison Avenue, New York, NY 10016, United States of America.

Library of Congress Cataloging-in-Publication Data
Names: Black, Ryan C., 1982– author. | Owens, Ryan J., 1976– author. | Wohlfarth, Patrick C., author.
Title: Cognitive aging and the federal circuit courts : how senescence influences the law and judges / [edited by] Ryan C. Black, Michigan State University; Ryan J. Owens, Florida State University; Patrick C. Wohlfarth, University of Maryland, College Park.
Description: First edition. | New York : Oxford University Press, 2024.
Identifiers: LCCN 2024024853 (print) | LCCN 2024024854 (ebook) | ISBN 9780197747025 (hardback) | ISBN 9780197747032 (epub)
Subjects: LCSH: Judicial process—United States. | Circuit courts—United States. | Appellate courts—United States | United States. Court of Appeals (Federal Circuit) | Clerks of court—United States. | Neurosciences—Law and legislation—United States. | Cognition—Age factors. | Aging—Physiological aspects.
Classification: LCC KF8751 .C64 2024 (print) | LCC KF8751 (ebook) | DDC 347.73/24019—dc23/eng/20240604
LC record available at https://lccn.loc.gov/2024024853
LC ebook record available at https://lccn.loc.gov/2024024854

DOI: 10.1093/oso/9780197747025.001.0001

To Dick and Sally. – RCB

To Karen. – RJO

To Emily, Vance, and Hazel. – PCW

Acknowledgments

We wish to thank a number of people who have helped on this project, which lasted far longer than any of us expected and during which we have aged cognitively—with perhaps some noticeable effects. We thank Miles Armaly, Christy Boyd, David Canon, Matt Cota, Scot Harvath, Rachael Hinkle, Tim Johnson, Jonathan King, Chris Krewson, Elizabeth Lane, Jessica Schoenherr, Marcy Shieh, Logan Strother, and Alex Tahk.

Chapters of this book were presented as papers at the American Political Science Association (2022, 2023), Midwest Political Science Association (2019, 2023), and the Southern Political Science Association (2020, 2023). We thank Susan Haire, Matt Hall, Morgan Hazelton, Rachael Hinkle, Kenneth Manning, Wendy Martinek, Ali Masood, and Logan Strother for providing their advice and feedback at those conferences.

We published a subset of the results reported in Chapter 11 in 2023 as part of a special issue of *New Political Science* on "American Constitution in Crisis." We thank Courtenay Daum, the guest editor of that issue, as well as two anonymous reviewers for their helpful feedback on that earlier work.

Black writes the following: I gratefully acknowledge a year-long research leave provided by the Department of Political Science at Michigan State University during the 2020–2021 academic year. I especially thank then-department chair Cory Smidt for advocating on my behalf to obtain this leave during a tumultuous time at MSU. I would like to think the time away provided a long-overdue opportunity to recharge my batteries. I thank both his predecessor, Chuck Ostrom, and successor, Jeff Conroy-Krutz, for their previous and ongoing support, as well.

My dedication is to Dick and Sally Jenkins, who are my father- and mother-in-law. The pairing of these titles along with the underlying topic of the book (i.e., cognitive decline) should *not* be read as to have any sort of hidden or tongue-in-cheek meaning! I am a jackpot winner in the "in-law lottery," and have been delighted to call them family for nearly a quarter century. I am particularly thankful to them for allowing me, Krista, Bailey, and Hunter to "boomerang" to their lake house basement during the first summer and early fall of COVID. They then graciously allowed us to live in their Arizona home that following winter. Since then, their support, understanding, and an endless supply of Rice Krispy Treats supported my contributions to completing this book.

Contents

1
Introduction

Judge Henry Friendly was among the most impressive appellate judges ever to have served on the federal judiciary (Posner 2016; Dorsen 2012). During his 27 years of service (1959–1986) on the United States Court of Appeals for the Second Circuit, he mentored numerous judges and lawyers, including future Chief Justice John Roberts and Attorney General Merrick Garland. After Friendly's death, Chief Justice Warren Burger paid him tribute, declaring: "In my 30 years on the bench, I have never known a [lower court] judge [who was] more qualified to sit on the Supreme Court" (Johnson 1986). Supreme Court justices relied on his perspicacity. They regularly cited Friendly's opinions. Justice Sandra Day O'Connor once stated that "when there was no Supreme Court case on point, she instructed her (law) clerks to find an opinion by Judge Friendly" (Mears 2012). By all accounts, Friendly was a judicial exemplar.

But like all humans, Friendly experienced the effects of cognitive aging. Toward the end of his career, he noted a decline in his reasoning abilities: "I seem to have greater difficulty in making up my mind than formerly" (Dorsen 2012, 341). Five years before Friendly died, he told a colleague: "I have indeed become concerned about slippage; I am conscious that I do not write with the same passion or verve as I did five years ago, and hope that someone will have the kindness to tell me when the time has come to quit" (Dorsen 2012, 341).[1]

Judge Richard Posner, too, was a judicial giant. The most cited judge in U.S. history (Shapiro 2021), Posner served on the Seventh Circuit Court of Appeals from 1981 until he retired in 2017 at the age of 78. Observers consistently rated him as among the most influential judges of his time (Choi and Gulati 2004*a*). Off the bench, he wrote hundreds of books and articles on a variety of topics. On the bench, judges and scholars regularly looked to his opinions for guidance. Like Judge Friendly, Posner wrote opinions that judicial liberals and conservatives seemed equally to respect and to invoke.

But as he aged, Posner also became erratic. After he served nearly 36 years on the bench, he abruptly announced his retirement the day before he left office, telling news outlets that he "was not getting along with the other judges" (Greene 2022). This once great judge simply turned on his heel and walked out the door without warning. Adding to the mystery, Posner published a book, not long before he retired, that relentlessly attacked the U.S. Supreme Court. He called Chief Justice Roberts inept, ridiculed Justice Kagan as "mawkish" in her praise for Justice Scalia (whom he also attacked), and stated: "I don't think [the Court is] well managed and I don't

[1] Unable to overcome the despair he felt from his wife's death, Friendly departed the court when he died by his own hand at the age of 82 (Gewirtz 1987).

Cognitive Aging and the Federal Circuit Courts: How Senescence Influences the Law and Judges.
Ryan C. Black, Ryan J. Owens, Patrick C. Wohlfarth, Oxford University Press. DOI: 10.1093/oso/9780197747025.003.0001

think the Justices are doing a good job" (Posner 2017, 66, 219). Posner always had been outspoken, but these comments were uncharacteristically acerbic. Perhaps it is no surprise that six months after he retired, Posner announced that doctors diagnosed him with Alzheimer's disease, whereupon he checked in to an assisted living facility (Greene 2022).

Judge Pauline Newman was appointed to the U.S. Court of Appeals for the Federal Circuit in 1984. Newman had led a remarkable life to that point. In 1947, she double majored in chemistry and philosophy at Vassar college. She then obtained a Master's Degree from Columbia University and a Ph.D. in chemistry from Yale University. She went on to earn a law degree at New York University.[2] She worked actively in trademark issues and held a series of government and private jobs related to trademark and intellectual property. On top of all that, she worked with President Reagan to create the Federal Circuit, a specialized federal court that would oversee trademark and related disputes. When Reagan appointed her to the court, experts breathed a sigh of relief, knowing that a serious person would serve on the bench.

Fast forward to 2023. At the age of 96, Judge Newman still served as an active judge on that same court. Only now, there were complaints that she was no longer up to the job. Staff and colleagues pointed to "evidence of memory loss, confusion, and lack of comprehension" as well as evidence of paranoia and agitation.[3] Newman's judicial colleagues demanded that she sit for a neurological exam. She refused and asserted that she was still up to the job. Her colleagues disagreed and suspended her from hearing cases for a year (Brittain and Raymond 2023). Whether they possessed the constitutional authority to do so is unclear. What is clear is that there were strong reasons to believe this once great judge lost cognitive capability.[4]

If these three stories suggest that cognitive aging influences the federal judiciary, the following data provide even further reason to believe it. Figure 1.1 shows the longitudinal trends in the distribution of age among all Article III judges from 1789 to early 2024.[5] Within the plot, the thick black line shows, for a given year, the median

[2] See https://www.fjc.gov/history/judges/newman-pauline. All web links included in the book were active and working as of March 2024.

[3] See https://tmsnrt.rs/3EMAOqC.

[4] Other judges have displayed similarly odd behaviors as they aged. As Justice Thurgood Marshall aged, he occasionally slipped and asked stunningly confused questions at oral argument. For instance, in *FTC v. Superior Court Trial Lawyers Association* (1990), he interrupted one lawyer, asking: "Who is in competition with the court?.... Who is in competition with the lawyers?" The audibly confused lawyer stammered: "The... there is no one in competition with the lawyers...." For the next two minutes, Marshall asked a series of perplexing questions until he conceded: "If I appear confused, I am." Justice Sherman Minton once told *Time* magazine: "Worst of all, it's [anemia] gone to my brain. It affects my power to concentrate and think and retain arguments in my mind" (Time 1956). Justice Hugo Black reportedly lost his memory five years before he retired, admitting to colleagues that "[m]y mind isn't as quick" as it had once been (Garrow 2000, 1050). In 2007, District Judge Richard Owen, who was 84 years old, claimed not to know what email was and asked the attorneys for help understanding it. Surprisingly, Owen recently had tried two cases whose outcomes hinged on a series of emails (Goldstein 2011). In other words, in a very brief period of time, Owen had forgotten what emails were.

[5] We obtained the underlying data used to make this figure from the Federal Judicial Center's Biographical Directory of Article III Federal Judges (downloaded on February 21, 2024). Like the FJC, we do not make a distinction between senior versus active judges as many of the former continue to decide cases at all levels (except the Supreme Court) within the federal judicial hierarchy.

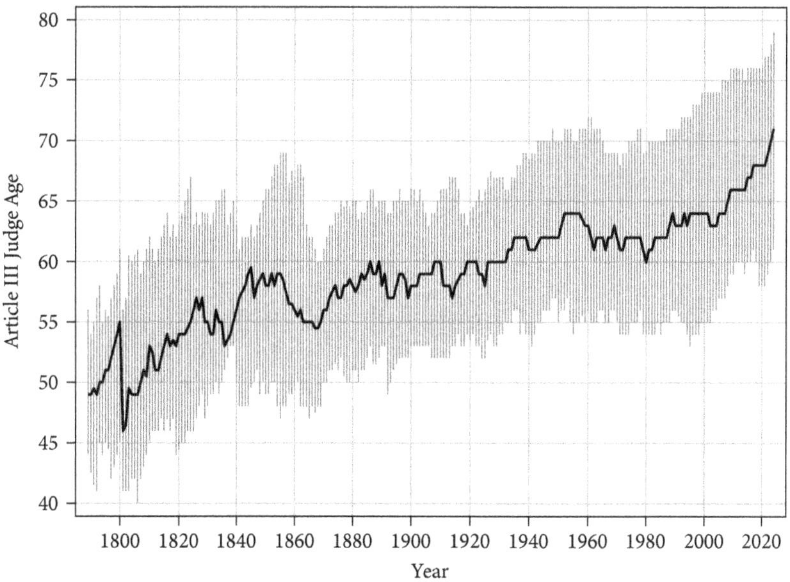

Figure 1.1 Average age of federal judges in the United States, 1789–2020. Vertical lines reflect the 25th and 75th percentiles. Data compiled by the Federal Judicial Center: https://www.fjc.gov/history/exhibits/graphs and maps/age-and-experience-judges.

age of an Article III judge. The vertical line segments show the interquartile range (i.e., the 25th and 75th percentiles). Prior to 2007, the general trend is upward, but with periods where it bounces up or down by a few years. For the twenty-year period from 1988 to 2007, there was considerable stability, with the median age holding at 63 or 64 years old. Since then, however, we observe a marked uptick in judge age. In 2023, the median age of a federal judge hit 70 for the first time in history. The 75th percentile is 78 years old, 10% of federal judges are 85 years or older, and in 21 of the last 28 years there has been at least one federal judge who is 100+ years old (and who would therefore be honored by Smuckers on the Today Show).

Figure 1.2 shows that federal circuit judges remain on the bench longer than ever before. During the 1950s, the average time served by a circuit court judge on the date of his or her termination was 15.3 years. In the 1960s, that average increased to 21.6 years. By the 1990s, judges served 22.9 years when they left; 25.5 years in the 2000s; 29.7 years in the 2010s; and—so far—29.3 years in the 2020s.

What is more, "senior judges" in the federal judiciary continue to proliferate (see, e.g., Aldisert 2013; Burbank, Plager, and Ablavsky 2012). Once federal judges reach 65 years of age and satisfy the "Rule of 80" (i.e., age plus years of service), they are eligible to assume senior status (Yoon 2006). This allows them to continue to decide cases but with a reduced workload and greater control over the types of cases they decide. When a judge takes senior status, that opens up a judicial vacancy for the president to fill. From 2013 to 2018, senior judges participated in roughly 20% of cases across the circuits. Some circuits have used them even more frequently. For instance, the Ninth

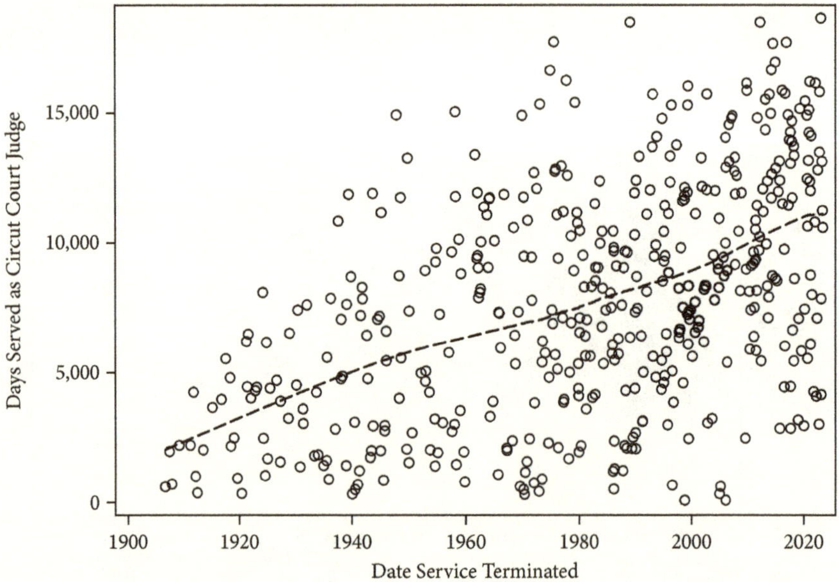

Figure 1.2 Total days served by United States Courts of Appeals judges, 1900–present. For judges who served in multiple circuit court roles (e.g., those who transferred circuits), the data reflect the combined years of service. The data exclude sitting judges (as of May 19, 2023), those who were impeached and removed, and judges who were elevated to the U.S. Supreme Court. Data collected from the Federal Judicial Center: https://www.fjc.gov/history/exhibits/graphs-and-maps/age-and-experience-judges.

Circuit employed senior judges in 36% of its cases in 2017.[6] As Figure 1.3 shows, since 2016, there have been over 600 senior judges serving in the federal judiciary. These trends look to continue. Indeed, as the top portion of Figure 1.4 shows, judges today are serving slightly longer until they take senior status than they did in the past. And as the bottom portion of Figure 1.4 shows, they are serving longer as senior judges than they did in the past.[7]

Cognitive aging effects all people (Gutchess 2019; Cabeza, Nyberg, and Park 2017; Kennedy et al. 2015; Reuter-Lorenz and Park 2014; Turner and Spreng 2011; Park 2000; Salthouse 1996; Weinberg 1989). Judges are people. Therefore, cognitive aging effects judges. And as the judiciary contains older and older judges, we can expect to observe more manifestations of cognitive aging.

Yet, scholars know next to nothing about the consequences of cognitive aging on judges. Only a few studies have investigated the topic. Some examine the conditions under which judges cite other judges' opinions (Bhattacharya and Smyth 2001; Kosma 1998; McCormick 1996; Posner 1995*a*), but they tend not to analyze age

[6] Case statistics come from the Administrative Office of the U.S. Courts: https://www.uscourts.gov/sites/default/files/data_tables/fcms_na_appcp0630.2018.pdf.

[7] Further, a substantial percentage and number of federal judges are dying while in office. For instance, in 2020, over 83% of departures from the federal judiciary came from deaths (35 out of 42 departures).

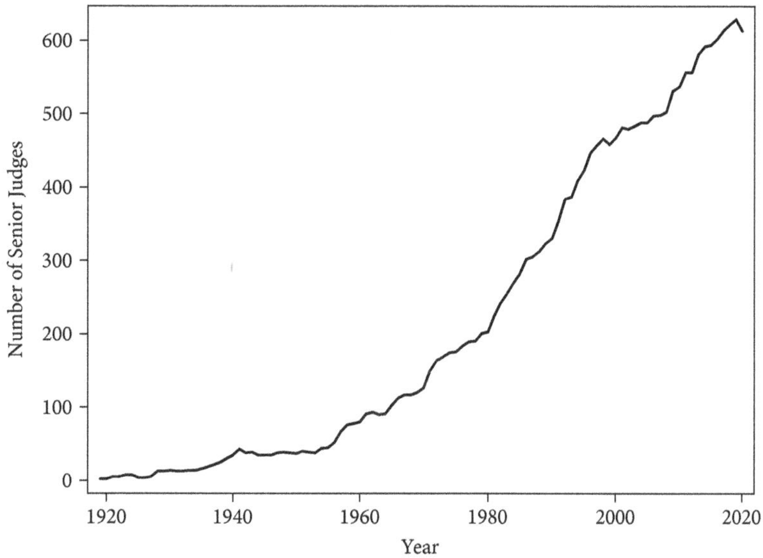

Figure 1.3 Number of senior judges in the United States. Data compiled by the Federal Judicial Center: https://www.fjc.gov/history/exhibits/graphs-and-maps/age-and-experience-judges.

effects. Other scholars evaluate productivity and judge aging (Teitelbaum 2006), or how judges' ideologies change with age (Kaheny, Haire, and Benesh 2008). Others examine whether judges rely on their clerks, with only a glancing reference to whether aging might be the cause (Wahlbeck, Spriggs, and Sigelman 2002). While all of these studies are useful starting points, they simply do not examine the effects of cognitive aging comprehensively. Given the age of today's federal judiciary, not to mention the three examples with which we led, it is time for a systematic look at cognitive aging on judges.

The central effort of this book is to examine the effects of cognitive aging on federal circuit court judges. We undertake a rigorous empirical approach, focusing on a variety of judicial behaviors, including opinion writing, bargaining, voting, and more. We conduct a series of cross-sectional analyses, comparing young versus old judges. And where possible, we employ longitudinal analyses, comparing older judges against their younger selves. We also design and execute novel survey experiments to consider the potential consequences of judge aging on public support for courts, judges, and the prospect of judicial reform.

Our population of interest throughout this book is United States Courts of Appeals judges. This is so for a handful of reasons. First, we focus on federal rather than state judges because unlike judges in nearly every state, federal judges enjoy lifetime tenure. Article III of the U.S. Constitution declares that "The Judges, both of the supreme and inferior Courts, shall hold their Offices during good Behaviour." Federal judges continue in office until death takes them, until they retire, or until Congress impeaches and removes them for treason, bribery, or other high crimes and misdemeanors (Whittington 1999; Tassel 1993). Simply put, because federal judges are entitled to

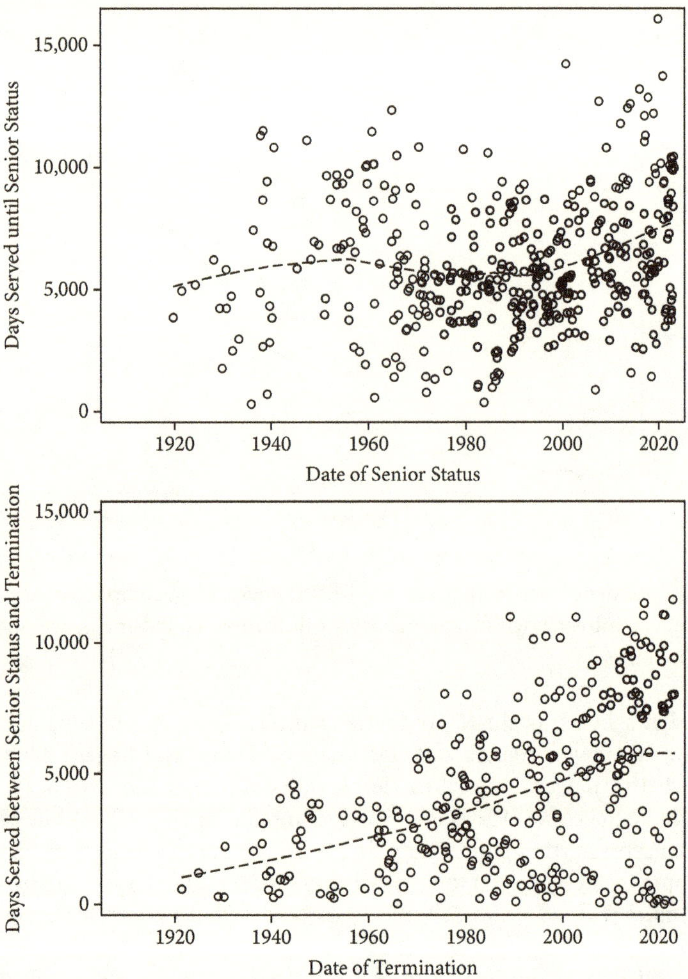

Figure 1.4 Top panel—Total days served between commission and senior status by United States Courts of Appeals judges, 1900–present. Bottom panel—Total days served between senior status and termination by United States Courts of Appeals judges, 1900–present. For judges who served in multiple circuit court roles (e.g., those who transferred circuits), the data reflect the combined years of service. The data exclude sitting judges (as of 5-19-2023), those who were impeached and removed, and judges who were elevated to the U.S. Supreme Court. Data collected from the Federal Judicial Center: https://www.fjc.gov/history/exhibits/graphs-and-maps/age-and-experience-judges.

serve for life—and often do—cognitive aging is more likely to influence them than judges who serve for periodic terms.

Second, because of their workloads, circuit court judges may be unable to mask the effects of cognitive decline. Justices on the United States Supreme Court can hide cognitive decline because they oversee a smaller workload and benefit from a large staff with significant resources. Circuit court judges must decide tens of thousands of cases and with fewer resources, making their cognitive load greater and their decline therefore more detectable.

Third, many people have served as circuit judges in the modern era. According to data from the Federal Judicial Center, around 835 individuals were appointed to a circuit court position from the late 1800s through the early months of 2024. For comparison purposes, there have been just 116 justices over the Supreme Court's entire history. This is an important consideration since although, as we discuss in the pages ahead, cognitive aging eventually affects everyone, there can be considerable variation in its onset and progression.[8]

Finally, because nearly all federal appeals terminate at the circuit-court level, the overall impact of cognitive aging on legal policy may be greatest there. In short, studying how aging effects circuit court judges allows us to understand cognitive aging at an observable and relevant level.

1.1 What Is Cognitive Aging?

We have mentioned cognition and cognitive aging a few times already but have not defined the terms. It turns out that cognition is not an easy concept to define, even for the experts who devote their academic careers to the topic. Most people broadly understand what cognition means—thinking and understanding—but, alas, a concise definition is tricky. Cognition consists of multiple processes and actions that take place in the brain, all of which must "fire" in proper order and timing, and which work together to allow us to perceive and act in the world. It is "a result of coordinated processing among distributed brain regions" (Bennett and Madden 2014, 187). Cognition is "all the processes by which the sensory input is transformed, reduced, elaborated, stored, recovered, and used" (Neisser 1967, 4).

Various cognitive domains combine to form cognition. Among them are: memory, attention, speech and language, visuospatial abilities, processing speed, and executive functioning.[9] And while all of these domains are important, some are more relevant to judging than others. Executive functioning is perhaps the most critical component of cognition for judges. It relates to the cognitive skills necessary to reason, to plan, and to moderate behavior (Baltes 1993). As Harada, Love, and Triebel (2013, 741) put it, executive functioning involves "the ability to self-monitor, plan, organize, reason, be mentally flexible, and solve problems." Processing speed also seems germane to judging. Processing speed focuses on "the speed with which cognitive activities are performed as well as the speed of motor responses" (Harada, Love, and Triebel 2013, 739). Processing speed involves the overall efficiency of the cognitive process. Someone with quick processing speed can take in arguments, evaluate them, and apply them with ease. But processing speed is not just about how quickly people can process information. As Gutchess (2019, 2) notes, "More than simply slowing down how long

[8] This statement should not be read as a reason for scholars to avoid examining the High Court. It simply means that one might expect less precision when examining it.

[9] Psychologists disagree even among themselves over all the cognitive domains that exist, but these are among the most well accepted and understood.

it takes to reach a solution for a problem or retrieve information from memory, speed of processing also could impact the *quality* of information processing" (emphasis in original). Cognition involves multiple domains, but executive functioning and processing speed are crucial for judges.

Cognitive aging, in turn, is simply what happens to people's cognitive capacities as they age. And on this, the literature is clear. Aging (senescence) is correlated with cognitive decline, even among otherwise "healthy" people (Gutchess 2019; Cabeza, Nyberg, and Park 2017; Kennedy et al. 2015; Reuter-Lorenz and Park 2014; Turner and Spreng 2011; Park 2000; Salthouse 1996; Weinberg 1989). Memory, attention, speech and language, visuospatial abilities, processing speed, and executive functioning nearly all show (mostly negative) aging effects (Harada, Love, and Triebel 2013; Reuter-Lorenz and Park 2010). Executive functioning undoubtedly declines with age. Indeed, "[t]here is a sharp decline in executive functioning abilities after the age of 60" (Drag and Bieliauskas 2010, 80). Powell (1994) finds that reasoning is an "early casualt[y] of the aging process" (86). Similarly, Salthouse (1991) finds significant declines in inductive reasoning (among other aspects of cognition) as individuals age. Further, slow processing speed is one of the most notable effects of cognitive aging (Harada, Love, and Triebel 2013). Studies have shown that people older than 55 have a 20% to 40% slower comprehension than people younger than 55 (Backes-Gellner, Schneider, and Veen 2011, 1106). Older adults simply take longer to process ideas and thoughts than younger adults (Salthouse 1996).

To be sure, aging does not lead *only* to negative cognitive outcomes, nor does it effect everyone uniformly. Research has shown tremendous plasticity in the brain and the brain's ability to adapt. For example, the brain can undertake certain compensatory actions (such as engaging both hemispheres) to mitigate the negative effects of aging (Cabeza 2002). In terms of aging's positive effects, older people tend to be happier and more emotionally stable than younger people (Scheibe and Carstensen 2010). What is more, the negative aspects of cognitive aging do not effect everyone the same way. Some hearty few people live well into their later years with little to no negative effects. Similarly, physically and mentally active people sometimes stave off the negative effects of cognitive aging. And some people experience negative effects in areas that are less relevant to judges (e.g., visuospatial abilities).

Overall, however, the research on cognitive aging leaves us melancholy. Judging is problem solving. It depends heavily on cognitive capacity. Appellate judges must read thousands of pages of legal text; they must understand that material; and they must apply what they learn. They must read and understand precedent, and reason through how cases before them interact with existing law. They must think and write, and write and think. All of this requires considerable cognitive exertion. To judge effectively, all of this requires a fertile and capable mind. But aging brains become less fertile and less capable.

The normative implications of cognitive aging among judges are profound. Consider the consequences on judicial decisions. A judge's inability to regulate her thoughts and to solve problems could be devastating because judges often interpret the scope of our constitutional rights. One judge's vote in a case could mean the difference between a right vindicated or a liberty lost. A cognitively declining judge who decides cases after dotage could fritter away our liberties and perhaps diminish the judiciary's legitimacy along the way.

Additionally, consider the qualities associated with the ideal judge. Chief among them is a practice of thoroughly and thoughtfully considering how the law applies to real-world situations that affect people's lives. A judge who takes shortcuts and relies on heuristics to compensate for cognitive loss arguably vitiates litigants' due process rights. In fact, studies show that though heuristics can often be harmless shortcuts, they also can lead to "incorrect" or problematic outcomes.[10] Tversky and Kahneman (1974) note in their seminal study that while heuristics can be "highly economical" (1131), they also can "lead to severe and systematic errors" (1124). That could be something to worry about when it comes to aging judges.

What is more, cognitively diminished judges can hamper judicial business. The expression "justice delayed is justice denied" seems apropos. Age-related increases in caseloads, if left unchecked, could contribute to delayed justice (e.g., Engel and Weinshall 2020). The backlog could become even more worrisome when one considers the additional cognitive toll it will impose on other judges (to work faster on more cases), thereby exacerbating the effects of whatever cognitive declines *they* endure. Relatedly, a backlogged judiciary also means greater uncertainty about the meaning of the law. The rule of law requires uniformity and clarity. Aging judges likely inhibit courts from achieving those goals.

All of this raises legitimate questions about whether and how to remove federal judges. The effects of cognitive aging particularly call into question the use of lifetime tenure for an institution where many of its officeholders continue to serve critical governmental functions long after the conventional retirement age. Perhaps it is time to consider term limits or a mandatory retirement age for federal judges. Alternatively, it may be necessary for Congress to consider diverting additional resources to the judiciary to compensate for aging's effects.

1.2 Plan for the Book

We have a tough task before us—to examine the effects of cognitive aging on federal circuit court judges. Judges, of course, will not undergo MRI exams for a bunch of academics. (We can't blame them.) Nor are they likely to reveal their personal cognitive issues to us. (Can't blame them there, either.) Consequently, we must rely on the broader neuroscience scholarship generally, apply it to judges specifically, and then make inferences from the results. In that vein, Chapter 2 gets right into it by introducing readers to some of the most relevant and recent neuroscience research on cognitive aging. Decades of scholarship shows that aging leads to cognitive decline

[10] Dancey and Sheagley (2013) discover that politically interested people who use heuristics are often able to identify their senators' voting behavior—but only when their senators vote to type. When their senator votes against type (i.e., against the party), short-cutters are the most likely people to arrive at wrong outcomes. "[W]hen heuristics go bad, it is the norm for the most attentive segment of the public to become the most misinformed, revealing an important drawback to heuristic" (312).

(Gutchess 2019; Cabeza, Nyberg, and Park 2017; Kennedy et al. 2015; Reuter-Lorenz and Park 2014; Turner and Spreng 2011; Park 2000; Salthouse 1996; Weinberg 1989). This literature shows that the brain's physical structures and efficiencies change over time, leading to cognitive declines. These declines "are fairly broad, begin early in adulthood, and are cumulative across the life span" (Salthouse 2004, 141). Even under "typical" circumstances, cognitive decline begins in a person's 40s or 50s (Hertzog et al. 2009). Chapter 2 walks the reader through these findings. It analyzes different cognitive domains, examines various parts of the brain, and summarizes how the brain changes with age.

Chapter 3 transports these neuroscience studies to the realm of political science. It hypothesizes how these findings apply to judging in the United States Courts of Appeals. We begin by discussing how the federal circuit courts operate and what scholars know about circuit judge behavior. We then hypothesize some of the ways cognitive aging may influence federal judges. Among our hypotheses are the expectations that older judges will require more time to accomplish their tasks, will rely more on heuristics and on others, and will become less influential. These and other hypotheses apply to the empirical chapters that follow.

Chapter 4 is the first of our eight empirical chapters,[11] the initial four of which analyze the opinion-writing process and the content of judicial opinions. Why focus so much on opinions? Legal opinions are perhaps the most visible judicial "outputs." They lay out a court's ruling, provide its rationale, and allow future litigants in similar situations to anticipate the likely outcomes of their behaviors. Opinion content also can influence a court's legitimacy (e.g., Popkin 2007; Zink, Spriggs, and Scott 2009), increase compliance with a court's decision (e.g., Baum 1976; Corley 2009), and help judges professionally advance up the judicial hierarchy (Black and Owens 2016; Choi and Gulati 2004*b*; Smelcer, Steigerwalt, and Vining 2013). Because opinions are the most important and visible acts of judging, we devote significant attention to them.

Chapter 4 examines how cognitive aging influences the bargaining and accommodation that take place privately as judges write their opinions and form coalitions. We investigate archival documents collected from the papers of Judge J. Skelly Wright on the Circuit Court of Appeals for the District of Columbia. Using those private records, we analyze two aspects of the opinion-writing process: the length of time it takes an opinion writer to circulate an opinion draft to his colleagues; and bargaining behavior in response to the opinion draft.

Next, in Chapter 5, we review a judge's writing style over time. We analyze hundreds of thousands of opinions that numerous judges wrote over the course of their careers as circuit court judges. We examine their writing style variation. Specifically, we evaluate the cognitive complexity of judges' opinions, and various measures of the length and tone of those opinions. As judges age, and as their abilities to reason reduce, their opinions should become less cognitively complex. Judges may move from interpreting events "in multidimensional terms" and "integrat[ing] a variety of evidence" (Tetlock, Bernzweig, and Gallant 1985, 1228) to making decisions

[11] Data and code to reproduce our statistical results are available on a Harvard Dataverse page (https://doi.org/10.7910/DVN/OFXC6W).

"on the basis of only a few salient items of information" (Gruenfeld 1995, 5). Similarly, their opinions may become shorter, consistent with their increased cognitive costs.

Chapter 6 analyzes whether, as they age, opinion-writing judges increasingly rely on others. We first examine whether judges rely more on their law clerks as they age. Judges often rely on clerks to write portions of their opinions. But aging judges may rely on them more than younger judges. Judge opinion variability allows us to examine how judges use law clerks. This is because each judge and each law clerk possesses his or her own linguistic fingerprint. By stylometrically examining the variability in those opinions, we can detect whether more or fewer people helped write them. We also evaluate the degree to which judges co-opt the language in party briefs. The parties' briefs would be natural sources of text from which aging judges might copy. The briefs address the case facts and the relevant law at issue in the dispute, offering ready-made cognitive shortcuts. We measure the similarity between a judge' opinion and the briefs filed in the case.

Chapter 7 examines how judges across the federal judiciary treat opinions written by old and young judges. Specifically, we analyze whether aging judges write opinions that receive fewer citations and positive treatments from their colleagues. Citations and positive treatments may reflect opinion quality. After all, judges should be more likely to cite and follow higher quality opinions. We examine more than 35 million "treating opinion-precedential opinion" pairings to understand the conditions under which judges cite other judges' opinions and, if they do cite them, whether they do so positively or negatively. We are also able to leverage the fact that intra-circuit opinions are binding within the circuit but persuasive outside the circuit. This dichotomy allows us to examine the effects of aging in cases where precedent is binding and in cases where it is merely persuasive.

Chapter 8 investigates how aging circuit court judges apply Supreme Court precedent. We seek to determine whether aged judges apply High Court precedent differently than younger judges apply it. The analysis focuses on whether aging judges are increasingly likely to apply Supreme Court precedent in an ideological manner. We examine data on how circuit judges treated a random sample of U.S. Supreme Court precedents from 1953–2000. Because we expect aging judges to rely increasingly on cognitive shortcuts, we believe they will be more likely to consider the ideological implications of Supreme Court precedent when they apply those precedents.

Chapter 9 considers whether aged judges are more (or less) influenced by panel composition than their younger colleagues. Panel effects occur when the composition of a three-judge panel influences the votes judges cast. Circuit courts usually decide cases using panels of three judges, randomly selected from among the pool of circuit judges within the circuit. As a consequence, different cases will observe different combinations of judges sitting on panels. And these combinations can influence how judges behave. For example, in sex discrimination cases, male judges are more likely to vote for the rights claimant when a female judge serves with them than when the panel consists only of men (Boyd, Epstein, and Martin 2010). We ask whether judge age similarly influences judges. We examine, first, whether judges become less successful at persuading their colleagues as they age, and, second, whether they are increasingly likely to be influenced by their panel colleagues as they age.

Chapters 10 and 11 then shift toward the broader policy debates over an aging judiciary. Chapter 10 presents a survey experiment that examines how the public perceives an aging judiciary as well as some proposed reforms to address the graying courts. We expose survey respondents to a series of newspaper-styled vignettes about court decisions. Included in those vignettes is information about a judge's age and cognitive health. We examine how respondents react to a hypothetical judge and to a hypothetical decision. We also evaluate public support for reforms (a retirement age or a term limit) that might reduce the number of aged judges in the federal judiciary.

In Chapter 11, we focus on public support for policy reforms. Beyond simply measuring whether the public believes mandatory retirement age or term limits are good ideas, we also manipulate arguments people advance both *for* and *against* those ideas. Chapter 11 presents a second survey experiment that tests people's support for judicial reforms. We ask people to rate their support for various reforms as a function of who proposed them, the costs associated with the reforms, and a series of arguments in support of or opposition to them.

Chapter 12 concludes. We summarize our findings, lay out the broader implications of those findings, and offer thoughts about our work's relevance. We highlight the tradeoffs that come with lifetime tenure, such as a lack of judicial accountability, non-majoritarian decisions, and most important for our purposes, the possibility that judges could serve well after their mental faculties have declined. We also discuss potential reforms to the federal judiciary, with a careful eye on incrementalism and the profound importance of judicial independence.

Before moving on, we are going to make a few points. We recognize that people may use our findings to attack the courts for political gain. This would be regrettable, but perhaps unavoidable in a highly charged, zero-sum political environment. Perhaps it is naive but we hope that people will respond reasonably to these findings and work toward positive solutions.

Along the same lines, we also recognize that aging is a sensitive issue. Federal and state laws protect people from age-related discrimination. Proper manners tell us that we should be respectful when discussing aging and its effects. Most federal judges are dedicated public servants who seek to protect and defend the U.S. Constitution as best they can. Nevertheless, judges are not immune from the same age-related policy discussions that occur among other professions. Pilots must retire by age 65 for fear of being unable to react to immediate dangers effectively; to prevent fatalities, air traffic controllers generally must retire by age 56.[12] FBI Special Agents and most federal law enforcement officials face a mandatory retirement age of 57.[13] Employees at the Department of State generally must retire at age 65.[14] These concerns are not limited to jobs with immediate physical harms.[15] People evaluate the president through the lens of age and cognitive capacity. A 2023 poll showed that 62% of the public overall

[12] See 49 U.S.C. §44729 and 5 U.S.C. §8335, respectively.

[13] See 5 U.S.C. §§8335, 8425.

[14] https://rnet.state.gov/cri2.htm.

[15] Even our own beloved positions as tenured professors were subject to mandatory retirement ages in the not too distant past. As recently as 1993, universities could require tenured faculty to retire at age 70; amendments to the Age Discrimination Act of 1967 eliminated this requirement (Larson and Diaz 2012).

(and 69% of Independents) believed that President Biden's mental fitness limited his ability to be president.[16] A special counsel report[17] even remarked on the president's increasing memory problems, leading 86% of Americans to believe the president was too old to be president.[18] Policymakers and the American people have decided that in some professions, the costs to society from cognitive aging simply are too risky to bear. There is no reason to exempt judges from these discussions.

A final point. Our findings likely under-represent the effects of cognitive aging. As we discuss throughout, we obtain our results even while accounting for so-called senior status. When judges reach the age of 65 and have at least 15 years of service, they can take senior status. Doing so allows them to hear a reduced caseload. We discuss the particulars of senior status more fully later, but the point is that we have found evidence of cognitive aging even in the face of current efforts to reduce it. Each chapter finds that cognitive aging influences judges. Some analyses find greater effects than other. But taken together, they point to some alarming trends.

[16] https://www.npr.org/2023/05/23/1177617666/more-than-6-in-10-say-bidens-mental-fitness-to-be-president-is-a-concern-poll-fi.

[17] See https://www.justice.gov/storage/report-from-special-counsel-robert-k-hur-february-2024.pdf

[18] See https://www.ipsos.com/en-us/majority-americans-think-both-biden-and-trump-are-too-old-serve-second-terms.

2
The Neuroscience behind Cognitive Aging

Time and use tend to reduce the quality of things. Gears and belts deteriorate. Ink fades. Iron rusts. Knives dull. And, unfortunately, senescence erodes cognition. Decades of research shows that aging leads to cognitive decline—even among neurologically "healthy" people (Gutchess 2019; Cabeza, Nyberg, and Park 2017; Kennedy et al. 2015; Reuter-Lorenz and Park 2014; Turner and Spreng 2011; Park 2000; Salthouse 1996; Weinberg 1989). "A clear body of evidence indicates that as individuals age a decline occurs in specific brain functions that cannot be attributed to disease processes in the brain, such as neurodegeneration from Alzheimer's disease or stroke" (Blazer, Yaffe, and Liverman 2015, 22). Cognitive declines "are fairly broad, begin early in adulthood, and are cumulative across the life span" (Salthouse 2004, 141). Even under "typical" circumstances, noticeable changes begin in a person's 40s or 50s (Hertzog et al. 2009). At best, these changes lead to slower processing speeds and minor cognitive inefficiencies. At worst, they can significantly reduce a person's cognition.[1]

Though cognitive aging is widespread, it is, as we will see, variable. As one study put it, cognitive aging "is a process of gradual, ongoing, yet *highly variable* changes in cognitive functions that occur as people get older" (Blazer, Yaffe, and Liverman 2015, 2) (emphasis added). It is "highly variable" because it affects some cognitive domains more than others (Park 2000). We will see, for example, that vocabulary awareness and the retention of general information remain relatively stable over time while some memory, reasoning, problem solving, and processing speed decline with age (Salthouse 2010*b*, 10). Unfortunately, the cognitive domains that aging hits hardest are those necessary for effective judging.

But before we can address cognitive *aging*, we must first discuss the concept and domains of *cognition*. Therefore, §2.1 of this chapter provides an overview of cognition and its various domains. §2.2 then discusses which of those domains decline with age and why. We identify which brain regions control the various domains of cognition and (generally) how they change over time. The studies we discuss reflect some of the most foundational research on cognitive neuroscience and cognitive aging to date.

[1] Humans are not the only species to experience cognitive aging. Other mammals such as rabbits (Solomon and Groccia-Ellison 1996), mice (Kelly et al. 2003), dogs (Milgram et al. 1994), and monkeys (Lyons et al. 2004) also experience the effects of cognitive aging (Samson and Barnes 2013).

Cognitive Aging and the Federal Circuit Courts: How Senescence Influences the Law and Judges.
Ryan C. Black, Ryan J. Owens, Patrick C. Wohlfarth, Oxford University Press. © Ryan C. Black, Ryan J. Owens, Patrick C. Wohlfarth 2024. DOI: 10.1093/oso/9780197747025.003.0002

2.1 Cognition and Cognitive Domains

Defining precisely what cognition is depends on who you ask. It is a little like asking someone to explain what love is. We all know generally what it is, but providing a precise definition is difficult.[2] One study defines cognition as "a result of coordinated processing among distributed brain regions" (Bennett and Madden 2014, 187). Another study defines it as "all the processes by which the sensory input is transformed, reduced, elaborated, stored, recovered, and used" (Neisser 1967, 4). A third study tells us that cognition "covers many mental abilities and processes.... Collectively, these different domains of cognition are critical for successfully engaging in the various activities involved in daily functioning" (Blazer, Yaffe, and Liverman 2015, 1). While each of these definitions (and others we could recite) define cognition slightly differently, they all agree that cognition involves multiple domains (Murman 2015). The major domains we address in this chapter include: memory, attention, speech and language, visuospatial abilities, processing speed, and executive functioning.[3]

Memory. Memory is the record of what a person has stored in his or her brain. Memory involves taking in and coding events and facts, storing them, and then retrieving that information later. More formally, it is "the re-creation of past experiences by the synchronous firing of neurons that were involved in the original experience" (Carter 2019, 156).

As Figure 2.1 illustrates, cognitive memory has several facets. Scholars have categorized memory into nondeclarative (or implicit) memory and declarative (or explicit) memory. Nondeclarative memory is memory a person can call up without having to express in words. It involves things people remember on "autopilot," such as how to ride a bicycle, how to tie a tie, or how to swim (Harada, Love, and Triebel 2013, 740). A person does not need consciously to remember how to do those things. "[O]ne can swim the backstroke without consciously recalling what he or she learned in swim lessons" (Drag and Bieliauskas 2010, 82). Classical conditioning is another example of nondeclarative memory. Once learned, the memory "sticks." It returns, when needed, without a person consciously seeking it out. There are few examples we can think of that would apply to judging because there are few (if any) judicial behaviors that operate on autopilot.

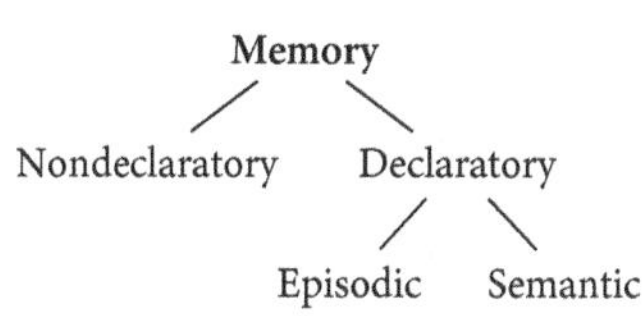

Figure 2.1 Multiple categories of memory.

[2] Indeed, the philosopher and poet "Haddaway" once publicly and to great fanfare asked the question: "what is love?" See https://www.youtube.com/watch?v=HEXWRTEbj1I.

[3] Our discussion of cognitive neuroscience surely is not exhaustive. Research in psychology and cognitive neuroscience constantly evolves.

Declarative memory, on the other hand, is the actual, volitional summoning of a previously learned or experienced thing (Harada, Love, and Triebel 2013, 740). It is "declarative" in the sense that a person can recall the memory and declare it out loud. There are two general kinds of declarative memory: episodic memory and semantic memory. Episodic memory is "the conscious recollection of experienced events, such as a 21st birthday party, a phone conversation from last week, or a word list from 30 minutes ago" (Drag and Bieliauskas 2010, 81). People perceive episodic memory in the first person. They associate it with time and place. A person may recall precisely where she was on September 11, 2001, when terrorists slaughtered 3,000 innocent people. Or, a person might recall what she did on February 6, 2011, when the Green Bay Packers gloriously defeated the Pittsburgh Steelers (31–25) in Super Bowl XLV. Judges might recall these same events. Or, as additional examples, they might recall where they were when a colleague circulated an objectionable opinion draft to them, or what they were doing when the U.S. Supreme Court rendered a significant decision.

Semantic memory, on the other hand, is the recall of factual, objective information. It "refers to the store of factual knowledge in memory... [such as] definitions of words, historical facts, and the names of all 50 state capitols" (Drag and Bieliauskas 2010, 81). Knowing that Aaron Rodgers was the Most Valuable Player in Super Bowl XLV involves semantic memory. One can think of semantic memory as akin to encyclopedic knowledge. It is not personalized in the way that episodic memory is. For judges, this kind of memory involves learning precedents and retaining their holding, understanding what the Founding era believed a particular constitutional phrase meant, or knowing what a particular rule of civil procedure means.

Attention. Attention is a second cognitive domain. Most readers surely know what attention generally is. It refers to the mind's ability to focus on a specific thing or set of things for a period of time (Gutchess 2019; Harada, Love, and Triebel 2013). As one study put it: "Attention causes you to select one item from the sensory inputs you are receiving and allows you to become more fully or sharply conscious of it" (Carter 2019, 182).

Researchers have created numerous categories of attention, some of which overlap conceptually. Selective attention, for example, refers to a person's ability to focus on one thing while ignoring irrelevant information. Holding a conversation in a noisy room or driving carefully while transporting screaming children are examples of selective attention (Harada, Love, and Triebel 2013, 739). Divided attention is the ability to focus on multiple things simultaneously. One might think of it as multi-tasking. A person would employ divided attention, for instance, if he simultaneously cooked eggs, bacon, and cinnamon rolls without burning them. A judge might employ divided attention to dictate an opinion while she skims proposed oral argument questions. Alternating attention (also called task switching) involves a person's ability to change focus effectively from one thing to another (Drag and Bieliauskas 2010). For example, alternating attention might involve reading an opinion but then shifting focus to writing a draft opinion. Sustained attention involves a person's ability to remain focused for an extended period of time (Blazer, Yaffe, and Liverman 2015, 36). Tasks associated with sustained attention are often called "vigilance tasks" and require the person to hold thoughts for some consistent period of time. Working through a logic problem, for example, requires sustained attention. Reading a legal brief (or set of briefs) might also require sustained attention.

Language. Language and speaking combine toward another cognitive domain. Language is "the mental faculty that many people consider most uniquely human and that most distinctly separates us from the other species that inhabit the earth" (Banich and Compton 2018, 224). When researchers speak of language skills, they refer to a whole host of different features, including: understanding spoken words, producing speech, reading, writing, and verbal reasoning (Blazer, Yaffe, and Liverman 2015, 40). Listening to speech involves four important features: phonological analysis and segregation of speech stream, determination of syntactic structure, development of conceptual coherence, and discourse comprehension (Park 2000, 177). As Shafto and Tyler (2014, 583) state: "understanding and producing language are crucial and complex human behaviors, essential for effective communication, that underpin almost all our social interactions." Obviously, this domain is important for judges, who must understand language and know how to communicate effectively.

Visuospatial abilities. This cognitive domain focuses on how well a person can think in two or three dimensions (Murman 2015). It involves the ability "to produce figures, to recognize familiar faces, to form relationships among spatial locations, and to copy and match objects and pictures" (Blazer, Yaffe, and Liverman 2015, 41). Visuospatial abilities are important for those who must navigate new areas, read maps, and remember objects' locations. Imagine that you must drive the confusing streets of Washington, D.C. (We wish you and your visuospatial abilities luck.) Only the most seasoned drivers can endure the bewildering mix of city quadrant addresses (647 A St., NE is two blocks away from 647 A St., SE), diagonal streets (all those "state" roads), missing sequential street letters (there is no "J" Street), and multi-lane traffic circles (some with far too many exits, like Dupont Circle's *ten*). Driving these roads would test a person's visuospatial abilities. This domain is less important for judges, we suspect. Other than using visuospatial skills to travel to a courthouse, the domain seems less relevant for judging, on the whole. (We could think of some cases where it might be important for a judge to understand three-dimensional features or maps, but those would be hen's tooth rare.)

Processing Speed. This domain involves the overall efficiency of one's mental, cognitive process. It addresses "the speed with which cognitive activities are performed as well as the speed of motor responses" (Harada, Love, and Triebel 2013, 739). Nearly everything humans do relies on processing speed. For example, "making the appropriate responses in driving, such as determining when to turn or when to stop at a red traffic light are heavily dependent on processing speed" (Blazer, Yaffe, and Liverman 2015, 33). As a less prosaic example, processing speed might also involve quickly taking in a legal argument and grappling with its implications. Debate, discussion, and deliberation—all critical skills for effective judges—require quick processing speed.

Executive Functioning. Executive functioning is like the control tower of the brain. Some scholars refer to it as "the guidance of control of behavior toward a goal" (Banich and Compton 2018, 334). It deals with the cognitive skills necessary to reason and to moderate behavior (Baltes 1993). As Harada, Love, and Triebel (2013, 741) put it, executive functioning involves "the ability to self-monitor, plan, organize, reason, be mentally flexible, and solve problems." That is, it involves the ability to learn, to manage, and to carry out a plan. Executive functions are higher-order mental operations that regulate other cognitive processes. "Although there is no consensus on how to best define executive functions, abilities such as self-regulation, sequencing of behavior, mental flexibility, response inhibition, planning, organization, and the ability to initiate, maintain, switch, and stop sequences of complex behavior are generally included" (Wecker et al. 2005, 345).

Reasoning is one important element of executive functioning. Reasoning involves logical thinking, the ability to solve problems, and the ability to draw appropriate conclusions from evidence. Blazer, Yaffe, and Liverman (2015, 39) call it "the process of drawing conclusions from information to inform problem solving or make decisions." Reasoning is a complex function that separates humans from other species. Abstract reasoning, in particular, is a complicated process that falls within the purview of executive functioning. Such reasoning often obtains in the legal world, where judges must apply abstract principles to specific facts in cases.

Working memory is another important element of executive functioning. Working memory is "the active and simultaneous processing and storing of information" (Hoyer 2015, 797). It "is a key component of cognitive tasks that require juggling lots of information at once" (797). Working memory is "the cognitive system that actively maintains several pieces of information in mind for immediate use in higher order processing tasks" (Reuter-Lorenz and Park 2010, 405). It is the ability to keep numerous pieces of information in one's mind while acting on them (Carstensen 2011, 58). Working memory is important because it allows us to store information and build upon it for later processing. As Park (2000, 10) put it, working memory is like "the amount of on-line cognitive resources available at any given moment to process information," and it can "involve storage, retrieval, and transformation of information." It "operates like a cook, switching among pots and pans to attend to the one requiring focus at any moment while other pots and pans simmer on the back burner" (Gutchess 2019, 57–58).

Researchers often point to solving math problems as an example of working memory. To solve a math problem, a person must know what the numbers mean and how they are arranged. When performing addition, a person may need to remember to carry the one, or to recall a negative sign. As Carstensen (2011, 58) puts it: "In order to put two and two together, we have to simultaneously remember both numbers." Using an example from the legal world, working memory might involve listening to an oral argument while thinking of how it weaves throughout the interstices of existing precedent. One must store the argument, maintain it while retrieving and thinking of existing precedents, and then retrieve the argument again.

2.2 The Effects of Aging on Cognition

Aging leads to cognitive decline. But as we noted earlier, research shows that aging effects some cognitive domains more than others. Here, we discuss what scholars know about the effects of aging on the major cognitive domains.

Memory. Cognitive aging leads to some memory declines, but not others. Non-declarative memory stays with us throughout our lives. Once a person learns to ride a bicycle or how to do the back stroke, that memory remains. Semantic memory also remains fairly stable—and can improve—with age (Park 2000). Like an encyclopedia with more and more entries, a person's reservoir of knowledge increases over time until very advanced age (Park et al. 2002). One study examined the number of words people could answer in a *New York Times* crossword puzzle. It found that vocabulary knowledge tends to peak around age 50 and then remains fairly stable until age 79 (Ryan, Sattler, and Lopez 2000). This particular finding, at least, is somewhat reassuring as it relates to aging judges.

Episodic memory, however, declines with age. It becomes more difficult to filter out the memories that are relevant and those that are not (Drag and Bieliauskas 2010). One study found that the difference in episodic memory quality between 18-year-olds and 80-year-olds is roughly the same as the difference in quality between 8-year-olds and 18-year-olds (Jones and Conrad 1933; Salthouse 2010*a*). Another study found that "adults in their 60s and 70s perform at an average level [on memory tests] nearly 1 standard deviation below that of adults in their early 20s" (Salthouse 2010*a*, 71). This decline in episodic memory also correlates with the increasing likelihood that older people create false recollections of their pasts (Gutchess 2019, 105).[4] Among the aged, episodic memory recall is worse under conditions in which there are fewer cues to aid them.

Attention. As with memory, some kinds of attention decline with age. Aging does not seem to impair sustained attention (Blazer, Yaffe, and Liverman 2015, 36). The ability to sustain attention drops in a person's 30s, but by the time he or she reaches 40, sustained attention remains stable. Carriere et al. (2010) conducted a study that examined people's sustained attention to certain tasks. They asked respondents to observe a series of presented numbers and press keys whenever a digit other than the number "3" appeared. Though older people took longer to perform the task than younger people, they were less likely to make errors.

Selective attention, divided attention, and task switching, however, all decline with age (Blazer, Yaffe, and Liverman 2015). Examining selective attention, one group of scholars showed respondents transparent images of faces and houses laid on top of each other. The respondents were instructed to determine whether the faces were male or female while ignoring the images of the houses that overlayed them. While the younger respondents differentiated easily between the two, the overlay distracted older respondents (Schmitz, Cheng, and Rosa 2010).[5] As it relates to divided attention, McDowd and Craik (1988) find that age exaggerates the effects of task complexity on divided attention. Older people require more time than younger people to retrieve memories of words under conditions of divided attention

[4] It also appears that cognitive aging makes it harder for people to acquire *new* memories (Harada, Love, and Triebel 2013, 740).

[5] Another way to measure selective attention is through the "Stroop Test." An example of this test is to show someone a black ball with white letters that spell the work "black" or some other color and ask them to say what color the words themselves are. These tests tend to reveal a decline in selective attention with age (Drag and Bieliauskas 2010, 80).

(Anderson, Craik, and Naveh-Benjamin 1998). They also are more likely than younger people to make errors in memory retrieval when tasked with recognizing pairs (Castel and Craik 2003). Finally, task switching declines with age. As Wecker et al. (2005, 350) put it: "... advancing age is associated with poorer performance on tasks of cognitive switching, even after parsing out the key component skills tapped by those tasks." The act of switching between tasks is more difficult for older adults than younger adults, particularly when a person is unable to predict the next task (see, e.g., Van Asselen and Ridderinkhof 2000; Kramer, Hahn, and Gopher 1999).

Language. In terms of aging and language, the results are mixed, with some good news and some bad news. On the positive side of things, cognitive aging does not diminish one's vocabulary—at least not until very old age (Tyler et al. 2010; Wingfield and Grossman 2006). Older people enjoy larger vocabularies than younger people (Verhaeghen 2013). They generally retain their understanding of words, even if their speed in retrieving them decreases with age. But the news is not all positive. Age does reduce at least some language-related cognitive processing. For example, aging reduces a person's ability to think of the right word at the right time—the so-called "tip of the tongue" problem (Burke et al. 1991). Elderly people also tend to employ words that lack imagery. They use shorter and simpler sentences than their younger selves. "Older adults produce propositionally and syntactically simpler speech than younger adults in natural contexts, use more vague terms, have more frequent and more empty pauses, and are slower to access phonological information in experimental contexts" (Shafto and Tyler 2014, 585). What is more, because the *spoken* word involves working memory, and working memory diminishes with age (see below), verbal communication suffers with age. Older people are able to hear and understand short declarative sentences without issue. But as those sentences become longer and require a greater reliance on working memory, aging adults have a harder time following along. "As the length, and syntactic complexity of sentences increase, older adults have significantly more difficulty than younger adults in sentence comprehension and accuracy of recall" (Wingfield 2000, 184–185, citing Norman et al. 1991).

Visuospatial abilities. Visuospatial abilities also decline with age. As Blazer, Yaffe, and Liverman (2015, 41) state: "Older adults do not perform as well as younger adults on spatial tasks requiring mental rotation, visualization abilities, or remembering the location of objects." If your grandparents or elderly parents venture to D.C., tell them to take the Metro (although we wish them luck navigating that too).

Processing Speed. Processing speed declines markedly with age (Schaie 1994). In fact, slower processing speed is one of the most notable symptoms of cognitive aging (Harada, Love, and Triebel 2013). Older adults simply take longer than younger adults to process ideas and thoughts (Salthouse 1996). For example, Verhaeghen (2013) examined the differences in mental processing speeds of 1,354 pairs of young versus old adults. He found that older adults moved with a speed that was between 1.2 and 1.7 times slower than young adults. Schaie (1989) timed respondents and asked them to find the letter "A" in an experimental context and to compare identical pictures. The study found a strong negative correlation with age, with older people taking significantly longer to complete the task than younger people.

Other studies likewise find strong evidence of processing delays with age. Park et al. (1996) had respondents perform a Digit Symbol Substitution test, in which participants used a code to interpret and write symbols. They also had respondents perform Letter Comparison tests and Pattern Comparison tests, in which participants compared letters and line patterns, seeking to finds matches. Their results showed that processing speed begins to decline in a person's 20s and then declines linearly for the remainder of one's life. As Park (2000, 6) put it: "[t]he declines are regular, generally linear, and of considerable magnitude." Other studies have shown a 20–40% slower comprehension after the age of 55 (Backes-Gellner, Schneider, and Veen 2011, 1106). Processing speed is so important to efficient cognition that some scholars believe the majority of cognitive decline is a function of decreased processing speed (Salthouse 1996).

Executive Functioning. Executive functioning also declines with age. Indeed, "[t]here is a sharp decline in executive functioning abilities after the age of 60" (Drag and Bieliauskas 2010, 80). In particular, older adults' working memory declines. Researchers typically measure working memory by asking respondents to complete tasks like solving math problems while remembering certain numbers in an equation (i.e., a computational span task) (Park 2000, 10). Individuals with better working memory are able to retain, and then recall, more numbers. Similar tests involve reading comprehension and backwards digit calculation. Salthouse et al. (1989) finds that older adults exhibited poorer working memory than young adults when task complexity increased and their limited processing resources took on a greater load. "Differences [between young and old] are pronounced when executive functions such as memory updating, reordering, or inhibition" are required (Reuter-Lorenz and Park 2010, 405). Daneman and Carpenter (1980) read a list of sentences to participants and asked them to remember the final word in each sentence. The test involved more and more sentences to increase the cognitive load on the respondents. The older the participants were, the poorer they performed (Park 2000, 183).[6]

Reasoning abilities also decline with cognitive aging. Powell (1994) finds that reasoning is an "early casualt[y] of the aging process" (86). Salthouse (1991) finds significant declines in inductive reasoning. Salthouse (2004) asked participants to reason which geometric pattern should follow in a matrix of patterns and found that older participants were significantly less likely to answer correctly than younger participants. Harada, Love, and Triebel (2013, 741) agree, noting that "[r]easoning with unfamiliar material... declines with age." In a longitudinal study, Schaie (2005) found a statistically significant decline in people's reasoning beginning at about age 53.

But, is it all bad? Does cognitive aging cause nothing but trouble? While the effects are overwhelmingly negative, cognitive aging is not all uncontrollably bad. Research shows that emotional stability and overall happiness increase with age. Older respondents report being as happy, or happier, than younger respondents

[6] Executive functioning also controls one's ability to inhibit responses—it allows people to hold their tongues when needed. This, too, declines with age. One relevant example shows the point. Federal District Judge J. Thomas Greene grew "more impulsive with age" (Goldstein 2011). When a prospective female juror announced that she did not recognize a defendant, the 76-year old Judge Greene retorted, "She didn't recognize you with your clothes on" (Goldstein 2011). Such behavior is consistent with typical cognitive aging, where a person loses the ability to focus on the relevant, keep a lid on the irrelevant, and withhold snarky and inappropriate comments.

(Buecker et al. 2023). They also are able to resolve interpersonal disputes more effectively than younger people (Luong, Charles, and Fingerman 2011). Why this is the case is not entirely clear; though, scholars have largely settled on a conceptual construct called socio-emotional selectivity theory. The theory holds that older people choose to be happier because they know they are nearing death. They sink more resources into positive activities as a consequence. Support for this theory can be found among younger people with terminal illnesses; they too focus on the positive when they know the end is near (Scheibe and Carstensen 2010). What is more, dopamine has less impact on people as they age, making them less emotional (Dang et al. 2017).

Additionally, people can take action to mitigate cognitive decline. Activities that lead to "cognitive enrichment," such as physical exercise and mental stimulation, can reduce the negative effects of aging (Hertzog et al. 2009). One longitudinal study showed that women who walk regularly are 30% less likely to suffer cognitive decline than physically inactive women (Yaffe et al. 2001). Other studies show that increased aerobic exercise can increase the volume of the entorhinal cortex (we promise this is a real thing), which is partially responsible for memory formation (Whiteman et al. 2016). Similarly, Hertzog et al. (2009) provide an excellent summary of the studies that find a correlation between increased mental stimulation and reduced cognitive decline. One study in particular observed 4,000 elderly people in a community who reported on their "cognitive activities" (or various forms of mental stimulation) over the course of years, and found less cognitive decline among the active (Wilson et al. 2003). Still, even among those with careers that are mentally stimulating, cognitive decline occurs. For example, Powell (1994) examined cognitive aging among medical doctors and the general population and found that doctors at age 70 scored 14% lower on cognitive tests than younger doctors, while those aged 75 or older scored 26% lower than younger doctors.

Similarly, older brains often compensate for some cognitive losses. They tend to show "networking activity" in *both* brain hemispheres where younger adults show activity only in *one* hemisphere or region. "With age, the distinction of brain systems breaks down, such that there are weaker connections *within* a system and stronger connections *between* systems" (Gutchess 2019, 31). While this compensatory action helps, it is not as effective as the original (younger) system (Gutchess 2019).

In short, while things like physical exercise and mental stimulation can mitigate some of the effects of cognitive aging, they typically cannot prevent them.

2.3 The Causes of Cognitive Decline

Just *why* aging leads to cognitive decline is the final section of this chapter. That question is still under analysis, but studies have made clear that the brain changes as people age—and those structural changes may lead to cognitive decline. As Gutchess (2019, 21) notes:

> At the most fundamental level, brain structures change with age. The volume of the brain is decreased, and the cortex thins. The overall weight of the brain decreases

and spaces in the brain, including the sulci, the grooves between different parts of the cortex, and the ventricles, spaces through which cerebrospinal fluid passes, become enlarged.

Other parts of the brain, such as the mylenation of the axons, also change, which could lead to some of the manifestations we observe with declines in processing speed (Bennett and Madden 2014).

To put this all into greater context, we must talk briefly about the brain. The brain consists of the cerebellum, the brain stem, and the cerebrum (Carter 2019; Gazzaniga, Ivry, and Mangun 1998). The cerebellum is a small area near the bottom of the brain, between the cerebrum and the top of the brain stem. It is primarily responsible for motor control (Banich and Compton 2018, 9). It is critical to the coordination of fine-skilled movement. Humans use it to maintain posture, to walk and balance, and to speak. It is important for learning motor behaviors and motor control. Evolutionarily, it is one of the older portions of the brain. The brainstem, or the medulla, connects the spinal cord and nerves to the rest of the brain. It regulates things like breathing, heart rate, blood pressure, sleep, swallowing, and hunger. It also regulates things like pain sensitivity. All the information that passes from the body to the cerebellum and cerebrum runs through the pathways in the brainstem (Banich and Compton 2018, 8–9).

We are most concerned with the cerebrum, as it controls most of the body's voluntary actions. The cerebrum is "the large pinky-gray wrinkled and folded structure that forms more than three-quarters of the brain's total volume" (Carter 2019, 53). The exterior portion of the cerebrum (the cerebral cortex) is called "gray matter" because of its color. The cortex is akin to the bark on a tree. Language, memory, and learning are cortical functions. The interior spaghetti-like portion of the brain is called "white matter" because of its color. The bulges seen on the cortex are called "gyri" while the small grooves are called "sulci" (Carter 2019, 66). (A very deep sulcus is called a "fissure.") Buried deeper in the core of the cerebrum are various subcortical systems, such as the hippocampus (largely dealing with episodic memory and spatial navigation) and the limbic system (largely dealing with emotions) (Banich and Compton 2018, 12).

The cerebrum is divided into two hemispheres, the left and the right. The "longitudinal fissure" is the long fissure that divides the two hemispheres which, themselves, are linked by a group of nerve fibers called the "corpus callosum." The corpus callosum consists of over 3 millions axons, which connect the brain cells with other parts of the brain and body. It allows the cortex of one hemisphere to coordinate actions with the cortex of the other hemisphere (Gazzaniga, Ivry, and Mangun 1998, 327–328).

Each hemisphere has four main divisions, or "lobes." The occipital lobe resides at the back of the brain and is responsible for vision and visual processing, taking in things like motion, color, and location. It helps us make sense of our visual perceptions, with spatial reasoning, and with depth and distances. The parietal lobe is at the back of the top part of the brain. It focuses on sensory input, processing "information about touch, pain, temperature sense, and limb proprioception (limb position)" (Gazzaniga, Ivry, and Mangun 1998, 49). It also is the area of the brain that works to read, write, and understand written language. The temporal lobe is situated near the ears on each side of the brain. It deals with hearing, allowing us to understand and interpret sounds. It also involves language comprehension, learning and memory, and some visual functions. The hippocampus, which helps with memory formation, resides in each hemisphere of the temporal lobe (Gazzaniga, Ivry, and Mangun 1998, 53).

Most important for our purposes is the frontal lobe. The frontal lobe sits at the very front of the brain. It is the largest of the four lobes (taking up about one-third of the cerebral cortex) (Gazzaniga, Ivry, and Mangun 1998). It contains areas such as the primary motor cortex, which initiates motor movement, as well as the premotor cortex, which plans motor movement.[7] The prefrontal cortex is the region of the brain that is responsible for executive functioning (Blazer, Yaffe, and Liverman 2015) and "the planning and execution of behavior, tasks that require the integration of information over time" (Gazzaniga, Ivry, and Mangun 1998, 49).

The various regions of the brain communicate with each other and the body via electrical pulses between brain cells. Each cell contains internal components (often called the "organelles") and "threadlike extensions" called "neurites" (Carter 2019, 70). The neurites ("dendrites" and "axons") are important for our purposes because they are involved with sending and receiving transmissions (Klingseisen and Lyons 2018). Dendrites receive nerve signals. Axons are like highways that transport messages from brain cells. They are covered in something fatty called myelin, which helps speed the transmission of information from brain cell to brain cell across the axons. (The myelin is white, thus giving the white matter its color.) We will return to axons shortly.

With that general summary of the brain and how it functions, we can now turn to the physical changes that occur in the brain over time. We are concerned with the physical changes in three areas of the brain: the prefrontal cortex, the hippocampus, and white matter. Ultimately, these changes may cause the declines we observe in terms of cognition (Desjardins and Wamke 2012; Reuter-Lorenz and Park 2010).

First, the prefrontal cortex shrinks as we age (Paraskevoudi, Balcı, and Vatakis 2018). For example, "after the age of 65, a reduction of 10–17% of the frontal cortex occurs" which represents "a selective deterioration of areas involved in high-level cognitive function" (Paraskevoudi, Balcı, and Vatakis 2018, 78). This is relevant because, as we discussed, executive functioning takes place in the prefrontal cortex (Paraskevoudi, Balcı, and Vatakis 2018). Studies have shown that people with smaller prefrontal cortex regions do worse on tests than those with larger cortex regions. Scholars have argued that the prefrontal cortex is where people learn to understand the consequences of their actions; it is where people learn to inhibit their actions. The prefrontal cortex is also involved in manipulating working memory (Banich and Compton 2018, 290–291). Importantly, older people have significantly less prefrontal cortical volume than younger people (Raz et al. 2004). Perhaps it should be no surprise, then, that executive functioning diminishes with age; the area of the brain responsible for executive functioning shrinks.

[7] The reader will note that the two need to work together for movement, with the premotor cortex sending a signal to the primary cortex to engage movement (Lu, Preston, and Strick 1994).

Indeed, studies have shown that people with damage to their frontal lobes are unable to adjust to non-routine events. For example, one study involved two patients with executive dysfunction who went to a buffet to eat dinner. The upper-class man who had eaten at restaurants in the past sat and waited to be served, not adapting to the fact that it was a buffet. The woman who had worked as a housekeeper began to serve the other guests. Neither had the executive function power to adjust (Lhermitte 1986, cited in Banich and Compton 2018, 334–335). Prefrontal shrinkage has been shown to correlate with worse executive functioning and processing in cross-sectional and longitudinal studies (Raz et al. 2007).

Second, the hippocampus becomes smaller as people age (Persson et al. 2012). For people aged 70–89, hippocampal volume declines at an average rate of 1.5% per year (Stark and Stark 2017). This decline is important because the hippocampus involves some memory processing (Gorbach et al. 2017). More specifically, the hippocampus is critical for episodic memory and long-term memories. Its shrinkage effects the retention of memory and memory creation.

Third, the brain loses white and gray matter volume as it ages. This reduction in white matter is especially important. As we stated above, white matter (myelin) covers the brain's axons. These axons are the highways that transmit information from one part of the brain to another and throughout the body. The myelin speeds up the travel time needed to send information across the brain and the body. As the white matter decays, the brain requires more time to process information; brain circuits become less efficient; they observe slower processing speed and problems with memory (Carter 2019, 214). Gutchess (2019, 29) summarizes the scholarship on white matter shrinkage thusly: "... impaired white matter integrity, particularly in frontal regions, can result in a disconnection syndrome, in which the various regions supporting subprocesses in memory cannot coordinate activity or share information effectively. Disconnection between regions ultimately slows reaction time during retrieval."[8] Studies which examine lesions on the white matter (called white matter "hyperintensities") show similar results. Such white matter abnormalities are associated with "attenuated performance on tasks of processing speed, immediate and delayed memory, executive functions, and indices of global cognitive functioning" (Gunning-Dixon and Raz 2000, 224).

Collectively, research shows that people's processing speeds decline because the white matter in their brains decays. Their episodic memory worsens as their hippocampi shrink. And, their reasoning abilities and executive functioning decline as their prefrontal cortexes lose volume. There is every reason to believe that these observed changes occur to judges as well as to the rest of us.

2.4 Conclusion

In our introduction, we discussed three legal giants: Judges Harry Friendly, Richard Posner, and Pauline Newman. Each of them experienced cognitive decline due to

[8] It is also the case that certain declines in the prefrontal area of the brain are related to speed of processing declines (Gutchess 2019, 30).

aging. Like all people, their processing speeds declined, their executive functioning worsened, and their corresponding reasoning abilities suffered. Simply put, cognitive aging influences all people. Judges are people. Therefore, cognitive aging influences judges.

The question to address now is how cognitive aging manifests among judges. What kinds of behavioral changes can we expect from older versus younger judges? The next chapter speaks directly to that question. It outlines the tasks that appellate judges regularly undertake and discusses the theoretical basis for cognitive aging's impact on judging. It lays out testable empirical hypotheses that we evaluate throughout the rest of this book.

3
How Cognitive Aging Applies to Judges

To be a good judge requires considerable effort, focus, and mental acuity. Judges must be able to recall facts quickly, handle multiple cases that involve different factual and legal issues, switch their attention to different issues with ease, and manage their time and workloads effectively. To illustrate, a court of appeals judge once wrote: "The judge questions, doubts, and searches for the truth. Between the lines he sees inferences that are missed by the novice and reaches conclusions that only an expert can find" (Wright 1973, 1180). A former judge serving on the U.S. Court of Appeals for the First Circuit described a day in the life of a federal judge:

> [T]he average day in the life of an active judge would be something like the following: From one to two hours as a member of a duty panel dealing with emergency motions or appeals, reviewing draft orders, screening cases to be decided without oral argument; another hour or two reviewing colleagues' drafts, writing or reviewing draft responses, receiving and making reports, correspondence, telephone calls, and attendance at meetings in connection with one's court, or a committee of the judicial council of one's state or circuit, or of the Judicial Conference of the United States; preparation for and participation in educational workshops and seminars; reading briefs for the next session of court; and, in between or after these activities, several hours consulting with clerks, reviewing their drafts, and doing research and writing on the draft opinions which the judge has undertaken to write in the first instance.
>
> (Coffin 1994, 181)

All of these actions require a competent mind and iron clad reasoning skills. So, how might cognitive aging play a role in all of this? The previous chapter analyzed research on cognitive aging and some of cognitive aging's effects. Here, we spell out our expectations of how cognitive aging shapes judges' behavior. We begin the chapter by describing the process that federal circuit courts generally employ when they decide cases.[1] In particular, we summarize what the prevailing literature teaches us about how circuit courts operate and how judges behave. We then present our hypotheses for the remaining empirical chapters in the book.

[1] We have discussed that process extensively elsewhere (see, e.g., Black and Owens 2013). We borrow much of that previous discussion in the paragraphs that follow. Not all courts employ these practices. Some employ variations of them. Overall, however, the procedures we discuss here reflect a good representation of those procedures.

Cognitive Aging and the Federal Circuit Courts: How Senescence Influences the Law and Judges.
Ryan C. Black, Ryan J. Owens, Patrick C. Wohlfarth, Oxford University Press. DOI: 10.1093/oso/9780197747025.003.0003

3.1 How Circuit Courts and Circuit Court Judges Operate

The United States Circuit Courts of Appeals are intermediate appellate courts that sit above U.S. District (trial) courts and below the U.S. Supreme Court. As Figure 3.1 shows, there are 12 federal circuits (including the D.C. Circuit) organized geographically. When a circuit court renders a decision, it has a binding effect on all federal courts within its geographic boundary. So, for example, when the Seventh Circuit (containing Wisconsin, Indiana, and Illinois) renders a decision, it binds all the federal district courts within those states. The decision also binds future Seventh Circuit Court panels.[2] For some courts, such as the Ninth Circuit, which oversees the federal courts in nine states and two territories, this reach is quite broad.[3]

Circuit courts review decisions of federal trial courts (and administrative agencies) within their geographical regions and are themselves subject to review by the U.S. Supreme Court. When a party files an appeal with the clerk of the circuit court that possesses jurisdiction over the legal dispute, the clerk dockets the case and randomly assigns it to a panel of three judges who will oversee, and rule on, the appeal (Breyer 1990, 29).[4] The parties then submit briefs to the three-judge panel. If the panel determines that the dispute would benefit from oral argument, the litigants each

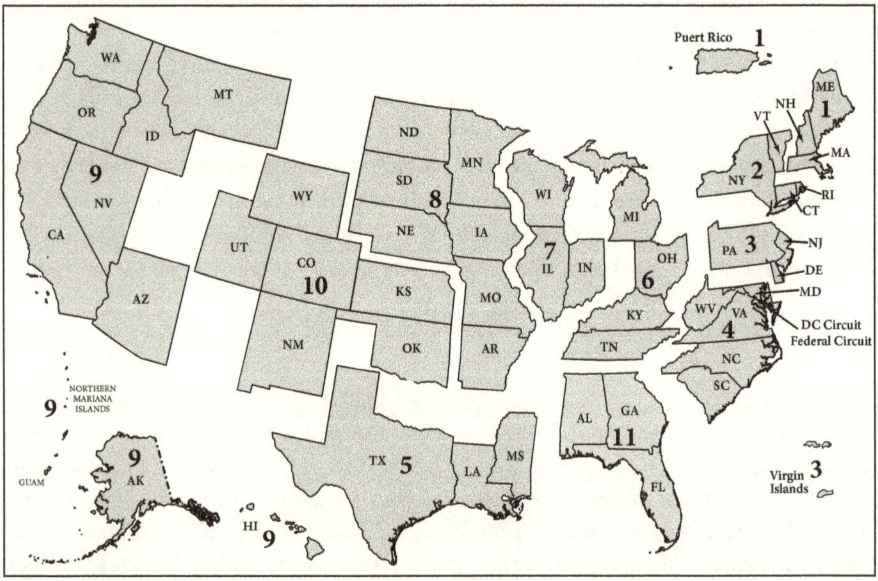

Figure 3.1 Circuit map of the United States Courts of Appeals.

[2] When circuits decide cases *en banc*—with the full complement of all judges (or most judges, in the Ninth Circuit)—they can overrule their existing precedents.

[3] The U.S. Court of Appeals for the Ninth Circuit oversees federal courts in Alaska, Arizona, California, Guam, Hawaii, Idaho, Montana, Nevada, Northern Mariana Islands, Oregon, and Washington.

[4] Not all circuits randomly assign judges to panels, though most today do (Hall 2009).

receive anywhere from 10 to 20 minutes to present their cases (Wald 1992). Following oral argument, the judges meet in brief "impression conferences" (Coffin 1994, 129) to discuss the day's cases, during which time they state their initial positions (Wald 1992, 177). At the conclusion of the conference discussion—when a collective disposition becomes clear—the presiding judge on the panel (i.e., the most senior) selects a judge to author the majority opinion.[5] The author then drafts an opinion which is supposed to reflect the conference disposition and rationale. Once the author completes the opinion draft, which can take from as little as one day to more than a year, she sends it to the other judges on the panel with the hope of gaining their approval (Coffin 1994, 191). After reading that draft opinion, her colleagues can join the opinion, seek changes to it, or simply refuse to join it and write a separate concurring or dissenting opinion. The opinion writer, of course, decides whether to accept or reject any proposed changes by her colleagues.

Circuit court judges hear and decide many cases each year. According to the Administrative Office of the United States Courts, the circuit courts of appeals disposed of 43,582 total cases in the 12-month period ending December 31, 2022.[6] They terminated 15,620 of those cases on procedural grounds and 27,962 of those cases on the merits. As Figure 3.2 shows, the circuits have terminated a total of 50,000

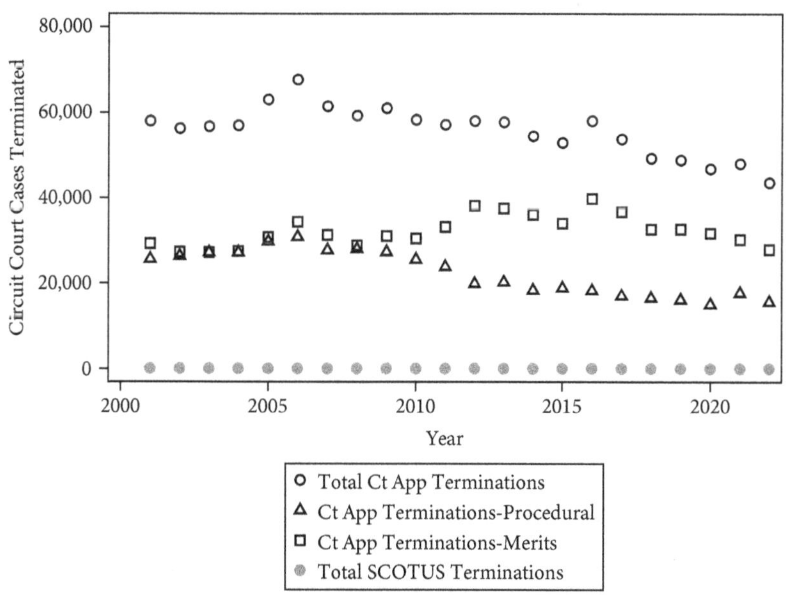

Figure 3.2 Cases Terminated by the United States Courts of Appeals. Data collected from the United States Courts (https://www.uscourts.gov/statistics-reports/caseload-statistics-data-tables) and the Supreme Court Database (http://scdb.wustl.edu/).

[5] The presiding judge is not always the opinion assignor. Some circuits require the presiding judge's assignment to be approved by the Chief Judge, while other circuits assign authorship by rotation or lot (Coffin 1994, 168).

[6] For these and similar data, see https://www.uscourts.gov/statistics-reports/caseload-statistics-data-tables.

to 60,000 cases per year over the last 20 years. Though not all of such cases received "full" treatment—meaning, extensive briefing and oral argument—many of them did. The circuits have terminated (on the merits) approximately 40,000 cases per year. To provide a reference point showing just how many cases these judges decide, we report the total number of cases the U.S. Supreme Court decided each term (displayed as gray, filled circles). (This number includes cases the Supreme Court terminated on the merits as well as cases it disposed of on the merits but without oral argument.) The number never comes close to 100. Put simply, circuit court judges hear and decide many cases each year, and this matters because the crushing workload may expose cognitive decline among them.

Scholars know a fair amount about what makes circuit court judges tick. Some of the features that explain their behaviors include: ideological considerations, workload, panel composition, whether they are visiting or senior judges, and various case characteristics. We discuss each in turn.

A judge's ideological preferences drive his or her behavior. Nearly 50 years of empirical research supports the notion that circuit judges pursue their ideological goals—at least in part—when they render decisions (Benesh 2002; Giles, Hettinger, and Peppers 2001; Songer and Haire 1992; Goldman 1966). Judges themselves have even suggested as much. Judge Patricia Wald once stated: "[T]he values by which judges make choices in areas of discretion will more often than not be in sync with that section of the political spectrum they inhabited in their former lives" (Wald 1992, 180). Howard's (1981) interviews with appellate court judges revealed that their personal views played a significant role in how they decided cases. What is more, not only do judges tend to vote based on their ideological preferences, they also bargain over opinion content with those preferences in mind (Black and Owens 2013).

While judges' ideological goals are important, their workloads also significantly influence their behavior (Hettinger, Lindquist, and Martinek 2006). Judge Wald once stated: "[T]ime and docket pressures very definitely constrict the judge" (Wald 1985, 10). Having to read through numerous briefs each week stretching into thousands of pages, these judges—even with the assistance of law clerks—simply do not have time to give every case their full consideration (Coffin 1994). As Hettinger and colleagues note, "Workload may matter because it is influential—if not determinative—of the time judges have to articulate disagreement with their peers" (2006, 40). A heavy workload can exacerbate other tensions. It can make busy judges take shortcuts. It can make them less likely to engage in effortful work. It can make them write shorter opinions and take longer to complete their tasks. In short, workload matters.

The composition of a panel of judges also can shape how judges decide cases. This phenomenon is known as a "panel effect." Panel effects occur when the composition of a three-judge panel influences the votes judges cast. For example, the presence of a particular judge (or judge "type") could lead the other judges on a panel to vote differently than they otherwise would. Empirical evidence suggests that the presence of a female judge on a three-judge circuit court panel can cause the two male judges to vote differently in sex discrimination cases than they would have voted in the absence of a female (Boyd, Epstein, and Martin 2010). Likewise, Sunstein et al. (2006) argue that the presence of a single Democratic-appointed judge sitting with two Republican appointees reduces the likelihood of the panel reaching a conservative outcome (see also, Cross and Tiller 1998; Cross 2007). Likewise, a lone Republican-appointed judge serving with two Democratic-appointed judges makes the outcome less likely to be liberal.

The presence of visiting judges also can influence circuit court judges. Federal law allows the Chief Justice of the U.S. Supreme Court and the Chief Judge in each circuit to assign federal district and circuit court judges temporarily to three-judge circuit court panels when needed. In other words, they can re-assign judges from other circuits, on loan, for a brief time. In recent years, visiting judges participated in nearly 20% of cases decided on the merits across the circuits (Brudney and Ditslear 2001, 565). Circuit courts invite these judges to serve in order to address ever increasing appellate court caseloads. Perhaps not surprisingly, visiting judges are less likely than active circuit judges to write majority opinions and dissent (Brudney and Ditslear 2001; Benesh 2006).

Much like visiting judges, those with senior status also seem to behave differently than active circuit judges. When an Article III judge reaches the age of pension eligibility, she has the option of remaining an active judge, retiring, or opting for "senior status" (Yoon 2005). Under current law, a judge becomes pension eligible according to the Rule of 80: A judge's age (if she is at least 65) plus her years of service must amount to at least 80. A judge who retires ceases to hear cases or otherwise work as a judge. She receives her pension, which is her full (current) salary for life. She is not eligible to receive any raises Congress grants to judges (Block 2007). Over the course of 12 months, a senior judge must undertake the amount of work an active judge performs in three months. Senior judges continue to receive their full salaries and are eligible for any cost of living adjustment and salary increase Congresses authorizes for judges (Block 2007). When a judge takes senior status, she creates a vacancy for the president to fill with a new (active) judge.

Senior judges continue to hear and decide cases, write opinions, and presumably, shape the law. The purpose of senior status is to open up a vacancy for a new judge to fill while allowing the judiciary to enjoy the benefits of an experienced judge. But the effects of senior status are unclear. A judge who takes senior status usually continues to hear cases but has much more control over the number and types of cases in which she would like to participate (Yoon 2005). Yet, even with that reduced workload, it appears that many senior judges are simply less engaged. Black and Owens (2013) find that senior judges are less likely to engage with opinion writers, for example. As such, we must account for senior status throughout the book.

The complexity and salience of cases can influence how judges behave. Circuit judges try to filter cases that require significant work from those that do not. One of the first things a judge does with a case is to engage in "rational triage" to determine whether it is "light," "moderate," or "heavy" (Coffin 1994, 172–175). The heavy, complex cases require more effort and time. The same is true for salient cases. More complex or salient cases influence how judges behave.

New judges exhibit different behavior than their seasoned colleagues. For instance, Hettinger, Lindquist, and Martinek (2003*a*) find that freshman effects are strong on the courts of appeals (see also Kaheny, Haire, and Benesh 2008). Likewise, Chief Judges have "internal" and "external" responsibilities beyond decision-making that keep them busy (Wasby 2003). Chief Judges must preside over cases and render decisions but also must attend to the needs of the circuit, supervise staff, participate in the Judicial Conference, oversee the district courts within the circuit, and engage in a host of additional administrative functions (Wasby 2003; Hettinger, Lindquist, and Martinek 2003*b*). These separate obligations take away from the judge's time to decide cases and lead Chiefs to behave differently than their colleagues. Finally, judges rated as highly qualified by the American Bar Association sometimes operate in ways that are different than their supposedly less qualified peers (Black and Owens 2013). We must account for this feature as well.

Despite this voluminous scholarship on circuit court judges, only a handful of studies examine the effects of aging on judges (Opeskin 2015). Some studies examine the effects of aging on opinion quality. In his book, *Aging and Old Age*, Posner (1995*a*) spends a chapter analyzing whether aged judges write poorer quality opinions than younger judges. To do so, he examines how often a judge is cited by other judges. (Note that his unit of analysis is the judge and not each opinion.) In his view, citation rates reflect judge quality; a judge who writes higher quality opinions will obtain more cites because fellow judges want to cite the best opinions. Posner finds evidence to suggest that "there is an age-related decline in judging [but] that it may not set in until an unusually advanced age" (188). In other words, citation rates per judge held fairly constant until old age. Other studies also examine whether older judges' opinions are cited more or less at the U.S. Supreme Court (Kosma 1998), in Canada (McCormick 1996), and in Australia (Bhattacharya and Smyth 2001). But beyond these and a handful of other studies we cite throughout the book, there is little work on how cognitive aging influences judges.

It should come as no surprise to think that age-related declines in cognition impact judges. After all, the practice of judging relies heavily on cognitive capacity. Appellate judges must read thousands of pages of case materials and legal briefs, digest them, and apply them to the cases at hand. They must read and understand precedent and reason through how the case facts before them interact with existing law. And they must commit those arguments to writing while clearly articulating a rationale in light of precedent. All of this requires significant cognitive effort. An excerpt written by Judge Frank Coffin alludes to just how much cognitive effort is required to be a good judge. He writes:

> After a term of court, my return to chambers signals a distinct change of style and pace in work, the onset of a period of solitary labors, enlivened by discussions with my clerks. My mind is buzzing with memories, impressions, and insights from the arguments of from forty to sixty lawyers and the questions and views of my colleagues, expressed both on the bench and in conference. Before memory fades, I try to analyze the extent of the workload added by the new opinions I have been assigned and to organize it so that we can come close to being "written up" when next I go to court for a new round of arguments. This goal is seldom fully realized, but continually monitoring my chambers production helps me avoid falling too far behind.... (Coffin 1994, 174)

Judges have spoken directly to the issue of cognitive aging as well. Consider the so-called "Breyer Report." In September 2004 Chief Justice William Rehnquist created the committee, chaired by Justice Stephen Breyer, to examine how effectively the federal judiciary implemented the Judicial Conduct and Disability Act. (We discuss this and similar legislation more fully in the book's conclusion.) The committee interviewed chief judges to determine how they dealt with concerns over aging judges' disabilities. Some chief judges conceded that aging effected their colleagues' behavior. One chief judge stated:

> I did face problems of the aging process, that's the most difficult by far to deal with.... In most cases, the judge recognized it and got off the bench. But not in all cases. I talked to family members. I got them to approach the judge. You can't slap a formal complaint at the end of his career on an 83-year old judge who has rendered distinguished service.... I tried to approach that with great delicacy, through family members. (Breyer et al. 2006, 102)

Another chief judge stated: "If using the family is a possibility, then you want to try that, but that's a mixed bag" (Breyer et al. 2006, 102).[7] These comments are similar to those made by chief judges in previous interviews. Barr and Willging (1993) reported that chief judges with whom they spoke could recall at least 25 instances of age-related disability, a number the study's authors viewed as an under-estimate. The chief judges' concerns "result[ed] from aging and amount[ed] to a natural byproduct of a system in which judges have life tenure" (Barr and Willging 1993, 140). In one particular passage, the authors highlight the sensitive nature of how to address aging colleagues:

> One chief judge, caught between the denial of a problem from a distinguished colleague and threats from other judges to file a formal complaint, met with the judge's spouse and persuaded her to convince the judge to end his career while his reputation remained outstanding.... [O]ne judge told a story of how a senior judge's death resolved the problem: "I knew he couldn't do any more work, but I didn't tell him. I knew he'd die soon. If I'd told him, he'd have died that day." Making judgments about situations like this is the largely untold story of responding to problems of disability and aging. (Barr and Willging 1993, 140)

Consider the controversy surrounding Judge Pauline Newman—a 96-year-old sitting judge who has served for more than 39 years on the U.S. Court of Appeals for the Federal Circuit. As we mentioned in the book's introduction, the court's Chief Judge—Kimberly Moore—appointed a special committee in March 2023 to investigate complaints about Judge Newman. Colleagues and court staff claimed that Newman impeded the resolution of cases and did not complete her opinions timely. Her delays reportedly occurred even after Newman's workload was reduced following a 2021 heart attack and a 2022 fainting spell that rendered her immobile (without physical assistance). The Chief granted her this reduction even though Newman was still an active judge (i.e., had not taken senior status). According to the committee's report, "From October 2021 through March 2023, Judge Newman

[7] Another chief judge noted that s/he sometimes observed age-related decline, stating: "[i]f someone on the court of appeals is losing it or is out of control, his colleagues see that..." (Breyer et al. 2006, 103).

authored (including her dissents) less than half the opinions of an average active judge (28 compared to 61 for an average judge) and her opinions took approximately four times as long to issue (199 days compared to 53 days for an average active judge)."[8] What is more, the report detailed multiple incidents where observers perceived that Judge Newman exhibited a loss of mental acuity. One portion of the report details particularly troubling concerns:

> These affidavits [from more than 20 interviews] detail staff reports of deeply troubling interactions with Judge Newman that sadly suggest significant mental deterioration including memory loss, confusion, lack of comprehension, paranoia, anger, hostility, and severe agitation.... The staff have reported that Judge Newman has been unable to remember from day to day how to perform simple tasks, such as bringing the standard materials (e.g., briefs and bench memos to court, logging onto the computer network, and locating files). The staff also reported that, when help has been offered on these matters, she has appeared "paranoid" and insisted that her devices are hacked and bugged, sometimes by the Court itself. She has appeared unable to comprehend or recall explanations that are given to her, and staff have had to address the same matters over and over with her. Staff across the Court have reported exchanges with Judge Newman in which they have had to answer the same questions from her repeatedly in the same or subsequent days (many recorded in email exchanges), because she has not remembered or understood the answers.[9]

To be sure, the legal contributions of distinguished federal judges like Pauline Newman over a long career are noteworthy and merit recognition. And, the various examples we cite here stand out as having received substantial public attention. Yet, there is reason to be concerned about the many aging judges in the federal judiciary. Given the documented effects of aging on human cognition, there is considerable reason to expect that these effects will manifest systematically among older judges.

Just what kind of imprint cognitive aging can leave is the focus of our next section.

3.2 Cognitive Aging and Delays

Our first expectation is that judges will require more time to perform judicial tasks as they age. Speed is important to the judicial decision-making process. As Posner (1995*a*, 197) writes: "Speed is important in judicial work...judges have to make many decisions in a limited amount of time...." The old adage "justice delayed is justice denied" speaks to the importance of dispatch. But, as we discussed in the previous chapter, processing speed declines with age. Verhaeghen (2013) examined the differences in mental processing speeds of 1,354 pairs of young versus old adults.

[8] The report can be found at: https://cafc.uscourts.gov/release-of-materials-in-ongoing-judicial-investigation-2/.

[9] This quote can be found at pages 3–4 of the July 31, 2023 report. See https://cafc.uscourts.gov/release-of-materials-in-ongoing-judicial-investigation-2/.

He found that younger adults moved with a speed that was between 1.2 to 1.7 times faster than older adults. Schaie (1989) asked respondents to find the letter "A" in an experimental context and to compare identical pictures. The study found a strong negative correlation with age, with older people taking longer to complete the task than younger people. Simply put, we believe that as they age, judges will take more time to complete their tasks. Cognitive aging leads to decreased processing speed. Decreased processing speed leads to increased amounts of time to complete judicial tasks. Therefore, cognitive aging leads to increased time to complete tasks.

In fact, the Breyer Committee's interviews with chief judges showed that delay was strongly correlated with aging. One chief focused directly on age-related delays: "... it's primarily delay, that's the most frequent problem. With delinquent cases, we'd have the clerk call and ask the [aged] judge about it" (Breyer et al. 2006, 102). Another chief judge made a similar remark: "If there is some concern about delay, there'll be a quick phone call. [An official at that particular court] will make that call, he has an easy manner" (Breyer et al. 2006, 102). Still another chief said that he "routinely reviewed the quarterly caseload reports for each district and circuit judge" within his circuit to make sure aging judges did not fall behind in their work (Barr and Willging 1993, 140). In another circuit, "the circuit executive brought the names of judges who appeared to have backlog problems to the attention of the chief judge. Together they would send a constructive letter, offering assistance to address the backlog" (Barr and Willging 1993, 140). A different chief judge created a "60-day" list which contained the names of cases—and their opinion authors—that lingered beyond 60 days. At monthly meetings, the chief judge would require lagging judges to explain their delays to their colleagues (Barr and Willging 1993).

This increased delay should be especially evident when judges write opinions. Opinion writing is arguably the most cognitively burdensome judicial task. Judges must master numerous issues across a variety of cases. When a judge hears a case, she must become fluent—or at least conversant—in the underlying legal content of that case. This requires cognitive effort. Appellate judges must be able to master a number and variety of concepts. Consider this: during the 12-month period ending on September 30, 2022, the circuit courts terminated on the merits just over 21,000 case. Among them were 2,500 civil rights cases, 4,143 prisoner petitions, 610 immigration offenses, 1,502 diversity of citizenship disputes, antitrust actions, tort cases, habeas corpus claims, tax suits, and a plethora of others.[10] That is a lot of information to learn and to synthesize.

This leads us to our first hypothesis: *As judges age, they will require more time to craft opinions and to exercise their judicial tasks.*

3.3 Cognitive Aging and Heuristics

We also believe that aged judges will be more likely than younger judges to rely on simplifying heuristics to help them make decisions. Studies show that "when faced

[10] See https://www.uscourts.gov/sites/default/files/data_tables/jb_b1a_0930.2022.xlsx.

with a difficult question, we often answer an easier one instead, usually without noticing the substitution" (Kahneman 2011, 12). People utilize decision-making shortcuts to simplify the world. Kahneman and Tversky identified what they call System 1 and System 2 thinking. System 1 is automatic and intuitive thought—if we can call it thought. It is often a knee-jerk reaction to something. System 1 thinking "operates automatically and quickly, with little or no effort and no sense of voluntary control" (Kahneman 2011, 20). System 2, on the other hand, is effortful, rational thought. It is the kind of thought that allows a person to know that a cute puppy might actually bite you, that a smiling stranger might not necessarily have kind intentions, and that $43 \times 82 = 3,526$. "Only the slower System 2 can construct thoughts in an orderly series of steps" (Kahneman 2011, 21). Kahneman even singles out "check[ing] the validity of a complex legal argument" as one example of a System 2 operation.

Within the political science literature, scholars have identified a variety of heuristics people use.[11] Voters use partisanship as a shortcut. People with low information and those without cognitive resources often use partisanship to decide their positions on issues and for whom they will vote. They rely on party "brands" as heuristic cues about candidates' ideologies (Popkin 1994; Downs 1957). Voters often know little about the specific policy positions of individual candidates, yet they often have general impressions of party positions and vote based on that knowledge. "Party-policy brands serve as heuristic cues about candidates' ideology" (Butler and Powell 2014). One study notes:

> For millions of Americans, the party label is the chief cue for their decisions about candidates or issues. It is the point of reference that allows them to organize and simplify the buzzing confusion and strident rhetoric of American politics. It shapes their perceptions and structures their choices; it relates their political values and goals to the real options of American politics (Beck 1997, 8).[12]

If voters know what a "Republican" usually stands for, and if they know that a particular candidate is a Republican, they can infer that candidate's policy positions.

People also rely on ideology as a cue (Sulfaro 1996). As Scheufele and Lewenstein (2005, 660) tell us, people "rely on heuristics or cognitive shortcuts, such as ideological predispositions, religious beliefs, and media portrayals, in order to form judgments about issues... that they know little or nothing about." Dahlberg and Harteveld

[11] Behavioral economists and psychologists have examined a number of interesting shortcuts. For example, they have analyzed the anchoring heuristic (your sense of something's numerical value can be effected by exposure to random numbers beforehand) (Guthrie, Rachlinski, and Wistrich 2001), availability bias (assessing risk based on how readily examples come to mind) (Thaler and Sunstein 2009, 25), representative bias (judging based on stereotypes) (Thaler and Sunstein 2009), and other shortcuts. With some notable exceptions (Owens 2023; Rachlinski and Wistrich 2017; Chen, Moskowitz, and Shue 2016; Guthrie, Rachlinski, and Wistrich 2007, 2001), few studies apply such work to judges.

[12] Parties know this, of course, and do what they can to enhance their brand names. Modern parties actually work to create and maintain strong brands to win elections (Cox and McCubbins 2005). Party members authorize party leaders to act as their trustees in creating legislative results that match party principles and create a positive brand for the party. It is important that the brand represent something identifiable.

(2016) show that knowledge of the ideological locations of parties allows voters to impute parties' specific views on issues. Taken together, these studies show that when the effort of learning about politics is steep, people rely on cognitive shortcuts like ideology. We suspect that judges are similar.

Consider the opinion-writing process. Each judge must decide whether to bargain with the opinion writer over the content of a draft opinion. Each opinion author must decide whether to accept or reject those suggestions. We suspect that those decisions become more cognitively taxing as judges age. Or, consider how judges apply precedent from upper courts or even sister circuits. They must understand that precedent and then apply it to the facts of the case before them. This practice can be intellectually challenging and also complicated when the judge strongly dislikes a precedent. Taken together, we expect that *judges will rely more on cognitive shortcuts as they age.*

3.4 Cognitive Aging, Law Clerks, and Briefs

We also expect that judges may be more likely to rely on others for assistance as they age. We have in mind two types of people on whom judges might become more reliant: the judges' law clerks and the attorneys in cases.

As they age, judges may rely more on the parties' briefs. Party briefs are among the most important sources of information for judges (Feldman 2017*a*). According to one important work, the brief is "the central feature of modern appellate practice" (Martineau et al. 2005, 770). Judge Paul R. Michel of the Federal Circuit has declared that he can reach a decision in roughly 80% of cases just from reading the briefs (Michel 1998, 21; quoted in Corley 2008, 468). First Circuit Court of Appeals Judge Frank M. Coffin once stated: "I know of no other field of human endeavor where a limited number of pages of written and structured argument can be so decisive as in appellate decision-making" (Coffin 1994, 107). Briefs are present for judges to use "from the beginning until the end of the case" (Feldman 2017*a*, 121). Briefs are useful for all judges but we expect them to be particularly so for aging judges. More specifically, we expect that *when they write opinions, aging judges will rely more on party briefs.*

Aging judges may also rely more on their law clerks. Law clerks today are surrogates for their judges. Judges delegate significant power to clerks. Those powers include (but are not limited to) reviewing whether the court possesses jurisdiction to hear the dispute before it, scrutinizing whether the parties are otherwise barred from bringing their suit, advising the judges on how they should vote, preparing them for oral argument, analyzing the law for them and, perhaps most importantly for our purposes, writing portions of the opinions.

Once again, Judge Coffin provides unique insight, here, on the role of clerks. "My first mission, on settling back into chambers, is to bring my clerks 'up to speed' on all the new cases by telling them the salient points discussed in the judges' conference" (Coffin 1994, 174). He goes on to note that because judges often lack sufficient time to spend on important cases, they assign these important cases to their clerks to research and write. "To give a great deal of responsibility to a law clerk is... a generally unavoidable consequence of today's demands upon an appellate judge" (Coffin 1994, 197).

If young judges assign hard or time consuming cases to their clerks, it seems reasonable to believe that they would rely more on their clerks as they age. Age-related decline is likely to influence how judges write opinions. And so we expect that *aging judges increasingly will rely on their clerks to write their opinions.*

3.5 Cognitive Aging and Decreased Legal Influence

We also suspect that aging judges will exert less legal influence than younger judges because the quality of their opinions will decline. As we stated in Chapter 2, the prefrontal cortex shrinks as we age (Paraskevoudi, Balcı, and Vatakis 2018). "[A]fter the age of 65, a reduction of 10–17% of the frontal cortex occurs" which represents "a selective deterioration of areas involved in high-level cognitive function" (Paraskevoudi, Balcı, and Vatakis 2018, 78). This is relevant because executive functioning takes place in the prefrontal cortex (Paraskevoudi, Balcı, and Vatakis 2018). Powell (1994) finds that reasoning is an "early casualt[y] of the aging process" (86). Examining the decline in inductive reasoning (among other aspects of cognition), Salthouse (1991) finds significant declines in inductive reasoning with age. Harada, Love, and Triebel (2013, 741) agree, noting that "[r]easoning with unfamiliar material... declines with age." Schaie (2005) found a statistically significant decline in people's reasoning at about age 53.

Aging judges may not write with the same zeal or quality as they once did; their influence over others and the law may wane. If so, we might observe this dynamic in the opinions they write. Those opinions may change in terms of style, content, and length. They may also diminish in terms of quality (see, e.g., Kosma 1998; Posner 1995*a*). Since executive functioning and reasoning skills have been shown to decrease with age, we expect to uncover evidence of decreased quality of opinions with judge age. We hypothesize that *as they age, judges will write opinions that are less cognitively complex and are less influential across the circuits.*

We also expect to see reduced influence as it relates to panel effects. Again, panel effects occur when the composition of a three-judge panel influences the votes judges cast. As we reported earlier, some evidence shows that the presence of a female judge can influence male judges. We suspect that age may create its own kind of panel effect. More specifically, we suspect age will matter when we examine counter judges and twain judges. A counter judge is someone who sits with two panel colleagues who were appointed by a president of the other party. A twain judge is a judge who shares appointment partisanship with another judge on the three-judge panel. Based on all the features we described in Chapter 2, we expect that *aging counter judges will be less likely to persuade twain judges to "switch" to their position.* We also expect that *when aging judges are among the twain judges, they will be more persuadable than younger twain judges.* (Of course, this could be a shortcut as well.) Aged judges may be more susceptible to panel effects than younger judges.

3.6 Conclusion

In this chapter, we laid out some of the likeliest observable manifestations of cognitive decline among federal circuit court judges. Older judges will take longer to complete their tasks; they will rely on shortcuts more than younger judges rely on them; they will rely on others more as they age; and their influence in the judiciary will wane. The chapters that follow test these claims.

We remind the reader that we do not expect to observe huge effects in each of the chapters that follow. Aging is gradual and its effects sometimes modest. Some people are affected by aging more than others, and some experience effects in different ways. We expect to observe effects across various aspects of judicial behavior. We expect them to be noticeable, if not extreme. And that is exactly what the remaining chapters show—across the board but sometimes modest effects across a wide swath of judicial behavior, and with enough consistency to raise serious questions about a greying judiciary.

4
Opinion Crafting and Cognitive Aging

On December 7, 1983, in a case called *Pope v. Railroad Retirement Board*, the U.S. Court of Appeals for the District of Columbia heard a dispute over attorney fees. In a previous decision that involved the same parties, the court had held that the United States Railroad Retirement Board did not use proper procedures when it sued Wilhelmina Pope and Edward Williams. The question now before the three-judge appellate panel was whether Pope and Williams could collect attorney fees from the recently-held-liable United States. Immediately after hearing oral arguments, the three judges on the panel—J. Skelly Wright, Earl Tamm, and Luther Swygert—held a private conference to discuss which party should win the case and why. They decided to reverse the district court judge who, they believed, ought to have awarded Pope and Williams attorney fees. Luther Swygert—a 79-year-old judge—received the responsibility of writing a short *per curiam* ("for the court") opinion.

Despite the fact that the panel had determined the opinion would be quick and easy, Swygert did not circulate his draft opinion until September 10, 1984, 278 days later. The delay was unusual. Judges typically circulate *per curiam* opinions within a week or two of assignment. Swygert required nine months. Also unusual was the response his draft opinion received from the other judges on the panel. Judge Wright told Swygert that his opinion unnecessarily needled the lower court judge, stating:

> I have read with interest your pc op. in [the] above case. I think it is excellent and does [the] job very well. I do think, however, that in [a] couple of places you come down [a] bit hard on the USDC [district court judge]. It might be better under [the] circumstances to eliminate those parts that might offend [the] USDC unless they are necessary for [the] op[inion].

The opinion eventually published on October 2, 1984. *See Pope v. Railroad Retirement Board*, 744 F.2d 868 (CADC 1984). It was short (roughly 1300 words), broke no new ground, and largely repeated much of the court's opinion from the previous case.

What explains Swygert's long delay? Was it the fact that he was 79 years old? As we indicated in earlier chapters, older adults experience slower processing speeds than younger adults; their executive functioning is less efficient than younger adults'; and their reasoning abilities tend to retrogress. There is little debate over whether aging correlates with overall reduced cognitive performance. Cognitive aging likely influences how judges craft opinions, the length of time it takes to write them, and how they negotiate with one another over them. Writing opinions is difficult and requires cognitive firepower. It requires cognitive exertion that can push even the most efficient brain to the max. So, was Swygert's delay a function of his age? Perhaps so.

Cognitive Aging and the Federal Circuit Courts: How Senescence Influences the Law and Judges.
Ryan C. Black, Ryan J. Owens, Patrick C. Wohlfarth, Oxford University Press. DOI: 10.1093/oso/9780197747025.003.0004

This chapter analyzes whether aging judges behave differently when they write opinions. Specifically, we examine whether, as they age, judges require more time to circulate opinion drafts and increasingly rely on cognitive shortcuts. The results show that the answer to both questions is yes.

4.1 Opinion Writing, Timing, and Shortcuts

When judges write opinions, they must master a variety of legal issues. A tax case requires a judge to digest tax law. A criminal case necessitates that the judge comprehend criminal law. And a telecommunications case demands the judge ascertain telecommunications. So it is with every issue in every case. In a recent year, the circuit courts decided 2,500 civil rights cases, 4,143 prisoner petitions, 610 immigration offenses, 1,502 diversity of citizenship disputes, antitrust actions, tort cases, habeas corpus claims, tax suits, and a plethora of others.[1] That is a substantial amount of information to learn, to command, and to synthesize. With the exception of judges who sit on specialized courts, federal appellate judges cannot limit themselves to particular cases or legal issues. That is, judges not on senior status lack the luxury to say "I don't understand this legal issue; someone else can decide it." (Judges on senior status have more control over their schedules and the types of cases they decide.) To be a capable judge, one must have the ability to learn many legal issues effectively—and quickly.

In addition to mastering a variety of legal issues, judges also must decide a large quantity of cases. In the 12-month period before March 31, 2023, federal appellate circuit courts terminated 41,906 cases.[2] There are 179 authorized circuit court judgeships today,[3] which means that each judge, sitting on a three-judge panel, must decide numerous cases.

As judges address a wide-ranging variety of issues and numerous cases, they simultaneously seek to write quality opinions that engender respect. This includes respect from their panel and circuit colleagues, judges on other courts, lawyers, and the public. Reputationally, judges want their opinions to survive scrutiny from broader audiences. Judges "want to be respected as professionals who are capable of doing their work well and who adhere to the norms of their job" (Baum 2006, 54). They want their colleagues and other judges to respect their work product. They want lawyers and law professors to evaluate their opinions positively. And many care whether their opinions will withstand public scrutiny (Owens and Wohlfarth 2019). Knowing that others will evaluate their work, judges have an incentive to build a respectable corpus of opinions.

All of these factors make opinion writing a cognitively demanding task. But as we note throughout this book, age-related declines reduce cognitive efficiencies, particularly the speed with which the brain processes information. Older adults take longer than younger adults to process ideas and thoughts (Salthouse 1996). At some point, judges likely require more time to maintain their workloads—even if they can rely on their law clerks for some assistance. But time and delays can gum up

[1] See https://www.uscourts.gov/sites/default/files/data_tables/jb_b1a_0930.2022.xlsx.

[2] See https://www.uscourts.gov/statistics/table/na/federal-court-management-statistics/2023/03/31.

[3] See https://www.uscourts.gov/file/21616/download.

the judiciary. As Ninth Circuit Court of Appeals Judge Eugene Wright once wrote: "Time—judicial time—is our most valuable commodity. We must employ it effectively and efficiently if we are to keep abreast of new developments in the law, new areas of litigation, and modern procedural improvements..." (Wright 1973, 1179).

Judges have admitted that age impacts the time it takes them and their colleagues to perform their tasks. The so-called "Breyer Report," undertaken in September 2006 to examine how the federal judiciary was implementing the Judicial Conduct and Disability Act, explored how chief judges addressed concerns over aging judges' disabilities. Chiefs not uncommonly reported concerns over age-related delays. They also discussed the informal actions they undertook to resolve those delays. (Elsewhere in the book, we address some of these informal actions, such as prevailing upon spouses to persuade their loved ones to retire.)

As they age, judges are likely to require more time to write their opinions. Opinion writing requires mental acuity. On top of that, circuit court judges decide a potpourri of legal issues—and many, to boot. They seek to acquire and maintain the approval of their colleagues and other audiences. Under "normal" conditions, opinion writing is difficult and time consuming. Under conditions of slow processing speed and reduced executive functioning, it is even more precarious. Taken together, this leads us to believe that as judges age, they are likely to require more time to write opinions.

We also suspect that aged judges, relative to younger judges, will be more likely to rely on cognitive heuristics when they bargain over the content of opinions.[4] After a panel holds oral argument in a case, the three judges meet in brief "impression conferences" (Coffin 1994) to discuss the day's cases. There, they declare their views on the case. The presiding judge then selects an opinion author. Once the author completes the draft opinion, she sends it to the other judges on the panel with the hopes of gaining their acceptance. Those judges can respond by joining the opinion without changes, by asking for changes (politely or threateningly), or by noting that they disagree and will write a separate opinion. If the opinion author wishes, she can accommodate the judges who suggest the change(s) or reject them and see what happens. This bargaining can be cognitively taxing and time consuming.

Importantly for us, people use heuristics when cognitive costs are high. Kahneman (2011, 12) argues that "when faced with a difficult question, we often answer an easier one instead, usually without noticing the substitution." Decades of studies by political scientists on the American voter show that voters use ideology and partisanship to make decisions (Sulfaro 1996). As Scheufele and Lewenstein (2005, 660) tell us, people "rely on heuristics... such as ideological predispositions... in order to form judgments about issues...." Dahlberg and Harteveld (2016) show that knowledge of the ideological locations of parties allows voters to impute candidates' specific views on issues. Similarly, voters rely on party brands as heuristic cues about candidates' ideologies (Butler and Powell 2014; Popkin 1994; Downs 1957). As one study put it: "Increasing the number of alternatives... should increase the complexity of the task, and increase the reliance on heuristics" (O'Brien and Harris 2014, 2706).

[4] For a more extensive discussion—and to see the language from which we borrow in this part—see Black and Owens (2013).

Like other people, judges also utilize shortcuts when they face cognitive demands. Posner (2008, 108) writes that under some conditions, "the cost [to a judge] of consciously processing...information may be so high that intuition will enable a more accurate as well as speedier decision than analytical reasoning would." Federal magistrate judges fall prey to anchoring effects, framing, hindsight bias, the representative heuristic, and egocentric biases (Guthrie, Rachlinski, and Wistrich 2001). Florida trial court judges "candidly admit[ted]" in a series of interviews that "time pressures present[ed] an enormous challenge, often inducing less-than-optimal decision making" (Guthrie, Rachlinski, and Wistrich 2007, 35). A related study found that "[j]udges, facing cognitive overload...are more likely to make intuitive rather than deliberate decisions because the former are speedier and easier" (Guthrie, Rachlinski, and Wistrich 2007, 35).

While judges may rely on a host of heuristics, we expect that their ideological preference in the case will be among the greatest. Judges are more likely to rely on ideology when cognitive costs increase. Judges already rely on ideology to decide cases (e.g., Songer and Haire 1992; Hettinger, Lindquist, and Martinek 2004, 2006). In fact, judges' ideological preferences have been shown to predict a considerable amount of behavior (Benesh 2002; Giles, Hettinger, and Peppers 2001; Songer and Haire 1992; Goldman 1966). Judges who display conservative tendencies often vote for right-leaning outcomes while judges who display liberal tendencies vote for left-leaning outcomes. Judges vote based on ideological preferences, and bargain with those preferences in mind (Black and Owens 2013). Our expectation, then, is that as judges age, they will increasingly rely on ideology when they negotiate with colleagues over opinion content.

4.2 Data and Measures

The only way to examine the time it takes judges to write opinion drafts or to determine how they bargain with each other is to obtain and evaluate the judges' private materials. We employ data from Black and Owens (2013), who gathered and content-analyzed the private papers of Judge J. Skelly Wright, a D.C. Circuit Court of Appeals judge from 1962 to 1988. Wright's archival data provide a treasure trove of materials. Among other things, his papers reveal: when (if at all) judges heard oral arguments in cases, their conference votes, who assigned opinions, who received opinion assignments, when writers circulated opinions, and the content of any bargaining and accommodation that occurred during the opinion crafting phase. Black and Owens (2013) analyzed case sheets from 2,728 unique docket numbers across Wright's tenure as a circuit judge.

4.3 Delays and Opinion Writing

We begin by evaluating whether cognitive aging leads to delays in opinion writing. The dependent variable in our first analysis captures the *Number of Days* between opinion assignment and the date the opinion author circulated his or her first draft.

To code this variable, we looked to Wright's docket sheets to determine the date the opinion was assigned and the date the opinion writer circulated the first draft opinion. The mean time to circulate a draft opinion in the sample is approximately 70 days. Our key covariate of interest is *Author Age*, which is the age of the opinion author at the time of opinion assignment in each case. To code the variable, we collected from the Federal Judicial Center's *Biographical Directory of Article III Federal Judges* the birth dates of each circuit judge in the sample.[5] We then identified the date of the opinion assignment. Finally, we computed the number of years between the assignment date and each judge's birth date, subtracting the birth year from the year of the assignment.

One important control variable we account for is another time-based characteristic—a judge's experience. Every additional year that transpires adds to a judge's age, but it also represents an additional year of experience on the bench. We can imagine that greater experience is likely correlated with greater efficiency in opinion writing. Failing to separate out the independent effects of aging versus experience could lead us to conclude erroneously that aging does not matter or, worse still, to err about the way in which it matters. To guard against this, we include *Opinion Author Experience*, which is the number of years an author has served as a judge at the time of opinion assignment.

We also include a number of control variables, consistent with Black and Owens' (2013) original models. We examine case complexity, as more complex and immportant cases likely require more drafting time. To capture complexity, we use the number of pre-draft memos circulated by the judges in a case and whether the court allowed the parties to offer oral argument. *Number of Pre-Draft Memos* is a count of the number of memos the judges circulated in each case after oral argument (if held) but prior to the circulation of the first opinion draft. *Orally Argued Case* takes on a value of 1 if the case received oral argument; 0 otherwise. For a similar reason, we code *En Banc Case* and assign a 1 to those decisions rendered by an *en banc* panel; 0 otherwise. In some highly important cases, all (or most, in the case of the Ninth Circuit) of the judges on the circuit will sit together—*en banc*—to decide a case.

We further include several dummy variables to capture different characteristics of the authoring judge. These measures also come from the FJC's *Biographical Directory of Article III Federal Judges*. We include controls for whether the opinion author was black (*Black Opinion Author*) or female (*Female Opinion Author*), assigning a 1 if the judge has such an identity (0 otherwise). *Guest Author* equals 1 if the authoring judge came from another circuit besides the D.C. Circuit; 0 otherwise.[6] *Senior Author* takes on a value of 1 if the judge had taken senior status before the circulation of the draft opinion; 0 otherwise. We similarly coded whether the authoring judge was a *Freshman* or *Chief* Judge. Again, we assign a 1 to judges with those characteristics. Freshman judges (those with less than two years' experience) may be finding their way and take longer to write; Chiefs might require more time to write because administrative obligations take up their time. We also controlled for the judge's perceived qualifications. When the president nominates someone to a

[5] See https://www.fjc.gov/history/judges.

[6] A handful of guest judges in this sample are district court judges sitting by designation. See https://www.americanbar.org/groups/committees/federal_judiciary/.

federal judgeship, the American Bar Association evaluates whether the nominee is not qualified, qualified, or well qualified for the position. *High Quality Author* takes on a value of 1 when the ABA rated the judge as well qualified; 0 if qualified or not qualified. *Author Panel Median* takes on a value of 1 if the opinion author was the median judge on the panel; 0 otherwise. According to the median voter theorem, median judges enjoy more institutional power than non-median judges and their actions may be different as a result. Finally, we account for the judge's workload by performing a series of searches on LexisNexis and counting the number of opinions written by the opinion author (*Author Workload*) that were released within 30 days after the author initially circulated the draft opinion. A judge with a larger workload may require more time to write her opinion.

We employ a Cox proportional hazards regression model with the Breslow model for handling ties. The Cox model is the most useful and analytically appropriate model to estimate how covariates affect the time it takes for an "event"—here, the circulation of the draft opinion—to take place. An additional useful feature of the Cox model is that, as a semi-parametric method, it does not require us to specify *ex ante* the underlying distribution from which the baseline hazard function is estimated. This model predicts the "risk" that an opinion author will circulate the draft opinion over time (i.e., the number of days since opinion assignment), given that the opinion draft has not already been circulated.

We estimate a total of three models and report parameter estimates for these models in Table 4.1. The first model is bivariate and includes only our *Opinion Author Age* measure; the second model is "trivariate" and includes both *Opinion Author Age* and *Opinion Author Experience*. Finally, the third model includes the full suite of controls. In the first two specifications, we fail to find a statistically significant effect for either the age or experience level of an opinion author. In the third model, however, we find effects that are both statistically significant and align with our theoretical expectations. Given this rather dramatic transformation, one might wonder about how sensitive our key result is to the specific inclusion of control variables. We provide a longer explanation in the chapter appendix for interested readers, but, for those of limited interested, the punchline is that we see no strong reason to be concerned.

Focusing on the fully specified model (i.e., Column 3), we uncover a negative coefficient on the key covariate of interest, *Opinion Author Age*, and the hazard rate (i.e., relative risk) that a judge circulates an opinion. When the relative risk of circulation decreases, it means that a judge is less likely to circulate the opinion and the amount of time until circulation increases. In other words, consistent with our theoretical expectation, the results indicate that aging opinion authors take *more time* to circulate their drafts. What's more, it is not as though older judges use that increased time to improve the quality of their opinions. As we show in Chapter 7, older judges' opinions are actually of lower quality than younger judges' opinions.

To help understand the substantive magnitude of this effect, we turn to Figure 4.1, which shows the probability that an opinion author has circulated her initial draft (y-axis), conditional on the number of days elapsed since assignment (x-axis), and her age at the time of opinion assignment (line type within the plot). The solid line represents an author who is among the youngest in our sample—50 years old, or the 5th percentile. The dashed line represents an author who is among the oldest in our

Table 4.1 Time to Circulate the First Opinion Draft

	(1)	(2)	(3)
Opinion Author Age	0.0025	0.0045	−0.0274**
	(0.0026)	(0.0036)	(0.0054)
Opinion Author Experience		−0.0031	0.0190**
		(0.0042)	(0.0059)
Pre-Draft Memos			−0.1095**
			(0.0404)
Orally Argued Case			−0.2768**
			(0.0792)
En Banc Case			−0.4356**
			(0.0674)
Black Opinion Author			−1.1983**
			(0.1062)
Female Opinion Author			0.5935**
			(0.1347)
Guest Author			−0.1911*
			(0.1054)
Senior Author			0.1592
			(0.1169)
Freshman Author			0.0433
			(0.0917)
Chief Author			0.1102
			(0.0730)
High Quality Author			−0.5516**
			(0.0627)
Author Panel Median			0.0464
			(0.0487)
Author Workload			−0.0361**
			(0.0152)
N	2,020	2,020	2,020
BIC	26,781.26	26,788.37	26,593.51

Note: Table entries are Cox Proportional Hazard regression coefficients with robust standard errors in parentheses. The dependent variable represents, for each case, the number of days between the opinion assignment and circulation of the first opinion draft. * and ** denote $p < 0.10$ and $p < 0.05$, respectively (two-tailed). Data come from the private papers of Judge J. Skelly Wright on the D.C. Circuit Court of Appeals, 1962–1988. Negative coefficients mean that the risk of circulation decreases which, in turn, means that the amount of time *increases*.

sample—74 years old, or the 95th percentile. We hold all other predictors constant at their median values. This figure provides us with a clear portrayal of the effect of an opinion author's age.

Consider the near-immediate production of an initial draft. There is a 0.144 probability that, by the end of the very first day after an assignment is made, a young opinion author has circulated her opinion. The likelihood that an older opinion author has done so is approximately half that value—i.e., a probability of about 0.075. Though this relative difference decreases steadily from there on out (i.e., the probability is never twice as high), the older judge continues to lag behind the younger judge in a substantively meaningful way. We estimate a 0.50 probability that after

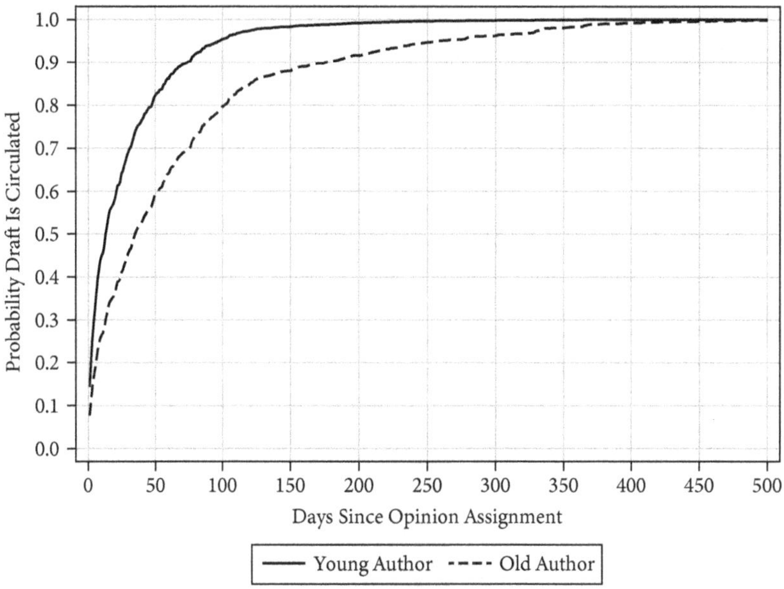

Figure 4.1 The impact of age on the time needed to write and circulate the first opinion draft. Figure reports the probability that the first opinion draft has circulated as a function of the days since opinion assignment, using results from Model 3 in Table 4.1. The darker, solid line represents a young opinion author (50 years old; 5th percentile) while the dashed line represents an older judge (74 years old; 95th percentile). All other variables were held at their median values.

just 13 days a young opinion author has circulated her draft. For an older opinion author, the probability of circulation after 13 days is only 0.30. It will take more than an additional 3 weeks—22 more days, to be exact—before an older opinion author has a greater than 0.50 probability of having circulated a first draft (she has a 0.501 probability after 35 days). And, at that point, we estimate a 0.74 probability that the younger opinion author has circulated a first draft. After 90 days, the older opinion author observes just a 0.77 probability of having circulated a draft compared to a 0.94 probability for the younger author. To put that in perspective, the 0.77 value is slightly greater than the probability that the younger judge has circulated *five opinions in that same period of time* (if we assume, for the sake of a dramatic splash, that each of these events is statistically independent (i.e., $0.94^5 \approx 0.73$)).

For another empirical perspective on these results, we calculate the expected duration of an opinion author's drafting time using the generalized additive model (GAM) approach proposed by Kropko and Harden (2020) and implemented via the `coxed` package in R (Kropko and Harden 2019). For this approach, we estimate the predicted duration for the same two opinion authors: one who is 50 years old and one who is 74 years old. All other model covariates are held at their observed values, so the only thing changing between the two sets of calculations is the opinion author's age. From this we learn that the average time-to-circulation for a young opinion author is approximately 46 days. For an older opinion author, however, the mean time-to-circulation is over 101 days. This difference of about 55 days is nearly two months long and is a relative increase of 120%.[7]

A skeptic might note that, by using the 5th and 95th percentiles, we have selected hypothetical values located in the tails of our sample. Fine. The analogous results from more modest comparisons are still noteworthy. If we look at the 25th and 75th percentile values of author age (56 and 69, respectively), we obtain average expected durations of around 55 days for the 25th percentile judge and 91 days for the older judge. The 36 days separating these two expectations constitutes a 65% relative increase. And, for those who prefer looking at discrete amounts above and below the average value of opinion author age, the expected duration for an author who is one standard deviation below the average age (i.e., 55 years old) is about 53 days compared to an expected duration of 95 days for an author whose age is one standard deviation above the mean (i.e., 71 years old). This is, remarkably, a 79% relative increase.

These individual case differences are noteworthy in and of themselves. Their substantive impact is all the greater when one considers that circuit judges decide many cases, which exacerbates these effects. The average annual number of written, signed decisions per (active) D.C. Circuit judge from 1992–2018 was approximately 21 opinions. Given this, we can predict that a judge who is 71 years old, which is just a single standard deviation above the average in our sample, is likely to expend *almost 16 additional months drafting opinions* compared to a judge who is 63 years old, which is the sample average. And justice delayed can often mean justice denied. Moreover, if these results offer any indication of the impact of aging among judges in the other circuit courts of appeals—many of whom decide *more cases* than the D.C. Circuit—the costs of cognitive aging there are likely to be even more severe.

Among our controls, we find a number of features that increase the amount of time to circulation. Complex cases that observe an increasing amount of pre-draft memos take longer to circulate, as do opinions in orally argued and *en banc* cases. Authors with greater workloads also, and unsurprisingly, take longer to circulate their opinions. We also find that black opinion authors tend to be slower to circulate their first drafts relative to non-black authors. Guest judges tend to take longer than home circuit judges to write opinions. And, somewhat surprisingly, judges whom the ABA rated as high quality tend to write slower than those rated not qualified. (Of course, this could mean that the baseline judges, those who are unqualified, write too quickly!) In terms of factors associated with greater writing speed, we find that additional experience is associated with faster time to circulation. We also find that female authors circulate their drafts quicker than do their male counterparts.

4.4 The Decision to Bargain

Our next analysis focuses on a responding judge's decision to seek changes to the draft opinion. That is, we shift units of analysis from focusing on the behavior of the authoring judge to how the other judges on the panel respond to the opinion draft.

[7] The median time-to-circulation for a young opinion author is approximately 27 days. For an older opinion author, the median time-to-circulation is over 90 days—a predicted difference of 59 days.

We evaluate two dependent variables. First, we examine whether each responding judge makes a substantive suggestion to the opinion author. If she does, then we code *Suggestion* as 1. If not, we code it as 0. We observe suggestion-seeking behavior in just under 16% of the responding judge-authoring judge dyads in our data. Our second dependent variable assesses whether a responding judge issued a threat to the opinion author. This language simply indicates that a responding judge will not fully join the majority opinion unless the author undertakes certain changes. We code *Threat* as 1 if a responding judge threatened to withhold a vote unless the author made certain changes to the opinion; 0 otherwise. This type of behavior is uncommon on the circuit courts. We observe it in only 111 out of the more than 6,111 author-responding judge dyads in our data, which works out to a rate of approximately just 1.8%.

Among our independent variables, *Responding Judge Age* is measured the same as above. *Responder-Author Ideological Distance* is the absolute value of the ideological difference between the opinion writer and the responding judge, using the Judicial Common Space (JCS) (Epstein et al. 2007). The JCS is a scaling procedure that allows scholars to compare the ideal points of Supreme Court justices, members of Congress, presidents, and, most important for our purposes here, lower court judges. Negative scores mean a judge is more liberal; positive scores mean a judge is more conservative. To determine the interactive effect of the two variables, we multiply *Responding Judge Age* with *Ideological Distance*.

Our controls predominantly come from the earlier model, but we also supplement them in light of the dyadic nature of these data and, particularly, the need to control for attributes of the responding judge. To that end, we now also include *Responder Panel Median*, which equals 1 if the judge making a suggestion in a case was the median judge; 0 otherwise. *Responder Workload* measures the number of opinions by the responding judge that were released within thirty days after the opinion author initially circulated the draft opinion. *Guest Responder* equals 1 if the responding judge came from another circuit besides the DC Circuit (0 otherwise).[8] To determine whether the responding judge had senior status, we examined the FJC website to determine whether the sitting judge took senior status before the circulation of the draft opinion. If so, *Senior Responder* takes on a value of 1; 0 otherwise. We similarly coded whether the responding judge was a *Freshman* or *Chief Judge*. We followed the same practice as before to code the responding judge's perceived quality.

Because both dependent variables are dichotomous, we estimate logistic regression models. Table 4.2 reports coefficient estimates for the *Suggestion* and *Threat* dependent variables. For each of these variables, we present an initial baseline specification that features our key covariates of interest—i.e., the age and ideology interaction—as well as the fully specified model that includes the full battery of statistical controls.

The interactive nature of our main independent variables makes them difficult to interpret from the table, so we turn to predicted probabilities. We begin by evaluating a responding judge's likelihood of offering a substantive suggestion to the opinion author, which we plot in Figure 4.2. The x-axis shows the responding judge's age at circulation. The y-axis reports the probability the responding judge makes a

[8] Again, a handful of guest judges in this sample are district court judges sitting by designation.

Table 4.2 Responses to Majority Opinion Drafts

	Suggestion		Threat	
	(1)	(2)	(1)	(2)
Responding Judge Age	−0.0331**	−0.0455**	−0.0804**	−0.0910**
	(0.0052)	(0.0086)	(0.0269)	(0.0317)
Ideological Distance	0.4042	0.2559	−4.6587**	−5.2747**
	(0.5567)	(0.5882)	(1.9028)	(1.7638)
Ideo. Dist. × Age	−0.0047	0.0004	0.1044**	0.1292**
	(0.0091)	(0.0095)	(0.0321)	(0.0311)
Judge Experience		0.0256**		−0.0095
		(0.0099)		(0.0249)
Pre-Draft Memos		0.0250		−0.0387
		(0.0455)		(0.1667)
Orally Argued Case		0.4746**		0.5669
		(0.1624)		(0.4976)
Freshman Judge		−0.0755		0.7111**
		(0.1354)		(0.3084)
Freshman Author		0.4039**		0.9437**
		(0.1485)		(0.2838)
Guest Judge		−0.6567**		
		(0.3178)		
Guest Author		0.8987**		2.9819**
		(0.2752)		(0.4107)
Senior Judge		−0.2511		−0.3248
		(0.1818)		(0.4753)
Senior Author		0.1057		−1.5977**
		(0.2362)		(0.8046)
Chief Judge		−0.1124		−0.4559
		(0.1438)		(0.3475)
Chief Author		−0.2242		−0.9233*
		(0.1432)		(0.5027)
High Quality Judge		0.5654**		1.2704**
		(0.0823)		(0.2088)
High Quality Author		0.1027		0.6870**
		(0.1052)		(0.2868)
Judge Workload		−0.0422		−0.0152
		(0.0270)		(0.0600)
Joint Service		0.0000		0.0004**
		(0.0000)		(0.0001)
En Banc Case		−0.7869**		−0.5617
		(0.1456)		(0.3695)
Author Panel Median		−0.4575**		0.2932
		(0.0988)		(0.2289)
Responder Panel Median		0.1213		0.3079
		(0.0856)		(0.2075)
Opinion Author Age		−0.0124*		−0.0078
		(0.0073)		(0.0176)
Constant	0.3168	1.1115	−0.0385	−1.8329
	(0.3207)	(0.7178)	(1.5307)	(2.1289)
N	6,111	6,111	6,111	6,111
BIC	5,262.74	5,182.32	1,082.575	1,125.13

Note: Table entries are logistic regression coefficient estimates with robust standard errors, clustered on each docket, in parentheses. Suggestion is whether a responding judges makes a suggestion to the opinion author. Threat is whether a responding judges threatens to withhold his vote unless a change is made. Both are coded such that 0 = no; 1 = yes. * and ** denote $p < 0.10$ and $p < 0.05$, respectively (two-tailed). Data come from the private papers of Judge J. Skelly Wright on the D.C. Circuit Court of Appeals, 1962–1988. Guest Judge is omitted from the Threat model due to perfect prediction of no threat being made.

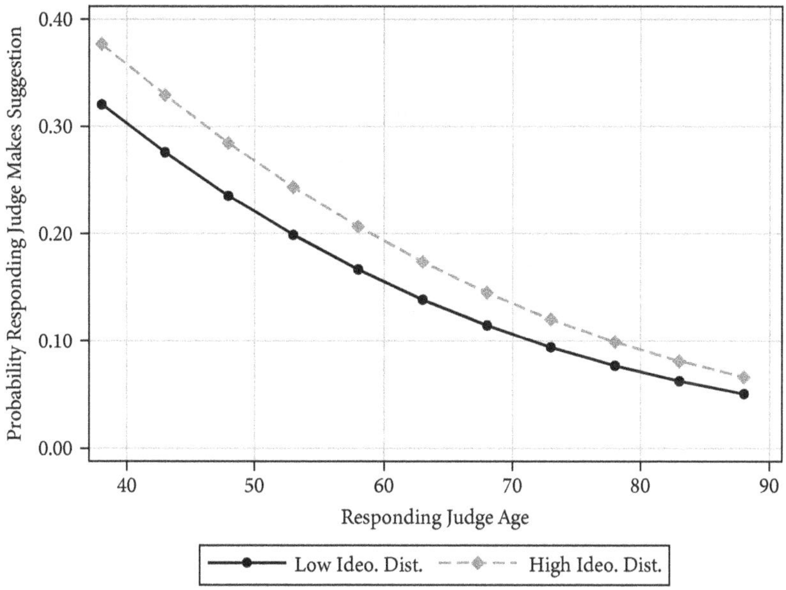

Figure 4.2 The effect of responding judge age and ideological distance from the authoring judge on the likelihood a responding judge offers a substantive suggestion. Figure reports the predicted probability the responding judge makes a suggestion using results from the suggestion Model 2 in Table 4.2. The effect of responding judge age is negative and statistically significant for all values of ideological distance, but there is no significant difference in the slope of these two lines.

suggestion. The line types show two hypothetical scenarios: one where ideological distance between the judges is low (solid line, circle points) and another where ideological distance is high (dashed line, diamond points). We define low ideological distance as being 0, which occurs around 14% of the observations in our sample, and high ideological as being 1, which is approximately the 95th percentile value in our data.

The slope of both lines is negative, which tells us that as judges age, they all become less likely to suggest changes to opinion drafts. This negative age-based effect is statistically significant for all values of ideological distance. For example, when ideological distance is at zero and a responding judge is 38 years old, we estimate a 0.32 probability that she makes a suggestion. If the responding judge is at the sample median of approximately 63 years old, that probability decreases to just 0.14—a relative decrease of 56%. When the responding judge's age approaches the sample maximum of 91 years old, the probability shrivels to a value of just 0.045. This is an 86% decrease relative to the youngest judge and a 68% relative decrease when compared to the median value of responding judge age. In general, a two-year increase in age is associated with roughly a 1% decrease in the likelihood of making a suggestion.

In terms of the interplay between ideological distance and responding judge age, the near-parallel nature of the lines in Figure 4.2 reveals no evidence of a significant interactive effect. An increase in ideological distance is, generally, associated with a somewhat elevated probability of making a suggestion, but the age of a responding judge neither attenuates nor exacerbates that effect in terms of ideology's effect on age.[9]

Among our controls, we find a positive effect for judge experience, whether the case was orally argued, if the authoring judge was a freshman or a guest author, and if the responding judge was of high quality (as rated by the ABA). Conversely, suggestions are significantly less likely to occur if the responding judge was not from the D.C. Circuit, if the case was decided *en banc* (versus as a three-judge panel), and if the authoring judge was the panel median.

We next assess responding judge threats in Figure 4.3. We construct this figure identically to the earlier suggestion figure, which is to say it shows the probability of a responding judge making a threat (y-axis), conditional on the age of the responding

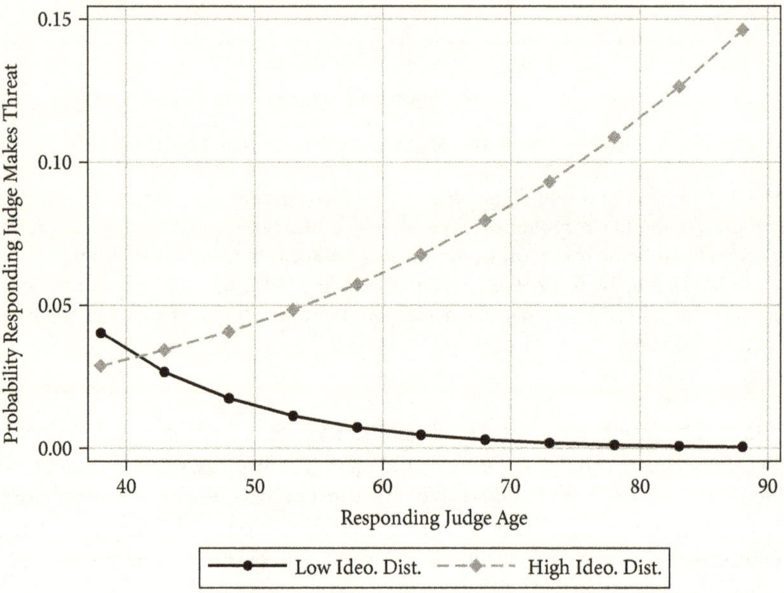

Figure 4.3 The effect of responding judge age and ideological distance from the authoring judge on the likelihood a responding judge makes a threat. Figure reports the predicted probability the responding judge makes a threat using results from the threat Model 2 in Table 4.2. The effect of responding judge age is positive and significant when ideological distance is high, but negative and significant when ideological distance is low. The difference in the slopes of these two lines is statistically significant.

[9] The estimated effect of a one-unit increase in ideological distance (i.e., going between the two lines in the figure) ranges from as much as +0.057 when responding judge age is 38 years old to as small as +0.014 when responding judge age is 91 years old. At these extreme values, however, the effect is neither statistically distinguishable from zero nor significantly different when compared to each other. The p-values for the individual marginal effects are 0.27 (young responding judge) and 0.35 (old responding judge); the p-value for the test of equality between the two is 0.48. The range of responding judge age over which the visual difference between the two lines *is* statistically significant runs from approximately 49 years of age until 73 years of age ($p < 0.10$, two-tailed test). This covers about 85% of the observations in our sample. The magnitude of the effect starts at +0.048 (young) and trends downward to +0.026 (old), but this difference is not statistically significant ($p = 0.47$).

judge (x-axis) and the level of ideological distance between the responding judge and the opinion author (lines within the plot). We see a modest negative slope when ideological distance is low but a strong positive slope when ideological distance is high, which suggests an interaction between ideological distance and responding judge age.[10] These visual differences are statistically significant, which is to say we can conclude that the effect of responding judge age is negative when ideological distance is low and positive when ideological distance is high. And, the difference in the slopes of these two lines is, itself, statistically significant.

Taken together, these results provide "double-barreled" evidence of how aged judges rely more heavily on ideological cues than their younger counterparts do. Older judges are more influenced by the *presence* of ideological distance between a responding judge and majority opinion draft author than are younger responding judges. When such a responding judge is young (38 years old), we estimate just a 0.029 probability that she threatens to withhold her vote. When the judge is at the median age (63 years old), by contrast, this probability more than doubles to a value of 0.068. And, when the judge is approaching the oldest age in our sample, the probability has, once again, more than doubled to a value of 0.159.[11] That is more than a five-fold increase over the probability of the youngest judge. In slightly different terms, it would take roughly 35 cases before we would expect to see a threat from a younger judge but it would take only seven cases before we would expect to see one from an older judge. Older judges leverage the cue of ideological distance much more than do younger judges.

Additionally, we find suggestive evidence that older judges exhibit complementary behavior when it comes to using the shortcut in the *absence* of ideological distance in terms of *not* making a threat. When ideological distance is low, a responding judge who is 38 years old has a 0.04 probability of threatening to withhold support for the draft majority opinion. When the responding judge is at the sample median age of 63 years, however, that probability has dropped to just 0.005 (i.e., one-half of one percent). And, a responding judge who is 91 years old, near the sample maximum, has just a 0.0004 probability of making a threat.[12] These are relative decreases of approximately 88% (youngest to median), 92% (median to oldest), and 99% (youngest to oldest). To put those numbers in perspective, in low ideological distance contexts, we would expect to see a threat from the young judge once in approximately 25 cases, but only once in every 200 cases for the median-aged judge, and only once in every 2500 cases for the oldest judge.

Our control predictors in the threat model exhibit significant and positive effects if either the responding judge or authoring judge were freshman and if either the responding judge or authoring judge were of high quality. Guest authors are more

[10] The effect of ideological distance is negative but not statistically significant when responding judges are 38, 39, or 40 years old ($p > 0.20$). It takes on positive values from 41 years old and greater. The p-value stays above 0.20 until 46 years of age, when it drops to 0.118 (46 years old) and then to 0.060 (47 years old); it is below 0.05 from 48 years old through the sample maximum of 91 years old.

[11] The difference in probability of a threat between the youngest and oldest judge when ideological distance is high is 0.131 and has a two-tailed p-value of 0.054.

[12] The difference between the probability of a threat when a judge is young versus old and ideological distance is low is roughly 0.04, which has a two-tailed p-value of 0.091.

likely to have threats made against them and as the duration of joint service between a responding-authoring pair of judges increases. Our results suggest just two negative correlates of making threats: whether the author of the opinion has taken senior status or whether the authoring judge was the Chief Judge of the circuit.[13]

4.5 Rejecting Colleagues

We next (and finally) analyze how aging majority opinion authors respond to the substantive changes their colleagues seek.[14] Once again, we estimate a logistic regression model. The dependent variable in this analysis takes on a value of 1 if the opinion writer *rejects* the substantive changes proffered by her colleague and 0 if she accepts them. The main independent variables include *Author Age* and *Responder-Author Ideological Distance* and the interaction of the two. Our other measures remain the same. Table 4.3 shows parameter estimates for both a baseline model (i.e., Model 1) as well as a second specification with all control variables (i.e., Model 2).

Figure 4.4 plots the predicted probability of rejection as a function of the ideological distance between a responding judge and the opinion author (x-axis) and the age of the opinion author (line type). There is a perceptible slope difference between the two plotted lines. When ideological distance is small (the left side of the figure), young opinion authors are (slightly) more likely to reject suggested changes from their colleagues than older opinion authors. But, when the opinion author and suggesting judge strongly disagree ideologically (the right side of the figure), the relative ordering reverses and the magnitude of the difference jumps. In terms of probabilities, for a young opinion author, we estimate a 0.123 probability of rejecting a suggestion if ideological distance is at its lowest versus a 0.186 probability when it is at its highest value; though, the difference is not statistically significant ($p = 0.39$). By contrast, when an opinion author is older, the probability of rejection jumps from just 0.080 when a colleague is ideologically proximate to 0.380 when the responding judge is ideologically distant. This nearly five-fold increase is statistically significant ($p < 0.05$) and we can conclude the visual difference in the slopes of the two lines is, itself, statistically significant ($p < 0.05$).

For another view, consider Figure 4.5, which reports the marginal effect of a one-unit increase in ideological distance (i.e., almost equivalent of going from sample minimum to maximum) across the range of our opinion author age variable. Ideology has essentially no impact on whether younger opinion writers reject a suggestion sought

[13] Though also bear in mind, per the caption to Table 4.2, whether a responding judge is a guest judge is a perfect predictor of not making a threat. This is to say that guest judge responder status, then, has the strongest possible negative effect on issuing a threat.

[14] Related analyses would look at the amount of time that elapses between the initial circulation of the majority opinion draft and when opinion-writing process concludes, or the complete duration from assignment until completion. We have assessed both of these dependent variables. We find that older opinion authors and older panels tend to have *shorter* amounts of time during which responsive accommodation is taking place (responses received until publication), but overall are associated with *longer* durations when it comes to the entire length of the opinion-writing process. See the chapter's appendix for a table of parameter estimates for these models as well as figures presenting the substantive effect of the results.

Table 4.3 Rejection of Substantive Changes by the Opinion Author

	(1)	(2)
Opinion Author Age	−0.0456**	−0.0195
	(0.0162)	(0.0285)
Ideological Distance	−2.3188	−2.2146
	(1.5234)	(1.9410)
Ideo. Dist. × Age	0.0507**	0.0562*
	(0.0238)	(0.0312)
Author Experience		−0.0105
		(0.0278)
Pre-Draft Memos		−0.1743
		(0.1598)
Orally Argued Case		−0.5680
		(0.4336)
Freshman Judge		−0.1335
		(0.3639)
Freshman Author		0.3626
		(0.3662)
Guest Judge		−0.4967
		(1.0477)
Guest Author		0.2004
		(0.5173)
Senior Judge		0.6075
		(0.4804)
Senior Author		−0.2120
		(0.7836)
Chief Judge		0.9539**
		(0.3105)
Chief Author		0.6369
		(0.4353)
High Quality Judge		−0.2302
		(0.2143)
High Quality Author		0.7782**
		(0.2862)
Author Workload		−0.2116**
		(0.0777)
Joint Service		−0.0001
		(0.0001)
En Banc Case		0.9174**
		(0.2939)
Author Panel Median		0.1895
		(0.2569)
Responder Panel Median		0.4241*
		(0.2407)
Judge Age		0.0023
		(0.0187)
Constant	0.7445	−0.9293
	(0.9862)	(1.7203)
N	804	804
BIC	721.53	800.74

Note: Table entries are logistic regression coefficient estimates with robust standard errors, clustered on each docket, in parentheses. The dependent variable is whether a majority opinion author rejects a substantive change from a responding judge (0 = no; 1 = yes). * and ** denote $p < 0.10$ and $p < 0.05$, respectively (two-tailed). Data come from the private papers of Judge J. Skelly Wright on the D.C. Circuit Court of Appeals, 1962–1988.

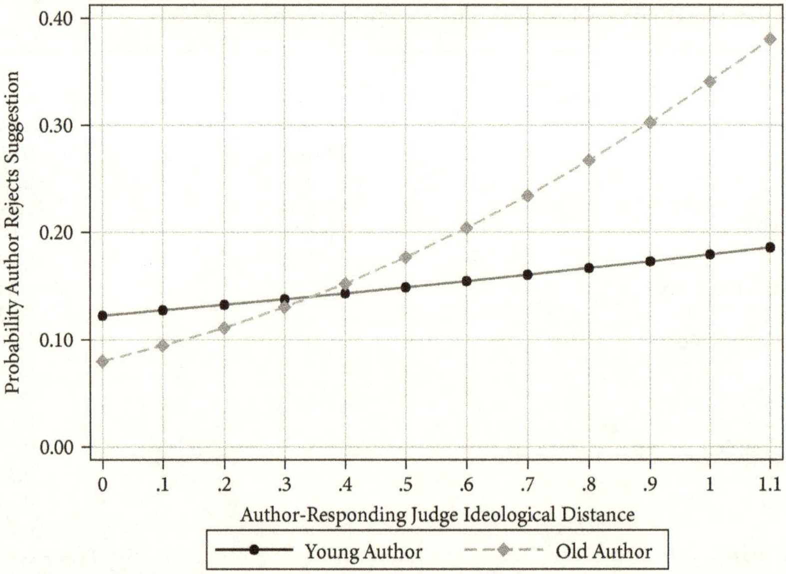

Figure 4.4 The impact of judge age and ideological distance on circuit court bargaining. Figure reports the predicted probability that a majority opinion author rejects a substantive request across the range of *Responder-Author Ideological Distance* using results from Model 2 in Table 4.3. Young Author and Old Author correspond to an author who is 48.3 years old or 74.7 years old; these are, respectively, the 5th and 95th percentile values in the sample. They differ from earlier models due to the subset of observations on which the model is estimated (i.e., only instances where a suggestion is made).

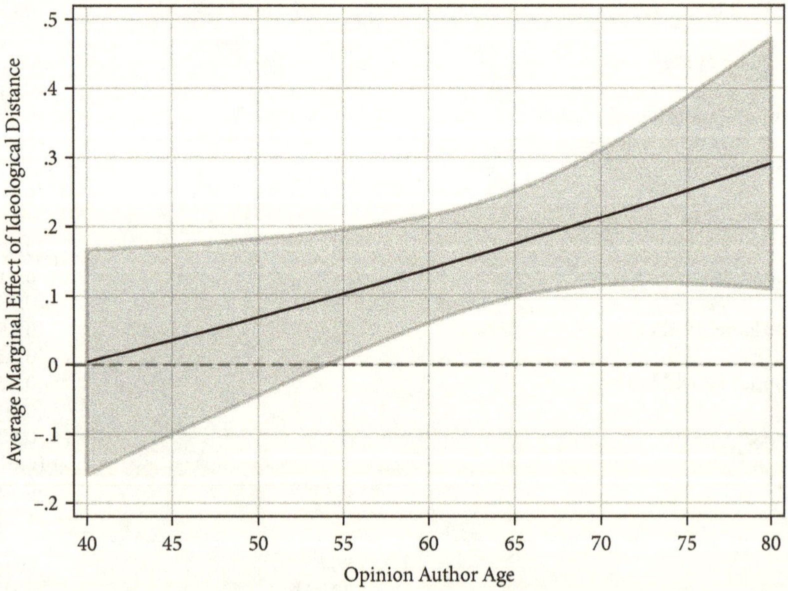

Figure 4.5 The marginal effects of ideological distance, conditional on judge age, on circuit court bargaining (with 95% confidence intervals). The y-axis shows the effect of a one-unit increase in ideological distance on the probability that an opinion author rejects a substantive change sought by a responding judge using results from Model 2 in Table 4.3.

by a colleague. As an opinion writer ages, the effect of ideology gains in strength and becomes statistically significant. Older opinion authors appear to consider ideology when determining how to respond to proposed changes whereas younger opinion authors do not.[15] We believe these results support our hypothesis that cognitive aging leads judges to rely on ideology as a cognitive shortcut.

Among our controls, we find that opinion authors are more likely to reject suggestions from Chief Judges (perhaps because they know the Chief is too busy to raise a fuss), in *en banc* cases, and when the responding judge was the panel median (which we did not expect). Authors rated higher by the ABA are also more likely to reject suggestions by their colleagues. Not surprisingly, authors with greater workloads are more likely to accept changes to their opinions (i.e., less likely to reject). Given their time constraints, this decision makes sense.

4.6 Conclusion

This chapter examined whether judges take longer to craft opinions as they age (they do) and whether they are more likely to rely on cognitive shortcuts as they age (they are). Adding up the time delays among older judges shows that a judiciary filled with aging judges will operate considerably slower than a judiciary of younger judges. That delay can harm litigants. As Wright (1973, 1193) notes: "Everyday that an appellate court opinion is delayed causes another day of injustice to some litigant. A well-disciplined judge will have set a time schedule for himself to meet." To be sure, time-to-circulation is not the only factor that matters. But the evidence here shows clearly that an aging judiciary will craft opinions more slowly than a younger judiciary.

What is more, the data suggest that older judges are more likely to rely on cognitive shortcuts than younger judges. As aging leads to increased cognitive costs on judges, they appear to rely more on cognitive heuristics. That feature is worrisome. We expect judges to overcome their impulses, to hunker down, and to impose reason in the law. That aging judges may be less able to do so than their younger counterparts is troubling.

But before we can confirm that is the case, we must continue our analyses. And so our next chapter turns to the final opinions judges eventually publish.

4.7 Appendix

4.7.1 Time to Initial Circulation Sensitivity Analysis

As we discuss in the chapter text, *Opinion Author Age*, our main independent variable of interest, is statistically significant and in the expected direction only in the fully specified model presented in Column 3 of Table 4.1. To determine the extent to

[15] We note that the null effect of ideology exists until age 51, 53, and 55 at the 0.20, 0.10, or 0.05 levels, respectively. This corresponds to between about 6% and 22% of the observations in our data, which we view as a modestly sized amount. We can also say that the visual difference in the marginal effects is statistically meaningful between a very young (i.e., 40 years old) and a very old (i.e., 80 years old) opinion author ($p = 0.058$).

which our results were driven by that particular specification, we conducted a model sensitivity analysis. We started with our full specification that contains 13 control variables in addition to our *Opinion Author Age* measure and iteratively estimated models that excluded each of those 13 controls while retaining the other 12 variables. For example, we first estimated a model that excluded the amount of experience the opinion author had and noted the direction (still negative) and significance (still $p < 0.05$) for this model. We then did another that added experience back while excluding *Pre-Draft Memos* (still negative, still $p < 0.05$). We then iteratively excluded all unique pairs (78 models), unique trios (286 models), unique quartets (715 models), unique quintets (1,287 models) and so on all the way down until we estimated another 13 models with only *Opinion Author Age* and a single control. All told, we estimated a total of 8,191 models.

For each of those models, we evaluated the directionality and significance of the *Opinion Author Age*. In terms of directionality, the effect was negative for 72.3% of the models. It was statistically significant at the 0.10 level (two-tailed) or better for 26% of the total models estimated (i.e., 2,157 out of 8,191). An additional 5% of models—400—had two-tailed p-values for age that were in the statistical "no-man's-land" zone of being above 0.10 but below 0.20. In general, we learn that the more under-specified a model is, the less likely it is to yield a significant result for *Opinion Author Age*. A majority of models with seven or fewer controls failed to yield what we would consider to be a non-null result (i.e., $p > 0.20$, two-tailed test). In evaluating what types of variables influence the results, we learn that controlling for various attributes of the opinion author is key. We estimated 31 models that include no author-level controls beyond the author's age. None of those models produced a statistically significant result. At the other end of the spectrum, we estimated 32 models that include the full slate of author-level controls. We find a negative and significant effect for opinion author age in 100% of those models.

4.7.2 Responsive Accommodation and Total Opinion-Writing Time

We also considered two alternative dependent variables that assess the potential that age might affect responsive accommodation during the opinion-writing process and the total time it takes to release the opinion: (1) the amount of time that elapses between the initial circulation of the majority opinion draft and when the opinion-writing process concludes; and (2) the complete duration from opinion assignment until completion. We, again, use a Cox duration model for each of these dependent variables. Table 4.4 reports the parameter estimates. Figure 4.6 shows the effects of opinion author age and the average age of the panel judges on the time that elapses between circulation of the initial draft and final release of the opinion. Figure 4.7 illustrates the results for the total duration of the opinion-writing process. In short, we find that older opinion authors and older panels tend to have *shorter* amounts of time during which responsive accommodation is taking place (responses received until publication), but overall are associated with *longer* durations when it comes to the entire length of the opinion-writing process.

Table 4.4 Responsive Accommodation and Overall Opinion-Writing Time

	Responsive Accommodation	**Entire Process Writing Time**
Opinion Author Age	0.0160**	−0.0191**
	(0.0062)	(0.0056)
Opinion Author Experience	0.0043	0.0179**
	(0.0068)	(0.0062)
Average Age of Panel Judges	0.0095**	−0.0184**
	(0.0042)	(0.0042)
Number of Judges on Panel	−0.0872*	−0.0483
	(0.0456)	(0.0393)
Chief Author	−0.2334**	0.0719
	(0.0855)	(0.0775)
Black Opinion Author	0.3424**	−1.0712**
	(0.1236)	(0.1106)
Female Opinion Author	0.3524**	0.8056**
	(0.1331)	(0.1323)
High Quality Author	0.1188*	−0.4627**
	(0.0624)	(0.0666)
Guest Author	−0.2330	−0.0759
	(0.1435)	(0.1106)
Freshman Author	0.1333	0.0449
	(0.0860)	(0.0840)
Senior Author	−0.1812	0.1151
	(0.1163)	(0.1223)
Author Workload	0.1051**	0.0183
	(0.0148)	(0.0150)
Pre-Draft Memos	−0.1150**	−0.1661**
	(0.0451)	(0.0486)
Orally Argued Case	−0.1917**	−0.2712**
	(0.0872)	(0.0870)
En Banc Case	−0.3481	−0.4296*
	(0.2798)	(0.2355)
Author Panel Median	−0.0644	−0.0179
	(0.0527)	(0.0496)
Time to First Draft	−0.0023**	
	(0.0003)	
N	1,881	2,012

Note: Table entries are Cox Proportional Hazard regression coefficients with robust standard errors in parentheses. Responsive accommodation is the number of days from initial circulation until the end of opinion writing. The entire process is the number of days between opinion assignment and the end of opinion writing. * and ** denote $p < 0.10$ and $p < 0.05$, respectively (two-tailed tests). Data come from the private papers of Judge J. Skelly Wright on the D.C. Circuit Court of Appeals, 1962–1988. Negative coefficients mean that the risk of the event decreases which, in turn, means that the amount of time *increases*.

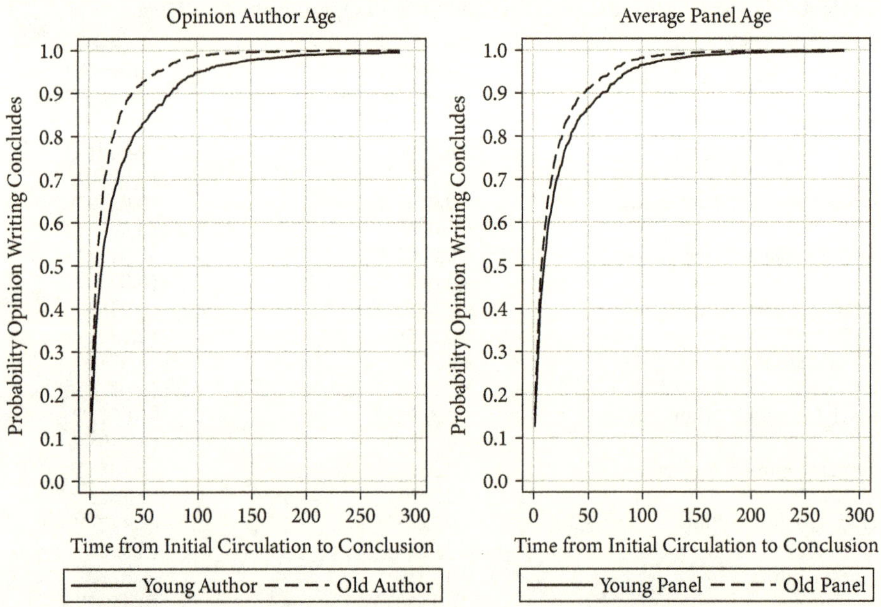

Figure 4.6 The impact of opinion author age (left panel) and average panelist age (right panel) on the time between when an opinion is initially circulated and the conclusion of the opinion-writing process. Figure reports the probability that the first opinion draft has circulated as a function of the days since opinion assignment, using results from the responsive accommodation model in Table 4.4. For the left panel, a young and old author are defined as judges who are 50 years old and 74 years old, respectively. For the right panel, a young and old panel are defined as those where the average panelist age is 54 years old and 73 years old, respectively. All other variables were held at their median values.

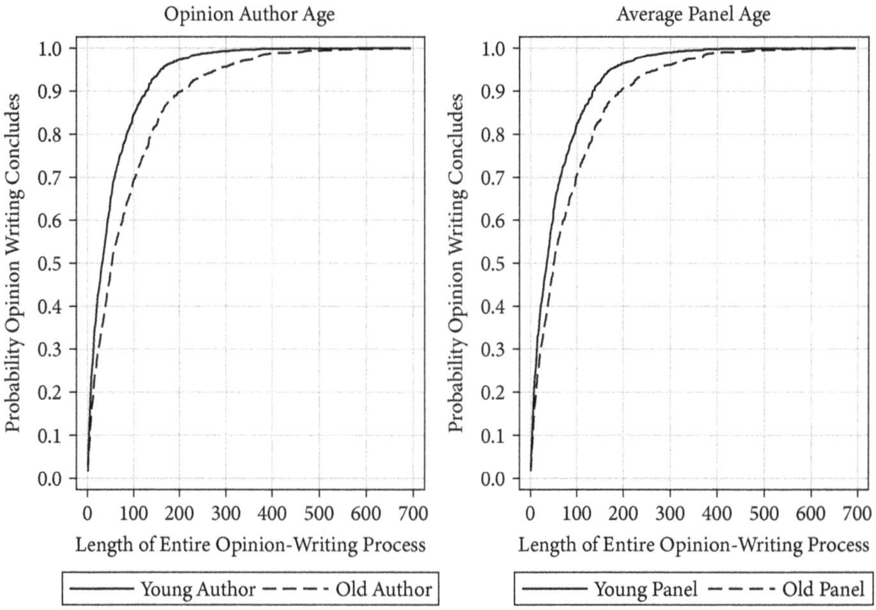

Figure 4.7 The impact of opinion author age (left panel) and average panelist age (right panel) on the time between when an opinion is assigned and the conclusion of the opinion-writing process. Figure reports the probability that the first opinion draft has circulated as a function of the days since opinion assignment, using results from the entire process writing time model in Table 4.4. For the left panel, a young and old author are defined as judges who are 50 years old and 74 years old, respectively. For the right panel, a young and old panel are defined as those where the average panelist age is 54 years old and 73 years old, respectively. All other variables were held at their median values.

5
Opinion Style

Co-authored with Alexander M. Tahk[1]

We began this book with a brief discussion of Judge Henry Friendly, who once told a colleague: "I have indeed become concerned about slippage; I am conscious that I do not write with the same passion or verve as I did five years ago, and hope that someone will have the kindness to tell me when the time has come to quit" (Dorsen 2012, 341). Friendly recognized that his writing abilities had declined with age. Of course, he was not the only judge ever to have noticed "slippage" in opinion writing. Others have been just as clear. Judge Posner, for example, once wrote that aging judges were even less equipped to perform than is commonly known. Some judges relied on their law clerks to write their opinions for them: "judicial ghostwriting—the delegation of opinion writing to law clerks—[...] is enabling a small number of senile judges, and a significant number of judges who are well past their prime though not yet senile (merely 'senescent'), to continue in office" (Posner 1995*a*, 181).

There is considerable reason to believe judges' opinions do change with time—and perhaps not for the better. If the research on cognitive aging has anything to say on the matter, we expect that as judges age, they write opinions that are less cognitively complex, are shorter in length, and are less sophisticated grammatically. Still, as we indicated earlier, cognitive aging does not generate *exclusively* negative outcomes. As people age, they report being happier and better able to manage personal relationships. Consequently, we expect that as judges age, their opinions will take on more positive tones. Our goal in this chapter is to determine if those expectations bear fruit.

And so we begin by explaining the opinion-writing process and, more specifically, factors that can shape opinions. We then discuss the literature on opinion content and the conditions under which judges employ some language versus other language. Then, we turn to our empirical analyses, where we focus on hundreds of judges, thousands of opinions, and millions of words.

5.1 Opinion-Writing Process

The circuit court opinion-writing process takes a series of twists and turns before the final opinion publishes (Black and Owens 2013). To begin, the parties must file an appeal with the clerk of the circuit court that possesses jurisdiction over the legal

[1] Associate Professor of Political Science and Director of the Tommy G. Thompson Center on Public Leadership, University of Wisconsin-Madison.

Cognitive Aging and the Federal Circuit Courts: How Senescence Influences the Law and Judges. Ryan C. Black, Ryan J. Owens, Patrick C. Wohlfarth, and Alexander Tahk, Oxford University Press. DOI: 10.1093/oso/9780197747025.003.0005

dispute. The clerk will docket the case and the court will randomly assign it to a panel of three judges (Breyer 1990, 29). The parties then submit briefs to that panel. If the panel wishes, it will schedule an oral argument (Wald 1992). Shortly thereafter, the judges hold a conference to discuss the case. Each judge states his or her views of the case and votes (Wald 1992, 177). Afterwards, the presiding judge on the panel (the most senior) assigns an opinion author. The author then drafts an opinion that is supposed to reflect the position of the conference majority.

An extensive and growing scholarship exists on a wide variety of features related to how judges write opinions and what those opinions say.[2] For example, recent studies show that courts choose to reference legal sources so as to protect their opinions. Black, Owens, and Brookhart (2014) find that the Supreme Court cites foreign sources of law more often in its controversial cases to provide extra support for its position. Corley, Howard, and Nixon (2005) show the Court is more likely to cite the *Federalist Papers* in controversial opinions. Horowitz (2011) finds that the Court is more likely, for strategic reasons, to cite authoritative case law when its decisions might be met with hostility from political actors and the public. Other scholarship shows that agencies and lower court judges alter the content of their opinions to avoid upper court review (Smith and Tiller 2002; Schanzenbach and Tiller 2006). And Epstein, Segal, and Victor (2002) suggest that the Supreme Court, when facing a hostile Congress, might rely on constitutional, rather than statutory grounds, to decide cases.

Other studies analyze whether the language judges employ is a function of external pressures. Owens, Wedeking, and Wohlfarth (2013) examine whether the separation of powers influences the clarity of Supreme Court opinions. They find that as the Court becomes increasingly distant ideologically from Congress, justices alter the readability of their opinions. They do so to increase the costs on Congress to read and react to the Court's opinions. Black, Owens, Wedeking, and Wohlfarth (2016) argue that courts write clear opinions to remove ambiguity that opponents can use to evade them (see also, Corley 2009). Staton and Vanberg (2008) argue that "[t]he more clearly an opinion states the policy implications of the decision, the easier it is to verify whether policy makers have faithfully complied, making it more likely that external actors can monitor and impose costs for noncompliance" (507). Spriggs (1996) shows that a comprehensible Supreme Court opinion makes it easier for litigants in cases involving federal agencies to take politically stubborn bureaucrats back to court (see also, Budziak and Lempert 2023; Goelzhauser and Cann 2014). As Vickrey, Denton, and Jefferson (2012) put it: "The challenge for the nation's judges... is to make sure that the public understands what is expressed in a supreme court opinion... [O]pinions serve as the court's voice because rulings communicate not

[2] Some studies simply conduct descriptive analyses of judicial opinion writing. For example, in his book *Evolution of the Judicial Opinion*, Popkin (2007) examines what he calls 'individual judicial styles.' He examines how some judges write with a technical voice, others write with a magisterial voice, and others write with a personal voice. He also provides anecdotal evidence that some judges write with different 'tones' than others.

only to lawyers, but also to the public..." (74). Not surprisingly, Benson and Kessler (1987) find that plain legal writing is more credible and persuasive than "legalese."

But, despite this relatively large corpus of research on judicial opinions, scholars know little about opinion content as a function of *judge aging*. One interesting and relevant study comes close. Wahlbeck, Spriggs, and Sigelman (2002) examined what they called "ghost writing" by law clerks at the U.S. Supreme Court. The authors argued that year-to-year variation in writing style showed that justices relied on their clerks, who worked at the Court for a year and then departed. They discovered that Justice Lewis Powell wrote opinions that employed similar language over his career. That is, the year-to-year differences in Powell's opinions were limited. The authors took these findings to mean that Justice Powell did not outsource much opinion writings to his clerks. (Or, if he did, he made sure they all employed his writing voice.) On the other hand, Justice Thurgood Marshall exhibited significant term-to-term variation in writing styles toward the end of his career. Those results suggested that Marshall relied more on his law clerks, who rotated every year, to write opinions as he aged. Though the study did not focus on the role of aging, its measurement approach revealed one way scholars might examine the effects of aging—by analyzing a judge's year-to-year variation in writing style.

Rosenthal and Yoon (2011*b*) performed a similar analysis but accounted for significantly more justices (see also, Li et al. 2013; Carlson, Livermore and Rockmore 2015; Bodwin, Rosenthal, and Yoon 2013*a*). They examined all published Supreme Court majority opinions from 1791 through 2011 that were greater than 250 words. They reported only on the most recent forty justices, however. Their results suggested that justices varied in their writings styles over the years. Some justices' opinions became increasingly variable with age, when comparing their first five year against their final five years. Justices Kennedy, White, Brennan, Stewart, Harlan, Warren, Clark, Frankfurter, Murphy, and Stone all varied more. Others showed less variability. Justices Souter, Burton, and Robert Jackson showed less variability in their opinions.

Only a small handful of studies systematically evaluate writing style on the federal circuits. Budziak, Hitt, and Lempert (2018) analyze writing style by measuring the reading difficulty, informality, affective language, and cognitive complexity of various circuit court opinions. They sought to determine whether judge variables (including age), case variables, or strategic variables correlated most strongly with a judge's writing style. Their results suggested that, overall, case variables accounted for the most variation in opinion content. Judge age played no significant role. Moyer et al. (2021) examined whether female or non-white circuit court judges write different opinions than white male judges. Specifically, they reviewed the length of opinions, the number of legal authorities those opinions cite, and whether the opinions engage in "deep" study of precedents. The findings suggested that female judges write longer opinions than male judges, that non-white judges cite more legal authorities than white judges, and that females and non-white judges engage in more deep citations than white male judges. Left untested was whether older judges write different kinds of opinions than younger judges and, if so, why.

5.2 Cognitive Aging and Opinion Writing

As we have pointed out, some cognitive domains decline with age. Some of the most important structural losses take place in the prefrontal cortex, which is responsible for executive functioning. Indeed, "[t]here is a sharp decline in executive functioning abilities after the age of 60" (Drag and Bieliauskas 2010, 80). Reading comprehension, abstract thought, reasoning, inhibition, and similar features all decline as a consequence. It is likely, then, that judges write opinions that are different (across various dimensions) as they age. We examine a host of possible differences, starting with the cognitive complexity of judges' opinions.

Cognitive complexity captures the level of "conceptual organization of decision-relevant information" (Gruenfeld 1995, 5) and refers to an individual's ability to "differentiate" and to "integrate" information (see also, Black, Owens, Wedeking, and Wohlfarth 2016, 44). Differentiation represents the degree to which an individual can see multiple perspectives or dimensions in an issue. It examines whether an individual perceives and explains events in black and white or in shades of gray. Integration represents the degree to which a person recognizes relationships and connections among perspectives or dimensions and integrates them into his or her decision or judgment. These two concepts scale into one dimension called "cognitive complexity." Less complex language relies on "one-dimensional, evaluative rules in interpreting events" in which actors make decisions "on the basis of only a few salient items of information" (Gruenfeld 1995, 5). On the other hand, with cognitively complex language, individuals tend to "interpret events in multidimensional terms and to integrate a variety of evidence in arriving at decisions" (Tetlock, Bernzweig, and Gallant 1985, 1228). We suspect that judges will write less cognitively complex opinions as they age.

Older judges may also write shorter opinions. Given that it takes aging judges longer to process information and that cognitive costs are simply higher for older judges, we suspect that their opinions will be shorter than opinions written by younger judges. Recall that processing speed declines markedly with age (Schaie 1994) and that slower processing speed is one of the most notable symptoms of cognitive aging (Harada, Love, and Triebel 2013; Salthouse 1996). Verhaeghen (2013) examined the differences in mental processing speeds of 1,354 pairs of young versus old adults. He found that older adults moved with a speed that was between 1.2 and 1.7 times greater than young adults. We expect that older judges will write shorter opinions just to keep up with their workloads. (As Chapter 4 pointed out, even that may not work.)

The sophistication of language, however, may not change with age. Research shows that cognitive aging does not diminish one's vocabulary—at least not until very old age (Tyler et al. 2010; Wingfield and Grossman 2006). Older people enjoy larger vocabularies than younger people (Verhaeghen 2013). They generally retain their understanding of words, even if their speed in retrieving them decreases with age. Given these findings, we expect that the sophistication of older judge opinions will be greater than or equal to that of younger judges.

We also know that emotional stability and overall happiness increase with age. Older adults report being as happy, or happier than younger adults (Buecker et al. 2023). They also are able to resolve interpersonal disputes more effectively than younger people (Luong, Charles, and Fingerman 2011). As such, we expect that older judges use more positive language than younger judges and that their opinions may be less emotional than younger judges' opinions.

5.3 Data and Measures

We collected raw opinion texts primarily from CourtListener,[3] which in turn collected opinions from one of four sources: (1) each circuit court's own website; (2) Public. Resource.Org (PRO), a non-profit that publishes public domain materials; (3) a donation from Lawbox, LLC; and (4) the Harvard Library Innovation Lab's Case Law Access Project.[4] CourtListener also provides metadata for these opinions, which identify the cases by docket number and citation (and other information). While this metadata includes variables for the judges, such data were missing for most opinions. The raw opinion from CourtListener frequently includes concurring and dissenting opinions along with the majority opinion as a single document.

The raw opinion texts were parsed using a combination of Python scripts and hand coding to separate out header information and individual opinions. The header information was parsed to identify the names and titles of the judges who decided the case and of the authors of each opinion. For visiting judges, the header information typically also identified their court of origin. Except for visiting judges or cases where more than one judge on the same court shared a surname, this typically only provided surnames of judges. The texts of the opinions were cleaned to correct formatting problems, such as removing double spacing and line numbers, and extracting citations to other cases.

We then matched the names and titles of judges taken from the opinions to data from the Federal Judicial Center's Integrated Database so as to identify judges who served on the appropriate court with matching name and title.[5] Where no exact match or multiple matches obtained, we identified judges by using fuzzy matching.[6] Visiting bankruptcy judges were not matched as the FJC's Integrated Database did not include these judges.

A small fraction of judges could not be identified (3,306 or about 0.5%). These appear to stem from one of four sources: (1) Some cases that originated from the Case Law Access Project did not include header text that would identify the judges.

[3] See https://www.courtlistener.com/.

[4] In some cases, these opinions were missing or corrupted. Corrections were made in these cases by redownloading such opinions from the court's website, from https://www.justia.com, or from https://casetext.com.

[5] Authorship was also sometimes identified as being "Per Curiam."

[6] The probability of a match was based on the Damerau-Levenshtein between surnames, common diminutives when first names were given (e.g., Tom matched with Thomas), initials when given, and the similarity between the titles (which could distinguish whether a judge held senior status and whether a judge was the chief judge on the court at the time).

(2) Some cases that originated from the Case Law Access Project contained OCR errors. (3) Some cases contained unresolvable ambiguity (e.g., identifying the judge as "Judge Hand" when cousins Learned Hand and Augustus Noble Hand both served on the Second Circuit). (4) Bankruptcy judges are occasionally not given that title explicitly in the text and are not in the FJC's Integrated Database. All together, we acquired a total of roughly 429,000 usable opinions published between 1924 and 2019.

5.3.1 Dependent Variables

Using these data, we investigate eight dependent variables. The first seven are: *Cognitive Complexity*, *Opinion Length*, *Sentence Length*, *Vocabulary Sophistication*, *Affective Words*, *Emotional Words*, and *Writing Tone*. We use these seven dependent variables in our first set of models. The eighth dependent variable is *Cognitive Inconsistency*, and we employ it in our second set of models. We address each specifically.

Cognitive Complexity. To measure *Cognitive Complexity*, we followed Owens and Wedeking's (2011) approach (with some minor modifications). First, using the Linguistic Inquiry and Word Count (LIWC) program, Owens and Wedeking obtained document-level estimates of ten LIWC language categories: "sixletter," "causation," "insight," "discrepancy," "inhibit," "tentative," "certainty," "inclusive," "exclusive," and "negations." Second, they standardized the values within those ten categories. Third, they collapsed those ten measures into a single score. By necessity, we deviate slightly from the Owens and Wedeking approach. As of this writing, LIWC-22 is the most recent version of the underlying linguistic software they used. Of the ten original categories they evaluated, only six remain in LIWC-22: "cause," "insight," "discrep," "tentat," "certitude," and "negate." A seventh category—"BigWords" (7+ letters)—is an obvious substitute for "sixletter" (but we have more to say on this measure later).

The remaining three categories from the Owens and Wedeking (2011) approach—"inhibit," "inclusive," and "exclusive"—were sunsetted by LIWC when the programmers updated their software.[7] We do, however, see LIWC-22 categories that are plausible substitutes for the removed "exclusive" and "inclusive" categories. LIWC-22 includes measures called "all-or-none" and "differentiation." We suggest these are approximately equivalent to the "inclusive" and "exclusive" categories, respectively. The software includes all four of these measures within the general category of cognitive processes and the examples provided in the software manual give us a high degree of confidence that the measures assess the same approximate quantities of interest.[8] Our review of the LIWC-22 categories reveals no clear substitute for the "inhibition" category.

[7] As they write in their 2015 manual: "For those who are familiar with LIWC2007, some of the LIWC2015 categories and results will be a bit jarring. Some of the original categories have been removed, largely due to their consistently low base rates, low internal reliability, or their infrequent use by researchers" (7). The researchers do not specify which of these attributes triggered the removal of the three measures used in the original Owens and Wedeking measure.

[8] Example words for "inclusive" and "exclusive" in LIWC 2007 were: and, with, include, but, without, and exclude. Example words for the LIWC-22 "all-or-none" and "differentiation" categories are: all, no, never, always, but, not, if, & or.

Although the LIWC-22 "BigWords" category is a strong substitute for the LIWC 2007 "sixletter" category, our theoretical expectations demanded that we omit it from the composite measure of cognitive complexity and examine it separately. Recall the neuroscience research which shows that vocabulary remains largely strong even in the face of cognitive aging. Thus, the relative frequency of longer, more sophisticated words is likely not to differ between younger and older judges (and may even go in the other direction and, thereby, counteract the negative effects we might otherwise observe).

Ultimately, our measure of *Cognitive Complexity* consists of eight LIWC-22 measures that are either directly borrowed from the earlier Owens and Wedeking approach (the initial six mentioned) or constitute approximations from the software they used ("all-or-none" and "differentiation" in lieu of "inclusive" and "exclusive"). Of the remaining two, we remove one because our theory ultimately demands it ("sixletter"), which leaves us with only one that is missing from our conceptual replication of their measure.

To generate our measure, we take opinion-level values of these eight measures and standardize them (i.e., subtract the mean and divide by the standard deviation), which produces z-scores for each opinion and each measure. We then use these eight measures to estimate an exploratory factor analysis model with iterated principal factors. From this we obtained a solution with a single factor with an eigenvalue greater than one. We then used these factor analysis results to generate factor scores for each of the opinions, which is our measure of *Cognitive Complexity*.

Opinion Length and *Sentence Length*. We estimate models for the length of each opinion, measured simply as the number of words in the opinion. Likewise, we measure the average length of the sentences contained within each opinion, which is equal to the total number of words in an opinion divided by the number of sentences within that opinion. Both of these measures come directly from LIWC-22 in the *WC* and *WPS* variables, respectively.

Vocabulary Sophistication. As we mentioned above, our theoretical expectation is that older judges will write opinions that employ vocabulary that is at least as sophisticated as the language younger judges use. We measure, for each opinion, the percentage of words that contain seven or more letters in them. This comes directly from LIWC-22 via its *BigWords* category.

Affective Words, *Emotional Words*, and *Writing Tone*. As we discussed above, we expect that older judges will show more control over their emotions relative to their younger counterparts. In fact, the tone of older judges' opinions may even be more positive than the tone of opinions written by younger judges. LIWC-22 offers a number of categories that measure these concepts. *Affective Words* and *Emotional Words* capture the relative frequency (i.e., percentage) of these types of words and come from the LIWC-22 categories of *Affect* and *Emotion*, respectively. The former consists of nearly 3,000 words that include examples such as: happy, hate, hope, and humiliation. The latter consists of approximately 1,000 words and includes examples such as: good, love, bad, hurt, and tired. While all emotional words are affective words, not all affective words are emotional words.[9] To sort out whether the tone of

[9] These two measures have a correlation of 0.47, which is just shy the 0.50 threshold for saying, according to one rule of thumb, that a moderate—as opposed to a low—relationship between the two measures exists

the judicial opinion is positive or negative in nature, we draw from LIWC-22's *Tone* category, which is a summary variable created that captures the degree of positive versus negative emotional tone within the writing.[10]

Cognitive Inconsistency. Our final dependent variable, which we use in a different theoretical approach, reflects the year-to-year variability in cognitive complexity among a judge's opinions. We start with the individual opinion-level values of *Cognitive Complexity.* We then aggregate these values per judge per calendar year in which the opinion was published. Following Owens and Wedeking (2011), we calculate the standard deviation of these values. We also look at several alternative approaches that capture dispersion, such as: the overall range (i.e., maximum minus minimum), the interquartile range (i.e., 75th percentile minus 25th percentile), and the median absolute deviation around the average. The latter two measures are resilient to outliers, which is a useful feature.

5.3.2 Independent Variables

Our main independent variable of interest is *Opinion Author Age*, which is the number of years old the author was at the time the opinion published.

To help protect our inferences from the influence of confounding features, we control for a bevy of additional variables. We control for *Opinion Author Experience*, which counts the opinion author's years of judicial experience on the court in which they sat when the opinion published. If the author was a circuit court judge, we use the date she received her first commission to be a circuit court judge. Circuit court judges authored 92.9% of the opinions in our data. For the remaining opinion authors, we use the date of their initial commission to either the district courts (6.8%) or another Article III non-district court (0.3%). This lattermost category includes, for example, individuals like Jane A. Restani, who was appointed to the United States Court of International Trade in 1983 by President Reagan and authored 377 opinions between 1990 and when our data end in 2019. To account for the fact that our experience measure pools judicial service on different courts, we also include dummy variables for each of these court types (i.e., circuit, district, or other) and then interact our experience measure with each of these dummy variables. In substantive terms, this parameterization allows the effect of experience to vary depending on whether, for example, an author's existing experience comes from the circuit court versus the district court.

Next, *Senior Status* assesses whether, at the time the opinion was published, the opinion author had taken senior status (yes = 1; no = 0). Senior judges authored about 19% of opinions in our data. To control for the preferences of the opinion

(Mukaka 2012). The Cronbach's alpha between the two measures is 0.40, which is well below the value of 0.70 threshold that is often utilized when attempting to discern whether two measures are driven by the same latent factor (Mukaka 2012).

[10] This is a proprietary, "non-transparent" aspect of the LIWC-22 output. If one tries to reverse engineer what drives it by simply comparing how *Tone* correlates with other LIWC-22 categories, it is, unsurprisingly, most strongly correlated with the standard positive/negative tone categories (0.50 and −0.67, respectively). Interestingly, however, no other categories have correlations with absolute values of 0.50 or more.

author, we look to the partisanship of the president (or presidents) who appointed that individual to Article III positions in the federal judiciary.[11] *Author Democratic* is the proportion of an opinion author's commissions that a Democratic president issued. This allows us to account for the fact that some judges received appointments from presidents of both parties. For example, President George H. W. Bush appointed Sonia Sotomayor to a district court judgeship in 1992. President Clinton then elevated her to a circuit court position in 1998. Values of 0 indicate that only Republican presidents appointed the author; values of 1 indicate that only Democratic presidents appointed the author. "Pure" Republican appointees authored 53% of our opinions. "Pure" Democrats authored 43%. Judges of mixed partisan appointments (like Sotomayor) authored the remaining 4%.

We also control for the opinion author's sex and race. Data for both of these measures come from the Federal Judicial Center's *Biographical Directory of Article III Federal Judges*.[12] We code *Female Author* as 1 if the author was female; 0 if he was male. We code *Non-White Author* as 1 if the opinion author was reported to be any value other than "White" from the FJC's *RaceorEthnicity* column. Female authors wrote approximately 13% of our opinions. Non-white authors wrote roughly 9% of our opinions.

Moving beyond the opinion author, we also control for attributes of the panelists with whom the opinion author served when she decided the case. This includes the cumulative age and experience of the non-author panelists. We also count the total number of non-author panelists who served in senior status, who were female, or who were non-white. We likewise control for panel partisanship by including the median value of the other panelists' individual partisanship scores, which we calculated as described above. And, since many of these measures are aggregations, we control for the number of judges in a case to account for the fact that some of the decisions in our data were *en banc* as opposed to the more typical three-judge panel.

Finally, we control for a number of case and opinion attributes. Given the substantial breadth of opinions included in this massive corpus, we are limited in our ability to include the "typical" sort of variables that scholars have grown accustomed to seeing in case-level analyses of both the Supreme Court and Courts of Appeals. But we can identify and control for a number of features. First, we include *Separate Opinion* to allow for the possibility that opinion content is different among majority opinions and separate opinions. This dummy variable takes on a value of 0 if the opinion was the majority opinion; 1 if the judge concurred, dissented, or some mixture of those. Second, we include a case-level control for whether the circuit court opinion reversed the court below it (most commonly a federal district court).

[11] In so doing, we part ways with arguably the most common approach, which is to use the Judicial Common Space to estimate. Those scores measure the revealed preferences of the senator(s) and president associated with that judge's appointment to the federal courts (see, e.g., Giles, Hettinger, and Peppers 2001; Epstein et al. 2007). We take our approach because the Epstein et al. JCS data do not provide scores for judges who authored opinions in the initial decades of our data. Using the JCS, then, would introduce avoidable missingness to our data. Nevertheless, we estimated our models on the subset of observations for which JCS scores do exist. We do not find any significant differences between the two sets of results, which, given the strong correlation between the two measures (i.e., 0.87), is not especially surprising. See page 84 in the Appendix for additional details and discussion.

[12] See https://www.fjc.gov/history/judges.

This measure, *Reverses Lower Court*, is a dummy variable that we code as 1 if the opinion provided any relief to the petitioner; 0 otherwise. To make this determination, we used regular expressions to search the content of the majority opinion for phrases such as "REVERSED," "the judgment must be and is hereby reversed," or "the decision of the District Court will be reversed."[13]

5.4 Methods and Results

We first report our results for the seven opinion-level measures. Each of the seven models we estimate is an ordinary least squares linear regression model. We chose OLS for its relative ease of substantive interpretation and consistency across our different dependent variables.[14]

We begin with the results from bivariate regressions, which appear in Table 5.1. We recover statistically significant relationships between our *Age of Opinion Author* variable and the outcome of interest for six of our seven dependent variables, with only *Affective Words* failing to reach conventional levels of statistical significance ($p = 0.14$, two-tailed test). These initial results suggest that opinions written by older judges tend to be less cognitively complex, shorter in terms of their overall length, longer with regards to average sentence length, contain a lower percentage of sophisticated words, have more emotional language, and are less positive in their tone. The latter three of these initial results are inconsistent with our initial expectations. We had expected that older judges would use the same or perhaps slightly more sophisticated language in their opinions, not less. Additionally, we hypothesized that older judges would write opinions with a lower percentage of emotional words but, to the extent there was emotive content in their writing, it would be increasingly positive as they aged.

Still, given the centrality of some of our control variables, especially *Opinion Author Experience*, we are not troubled by the mixed initial results. Instead, we proceed to a multivariate model that includes our controls. As Table 5.2 shows, we continue to find that opinions authored by older judges are less cognitively complex, shorter in overall length, and employ longer sentences. (More on these findings soon.) The earlier significance of the vocabulary sophistication measure now is negative and falls in statistical no-man's-land where, with a p-value of 0.12, we have insufficient evidence to reject the null hypothesis that an effect exists, but have "too much" evidence to be willing to consider accepting the null hypothesis of no relationship.

[13] All told, we looked for approximately 160 unique phrases that we identified through an iterative trial and error process. Page 82 of the chapter appendix contains additional discussion and results about the challenges of measuring this variable. We provide this in the interest of transparency and replication, but the conclusion is that our results are not at all driven by measurement decisions regarding how we measured this control variable.

[14] Strictly speaking, a number of our outcome variables are constrained within certain values. The *Vocabulary Sophistication* and *Affective Words* variables, for example, consist of the percentage of words in an opinion that were sophisticated (i.e., seven or more letters) or affective in nature. This means these measures only take on values between 0 and 100, which might make a more sophisticated model such as a tobit regression the most appropriate. We have estimated those models and none of our results differ appreciably with them.

Table 5.1 The Impact of Opinion Author Age on Opinion Style—Bivariate Results

	Cognitive Complexity	Opinion Length	Sentence Length	Vocabulary Sophistication	Affective Words	Emotional Words	Writing Tone
Opinion Author Age	−0.0038**	−5.1288**	0.0132**	0.0124**	0.0003	0.0004**	−0.0120**
	(0.0001)	(0.4394)	(0.0007)	(0.0006)	(0.0002)	(0.0001)	(0.0018)
Constant	0.3156**	3616.7247**	16.3309**	26.3746**	2.4453**	0.4235**	22.6706**
	(0.0083)	(28.1129)	(0.0434)	(0.0362)	(0.0119)	(0.0040)	(0.1172)
N	428,794	428,794	428,794	428,794	428,794	428,794	428,794
BIC	1,049,437	8,037,792	2,491,367	2,324,565	1,427,424	397,379	3,318,720

Note: Table entries are ordinary least squares regression coefficients with robust standard errors in parentheses. The dependent variable represents the value for each individual opinion content indicator. ** and ** denote $p < 0.10$ and $p < 0.05$, respectively (two-tailed).

Table 5.2 The Impact of Opinion Author Age on Opinion Style—Multivariate Results

	Cognitive Complexity	Opinion Length	Sentence Length	Vocabulary Sophistication	Affective Words	Emotional Words	Writing Tone
Opinion Author Age	−0.0064**	−3.7955**	0.0321**	−0.0014	−0.0063**	−0.0019**	0.0092**
	(0.0002)	(0.6870)	(0.0011)	(0.0009)	(0.0003)	(0.0001)	(0.0029)
Opinion Author	0.0049**	2.4704**	−0.0112**	0.0091**	0.0079**	0.0029**	−0.0371**
Experience	(0.0002)	(0.8068)	(0.0013)	(0.0010)	(0.0004)	(0.0001)	(0.0033)
District Court	−0.1777**	−683.6674**	−0.2791**	0.8883**	−0.0362*	0.0009	−0.9447**
	(0.0114)	(28.2097)	(0.0551)	(0.0528)	(0.0207)	(0.0047)	(0.1354)
Other Court	0.1504**	−499.9362**	0.5777**	−1.1131**	−0.1656**	−0.0594**	0.0773
	(0.0494)	(98.8226)	(0.2311)	(0.1458)	(0.0425)	(0.0127)	(0.4656)
District Court × Author	0.0036**	−2.6490*	−0.0093**	−0.0126**	−0.0009	−0.0008**	0.0543**
Experience	(0.0006)	(1.6038)	(0.0030)	(0.0028)	(0.0011)	(0.0003)	(0.0078)
Other Court × Author	−0.0145**	−7.7243	−0.0648**	0.0550**	0.0041*	0.0004	0.0517**
Experience	(0.0021)	(5.4671)	(0.0097)	(0.0067)	(0.0021)	(0.0007)	(0.0238)
Author on Senior Status	−0.0355**	3.6148	−0.4457**	0.3526**	0.0637**	0.0207**	−0.0058
	(0.0042)	(14.5803)	(0.0226)	(0.0189)	(0.0077)	(0.0020)	(0.0600)
Author Democratic	−0.0056**	16.1962*	0.3269**	−0.1268**	−0.0346**	−0.0184**	0.2432**
	(0.0026)	(9.1244)	(0.0144)	(0.0118)	(0.0044)	(0.0012)	(0.0378)
Author Female	−0.0004	506.3981**	−0.4999**	0.5389**	0.0942**	0.0560**	−0.8383**
	(0.0035)	(15.2464)	(0.0171)	(0.0152)	(0.0064)	(0.0020)	(0.0575)
Author Non-White	−0.0599**	466.5021**	−0.7246**	0.6411**	0.1088**	0.0478**	−0.8429**
	(0.0042)	(17.2384)	(0.0207)	(0.0184)	(0.0083)	(0.0022)	(0.0670)
Age of Panel Judges	0.0007**	−8.6597**	0.0154**	−0.0105**	−0.0023**	−0.0011**	0.0176**
	(0.0001)	(0.4801)	(0.0007)	(0.0006)	(0.0003)	(0.0001)	(0.0019)

Continued

Table 5.2 *Continued*

	Cognitive Complexity	Opinion Length	Sentence Length	Vocabulary Sophistication	Affective Words	Emotional Words	Writing Tone
Experience of Panel Judges	0.0007**	13.8055**	−0.0214**	0.0125**	0.0040**	0.0023**	−0.0469**
	(0.0002)	(0.5338)	(0.0008)	(0.0006)	(0.0004)	(0.0001)	(0.0021)
Senior Judges on Panel	−0.0479**	218.8231**	−0.3964**	0.4777**	0.1046**	0.0251**	−0.0730*
	(0.0028)	(10.3202)	(0.0150)	(0.0122)	(0.0093)	(0.0013)	(0.0414)
Female Judges on Panel	0.0129**	227.8863**	−0.6675**	0.4841**	0.1074**	0.0419**	−0.6250**
	(0.0026)	(10.1620)	(0.0124)	(0.0110)	(0.0075)	(0.0013)	(0.0378)
Non-White Judges on Panel	−0.0234**	331.8021**	−0.7233**	0.6177**	0.1123**	0.0339**	−0.2588**
	(0.0034)	(11.8378)	(0.0147)	(0.0136)	(0.0073)	(0.0015)	(0.0446)
Median Panel Democratic	0.0143**	−125.0540**	0.4868**	−0.5185**	−0.0892**	−0.0348**	0.1888**
Appointments	(0.0036)	(12.1217)	(0.0192)	(0.0155)	(0.0052)	(0.0016)	(0.0500)
Size of Panel	−0.0435**	463.1364**	−0.5296**	0.3540**	0.0915**	0.0406**	−0.5790**
	(0.0078)	(26.9141)	(0.0412)	(0.0324)	(0.0142)	(0.0034)	(0.1054)
Separate Opinion	0.5360**	−1.42e+03**	0.8533**	−0.7490**	0.1446**	0.0168**	1.2587**
	(0.0050)	(13.5137)	(0.0281)	(0.0195)	(0.0070)	(0.0023)	(0.0682)
Reverses Lower Court	0.0801**	246.3329**	0.1089**	−0.3267**	−0.0231**	−0.0212**	0.2208**
	(0.0038)	(15.1174)	(0.0233)	(0.0165)	(0.0054)	(0.0019)	(0.0597)
Constant	0.3736**	3256.4086**	15.1155**	27.2253**	2.7063**	0.5221**	21.8890**
	(0.0113)	(39.6002)	(0.0617)	(0.0486)	(0.0185)	(0.0055)	(0.1656)
N	428,794	428,794	428,794	428,794	428,794	428,794	428,794
BIC	1,027,432	8,017,253	2,476,043	2,307,255	1,420,672	386,314	3,315,890

Note: Table entries are ordinary least squares regression coefficients with robust standard errors in parentheses. The dependent variable represents the value for each individual opinion content indicator. * and ** denote $p < 0.10$ and $p < 0.05$, respectively (two-tailed).

As we suspected, the inclusion of the controls causes significant changes in the performance of the dependent variables that assessed affective language, emotional language, and the overall positive (or negative) tone of an opinion. As Table 5.2 reveals, all three of these measures now are statistically significant and in the predicted direction. Having an older judge author the opinion is associated with a significant *decrease* in affective words and emotional words. As to the tone of the opinion, we now find that an increase in opinion author age is expected to yield more positive tone within that opinion. These are the results that we had expected to find, per the literature on cognitive aging and our resultant hypotheses.[15]

To understand the substantive impact of author age on these measures more clearly, we calculate and graph predicted values. We begin with our finding that older judges tend to author opinions that are less cognitively complex. Figure 5.1 portrays the age of an opinion author on the x-axis. The youngest opinion author we observe in our data—Ricardo Hinojosa, a district court judge sitting by designation—was just 35. The oldest judge in our data—Wesley Brown, also a district court judge sitting by designation—was 99. The y-axis in the plot is the predicted level of cognitive complexity.

Starting with the youngest judge in our data, we predict a cognitive complexity score of approximately 0.26. This is roughly the 63rd percentile of the distribution.

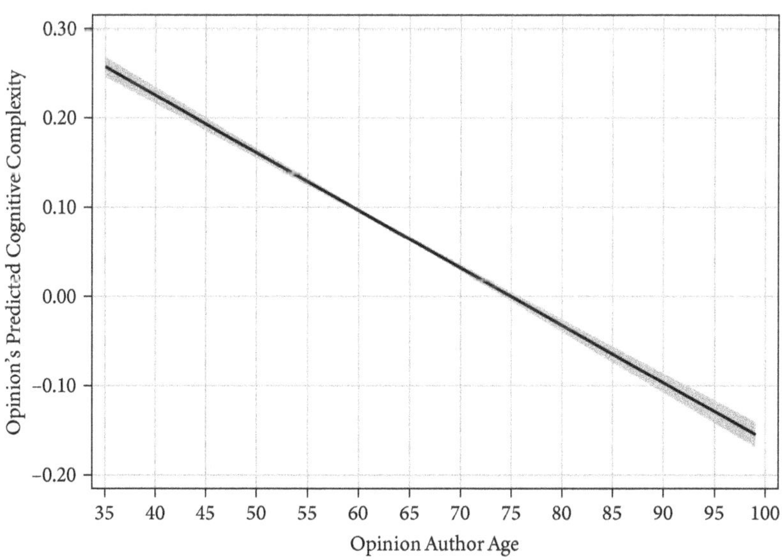

Figure 5.1 The impact of opinion author age on opinion cognitive complexity. Figure reports the predicted level of opinion cognitive complexity (with 95% confidence intervals) using results from Table 5.2. All other variables were held at their median values.

15 One might wonder what exactly it is about the fully specified model that triggers these variables to change. The short answer is that controlling for an opinion author's level of experience produces these results. See the chapter appendix on page 83 for additional discussion.

If, by contrast, the oldest judge in our data wrote the opinion, then the predicted level of cognitive complexity drops to −0.16. This would be roughly the 36th percentile of the distribution. This is a relative change of just over 160% and is equivalent to a bit more than one-half a standard deviation in our cognitive complexity measure. Of course, these are the most extreme values within our data. Modest shifts produce similarly modest changes in the predicted level of cognitive complexity. The 25th and 75th percentile values of our author age variable are 56 years and 70 years, respectively. These values yield estimated cognitive complexity scores of 0.12 and 0.03, which are the 54th and 48th percentiles of the cognitive complexity distribution. Taken together, these results show that although an author's age is by no means the *sole* driver of opinion cognitive complexity, age does influence cognitive complexity.

We next consider *Opinion Length* and *Sentence Length*, which we showcase in the left and right panels of Figure 5.2. The x-axes in both panels remain the same—*Opinion Author Age*. There is a negative relationship between opinion author age and opinion length. A 35-year-old author writes opinions that are approximately 3,400 words. A 99-year-old author writes opinions that are approximately 3,155 words. This is an absolute change of 245 words, which is roughly equivalent to one page of double-spaced text. In relative terms, the effect is a 7% decrease and is substantively the equivalent of changing from the 64th percentile of length for the very young judge to the 60th percentile of length for the very old judge. Age exerts an admittedly slight substantive effect even at its most extreme values. Movement from the 25th percentile to 75th percentile values of age (i.e., 56 years and 70 years, respectively) yields, predictably, an even subtler change of just 54 words (i.e., 3,320 words versus 3,266 words), which is just a 1.6% relative change and moves from the 63rd to 61st percentile in our opinion length measure. Of course, the effect of aging on opinion length is potentially better conceptualized by recognizing that judges author dozens of opinions a year. Judges on the circuit courts averaged, over a recent six-year period, just over 43 signed written opinions each year. Applying that information to our results suggests that a 56-year-old judge will produce 2,300+ additional words during

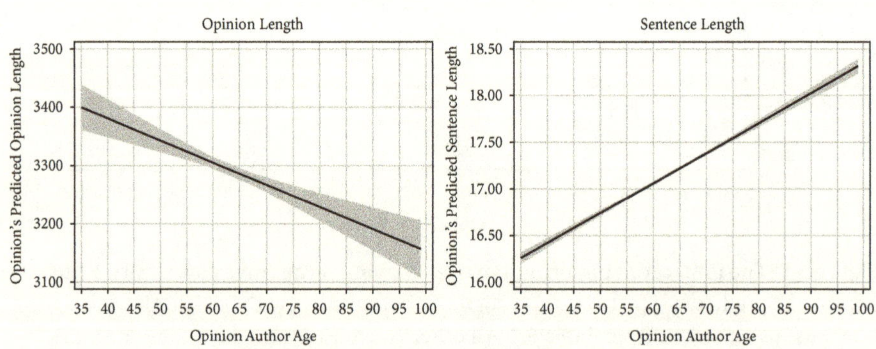

Figure 5.2 The impact of opinion author age on opinion length and sentence length. Figure reports the predicted number of words and words per sentence, respectively (with 95% confidence intervals) using results from Table 5.2. All other variables were held at their median values.

that year as compared to a 70-year-old counterpart, which is equivalent to about nine extra pages of text. Not a huge effect, but another link in the chain.

Judicial aging is not associated with the use of more sophisticated (i.e., longer) words, but it is associated with longer sentences. As the right panel of Figure 5.2 shows, older judges tend to write longer sentences than their younger counterparts. Opinions by the youngest judge in our data have an average of 16.3 words per sentence. Opinions by the oldest judge have an average of 18.3 words per sentence. This is a 12% relative increase and represents movement from the 45th to 68th percentile in the underlying *Sentence Length* measure. In other words, though two words per sentence and a low-double-digit percent change might not seem substantively noteworthy, the measure itself is rather tightly concentrated, so it is still a meaningful change across the measure's distribution. Changing the opinion author's age from the 25th to 75th percentile produces a 3% relative increase in sentence length, which moves from the 53rd to the 58th percentile in the measure (i.e., 16.9 to 17.4 words per sentence).

Lastly, we consider the amount of affective and emotional words as well as the net positivity of a judge's written opinion. Figure 5.3 plots these quantities of interest. As before, an opinion author's age appears on the x-axis. The y-axes for the first row of plots is our prediction of the percentage of words of that type appearing in a judge's

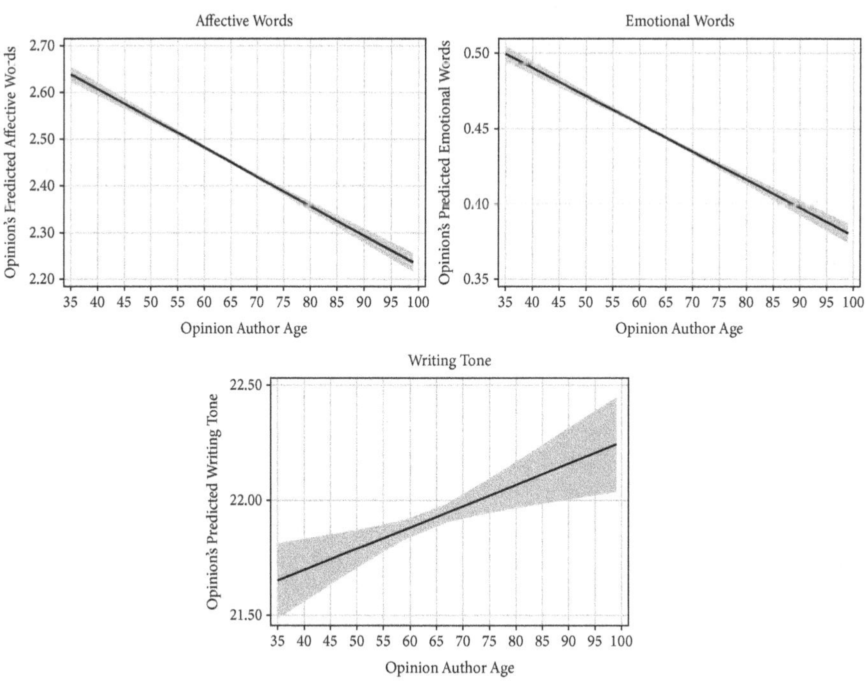

Figure 5.3 The impact of opinion author age on the use of affective words, emotional words, and writing tone. Figure reports the predicted percentage of words that are affective, emotional, and degree of positivity, respectively, (with 95% confidence intervals) using results from Table 5.2. All other variables were held at their median values.

opinion. As a preliminary matter, it is worth noting the overall rarity with which these words appear *at all* in an opinion. This rarity should not be surprising. Lawyers are told to focus on logical language in their briefs and to eschew emotional appeals. Failing to do so actually is associated with a lower likelihood of winning a case (Black, Hall, Owens, and Ringsmuth 2016). It would be odd for judges to deviate from their own advice here. With an overall sample mean of just 2.4% for *Affective Words* and only 0.4% for *Emotional Words*, our data suggest judges follow their own advice.

But, despite the overall low levels, we still observe statistically significant effects for opinion author age. For both *Affective Words* and *Emotional Words*, we observe a negative relationship between an opinion author's age and the relative frequency with which these words appear in her opinion. Of the words in opinions by the youngest authors, roughly 2.65% are affective; 2.25% of the words in old judges' opinions are affective. This absolute change is minuscule, but, just like sentence length, the underlying measure is compact, so even this small change results in moving from the 63rd to the 45th percentile. A smaller change from the 25th to 75th percentile in opinion author age yields an analogous change from the 57th to the 53rd percentile in the *Affective Words* measure. Results for *Emotional Words* tells the same basic story: small absolute changes but non-trivial changes in terms of the dependant variable's distribution.[16]

The lone panel in the second row of Figure 5.3 portrays the results for *Writing Tone*. Smaller values correspond to more negative writing tone whereas larger values suggest greater overall positivity. Although we find that older authors' opinions are less emotional than those of younger authors, to the extent such content is present in older judges' opinions, it is more positive. This is a statistically significant result but one that is substantively the slightest of those we obtained. The underlying measure can range from 0 to 100. Within our sample, the median value is 20.9 and the 25th and 75th percentile values are 14.5 and 28.1, respectively. Thus, the change in tone from our youngest author to our oldest author (i.e., 21.6 to 22.2) is objectively small and is the equivalent of moving from the 54th to 58th percentile in the tone measure.

We also expected that as judges age, they will show higher levels of *inconsistency* in their cognitive complexity as they rely more and more on their rotating clerks to write their opinions. (Remember, clerks tend to work for judges for one year and then depart, only to be replaced by another clerk.) In this next analysis, we examine the year-to-year (in)consistency of judges' opinions. Unlike our earlier analyses, which used each of the more than 400,000 opinions in our sample, testing our cognitive consistency hypothesis requires some aggregation across these opinions. We collapsed the data to the judge-year unit of analysis. This left us with slightly more than 19,600 observations.[17] To examine cognitive inconsistency, we created four dependent variables, each a standard measure of dispersion. These include: the

[16] Here, the youngest author's predicted value is the 68th percentile, but the oldest author's predicted percentile is the 53rd. Percentiles in emotional language for the less extreme counterfactual are the 64th (author is 56 years old) and the 60th (author is 70 years old).

[17] Strictly speaking, we had around 23,100 judge-year dyads. Approximately 15% of these observations, however, are instances where the judge authored only a single opinion in a year. This means there is not any variation to evaluate, so we exclude them.

Table 5.3 The Impact of Opinion Author Age on Opinion Cognitive Inconsistency—Bivariate Results

	Standard Deviation	Overall Range	Median Absolute Deviation	Interquartile Range
Opinion Author Age	0.0014**	−0.0002	0.0004**	0.0014**
	(0.0003)	(0.0011)	(0.0002)	(0.0004)
Constant	0.5543**	2.3646**	0.3270**	0.7190**
	(0.0192)	(0.0747)	(0.0112)	(0.0277)
N	19,602	19,602	19,602	19,602
BIC	20,102	75,924	−1,445	34,193

Note: Table entries are ordinary least squares regression coefficients with robust standard errors in parentheses. The dependent variable represents the value for each individual opinion content indicator. * and ** denote $p < 0.10$ and $p < 0.05$, respectively (two-tailed).

standard deviation, overall range, interquartile range, and median absolute deviation of the cognitive complexity of a judge's opinions in a given year. The first two are more commonly used than the latter two, but outliers can influence them. Outlier status is a potential concern since the median number of opinions for our judge-year dyad is 12 and roughly 47% of our observations have five or fewer opinions in a given year.

As before, we begin by evaluating the bivariate relationship between *Opinion Author Age* and our measures of dispersion. Table 5.3 shows a positive and statistically significant effect for three of these four measures. Increased opinion author age is associated with greater annual standard deviations in the cognitive complexity of a judge's opinion's, larger median absolute deviations, and a larger interquartile range among her opinions. The sign on the *Overall Range* measure is negative but not close to reaching statistical significance.

To probe the strength of these results we re-estimate the models with a number of control variables. We include the same control for the judge's experience, which is interacted with a series of dummy variables for the type of court on which the judge accumulated that experience. We also control for whether a judge was on senior status during that year. If not, the variable takes on a value of 0. If the judge had already taken senior status, it takes on a value of 1. Values in-between only occur if that was the year in which the judge made the transition from active to senior status and are equal to the proportion of opinions written during that year where a judge had senior status. Such was the case for fewer than 2% of the judge-year observations in our data. We also retain our earlier controls for the partisan affiliation of the judge, whether the judge was female, and whether the judge was non-white. Our data consist of about 50% of judge-years that were fully Republican appointees, 46% that were fully Democratic appointees, and about 4% that were judges with a mixed partisan background. Female and non-white judge-years account for 11% and 9% of our observations, respectively. We also control for the relative mixture of opinions authored in a given judge-year combination that were separate opinions and instances where the circuit court reversed the decision of the court it reviewed. These variables are coded as the mean of the case-level dummy variables. Across the 19,600 judge-year observations, the average of both variables is about 11%. Finally, we control for the number of opinions each judge wrote per calendar year.

Results for these models appear in Table 5.4. The introduction of statistical controls decreases the size of the coefficient on the *Standard Deviation* measure and also increases the size of its standard error. These forces combine to take a result that was statistically significant ($t = 4.81$) and push it even beyond the no-man's land level of significance ($t = 1.09$, $p = 0.28$). Interestingly, we observe the opposite for the *Overall Range* measure, which was negative and not significant in the bivariate model, but is now positively signed with a two-tailed p-value of 0.13. Neither of our outlier-robust measures, *Mean Absolute Deviation* and *Interquartile Range* exhibit any

Table 5.4 The Impact of Opinion Author Age on Opinion Cognitive Inconsistency—Multivariate Results

	Standard Deviation	Overall Range	Median Absolute Deviation	Interquartile Range
Opinion Author Age	0.0005	0.0026	0.0006**	0.0014**
	(0.0005)	(0.0017)	(0.0003)	(0.0007)
Opinion Author Experience	0.0007	0.0032*	0.0000	−0.0001
	(0.0005)	(0.0018)	(0.0003)	(0.0007)
District Court	0.0230	−0.5407**	−0.0036	0.1519**
	(0.0147)	(0.0395)	(0.0093)	(0.0226)
Other Court	0.0912	−0.0335	0.0534	0.1601
	(0.0700)	(0.1708)	(0.0461)	(0.1063)
District Court × Author	−0.0006	0.0064**	−0.0002	−0.0028**
Experience	(0.0008)	(0.0022)	(0.0005)	(0.0012)
Other Court × Author	−0.0031	−0.0114*	−0.0021	−0.0016
Experience	(0.0025)	(0.0062)	(0.0017)	(0.0038)
Author on Senior Status	0.0219**	0.0247	−0.0067	0.0129
	(0.0091)	(0.0316)	(0.0052)	(0.0134)
Author Democratic	0.0127**	0.0876**	0.0076**	0.0127
	(0.0061)	(0.0218)	(0.0035)	(0.0086)
Author Female	−0.0458**	−0.1015**	−0.0283**	−0.0865**
	(0.0089)	(0.0389)	(0.0048)	(0.0112)
Author Non-White	−0.0241**	−0.1323**	−0.0187**	−0.0255
	(0.0109)	(0.0369)	(0.0058)	(0.0161)
Separate Opinion	0.3742**	1.1730**	0.1878**	0.4240**
	(0.0301)	(0.0874)	(0.0186)	(0.0424)
Reverses Lower Court	−0.0436**	−0.0588	0.0160	−0.0636**
	(0.0218)	(0.0622)	(0.0137)	(0.0322)
Number of Opinions	0.0022**	0.0375**	0.0010**	0.0011**
	(0.0002)	(0.0007)	(0.0001)	(0.0002)
Constant	0.5092**	1.3130**	0.2742**	0.6265**
	(0.0279)	(0.0991)	(0.0156)	(0.0404)
N	19,602	19,602	19,602	19,602
BIC	19,666	69,616	−1,827	33,967

Note: Table entries are ordinary least squares regression coefficients with robust standard errors in parentheses. The dependent variable represents the value for each individual opinion content indicator. * and ** denote $p < 0.10$ and $p < 0.05$, respectively (two-tailed).

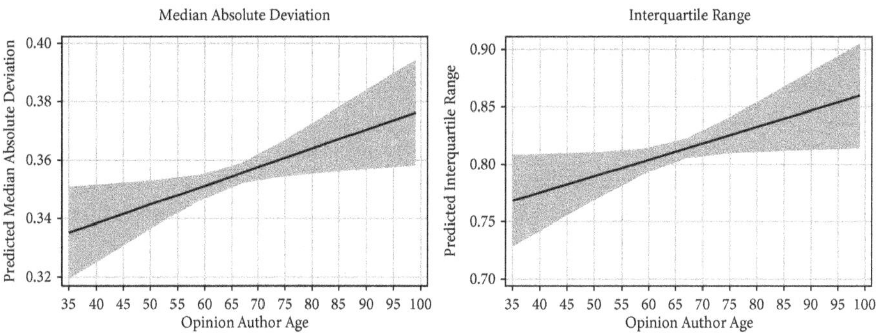

Figure 5.4 The impact of opinion author age on opinion cognitive inconsistency. Figure reports the predicted level of cognitive inconsistency—median absolute deviation and interquartile range, respectively—(with 95% confidence intervals) using results from Table 5.4. All other variables were held at their median values.

appreciable changes upon the introduction of statistical controls.[18] They continue to show increased inconsistency with increased age.

The two panels of Figure 5.4 show the substantive magnitude of these two measures. Along the x-axis, we plot the opinion author's age. The y-axis shows the specific measure of dispersion considered. Starting with *Median Absolute Deviation*, we predict that opinions authored by the youngest judge in our data have a median absolute deviation just shy of 0.34 above (or below) the median level of cognitive consistency for that judge's opinions in a given year. This is equivalent to approximately the 49th percentile value among our dataset. If we examine the analogous value for the oldest judge in our data, we predict an increase to just below 0.38, which is a 12% relative increase. In percentile terms, this 0.38 value clocks in around the 60th percentile value.

Moving to the *Interquartile Range* measure, we estimate that the corpus of opinions authored by the youngest judge in our data would have a gap of roughly 0.77 units in cognitive complexity between the 75th and 25th percentile values for that judge's opinions. This is equivalent to approximately the 56th percentile value among our dataset. If we examine the analogous value for the oldest judge in our data, we predict an increase to about 0.86, which is a 12% relative increase. This 0.86 value is, percentile-wise, equal to the 67th percentile. More modest changes in judge age yield more modest substantive differences.

5.5 Conclusion

This chapter sought to examine how the content of judges' opinions change with age. It turns out that opinion content changes much as we—and the neuroscience literature—anticipated. As judges age, and as their abilities to reason decline, their opinions become less cognitively complex. Judges move from interpreting events

[18] The interquartile range result is robust to using percentile "bookends" other than the 25th and 75th percentile. See the chapter's appendix for additional discussion.

"in multidimensional terms" and "integrat[ing] a variety of evidence" (Tetlock, Bernzweig, and Gallant 1985, 1228) to making decisions "on the basis of only a few salient items of information" (Gruenfeld 1995, 5). Similarly, judges' opinions decrease in length with age.

At the same time, older judges' opinions employ fewer affective and emotional words and a slight increase in the relative use of positive words. That is potentially good news. After all, judges counsel lawyers to avoid such language. Scalia and Garner (2008) once declared that making appeals to judges' emotions "is misguided. . . . Good judges pride themselves on the rationality of their rulings and the suppression of their personal proclivities, including most especially their emotions" (32).

When it comes to examining the year-to-year variation in judges' opinions, the results provide some support for our claims. We observe more deviation in judges' opinions as they age, at least according to two measurements. These findings add to the results we obtain throughout the book. As judges age, they behave differently and their work product changes. Sometimes, these changes are large; other times, the changes are more modest. But all the changes point in the same general direction.

5.6 Appendix

5.6.1 Measuring Reverses Lower Court

Common databases like the Supreme Court Database and the Courts of Appeals Databases provide definitive answers to whether a decision of those courts resulted in a reversal of the lower court whose decision was under review (see, e.g., *lcDisposition* in the Supreme Court Database). Because our data are bespoke and rather plentiful in nature, we lack such an elegant answer. The prospect of by-hand coding of 430,000 opinions wasn't terribly appealing, so we instead leveraged some regular expressions to determine whether the majority opinion provided any relief to the appellant. As it turns out, there are many, many different ways opinions author express this sentiment. Some say "the judgment below must be reversed." Others, seeking to imbue a bit more logic, will say "the judgment below *therefore* must be reversed" (emphasis ours). We used trial and error and a modest amount of bourbon to identify a list of around 160 phrases that authors used to indicate the outcome was not a complete win for the appellee.

We then search all of our opinions for those phrases. Because these phrases could also appear earlier in the opinions and might yield a false positive (e.g., if they were quoting from another case), our search code also captured the relative location of the potential search hit within the opinion. For example, a hit at the very beginning would have a value like 0.03 versus one that is literally the last phrase in the opinion, which would have a value of 1.0. A by-hand review of nearly 430,000 opinions was not feasible, so we instead conducted a sensitivity analysis where we varied the threshold used for determining whether the reversal search result hit should trigger a coding of "reversal" for the case. A value of 1.0, for example, requires that the search hit was the last content in the opinion. A value of 0.90, however, would also allow search hits that appear in the last 10% of the opinion. As a practical matter, this meant that the rate of relief for the petitioner ranged from 0.10—when the threshold was set to 1.0—to 0.36 when the threshold was set to just 0.05. For every 0.05 threshold between 0 and 1 we estimated the models we report in the chapter text to see whether the result of our age variables changed. None did. Each "flavor" of the reversal variable always retained the sign and approximate coefficient that it does in the models we report in the main chapter text. And, more important for our specific inquiry, the effect of *Opinion Author Age* is also invariant to these different specifications.

5.6.2 Differences between Bivariate and Multivariate Results

As we note in the chapter text, it is only upon including statistical controls that we obtain results consistent with our hypotheses for the relationship between *Opinion Author Age* and three of our dependent variables: *Affective Words*, *Emotional Words*, and *Writing Tone*. In footnote 15, we report that it is the inclusion of our *Author Experience* control that produces these results.

To reach this conclusion, we conducted a model specification sensitivity analysis. In particular, for each of the three dependent variables where the *Opinion Author Age* results changed between the bivariate and multivariate versions, we estimated models with every possible unique subset of the multivariate controls. That is, our reported specification in Table 5.2 features 14 controls in addition to our *Opinion Author Age* variable. We estimated 14 different models that iteratively excluded each of those controls (i.e., there were 13 controls included in each of them). We then estimated another 91 models that excluded all of the unique combinations for any two of those 14 controls (e.g., exclude both *Author Democratic* and *Author Female*, then exclude both *Author Democratic* and *Author Non White* but include *Author Female*). Then we estimated 364 models excluding any three of the controls, 1001 models excluding any four, 2002 models excluding any five, . . . and so on. All told, we estimated 16,383 separate models (and did so for each of the three dependent variables).

With model estimates in hand, we then looked to see how often the *Opinion Author Age* variable was both in the hypothesized direction (i.e., negative for affective and emotional language; positive for overall opinion tone) and statistically significant ($p < 0.10$, two-tailed test). Of the nearly 17,000 models we estimated, such results occurred 79% for the *Affective Words*, 74% for *Emotional Words*, and just 50% for *Writing Tone*.

At first blush, this might seem concerning, especially for the literal coin-flip results we obtain for the tone dependent variable. However, this overall accounting assumes that each of the candidate models should be considered equally plausible in terms of representing the most accurate characterization of this data-generating process. That is, it does not consider the theoretical importance of individual controls. This is, almost certainly, not the correct way to approach considering these results.

To wit, if the feedback we have received on various facets of this project have taught us anything, it is that discussants, panel attendees, and reviewers very much believe that controlling for a judge's experience is necessary if we are to make any realistic conclusions about the independent influence of her age. With that in mind, we focus on the 8192 model specifications that included the control for the amount of previous judicial experience, the type of court on which that experience was obtained, and the interaction of those variables. This includes, for example, the singular model where it is the only control, the 13 models where it is accompanied by one additional control, the 78 models where it is with two other controls, all the way up to the singular model where it is included with the full 13 additional controls. For 100% of those models for all three dependent variables (i.e., 24,576 models in total) we find that *Opinion Author Age* performs as our theory suggests it would in relation to the dependent variable. This means it is negative and statistically significant for *Affective Words* and *Emotional Words* and positive and statistically significant for *Writing Tone.* Thus, although the desired relationship emerges only after we engage in some form of statistical control, the type of control we include is one that we ultimately believe is theoretically essential in any analysis where a judge's age is the feature of interest.

Finally, for the sake of completeness, we also looked at the performance of *Opinion Author Age* in the other 8191 models that *excluded* a control for a judge's amount of judicial experience. Again, our belief, and that of reviewers and commenters of our work, is that such a model is unacceptably underspecified, but we wanted to leave no stone unturned. The age variable is significant and in the hypothesized direction 57% of the time for *Affective Words*, 47% of the time for *Emotional Words*, and 0% of the time for *Writing Tone.* The inclusion of the experience control is always a "sufficient condition" but is also, to a varying degree, a "necessary condition" to yield results that accord with our hypothesized effect for the age of an opinion author.

5.6.3 Measuring Judicial Ideology: Judicial Common Space Robustness

The 249 judges with JCS scores missing from both the Epstein et al. (2007) and Boyd (2015) data account collectively for more than 30,000 in our data. These are not observations missing at random, but rather are concentrated in the early decades of our opinion data. We have missingness rates above 90% from 1924 through 1937. The rate then stays above 50% through 1947 and only falls below 10% from 1961 onward.

Table 5.5 shows our author age variable along with the two candidate ideology measures for each of the seven dependent variables described in the main chapter text. We also included the same array of control variables featured in Table 5.2, but omit them here for the sake of simplicity. We estimated both models on the same subset of observations for which JCS score data were available. We do this because comparing the JCS observations only model against the full model would not be an apples-to-apples comparison (i.e., both the ideology measure and the observations included are changing). As the table reveals, coefficients for *Cognitive Complexity, Sentence Length, Vocabulary Sophistication, Affective Words*, and *Emotional Words* are identical or nearly identical.

For *Opinion Length*, both variables are negatively signed, which is consistent with our main model, but, in this subset of the data, they are statistically insignificant. Since the results are identical for the two different parameterizations of ideology, we do not read anything into that null effect other than the fact that, for a non-random subset of the data, there appears to no evidence that aged judges author shorter opinions versus their younger counterparts.

Table 5.5 The Impact of Opinion Author Age on Opinion Style—Robustness Results

	Cognitive Complexity		Opinion Length		Sentence Length		Vocabulary Sophistication		Affective Words		Emotional Words		Writing Tone	
Age of Opinion Author	−0.008**	−0.008**	−0.670	−0.868	0.016**	0.015**	0.005**	0.005**	−0.005**	−0.005**	−0.002**	−0.002**	0.007**	0.004
	(0.000)	(0.000)	(0.744)	(0.747)	(0.001)	(0.001)	(0.001)	(0.001)	(0.000)	(0.000)	(0.000)	(0.000)	(0.003)	(0.003)
Author Democratic	−0.000		13.498		0.380**		−0.199**		−0.039**		−0.020**		0.284**	
	(0.003)		(9.607)		(0.014)		(0.012)		(0.005)		(0.001)		(0.039)	
Author JCS		0.016**		−44.725**		−0.589**		0.292**		0.015**		0.021**		−0.625**
		(0.003)		(12.288)		(0.017)		(0.014)		(0.006)		(0.002)		(0.049)

Note: Table entries are ordinary least squares regression coefficients with robust standard errors in parentheses. The dependent variable represents the value for each individual opinion content indicator. ** and ** denote $p < 0.10$ and $p < 0.05$, respectively (two-tailed). These models also include the additional controls from Table 5.2. The number of observations for all models is 398,472.

Table 5.6 The Impact of Opinion Author Age on Opinion Cognitive Inconsistency—Alternative Approaches to Measuring Percentile Spread

	20th–80th Percentile	15th–85th Percentile	10th–90th Percentile	5th–95th Percentile	1st–99th Percentile
Opinion Author Age	0.0016**	0.0026**	0.0028**	0.0035**	0.0027
	(0.0007)	(0.0008)	(0.0010)	(0.0012)	(0.0017)
Opinion Author	0.0000	−0.0007	0.0003	0.0016	0.0031*
Experience	(0.0008)	(0.0009)	(0.0011)	(0.0014)	(0.0018)
District Court	0.1147**	0.0159	−0.1649**	−0.5190**	−0.5588**
	(0.0251)	(0.0276)	(0.0303)	(0.0351)	(0.0399)
Other Court	0.1290	0.0641	0.1187	0.0005	−0.0444
	(0.1184)	(0.1237)	(0.1591)	(0.1782)	(0.1712)
District Court × Author	−0.0018	0.0007	0.0033*	0.0068**	0.0067**
Experience	(0.0014)	(0.0016)	(0.0018)	(0.0020)	(0.0022)
Other Court × Author	−0.0013	0.0000	−0.0055	−0.0106*	−0.0115*
Experience	(0.0043)	(0.0047)	(0.0056)	(0.0063)	(0.0062)
Author on Senior Status	0.0349**	0.0681**	0.0955**	0.0879**	0.0191
	(0.0150)	(0.0173)	(0.0202)	(0.0261)	(0.0317)
Author Democratic	0.0163*	0.0146	0.0296**	0.0661**	0.0860**
	(0.0097)	(0.0112)	(0.0127)	(0.0162)	(0.0218)
Author Female	−0.0921**	−0.0974**	−0.1015**	−0.0977**	−0.1000**
	(0.0127)	(0.0144)	(0.0170)	(0.0230)	(0.0389)
Author Non-White	−0.0346**	−0.0454**	−0.0544**	−0.0614**	−0.1313**
	(0.0176)	(0.0196)	(0.0222)	(0.0292)	(0.0369)
Separate Opinion	0.4713**	0.5294**	0.6200**	0.7989**	1.1731**
	(0.0460)	(0.0503)	(0.0549)	(0.0653)	(0.0875)
Reverses Lower Court	−0.0374	−0.0216	0.0391	0.0869	−0.0642
	(0.0360)	(0.0407)	(0.0459)	(0.0553)	(0.0624)
Number of Opinions	0.0019**	0.0035**	0.0058**	0.0109**	0.0368**
	(0.0003)	(0.0003)	(0.0004)	(0.0005)	(0.0008)
Constant	0.7716**	0.8933**	1.0846**	1.3548**	1.3297**
	(0.0444)	(0.0494)	(0.0556)	(0.0705)	(0.0994)
N	19,602	19,602	19,602	19,602	19,602

Note: Table entries are ordinary least squares regression coefficients with robust standard errors in parentheses. The dependent variable represents the spread indicator for opinion cognitive inconsistency. * and ** denote $p < 0.10$ and $p < 0.05$, respectively (two-tailed).

Lastly, we observe that for *Writing Tone*, age is positive and significant in the *Author Democratic* model but not the *Author JCS* model. This is also not, from our perspective, worrisome. The two-tailed p-value in the lattermost model is 0.18, which is below the threshold one would need to consider accepting the null hypothesis of no effect. What is more, if we instead ask whether the coefficient of our author age variable is significantly different not from 0, but rather from 0.007, which is what we obtain in the *Author Democratic* model, we cannot reject the null hypothesis of no difference ($p = 0.48$).

5.6.4 Interquartile Range Robustness

The 25th and 75th percentile bookends of the interquartile range are an elegant, though ultimately somewhat arbitrary, choice. Yes, it's where 50% of the data live, but one could just as easily set the bookends at 15th and 85th percentile to look at where the middle 70% of the data are distributed. And, as we discussed in the text, our no-man's land result for *Overall Range* measure suggests that the inclusion of outliers in the calculation decreases the crispness of our results. With that in mind, we also evaluated alternative dependent variables that looked at the following percentile gaps 20–80, 15–85, 10–90, 5–95, and 1–99. This is to say these were capturing the middle 60, 70, 80, 90, and 98 percentages, respectively, of a judge's opinion's cognitive complexity scores for a given year. The resulting models, parameter estimates for which appear in Table 5.6, yield positive coefficients across the board and stay at the 0.05 level of significance or better until we look at the gap between the 1st and 99th percentile, which has a two-tailed p-value of 0.11. In short, our percentile spread result is robust to alternative conceptualizations.

6
Cognitive Aging, Law Clerks, and Party Briefs

In nearly every case that court of appeals judges decide, they must determine not only who wins and loses but also *why* those parties win or lose. What is more, at least one judge in the majority must then commit the logic of that determination to writing. As we already have discussed, that writing process requires cognitive exertion. And, sometimes that cognitive effort requires judges to rely on assistance.

Judges often rely on law clerks to lighten their loads (Ward and Weiden 2006). Law clerks tend to be recent law school graduates who work for a judge for one intense year (sometimes two). As Peppers (2006, 145) puts it, the modern law clerk "is relied on to master complex areas of the law. . . ." Clerks prepare their judges for oral argument, help them research the law, and most importantly for our purposes here, help judges write their opinions. At times, clerks write major portions of the opinions. Few judges would demur that without law clerks, the modern judiciary could not function.

Litigant briefs also assist judges. Briefs provide judges with legal and policy information about precedent, the facts of cases, and the likely consequences of judicial decisions. Justice Samuel Alito made the point succinctly when he stated: "[W]hat I am looking for in briefs is a roadmap for me to follow in deciding the case. . . . I am thinking about what I would say if I am assigned the opinion. . . . I am looking for as much help as I can get. . . ." (Alito 2008, cited in Feldman 2017*a*, 106). Briefs lay out the choices for judges and can provide them language to use in their opinions.

In this chapter, we examine whether aging leads judges to lean more on their law clerks and briefs. As we have discussed throughout this book, aging leads to reduced cognitive capacity. To try to keep up with all their obligations, judges will rely more on these resources.

6.1 Opinion Writing, Law Clerks, and Party Briefs

Judges rely on their law clerks to help them accomplish numerous tasks (see generally Ward and Weiden 2006; Peppers 2006). Clerks provide background research for judges. Such research informs judges what the legal precedents in the case suggest, whether other circuits have adopted the positions the parties advocate and if not, why not. This research also alerts judges to whether the Supreme Court has overruled or cast doubt on any relevant precedents cited. Clerks read through the lower court decisions and examine the procedural history of cases to determine whether the circuit court actually has the power to hear the case and whether the parties and lower court judge complied with proper procedures. They examine the facts of each

Cognitive Aging and the Federal Circuit Courts: How Senescence Influences the Law and Judges.
Ryan C. Black, Ryan J. Owens, Patrick C. Wohlfarth, Oxford University Press. DOI: 10.1093/oso/9780197747025.003.0006

case so as to ensure nothing is lost. As Smith (1973, 1204) states, clerks must always "verify every statement of fact that goes into the opinion. If the clerk discovers any reason to think that the judge was mistaken in his understanding of a factual issue, it is imperative that the clerk bring the matter to the judge's attention." Clerks also write bench memos for judges. These memos prepare the judges for oral argument. They provide judges with the relevant facts of the case, important precedents, and possible questions judges can ask at oral argument to address uncertainties in the briefs. One other task clerks perform (but surely not the only other task) is to help judges write judicial opinions. Nearly every federal appellate judge today relies on his or her law clerks to help write judicial opinions. Some clerks actually write substantial portions (if not all) of judges' opinions.

Whether and the extent to which each judge uses clerks to write opinions is unclear. As Judge Abner Mikva once stated: "I think many lawyers and others think clerks write the opinions and that the clerk's word is the final word in opinions. But I know very few judges who abdicate their responsibility that way. In fact, I really don't know any" (Mikva 1995, 11). He went on to say: "My clerks were not writing in any kind of unsupervised way—they didn't have a blank slate on which they could write anything they wanted" (11).

Other judges suggest, on the contrary, that clerks may play a profound role in writing judges' opinions. Posner argues that "it is generally true that whoever does the basic drafting of a document—a judicial opinion or anything else—will have a big impact on the final product" (Posner 1995*b*, 29). He continues: "as the ratio of law clerks to judges has grown, the tendency has been for more and more of the initial opinion-drafting responsibility to be delegated to law clerks, transforming the judge from a draftsman to an editor" (32). During his discussions with court of appeals judges, Cohen (2002, 117) found: "Only two of the judges with whom I spoke indicated that they always wrote their own first drafts. . . ." Clerks seem to write the drafts of many opinions. In fact, the clerk charged with writing opinions sometimes receives little guidance from the judge (Cohen 2002, 117). Not for nothing, Judge Alvin Rubin called law clerks: "para-judges," stating that "there are appellate judges whose literary style appears to change annually" (Rubin 1976, 456). His intimation, of course, was that clerks undertook the writing for their judges. Elsewhere, Posner (1995*a*, 181) has argued that ghostwriting by law clerks "enabl[es] a small number of senile judges, and a significant number of judges who are well past their prime though not yet senile . . . to continue in office." These interviews suggest that judges rely heavily on clerks when they write opinions.

Empirical studies concur. Wahlbeck, Spriggs, and Sigelman (2002) examined "ghost writing" by Supreme Court law clerks. They found that Justice Thurgood Marshall exhibited significant term-to-term variation in writing styles toward the end of his career, suggesting that Marshall relied more on his law clerks, who come and go every year, to write his opinions. Rosenthal, and Yoon (2011*a*) also analyzed the variability in justices' opinions. They found that Justice Kennedy, for example, showed more writing style variability than did Justice Scalia, confirming the authors' hypothesis that Kennedy relied more on law clerks to write his opinions than did Justice Scalia. Interestingly, they also found that the Court's opinions have become increasingly variable over time, suggesting that modern clerks now write more and more of the Court's opinions than past clerks.

Rosenthal and Yoon also examined within-justice variability. They compared a justice's opinion variability before the age of 65 versus his or her opinion variability after turning 65. They found "... no dominant trend comparing Justices pre- and post-sixty-five"; they go on to conclude that "older age does not manifest itself in greater variability in writing style" (2011, 1331). As we show below, however, our application of their approach to circuit court judges obtains a different result.

Only a handful of studies examine the use of law clerks to write opinions in courts other than the U.S. Supreme Court. Serioussi, Smyth, and Zukerman (2011) examined opinions on Australia's High Court to settle ghost-writing rumors. They found that Sir Owen Dixon ghostwrote a number of opinions for other judges. Holvast (2014) canvassed the consequences of using judicial assistants in Dutch courts. Bodwin, Rosenthal, and Yoon (2013*a*) conducted a similar analysis on the Canadian Supreme Court. Closer to home and more on point, Bodwin, Rosenthal, and Yoon (2013*b*) examined the opinions of Judge Frank Easterbook. Easterbrook allowed his clerks to write only one opinion each term for him. Knowing this, Bodwin, Rosenthal, and Yoon (2013*b*) used the corpus of Easterbrook's opinions to identify the opinions his clerks wrote (see also, Choi and Gulati 2005).

No study of which we are aware, however, systematically investigates the effects of aging on circuit court judges' use of their law clerks. This absence is strange because the literature is so clear that aging influences cognitive capacity. As we noted in earlier chapters, the brain changes with age. The prefrontal cortex shrinks. White matter lesions appear on the brain and myelin diminishes. These changes are associated with decreased working memory, reduced abilities to regulate and to think critically, slower processing speeds, and other negative effects. Older adults do what they can to compensate but ultimately, cognition declines. Surely, all of this influences judges' abilities to write opinions.

Anecdotal evidence suggests that aging judges may lead judges to rely more on their clerks. Posner (1995*b*, 112) writes: "Appellate judges ... are largely although not entirely shielded from direct evaluations of their work.... As long as they can pick competent law clerks they will be able to churn out, regardless of their own efforts or ability, professionally adequate opinions ...." We suspect that as they age, judges will become increasingly likely to rely on their law clerks to write their opinions.

We also suspect that judges will rely more on party briefs as they age. Judges need information to make well-reasoned legal decisions. Briefs do that. Tailored to the particular dispute in each case, briefs offer judges information that is directly relevant to the resolution of the legal controversy before them. As Hazelton, Hinkle, and Spriggs (2019, 126) put it, briefs aid judges to "assess facts, precedent, likely outcomes of policy alternatives, and probable reactions of other branches and the public ...." (see also, Hazelton and Hinkle 2022). Briefs furnish legal and extralegal information, both of which aid judges.

Legal information in the briefs includes information on what the law compels (or does not compel). This covers precedents, administrative rules, statutes, constitutional doctrines, and related legal matter. Briefs help judges determine the most appropriate legal outcomes in cases and provide judges legal information about the relevant precedents involved. Judges cite those precedents, discuss them, and apply them to the facts of the cases before them. In other words, briefs explain to judges *why* the law counsels toward one outcome versus another.

Consider *Bevis v. City of Naperville* (2023). This Seventh Circuit case addressed whether a city's prohibition on assault weapons and large-capacity magazines violated the Second Amendment to the U.S. Constitution and conflicted with the Supreme Court's recent decision in *New York State Rifle & Pistol Association Inc. v. Bruen* (2022). The brief's table of authorities referenced 45 cases, the Constitution, and other similar matter. Throughout the brief, Bevis discussed and applied numerous precedents. Figure 6.1 shows a page from that brief, revealing just how parties can reference cases to make their arguments.

At the same time, briefs can provide judges with information about the broader policy and political implications of rulings. Judges may need information to forecast how their decisions will translate into "real world" outcomes. For example, if they vote to strike down a particular legal provision, they may need to know whether that decision will undercut the constitutionality of other laws. Similarly, a pro-defendant ruling may place greater demands on the resources needed to prosecute crimes.

> statute that is probably unconstitutional. *Id.* So "the analysis begins and ends with the likelihood of success on the merits" of the constitutional claim. *Id., citing Korte v. Sebelius*, 735 F.3d 654, 666 (7th Cir. 2013).
>
> This Court reviews the district court's legal conclusions de novo and its balancing of the injunction factors for an abuse of discretion. *Ezell*, 651 F.3d at 694.
>
> **II. *Friedman* is no Longer Good Law**
>
> Plaintiffs will begin with a point of agreement. The district court held that the panel opinion in *Friedman v. City of Highland Park*, 784 F.3d 406 (7th Cir. 2015), "cannot be reconciled with *Bruen*." ECF No. 63, p 16. That conclusion is surely correct.
>
> The State disagrees,[2] but the State's argument on that score is wrong. In *Friedman*, the majority upheld an assault weapons ban that is materially identical to the laws challenged in this case. However, "[s]tare decisis cannot justify adherence to an approach that Supreme Court precedent forecloses." *Fed. Trade Comm'n v. Credit Bureau Ctr., LLC*, 937 F.3d 764, 767 (7th Cir. 2019). *See also United States v. Wahi*, 850 F.3d 296, 302 (7th Cir. 2017) ("When an intervening Supreme Court decision unsettles [the Seventh Circuit's] precedent, it is the ruling of the [Supreme] Court that . . . must carry the day.").
>
> [2] Intervening State Appellee's Opposition to Plaintiffs' Motion for Injunction Pending Appeal ("State Opp."), 2.

Figure 6.1 Page from appellant's brief in *Bevis v. City of Naperville* (2023). Briefs collected from Westlaw.com.

Politicians may be hankering to punish a court over a particular ruling, and judges may desire to know that (Johnson 2003).

Not surprisingly, then, court watchers have declared the brief to be the most important communicative tool between lawyers and judges today. It is "the central feature of modern appellate practice" (Martineau et al. 2005, 770). Federal District Court Judge Mark Kravitz once stated that briefs carry "the lion's share of the persuasion load" in court (Kravitz 2009, 268; cited in Feldman 2017). Judges and clerks "report that they review the briefs many times after arguments when coming to their decisions" (Feldman 2017*a*, 122). The attorneys' frontal assault hinges on their briefs. Perhaps it is no wonder that law schools increasingly emphasize to student how to write effective briefs (Hazelton, Hinkle, and Spriggs 2019; Corley 2008) and that judges commonly write law review articles aimed at improving brief writing among lawyers (Scalia and Garner 2008; Rehnquist 1999).

The fact that briefs are *written* heightens their value to aging judges. Older people have an easier time answering questions presented to them in written form than in auditory form (Park 2000, 11). The written format provides older judges "environmental support" and demands less from their working memory. Recall that working memory is "the active and simultaneous processing and storing of information" (Hoyer 2015, 797). It allows us to keep one thing in mind as we turn to another. But, working memory is one of the most well known age-related declines. Because briefs are present for judges to use "from the beginning until the end of the case" (Feldman 2017*a*, 121), they are particularly useful for older judges.

Given the importance of legal briefs in the appellate process and to older judges in particular, one might think that scholars have studied them thoroughly. They have not (Feldman 2017*a*, 107). The quantitative analyses that examine briefs tend largely to focus on the Supreme Court (Hazelton and Hinkle 2022; Feldman 2017*b*; Black, Hall, Owens, and Ringsmuth 2016; Collins, Corley, and Hamner 2015, 2014; Wedeking 2010; Collins 2008b; Spriggs and Wahlbeck 1997). In their analysis of the death penalty, Epstein and Kobylka (1992) find that well-made arguments in the attorneys' briefs persuaded at least some justices to affirm the constitutionality of Georgia's reformed death penalty laws in the 1970s. Justices often "borrow" language from briefs, especially from those written by the Solicitor General and elite, experienced attorneys (Corley 2008; Black and Owens 2012). Hazelton, Hinkle, and Spriggs (2019) find that "briefs presenting shared information are more likely to have that information adopted in the Court's majority opinion" (126) (see also, Oldfather, Brockhorst and Dimmer 2012; Evans et al. 2007).

Only a few studies analyze briefs and court of appeals judges. Samaha, Heise, and Sisk (2020) find that longer appellant briefs correlate positively with judges' votes to reverse in the Second and Ninth Circuits, but not in the Eighth Circuit. They also find evidence that longer appellee briefs might have made the Second Circuit less likely to reverse its lower courts. Those findings seem to confirm Sisk and Heise (2015) that longer appellant-side briefs are associated with Ninth Circuit judges voting to reverse.

These studies, however, do not address the question we raise here—whether judges are more likely to borrow language from party briefs as they age. To be sure, one study finds that Supreme Court justices borrow more language from briefs as they age (Feldman 2017*a*), but the *reason* why that is the case is not explained. (And, of course, that study examines the Supreme Court.) Because cognitive aging causes declines in processing speed, executive functioning, and reasoning abilities, and because judges are more likely to employ cognitive shortcuts as cognitive demands increase, we expect that as they age, judges will author opinions that: (1) are more similar to the party briefs in that case; and (2) borrow more language from (i.e., plagiarize) the party briefs.

6.2 Law Clerks: Data and Measures

To assess whether judges, as they age, rely more upon their law clerks, we follow the approach Rosenthal, and Yoon (2011*a*) developed to examine how Supreme Court justices use their law clerks (see also Rosenthal and Yoon 2011*b*).[1] This approach is a stylometric one and centers on the use of "function words" in opinions. Function words are "filler words of the language such as articles, conjunctions, and prepositions" (Mosteller and Wallace 1963, 279). Critically, the "usage frequencies are largely independent of subject matter" (Rosenthal and Yoon 2011*b*, 1314). Whether the case touches search and seizure, corporate taxation, or the right to privacy does not influence the relative rate with which the judge utilizes function words. In short, because each judge uses function words in an approximately constant manner, those words leave a "linguistical fingerprint."

Rosenthal and Yoon suggest that one can analyze judge opinion variability to examine how judges use law clerks to write their opinions. This is because each law clerk also possesses his or her own linguistic fingerprint. Applying this method to the Supreme Court,[2] Rosenthal and Yoon find strong facial validity for their approach. Justices who are thought to have written most of their opinions (e.g., Douglas and Holmes) displayed lower variability scores than justices thought to have delegated opinion writing tasks to their clerks (2011*b*).

To conduct our analysis, we utilize a subset of the opinion corpus we analyzed in Chapter 5 (where we assessed variation in stylistic features of judges' written opinions). In particular, we follow Rosenthal and Yoon and limit our analysis to majority opinions that are at least 250 words long. This filter leaves us with just over 370,000 opinions authored by approximately 2,430 unique judges. To provide the observed counts of function words, we created a custom dictionary of 71 words and then used the software program Linguistic Inquiry and Word Count (LIWC) to count the frequency with which these words appeared in opinions.[3]

[1] Bodwin, Rosenthal, and Yoon (2013*a*) apply this methodology to the Canadian Supreme Court and find strong evidence of clerk opinion writing that dates back to the late 1960s.

[2] Although their substantive interest is the role of law clerks in Supreme Court opinion writing, Rosenthal and Yoon examine function word variability for Court of Appeals judges Frank Easterbrook and Richard A. Posner, two judges commonly thought to write their own opinions. They show lower variability than any modern Supreme Court justice, which supports the validity of the Rosenthal and Yoon method (2011*b*, 1325–1326).

[3] In their examination of U.S. Supreme Court opinion writing, Rosenthal and Yoon start with an initial list of 72 function words, which was developed by Mosteller and Wallace (1963) in their seminal study of authorship of the individual essays in the *Federalist Papers*. Rosenthal and Yoon then removed nine words from this list that rarely appeared in their corpus of opinions. If we apply the same cutoff value used by

6.3 Law Clerks: Methods and Results

Data in hand, we use Rosenthal and Yoon's formula to calculate function word variability for a given subset of a judge's opinions.[4] We will elaborate on the "given subset" aspect in greater detail below. For now, we will begin by comparing opinions written by an individual judge before reaching 65 (the conventional retirement age in the U.S.) versus opinions written *by that same judge* after reaching retirement age.[5] If every judge has a stylometric fingerprint that is detectable regardless of a case's subject matter, then the judge who writes all of her own opinions will possess small variation scores. By contrast, the judge who farms out her opinions to others, each of whom have their own fingerprints, will reveal larger variability scores. To be included in this analysis, a judge needed to have written opinions on both sides of the 65 year old cut-point. We further limited the analysis to judges who had written at least 10 opinions in both of these periods. We took this step so as to reduce the risk of examining outlier opinions that might skew the results.[6] After these winnowing steps, we were left with a total of 569 judges who collectively wrote more than 170,000 opinions before they turned 65 years old and over 141,000 opinions from judges 65 and older. At the individual judge level, the median number of pre- versus post-65 opinions is 239 and 194, respectively.[7]

We begin our presentation of the results in Figure 6.2. The vertical axis shows our function word variability measure. If a judge is perfectly consistent in her use of function words, the variability should be equal to a value of 1.0, which appears at the very bottom of the plot. (There is no limit to the maximum the value can take.) The left side of the horizontal axis shows opinions authored before a judge turned 65 years old; the right side shows opinions written when she was 65 years or older.

Consider the overall averages in our sample of 569 judges. Comparing these two values tells us whether, as a whole, judges 65 and older seem to use law clerks more than judges younger than 65. These sub-sample means appear toward the top of the figure (i.e., "Sample Averages"). The average variability score for our full complement of pre-65 judges is 3.13. The average variability score of judges 65 and older is

Rosenthal and Yoon (i.e., 0.1% or lower), then we need to exclude only a single word—"whilst." All other function words appear in at least 14% of our opinions. See the chapter appendix for a full listing of the function words.

[4] See the chapter's appendix for this formula.

[5] Pension vesting is a tremendously important predictor of retirement—especially among lower court judges (Yoon 2006).

[6] We determined this value by examining our results using different thresholds. We sought a threshold that avoided variability scores less than 1, which is the value that should obtain if a judge is perfectly consistent in her function word usage. Values below 1 occur if many of the expected values for functions word equal zero. This happens when the number and length of opinions written by a judge are both very low.

[7] Fully importing the Rosenthal and Yoon approach to the circuit court judges raises a consideration that they did not need to consider in their Supreme Court-centric research: senior status. Although all federal judges—including Supreme Court justices—can avail themselves of this semi-retired status, only lower court judges can elect to fulfill their reduced workload responsibilities by continuing to decide cases at their appointed level or, in the case of senior status district court judges sitting by designation, potentially even higher. Since senior judges' opinions still carry the same weight as those of active judges, we leave them combined for the sake of efficiency and parsimony. But for those who are curious about the effect of senior status on variability, see the chapter's appendix for results.

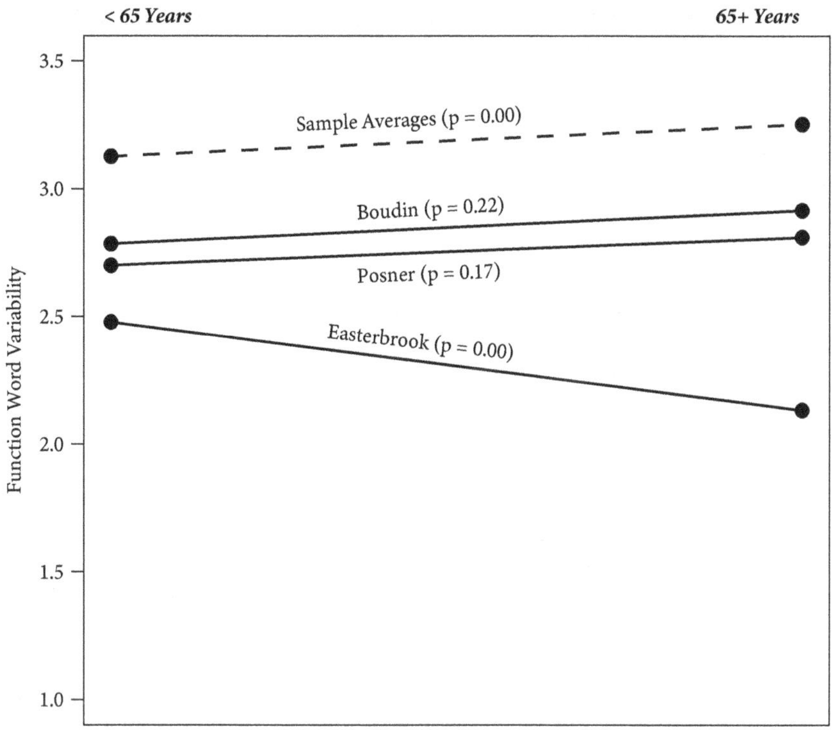

Figure 6.2 Variability by retirement age status. Vertical axis shows function word variability measure. Horizontal axis shows two types of opinions: those authored before a judge turned 65 years old (left side of plot) and those written when she was 65 years or older (right side of plot).

3.25. This difference (i.e., 0.12) is statistically significant in a paired t-test ($t = 5.66$, $p < 0.001$), which we note in the parentheses that appear in the plot.[8] Thus, we can conclude that, on the whole, judges older than 65 seem to use their law clerks to write opinions more than judges younger than 65.

For comparison and robustness purposes, the figure also shows three particular judges: Judges Boudin, Easterbrook, and Posner. By all accounts, they retained exclusive or near-exclusive ownership of their opinions. As expected, all three judges' variability scores—both before and after turning age 65—are significantly below the sample averages.[9] As to changes in opinion variability after they turned 65 years old, both Boudin and Posner show no significant change. Easterbrook's variability actually *decreases* by roughly 14%, a difference that is statistically significant. Easterbrook was

[8] To determine statistical significance, we follow the approach of Rosenthal, and Yoon (2011*a*); Rosenthal and Yoon (2011*b*) and use bootstrapping. See the chapter's appendix for additional details.

[9] To make this statement, we calculated the proportion of bootstrap samples for each of these judges that were less than the relevant sample means (i.e., 3.13 for pre and 3.25 for post). For the pre-65 values, 100% of the bootstrap samples for all three judges were below 3.13. For the post-65 values, 99.3% of the samples for Boudin were below 3.25; for Easterbrook and Posner, all 100% of the samples were less than 3.25.

systematically *less* variable in his opinion writing after turning 65 years old. Taken together, these results provide strong facial validity for the approach we take.

We now deploy the within-judge comparisons we just performed on Boudin, Easterbrook, and Posner to assess variability score changes across the other 566 judges in our data. In terms of point estimates, fully 61% (i.e., 346) of the 569 judges in our sample displayed greater opinion variability after they turned 65 relative to their pre-65 opinions. The remaining 39% (i.e., 223) display less variability in their 65 or older opinions.[10] When we burrow into whether these pre-65 versus post-65 differences are statistically different from zero, we find that 37% of the judges in our sample show significant increases in variability. Conversely, just 20% of our sample judges show a significant decrease in variability. The remaining 43% of judges have p-values that fall outside of common thresholds for statistical significance.[11] Thus, although a plurality of judges show neither a significant increase nor decrease, among those that do show significant movement one way or another, fully 85% show significantly greater use of law clerks as they age.[12]

While the foregoing establishes that opinions by aged judges show greater evidence of law clerk assistance than opinions by younger judges, we sought to provide a finer-grain analysis of opinion variability. So, we returned to our original corpus of data to examine decade-long sub-samples for judges. We calculated separate variability scores for opinions a judge wrote when she was 40–49 years old, 50–59 years old, 60–69 years old, and so on. To be sure, one could use either wider (e.g., 15 or 20 years) or narrower (e.g., 5 years) windows for these calculations. Existing studies of cognitive aging provide no guidance on how to parameterize aging. We ultimately selected 10-year windows because that struck us as a middle ground between providing additional variation in age while still maintaining a reasonable number of opinions both within an individual judge (e.g., Posner from 50–59 versus Posner from 60–69) and also between judges when evaluating overall patterns (e.g., comparing average variability in judges in their 50s versus their 60s).[13]

A total of 759 of the judges in our corpus have two or more decade windows in which they authored at least 10 majority opinions of length greater than or equal to 250 words. The total number of opinions across these judges was over 346,000.[14]

[10] None of the judges in our sample have exactly the same variability scores in their two samples, but 13 have differences that are less than one-hundredth of a point (e.g., 0.008 or −0.004). Five of these are lower variability between pre- versus post-65 years old and eight are higher variability.

[11] If we instead use a more permissive 0.20 threshold (i.e., right below what one might need to consider accepting the null hypothesis), then number of significant increases goes to 248 (i.e., 44%) and the number of significant decreases goes to 147 (i.e., 26%).

[12] It is also the case that the magnitude of the significant increases is larger than the magnitude of the significant decreases. The median decrease in the 115 judges with significant decreases is 0.44. The analogous value among the 208 judges with significant variability increases is 0.54, which is about 23% larger.

[13] See the chapter's appendix for additional discussion about the considerations involved in selecting a window length.

[14] The total word count of this corpus is approximately 1.2 billion words. The seven books in the Harry Potter series have a total of nearly 1.1 million words, so we are roughly 1100 times longer. Ten seconds on Google tells us that the average human speaks at 150 words per minute. One of us—Wohlfarth—hatched a child as we were putting the finishing touches on this book. If he were to read the entire corpus to his son, without ever stopping, his child would be almost 16 years old when he finished (though, he surely would have slept through all of it).

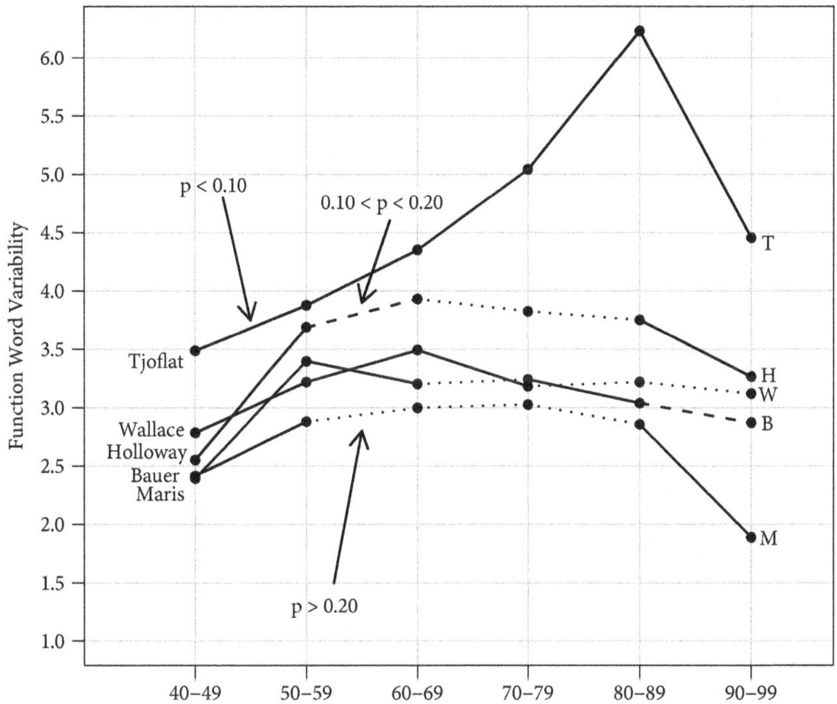

Figure 6.3 Variability by judge age for five judges. Figure shows judge-level opinion-writing variability scores, by decade. Dots display the variability scores. A dotted line represents a p-value that is larger than 0.20; a dashed line signifies a p-value between 0.10 and 0.20; and a solid line means the p-value is less than, or equal to, 0.10. The plotted values for Bauer and Maris for opinions written while 40–49 years of age are essentially identical (i.e., we didn't just forget to plot one of them).

There are 330 judges with two decades, 249 judges with three decades, 133 judges with four decades, 42 judges with five decades, and five judges with six decades of opinion writing. All told, we have a total of 2,179 judge decades worth of data.

We begin by showcasing in Figure 6.3 the five judges for whom we have data from their 40s through their 90s. Along the x-axis, we identify each of the six decade-long windows. The judge-level variability scores per decade appear on the y-axis. Within the plot, we show each of the five judges, whose last names appear on the far left of the plot. (Letters on the far right identify the judge for easier visual comparisons across time—e.g., T is for Tjoflat and B is for Bauer.) The dots in the plot show the variability scores. We use the style of line segment that connects two points to indicate whether a change is statistically significant. A dotted line means the p-value is larger than 0.20. A dashed line means the p-value is in the gray-zone (too small to ignore but too large for conventional levels of significance). A solid lines means the p-value is less than or equal to 0.10.

Our analysis suggests that Gerald Tjoflat steadily increased his use of law clerks in four of the five comparisons we examined. His variability score, which started at

3.49 in his 40s, increased significantly to 3.88 in his 50s. We then observe three more rounds of significant increases: to 4.35 in his 60s, to 5.04 in his 70s, and then, once more, to 6.23 in his 80s. His final progression suggests a rather dramatic reduction, when his score decreased to 4.45 in his 90s. More on that in a just a bit. The other four judges show a statistically significant increase when comparing opinions they wrote in their 40s to those they wrote in their 50s, and three of the five (including Tjoflat) show some evidence of a second, consecutive increase in variability when progressing from their 50s to their 60s. Beyond that period, we tend to see stability over the next few decades.

What are we to make of the reduction we see when the judges moved from their 80s to their 90s? Three of these reductions—Tjoflat, Holloway, and Maris—are statistically significant (i.e., solid lines) and one—Bauer—is in the gray-zone (i.e., dashed line). Should we be concerned about the veracity of our general claim about cognitive aging and clerk influence? We believe not. As these judges transitioned from their 80s to their 90s, their workloads reduced dramatically. Though opinion counts during our judges' 80s ranged from as few as 48 to as many as 392 opinions, they dropped precipitously during their 90s. Only one of the five judges (William Bauer) authored more than 18 opinions in his 90s.[15] As they scaled back on their workload, it stands to reason that they received lower levels of law clerk support. In describing senior judges, Levy (2021, 1243) notes: "... they may maintain a set of chambers and staff, though the number of staff they are allotted generally depends upon the workload they take on each year" and then continues to state in a footnote: "A few circuits have their own policies regarding staffing. For example, senior judges are 'generally' permitted two law clerks in the Eighth Circuit" (ibid.). Active judges may hire three. Losing a clerk would produce a lower variability score, as drafting duties would then be concentrated in a smaller number of individuals within a judge's chambers. (Of course, when we compare these judges' last window of opinions to their first window opinions, we still find that most judges observe significant increases.)[16]

Though these five judges nicely illustrate the usefulness of our approach, we are more interested in making broader characterizations of the other 750+ judges in our data. Simultaneously plotting this many lines, as we just did for the six decade club members, yields a figure that resembles a big plate of spaghetti but is, otherwise, pretty useless.[17] Instead we focus on the summarizing the extent to which judges' law clerk usage (i.e., variability) increases as they aged. That is, when an older judge is compared to a younger version of herself, do we find compelling evidence of more law clerk usage? To answer this question we offer Figure 6.4, which presents a barplot that summarizes more than 1,400 comparisons of judges during their youngest decade of opinion writing versus subsequent decades.[18] We identify these comparisons along

[15] The judge-level values for their 80s and 90s are: Bauer (392, 145), Holloway (83, 18), Maris (48, 18), Tjoflat (183, 15), and Wallace (126, 13).

[16] Bauer, Holloway, and Tjoflat all have significant increases, Wallace has a non-significant increase ($p = 0.16$), and Maris has a significant decrease.

[17] But, what's that you say? You're intensely curious about what our results look like for [insert your (least) favorite judge here]? You can access those via the book's online supplement on the Harvard Dataverse.

[18] An alternative would be to examine changes in variability in sequentially successive decades. This would look at 40s vs. 50s and 50s vs. 60s instead of 40s vs. 50s and 40s vs. 60s (i.e., move both the baseline

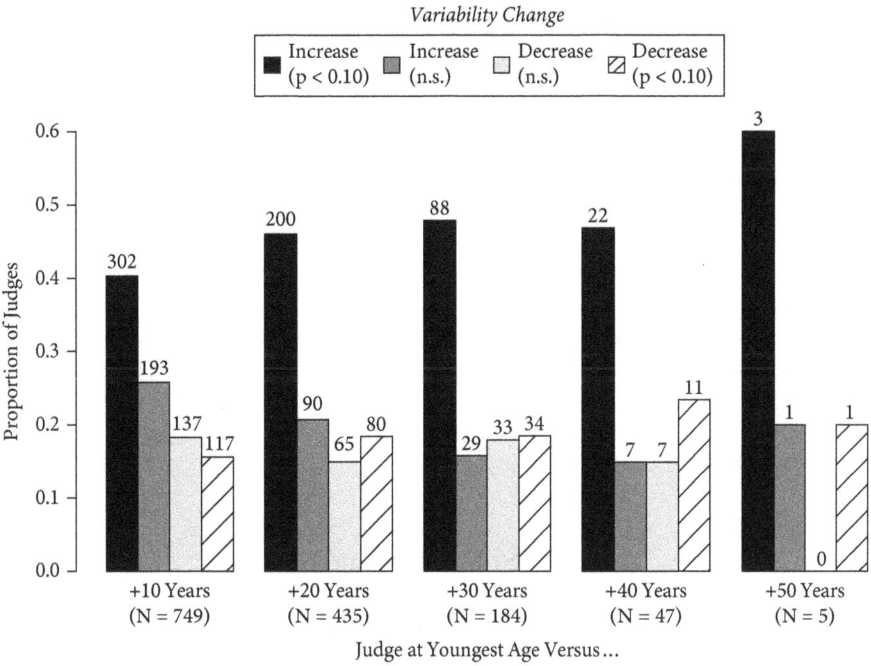

Figure 6.4 Variability changes for a 10-year increase in judge age. Figure reports within-judge opinion-writing variability comparing a judge's first decade on the court to subsequent decades. A black bar represents a statistically significant increase in variability; a dark gray bar indicates a non-significant increase; a light gray bar reflects a non-significant decrease; and a white bar with diagonal lines means a statistically significant decrease. The number at the top of a bar reports the frequency of judges represented within that bar.

the x-axis, which displays how many years forward the comparison set has moved, ranging from 10 years (i.e., one window) to the maximum of 50 years (i.e., five windows, which we presented with our quintet of judges above). Numbers in parentheses below these labels identify the number of judges used to make this comparison. The bars within the plot aggregate the results of these within-judge comparisons, with black bars indicating a significant increase in clerk usage, dark gray indicating non-significant increases, light gray indicating non-significant decreases, and white bars with diagonal lines indicating significant decreases. Numbers appearing at the top of each bar report the frequency of judges represented within that bar.

As the figure makes clear, for every single comparison group, the modal outcome is evidence of significantly greater law clerk usage by the aged judge as compared to the

and the comparison window forward). We believe the approach we use in-text better addresses the overall trajectory of cognitive aging and clerk usage. Nevertheless, results from the alternative support the same conclusion—judges tend to use law clerks more as they age. See the chapter's appendix for an analogous figure and discussion.

youngest version of that same judge. That is, the height of the black bar is always the tallest for each comparison. Even advancing forward by just a single window (+10 years) shows significant increases for 40% of the judges in our data. Only 16% of judges show evidence of significantly reduced law clerk usage. Moving another ten years out and comparing a judge's opinions in her third decade on the bench reveals even stronger results, with fully 46% of judges showing greater variability in that period relative to his or her first decade of opinion writing. This percentage increases once more—albeit slightly—when we see that 48% of judges' opinions written forty years later are more variable than those written in their earliest decade. And, as we noted just a bit ago, among the handful of judges for whom we have 60 years of opinions, three of the five show significant increases in variability.

If we aggregate across all five of the comparisons presented, fully 43% of the changes show a significant increase in clerk usage compared to just 17% that show a significant decrease. Put simply, we uncover compelling evidence that aging judges increasingly rely on their law clerks to write their opinions.

6.4 Briefs: Data and Measures

We turn, now, to examine how aging judges increasingly rely on the litigants' briefs to lessen their cognitive burdens. Although court opinion data are relatively easy to obtain, wrangling readily usable data on attorney briefs is far more difficult. Electronic databases such as Lexis and Westlaw provide inconsistent and often incomplete coverage.[19] And, as of this writing, no bulk download option readily exists, either. (Let's get with the program, people!) Thus, we needed to blaze our own trail to collect circuit court brief data. We started by creating a list of judges from which to sample. We constrained that list to include only judges confirmed in 1975 or later.[20] We also limited the list to judges in one of the 12 geographically defined U.S. Court of Appeals, thus excluding speciality courts like the Federal Circuit. We randomized the 416 judges on that list and then began collecting their written opinions. The results we report below come from 43 unique circuit court judges on that list.

We analyze signed majority opinions or orders (including both published and unpublished filings) in unanimously decided cases.[21] Our cases thus come from a sample of the second-most frequent type of judicial outcome on the U.S. Courts of

[19] Even studies of litigant briefs at the Supreme Court have to contend with these issues. Hazelton, Hinkle, and Spriggs (2019, 135) report that their analysis of 1988–2005, not an especially wide or ancient window of time, encountered nearly 10% of briefs that were unavailable through either Lexis or Westlaw and had to be obtained from one of the nine depositories of printed Supreme Court briefs.

[20] We exclude judges who began prior to 1975 because, though we believe there is merit in understanding circuit court decision making in the early and middle parts of the 20th century, the normative nature of the project demands greater attention to recent activity. What is more, Songer, Sheehan, and Haire (2000) show that circuit courts became more active starting in the 1970s. Further, data are less available the farther back in time we examine.

[21] A signed opinion is one where all the judges indicate their positions on it (i.e., join, concur, dissent). This is the opposite of a *per curiam* opinion, in which the judges' individual positions are not known and the opinion is released on behalf of all the judges. In 2022, a total of 17,345 unsigned opinions were filed across the circuits compared to 8,001 signed opinions. These figures include both published and unpublished opinions.

Appeals (with the first being an unsigned opinion). Our sample consists of 1,630 opinions and 5,230 briefs submitted in these cases (i.e., approximately 3.2 briefs per case). We obtained the opinions and the briefs from Westlaw. The decision dates among our cases range from 2005 to 2022, but the vast majority—about 83%—were decided in 2017–2019, inclusive.

Our models employ two dependent variables. The first—*Opinion-Brief Similarity*—measures the degree of similarity for each brief-opinion dyad. That is, it measures how similar each opinion is to each party brief in each case. To calculate the measure, we follow Hazelton, Hinkle, and Spriggs (2019) and Hazelton and Hinkle (2022) and calculate the cosine distance between each document. We do using the `cosine_distance` command in the `textTinyR` package. We standardize the values to facilitate easier substantive interpretation of the results. Larger values represent greater similarity between the opinion and the brief under consideration. The 5th and 95th percentile values are −1.40 and 0.87, respectively, and the median value is 0.22.

Our second dependent variable—*Borrowed Language*—measures the amount of language the opinion *copied* from the brief. We use Bloomfield's (2016) CopyFind program to calculate the amount of exact overlap between each brief-opinion pairing. CopyFind is the command-line version of Bloomfield's WCopyFind program, which offers a point-and-click interface. The "innards" of the two programs are identical. Both programs allow users to tune a number of parameters, but we make no significant deviations from the standard settings recommended by Bloomfield. (See the chapter's appendix for those particular values.) We utilize the output from Copyfind "as is," which means our measure is the number of matching words between each brief-opinion pairing. *Borrowed Language* ranges from a minimum of seven words to a maximum of 3,325 words; the 5th, 50th, and 95th percentile values are 41, 230, and 800 words, respectively (note that our statistical models will control for the length of each brief and the length of the court's opinion per case).

Moving to our independent variables, our primary interest lies in the opinion author's age. *Opinion Author Age* is the difference between the author's year of birth, which we obtain from the Federal Judicial Center data, and the year in which the opinion was filed, which we obtain from the opinion itself. *Opinion Author Age* in this sample ranges from a minimum of 40 years old to a maximum of 88 years old. The 5th, 50th, and 95th percentile values are 49, 63, and 79 years old.

In terms of statistical controls, we account for a number of relevant features. First, *Opinion Author Experience* allows us to isolate temporal patterns. Suppose an attorney seeks to woo a judge by using that very judge's past writing. The judge, in turn, might side with the attorney and, in writing the majority opinion, quote those past writings. Judges who have served longer on the bench will have a larger corpus from which strategic attorneys might draw.[22] We must account for that. In our sample of judges, the median level of experience is 13 years, with 5th and 95th percentile values of 2 and 34 years. The minimum is zero years and the maximum is 40 years of experience.

We also expect that the prevailing party's brief will be more informative to an opinion writer than the losing party's brief. To capture and control for this dynamic,

[22] We thank Deborah Beim for proposing this argument.

we measure *Brief for Appellant*, which takes on a value of 1 if the brief supported the appellant; 0 otherwise (i.e., for appellee). We then include *Appellant Win*, a dummy variable coded as 1 if the appellant received any relief in the case and 0 if it was a pure win for the appellee. We next create the interaction between these two covariates.[23]

Additionally, we include *Brief by United States*, which is coded as 1 if any attorney for the U.S. authored the brief under analysis; 0 otherwise. This control captures the outsized influence of the U.S. as a party in the federal courts (see, e.g., Black and Owens 2011, 2012; Wohlfarth 2009). The U.S. submitted approximately 8% of the briefs in our data, but at the case level, fully 22% of the cases in our data involved the U.S. *Case in West Reporter* takes a value of 1 if West's Federal Reporter published the opinion; 0 if not. This control captures potentially different dynamics in cases of extremely low salience (i.e., those that are not published). Approximately 8% of opinions in our data were unpublished. Finally, we included the full gamut of measures available through LIWC. We used the 2022 version of the software and, as a robustness check, include the nearly 120 measures in one of the specifications estimated below (Boyd et al. 2022).[24]

6.5 Briefs: Methods and Results

Because our first dependent variable (*Opinion-Brief Similarity*) is approximately continuous, we estimate an ordinary least squares regression model.[25] Table 6.1 reports the results from three different model specifications. Model 1 shows the bivariate relationship between *Opinion Author Age* and *Opinion-Brief Similarity*. Model 2 adds our non-linguistic control variables. Model 3 is the full model that adds the litany of LIWC (linguistic) covariates. Regression coefficients appear above their robust standard errors, which we report in parentheses.[26]

As Table 6.1 shows, across all three models, a positive and statistically significant relationship exists between the age of an opinion author and the similarity between her opinion and the briefs in each case. The older a judge is, the greater the similarity

[23] We evaluated whether there was any value in disaggregating cases with "mixed" outcomes such as "affirmed in part, reversed in part" from this more parsimonious approach. There is not. The marginal effect of an appellant brief is statistically indistinguishable in cases where the appellant wins fully versus winning partially ($p = 0.82$).

[24] There is also a practical reason for this particular specification. Litigant briefs—especially at the circuit court level—vary wildly with respect to their organization, content, and formatting consistency. The results we report here use the full text file of the entire brief, which includes, if present, things like the table of contents and table of authorities. Some of the useful LIWC categories include different types of punctuation, which will help to protect our similarity measure from being contaminated by this measurement error.

[25] Since the variable is not *strictly* continuous, we checked our results by estimating a Tobit regression. The results are identical. "Fun" fact we didn't know: the person who created the Tobit regression was actually named Tobi*n*. Bonus facts: His first name was James and he won a Nobel Prize in Economics in 1981.

[26] Our statistical inferences are unaltered if we instead use standard errors of the classical variety. Relatedly, clustering the errors on the 1630 cases in our data does not appreciably change anything. If we cluster on the 43 judges, however, the p-values for our *Author Age* variable *increase* to 0.24 in Model 1, 0.04 in Model 2, and 0.08 in Model 3.

Table 6.1 The Relationship Between Judge Age and Opinion-Brief Textual Similarity

	(1)	(2)	(3)
Opinion Author Age	0.008**	0.018**	0.011**
	(0.001)	(0.002)	(0.001)
Opinion Author Experience		−0.011**	−0.004**
		(0.002)	(0.001)
Appellant Win		0.136**	0.030
		(0.034)	(0.031)
Brief for Appellant		−0.287**	−0.272**
		(0.031)	(0.023)
Appellant Win × Brief for Appellant		0.106*	0.163**
		(0.057)	(0.040)
Brief by United States		0.135**	−0.091**
		(0.044)	(0.035)
Case in West Reporter		1.056**	0.838**
		(0.066)	(0.052)
Constant	−0.492**	−1.802**	−12.341**
	(0.089)	(0.137)	(1.255)
LIWC Brief Measures	No	No	Yes
N	5,230	5,230	5,230
BIC	14,827	14,276	10,127

Note: Table entries are ordinary least squares regression coefficients with robust standard errors in parentheses. The dependent variable is the cosine distance (i.e., text similarity) for each opinion-brief dyad; larger values represent greater similarity. ** and * denote $p < 0.05$ and $p < 0.10$, respectively (two-tailed).

between that judge's opinions and the parties' briefs.[27] To understand the substantive nature of the relationship, we present predicted values in Figure 6.5. These results come from Model 2, which includes controls but excludes the LIWC measures. The horizontal axis displays the full range of *Opinion Author Age*. The vertical axis shows the predicted level of similarity between a judge's opinion and an individual brief, conditional on a given value of age (while holding all other predictors constant). The black line reveals our point estimates; the gray region denotes the 95% confidence interval around those estimates.

We estimate that an opinion author at the sample minimum—40 years of age—writes an opinion with a brief similarity score of approximately −0.40. An opinion author at the sample maximum of 88 years old, by contrast, is likely to produce an opinion that has a similarity score of roughly +0.42. Since our dependent variable is standardized, this predicted change in opinion-brief similarity implies an effect that is equivalent to about eight-tenths of a standard deviation in the dependent variable. In percentile terms, −0.40 is near the 19th percentile and +0.42 is at around the 66th percentile within the sample, which is to say the effect covers nearly 50% of the range

[27] Given the results of the first half of this chapter, one might wonder whether it is the judge doing the borrowing or if it is "merely" her clerks. One could argue that such is a distinction without a difference since cognitive aging manifests both outcomes. Nevertheless, auxiliary analyses we conducted suggest it is a mixture of both the judge and the law clerks. See the chapter's (increasingly long) appendix for additional discussion and results.

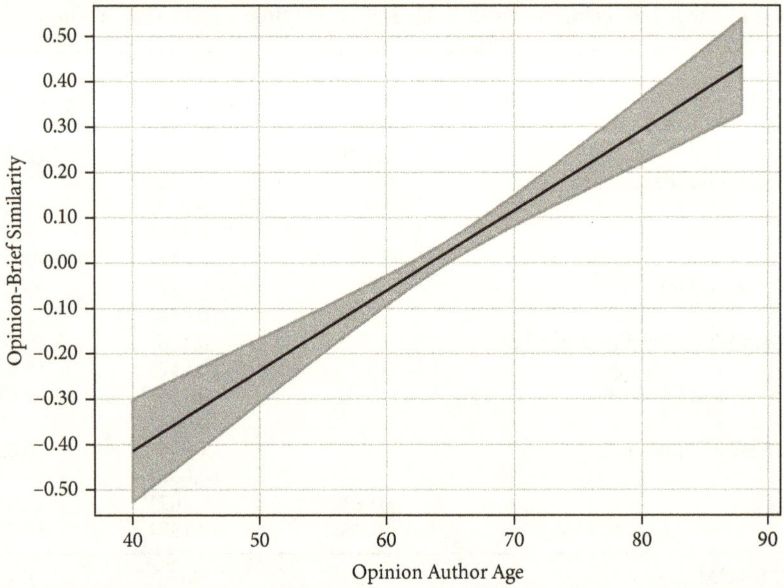

Figure 6.5 Opinion-brief textual similarity increases with opinion author age. Figure reports the predicted level of similarity between a judge's opinion and an individual brief (with 95% confidence intervals), conditional on a given value of age (while holding all other predictors constant), using results from Model 2 in Table 6.1.

in the underlying measure. In short, the empirical results indicate a moderate, yet meaningful effect of a judge's age on opinion-brief similarity, as we hypothesized.

One might be concerned that older judges are simply being assigned "easier" or more fact-bound cases. Such could explain greater similarity (and increased outright copy-pasting). Our similarity analyses account for this by examining only unanimous panel opinions. Of course, we recognize that some unanimous cases will be easier than others. Still, our auxiliary analyses suggest that our findings are not driven by "super easy" cases. To assess this possibility, we use opinion length as a(n admittedly coarse) surrogate for case difficulty. We then estimated our model excluding the bottom 10% of opinions and assessed whether (a) our author age variable is statistically significant and (b) whether the magnitude of the coefficient we estimate in the full model decreases. We still find a significant effect and fail to find evidence of a significant change in the magnitude of the coefficient (see also, footnote 30). Another way to address this concern would be to examine whether older judges depend more heavily on the winner's brief. Doing so might provide the clearest roadmap for a judge. Yet, in both the similarity model and the plagiarism model (as we explain below), they do not. It just does not appear that older judges are being assigned simpler cases.

In terms of our control measures, we find that the brief with the highest level of similarity is an appellee brief when the appellant wins (similarity is 0.28). Why this is the case, we cannot be sure. Perhaps judges use the appellee's brief to ease the loss; perhaps they use it to knock down the appellee arguments more precisely. More work is needed to explore this result. The brief with the lowest predicted value of similarity is one for the appellant when the appellee wins (similarity is −0.14). Nestled between these bookends is a winning appellant brief (similarity is 0.10) and a winning appellee brief (similarity is 0.14).

Interestingly, our inference about the effect of having a brief authored by the U.S. hinges on the inclusion of the suite of LIWC-22 controls. In a model that excludes them, we find the U.S. briefs are associated with a significantly higher similarity score. If, however, we include the LIWC-22 variables, we find a *negative* and statistically significant effect. Why this obtains is beyond the scope of our inquiry here.

Finally, across all model specifications, we observe greater brief-opinion similarity among those opinions in cases that were reported by the West Federal Reporter, relative to those cases that were not reported.

The foregoing results suggest that as judges age, they increasingly write opinions that are similar to the briefs (and that is not a function of experience). The substantive virtue of this approach, beyond its fidelity to the most recent work on U.S. Supreme Court briefs, is that it has the potential to detect more subtle forms of overlap versus verbatim borrowing or plagiarism measures. A skeptic, however, might argue that we simply "lowered the bar" to recover our hypothesized relationship. (It is also a bit unsatisfying trying to interpret cosine similarity scores.) To that end, we consider our more exacting *Borrowed Language* measure. Because this measure is a word count (i.e., the number of words copied), we estimate a negative binomial regression model.[28] Table 6.2 provides parameter estimates for the same three general models we estimated earlier.[29] It shows that even when we analyze exact language borrowing, we still uncover statistical support for our hypothesized relationship.[30] Across all three specifications, there is a positive and statistically significant relationship between the opinion author's age and how much that judge copies language from the briefs.[31]

As before, we turn to predicted values to translate the substantive magnitude of this statistically significant result. Figure 6.6 illustrates results that come from Model 2, which includes controls but excludes the LIWC measures. The horizontal axis displays the full range of *Opinion Author Age*. The vertical axis shows the predicted level of verbatim borrowing between a judge's opinion and an individual brief, conditional on a given value of age while holding all other predictors constant. The gray shaded region denotes the 95% confidence interval around the point estimates, which we again show with the black line.

Our model predicts that the youngest judge in our sample copies about 219 words from an individual brief. The oldest opinion author copies approximately 318

[28] All of the results we report in Table 6.2 are substantively unchanged if we instead estimate a good old fashioned ordinary least squares regression model.

[29] Since our dependent variable is the number of words borrowed, we now include controls for the length of the opinion and the length of the brief in that specific dyad. And, to account for the non-linear nature of this effect, we measure each of these as being the natural logarithm of those counts.

[30] We re-estimated our model while excluding the shortest 10% of opinions. *Opinion Author Age* remains statistically significant. We have no significant evidence that the coefficient becomes any smaller (or larger) when the model is estimated on longer opinions.

[31] Our inferences regarding statistical significance are unchanged if our standard errors are either classical (i.e., non-robust) or case-clustered. As before, cluster on the individual judge results in larger p-values for our age variable: 0.45 in Model 1, 0.23 in Model 2, and 0.21 in Model 3.

Table 6.2 The Relationship Between Judge Age and Borrowed Language in the U.S. Courts of Appeals

	(1)	(2)	(3)
Opinion Author Age	0.005**	0.008**	0.007**
	(0.001)	(0.001)	(0.001)
Opinion Author Experience		−0.006**	−0.005**
		(0.001)	(0.001)
Appellant Win		−0.082**	−0.087**
		(0.032)	(0.030)
Brief for Appellant		−0.372**	−0.341**
		(0.021)	(0.021)
Appellant Win × Brief for Appellant		0.293**	0.290**
		(0.041)	(0.038)
Brief by United States		0.201**	0.045
		(0.033)	(0.032)
Case in West Reporter		0.641**	0.583**
		(0.045)	(0.041)
Opinion Length		0.045**	0.055**
		(0.003)	(0.004)
Brief Length		0.085**	0.073**
		(0.003)	(0.003)
Constant	5.427**	3.861**	−0.157
	(0.081)	(0.084)	(0.899)
$\ln(\alpha)$	−0.474**	−1.098**	−1.271**
	(0.018)	(0.022)	(0.023)
LIWC Brief Measures	No	No	Yes
N	5,230	5,230	5,230
BIC	69,852	66,236	66,240

Note: Table entries are negative binomial regression coefficients with robust standard errors in parentheses. The dependent variable is the number of words copied for each opinion-brief dyad. ** and * denote $p < 0.05$ and $p < 0.10$, respectively (two-tailed).

words—about a 45% relative increase. This is an absolute gain of 99 words, which is equivalent to about 36% of one-standard deviation in the underlying measure. While the substantive significance is not exactly overwhelming, it still provides us with corroborating evidence that accords with the textual similarity results. Our inferences appear robust.

Among the control predictors, the results suggest that judges copy the least amount of language from the appellant's brief when that party loses (285 words). Somewhat paradoxically, however, the *highest* amount of language is copied from the appellee's brief when the appellee loses (414 words). In the space between these two are the appellee's brief when the appellant wins (382 words) and the appellant's brief when the appellant wins (353 words).

In terms of the effect of U.S.-authored briefs, Model 2 mirrors the results we obtained in the earlier similarity measure—i.e., greater borrowing. Here, however, the

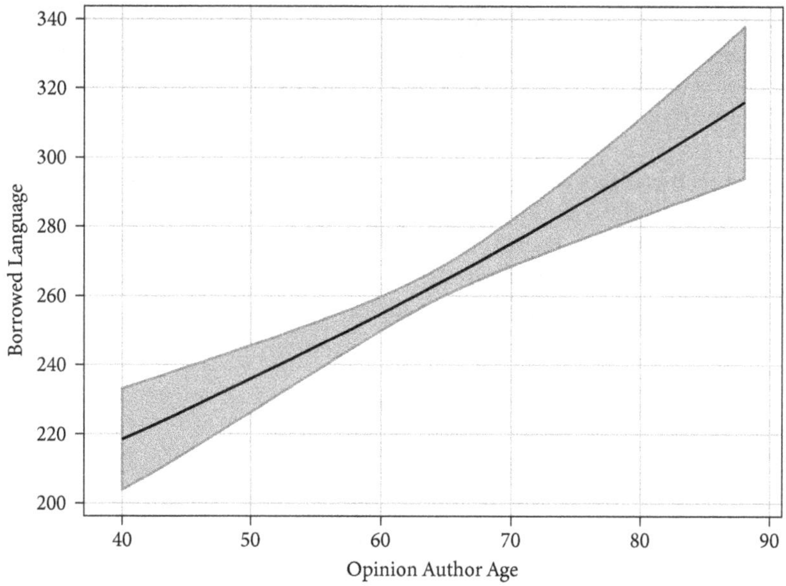

Figure 6.6 Language borrowing increases with opinion author age. Figure reports the predicted level of verbatim borrowing between a judge's opinion and an individual brief (with 95% confidence intervals), conditional on a given value of age (while holding all other predictors constant), using results from Model 2 in Table 6.2.

inclusion of the LIWC controls merely renders the effect null as opposed to reversing the nature of the effect altogether. Once again, opinion authors are more likely to copy language in cases that were reported by the West Federal Reporter. Lastly, as expected, opinions exhibit more copied language when those opinions and the briefs are themselves longer.

6.6 Conclusion

The judiciary demands conscientious judges (Black et al. 2020) who are able to contemplate each case fully and make complex decisions. But as we have stated throughout the book, the federal judiciary is becoming older and with that aging, judges have begun to rely more heavily on cognitive shortcuts.

This chapter reveals that when aging judges write judicial opinions, they are increasingly likely to rely on their law clerks and the party briefs. The variability among individual judges' opinions appears to increase with age. This is noteworthy, of course, since even in their early years on the court, judges will rely on their clerks. In other words, the increased reliance our data reveals is on top of the law clerk use that exists among the non-aged judges.

What is more, our findings suggest that the opinions written by older judges are systematically more similar to party briefs than the opinions written by younger judges. Though we do not wish to put too fine a point on it, it seems troubling that judges increasingly borrow from attorneys. After all, judges—not attorneys—are confirmed by the Senate to serve as constitutional officers. If aged judges increasingly outsource portions of their work product to attorneys, that raises constitutional concerns.

To be sure, the effects we observe in this chapter are not especially large. But one must think about these findings in relation to all the other chapters in the book. Think of each chapter as a puzzle piece. Alone, each represents a small portion. Taken together, they create a bigger picture. That picture is coming into view. Older judges simply behave differently than younger judges. And the results are concerning.

6.7 Appendix

6.7.1 Function Words

The following list presents all 72 words. We use italics to indicate which words were removed by Rosenthal and Yoon due to their infrequency. "Whilst" is the only word that we excluded from our analysis. The 72 function words are: a, all, also, an, and, any, are, as, at, be, been, but, by, can, do, down, even, *every*, for, from, had, has, have, her, his, if, in, into, is, it, its, may, more, must, *my*, no, not, now, of, on, one, only, or, our, *shall*, *should*, so, some, such, than, that, the, their, then, there, things, this, to, up, *upon*, was, were, what, when, which, *while*, *whilst*, who, *will*, with, would, *you*.

6.7.2 Function Word Variability Formula

What follows below is reproduced in near-verbatim form from Rosenthal, and Yoon (2011*a*, 1315). We have modified the formulae throughout to account for the larger number of function words we use as compared to what Rosenthal and Yoon used. That is, wherever you see the value 71 below, for the original formula it was 63.

> The seventy-one function words are numbered from $j = 1$ to $j = 71$. Suppose a given Justice has written opinions numbered from $i = 1$ to $i = K$ Let w_1 be the total number of words in judgment i and c_ij, be the number of times that function word j appears in judgment i. We further define
>
> $$e_{ij} = w_i\left(\frac{c_{1j} + c_{2j} + \ldots + c_{Kj}}{w_1 + w_2 + \ldots + w_K}\right)$$
>
> where e_{ij} is the expected number of times that function word j would have appeared in judgment i. The null hypothesis is that the total number of $c_{1j} + c_{2j} + \ldots + c_{Kj}$ appearances of j were each equally likely to occur in any of the total number of $w_1 + w_2 + \ldots + w_K$ words in all of Justice K's combined judgments.

The chi-squared statistic is the following:

$$chisq = \sum_{i=1}^{K} \sum_{j=0}^{71} \frac{\left(c_{1j} - e_{ij}\right)^2}{e_{ij}}$$

Under the null hypothesis, *chisq* should follow a chi-squared distribution with $(71 + 1 - 1)(K - 1) = 71(K - 1)$ degrees of freedom, and therefore mean $71(K - 1)$. This summation also includes $c_{i0} = w_i - c_{i1} - \ldots - c_{iK}$, the number of words in judgment i that are *not* function words.

Our variability measure is accordingly:

$$V\,score = \frac{chisq}{df} = \frac{chisq}{71(K - 1)},$$

which should approximate one under the null hypothesis and exceed one for opinions that collectively exhibit greater variability in writing style.

6.7.3 Statistical Significance and Variability

Although individual variability scores are reasonably informative, as Rosenthal and Yoon observe, "they do not establish whether the scores themselves are meaningfully different from one another" (2011*b*, 1327). To do so, they advocate for a bootstrap test to assess statistical significance. We follow this approach by taking 1000 random samples (with replacement) of *K* opinions from each judge's sub-corpus of opinions, where *K* denotes the total number of opinions in that sub-corpus. For each of these random samples, we calculate the function word variability statistic.

For example, before turning 65 years old, Judge Michael Boudin authored 458 opinions. We took 1,000 random samples—with replacement—of 458 opinions from that corpus. One of our samples contained 288 unique opinions, with 167 opinions appearing once, 83 opinions showing up twice, 28 opinions three times, 9 opinions four times, and one opinion was included five times (again, this is possible because of the with replacement aspect of our sampling procedure). The variability score for that sample was 2.78. The second sample had 292 unique opinions and yielded a variability score of 2.83. And so on.

We then repeated this same process on the 384 opinions Boudin wrote after turning 65 years old. This yields two vectors, each with 1000 variability scores. We then calculated the proportion of the 1,000,000 pairings of these values (i.e., $1{,}000 \times 1{,}000$) where Boudin's post-65 variability was higher than his pre-65 variability and then take one minus that proportion to generate our p-value (i.e., 0.22). Note that if a judge's opinions became systematically *less* variable as she aged, then the initial proportion we calculate in the previous step will be very low (e.g., 0.04) and one minus that value will be very high (i.e., 0.96). To make easier immediate interpretation, for those judges we do not take the last conversion step of subtracting by one, which keeps the p-value on a scale readers are more accustomed to seeing (i.e., lower values mean significance).

6.7.4 Senior Status and Variability

As we note in the text, we combine all opinions written by a judge after she turned 65 years old. This means that for some judges, we pool their post-65 *active* status opinions with their post-65 *senior* status opinions. We did so because opinions written by a senior status judge still carry the full weight of the law. In terms of theorizing about the possible impact of senior status, we recognize that there are stories to be told that go in both directions.

On the one hand, cognitive aging doesn't particularly care if you have decided to take your foot off the gas and opted for a reduced workload. The decline in capabilities will continue to proceed. This would suggest that senior judges will continue to rely more heavily upon their law clerks than they did in their active status years. On the other hand, since senior status judges hear, on average, a fraction of cases relative to their active status counterparts (Yoon 2005, 518–519), one might imagine that the reduced workload would lead them to take a heightened role in opinion writing for those cases. The reduced workload might lead to a reduced cognitive load.

In any case, the effect of senior status ultimately is an empirical question. And so we returned to our opinion corpus and generated two judge-level sub-samples: (1) opinions written after age 65 while on active status and (2) opinions written after age 65 while on senior status. A total of 307 of our original 569 judges had a sufficient number of opinions in both samples (i.e., 10 or more) to be retained. Of those, 59% show some level of *increase* in their opinion variability after taking senior status relative to active status. The remaining 41% show some level of decreased variability. These values are strikingly similar to the basic results we obtained in our pre-65 versus post-65 comparisons reported in the chapter. As to statistically significant changes in opinion variability, 36% of judges show evidence of significantly greater reliance on their law clerks compared to just 19% of judges who show significantly less use of law clerks.

Thus, although there are plausible stories for both increased and reduced usage of law clerks by a judge in her senior status years versus active status years, our results suggest that the forces of cognitive aging tend to swamp whatever effects there are for a reduced workload among circuit court judges.

6.7.5 Age Window Length Selection

In a perfect world, we would use a smaller window. Rosenthal and Yoon's analysis uses, at various points, annual windows for the justices, but their opinions tend to be much longer than circuit court judges. And, more importantly, Rosenthal and

Yoon do not attempt to discern whether significant differences exist from year-to-year. We suspect had they done so, they would have found themselves statistically underpowered. Yearly windows, then, were a no-go.

Our preference would have been to use, at the most, a 5-year window. When we attempted to do so, however, we discovered that we would need to increase the minimum opinion threshold by 50% (i.e., from 10 to 15) in order to avoid the problematic variability values we discuss in footnote 6. This, in turn, meant that we were losing a higher proportion of the judge-age sub-samples from our data. Under a five-year approach, there are 13 possible windows (e.g., 35–39, 40–44, . . . ,95–99). Because of the more observations required, however, we would have coverage rates less than 50% for seven out of those 13 values (i.e., 54% of the windows). That is, we would need to omit more than a majority of the possible judge sub-samples for age windows such as 45–49, 55–59, and 90–94, to name a few.

Using full decades means there are eight windows (e.g., 30–39, 40–49, . . . , 90–99). Under this approach we have just two values out of eight (i.e., 25%) for which we retain fewer than 50% of the observations. They are 30–39 and 40–49. For all other age windows, we keep at least 50% of the possible judge sub-samples for that window (e.g., 50–59, 90–99). This approach, we believe, best threads the needle between being generalizable (i.e., more judges) and being granular (i.e., narrower windows).

6.7.6 Alternative Presentation of Decade Window Results

As we mention in footnote 18, an alternative way of aggregating our results would be to compare sequential consecutive decades of opinion writing variability. By this approach, we would look at a judge in her 40s vs. 50s, 50s vs. 60s, 60s vs. 70s, and so on. Figure 6.7 does precisely that. The setup to the figure is identical to its earlier counterpart, except now the x-axis shows the six decade-to-decade age transitions present in our data. A key takeaway is that we see, overall, appreciably more evidence of increased reliance on law clerks as opposed to reduced reliance. The figure plots a total of 1,409 judge-decade-transitions. Fully 800 of those are increases (i.e., 57%) and 460 of those 800 are increases that are statistically significant. That is, of the 1,400+ windows we examined, we found significant increases in opinion variability for approximately 33%. At the same time, we found significant decreases for 326 windows, which is approximately 23%. That's just over 40% more increases in variability than we observe decreases. What is more, roughly 30% of the significant decreases we observe take place in either the 70-to-80 or 80-to-90 window. This is noteworthy given our earlier finding of a pronounced decrease once a judge dramatically reduced her workload in her final decade of judicial service.

6.7.7 CopyFind Parameter Values

We use the following specific tuning values for our implementation of CopyFind: minimum phrase length = 6, fewest matches to report = 1, ignore letter case = yes,

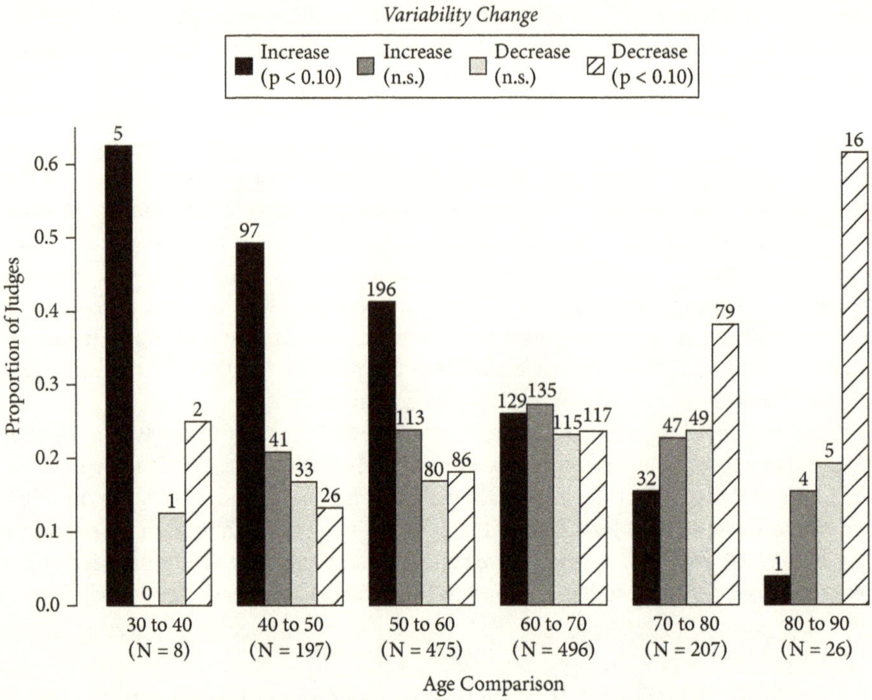

Figure 6.7 Variability changes for a sequential 10-year increase in judge age. Figure reports within-judge opinion-writing variability comparing judges' sequential decades on the court. A black bar represents a statistically significant increase in variability; a dark gray bar indicates a non-significant increase; a light gray bar reflects a non-significant decrease; and a white bar with diagonal lines means a statistically significant decrease. The number at the top of a bar reports the frequency of judges represented within that bar.

ignore numbers = no, ignore outer punctuation = yes, ignore punctuation = no, skip long words = no, skip non-words = no. We selected the options for the letter case, outer punctuation, and numbers parameters based on our desire to find matches "despite minor editing" (Bloomfield 2016). If one were to desire only absolute matches, then Bloomfield advises choosing the opposite states.

Two additional parameters that we did not utilize are the minimum percentage of matching words and most imperfections to allow. Copyfind produces two sets of estimates: perfect matches and observed matches. The former returns only perfect matches (conditional on the phrase length and ignore/skip parameter values). The latter allows for the user to allow a specified number or percentage of imperfections. Our measure comes from the perfect match value, so the settings for the imperfection values are irrelevant.

6.7.8 Who Dunnit? Clerks as Opinion Drafters and Plagiarizers

The first half of this chapter offers what we believe is compelling evidence of increased use of law clerks in opinion writing as judges age. In the second half of the chapter, we examine the overlap between judicial opinions and the parties' briefs, finding that older opinion authors show higher general and specific similarity versus younger judges. To what extent is it a judge's law clerks who are driving this result? As we argued in the footnote that led you here, our view is that it is simply a question of a direct (i.e., the judge's age) versus an indirect (i.e., the judge's age leads to greater clerk usage) effect for cognitive aging.

Still, we acknowledge that, as an empirical matter, it might be interesting to know about the relative contributions of judge age versus judge law clerk usage. To that end, we merged the chapter's two datasets together and re-estimated our language borrowing models with *Judge Opinion Variability* as an additional covariate. The specific value we use is a judge's variability score for the decade window in which she wrote the opinion. For example, if the judge was 63 when she wrote an opinion, then she gets the variability score derived from all of the opinions she wrote from 60 to 69 years of age.

We acknowledge that this will introduce some circularity into our models. Our dependent variables tap into the similarity between the opinion, which is authored by a mixture of the judge and her clerks, and a brief, which is authored by others. If an opinion has high overlap with a brief, then that's going to nudge the needle upward on this judge's variability score. This is because there are more fingerprints represented in the text of the opinion. That slightly higher variability score, in turn, is affecting the *Judge Opinion Variability* measure. Nevertheless, we see little need to sound the "bad social science" alarm or call the folks at Data Colada. The opinions for the brief similarity analysis are a subset of the judge's full corpus, which is to say that we have significantly more data to estimate a variability score than just the opinions for which we have brief similarity data. On average, we're using seven times the number of opinions to measure variability as we are to examine brief similarity.

With these prefatory remarks out of the way, on to the results. Starting with opinion-brief similarity (i.e., the cosine scores), we continue to find a significant and positive effect for *Opinion Author Age* even after controlling for *Judge Opinion Variability*, but as Figure 6.8 reveals, its inclusion attenuates the effect of author age.[32] When we exclude *Judge Opinion Variability*, a one-year increase in author age is associated with a 0.014 increase in opinion-brief similarity. By contrast, when we include variability the marginal effect decreases to 0.008, which is a relative decrease of about 43%. Given this, it probably comes as little surprise that the *Judge Opinion*

[32] An incredibly attentive reader might observe the solid line has different values compared to the solid line in the main text of the chapter. If that's you, well spotted. This is because we lose some observations in our briefs data associated with judges for whom we do not have a decade-level variability score. To ensure we're making apples-to-apples comparisons, we estimated the "no variability" model on the same observations for which we have that measure available.

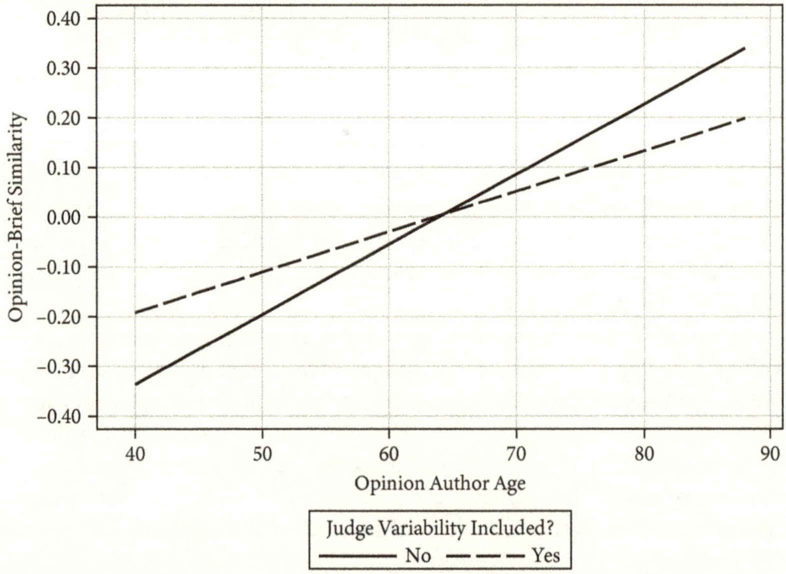

Figure 6.8 The impact of judge variability on cognitive aging for opinion similarity. Figure reports the predicted level of similarity between a judge's opinion and an individual brief, conditional on a given value of age (while holding all other predictors constant) and whether controlling for judge variability, using results from Model 2 in Table 6.1.

Variability coefficient is positive and statistically significant. In terms of its substantive effect, going from the 1st percentile to the 99th percentile in variability moves the predicted level of similarity from −0.163 to 0.314. These represent approximately the 16th and 58th percentiles in the estimation sample, so the relative magnitude is not small.

Figure 6.9 provides the analogous visualizing for exact borrowing between each litigant brief-opinion dyad. The story here tracks what we just found for the similarity measure. Our *Age of Opinion Author* variable continues to be positively signed and statistically significant ($p = 0.08$). The substantive magnitude of age, however, decreases. A one-year increase in author age in a model without judge variability corresponds to a 2.81 word increase in the expected amount of language verbatim borrowed from a litigant brief. Once one controls for judge variability, that one-year increase in age comes with just a 0.89 word increase in the amount of copied language—a relative decrease of about 68%. As to the effect of *Judge Opinion Variability*, its effect is both positive and statistically significant. The same 1st–99th percentile change in variability yields predicted language borrowing values of 265 and 449 words, which is equivalent to the 55th and 78th percentile in the dependent variable.

Taking a step back, these results continue to provide strong support for the role of cognitive aging in the opinion-writing process. Aged judges, all else equal, continue to write opinions that are generally more similar to and copy specific language from litigant briefs relative to judges who are younger. But we can also say that part of

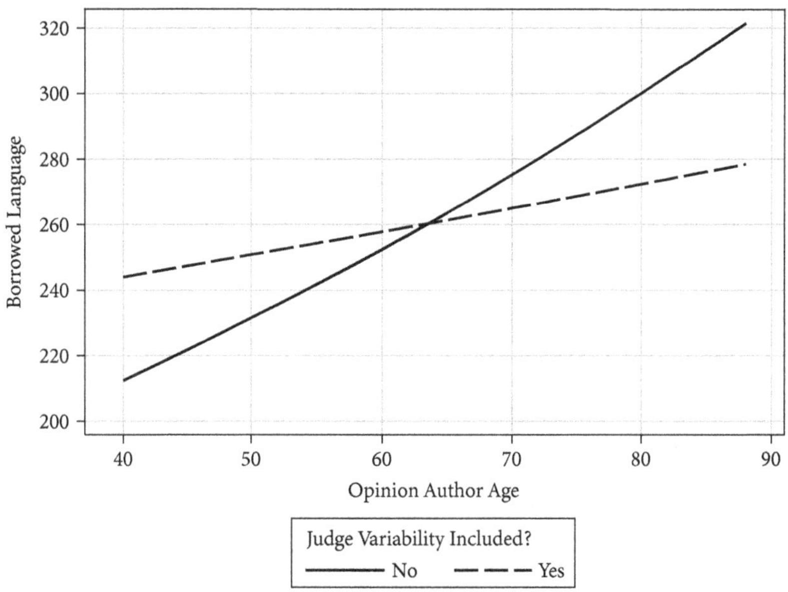

Figure 6.9 The impact of judge variability on cognitive aging for opinion language borrowing. Figure reports the predicted level of verbatim borrowing between a judge's opinion and an individual brief, conditional on a given value of age (while holding all other predictors constant) and whether controlling for judge variability, using results from Model 2 in Table 6.2.

the mechanism for this comes from their increased reliance on law clerks who also deploy these shortcuts. Why the clerks do so is beyond the scope of our inquiry, but one possibility is that although they do not experience the same cognitive challenges as an aged judge, a clerk who works for a judge who leans more heavily on her clerks for opinion drafting potentially has a higher workload than those who work for a judge more actively involved. This workload pressure could then mirror the effects of cognitive aging in terms of motivating the clerk to consider a variety of shortcuts.

7
Aging, Opinion Quality, and the Diffusion of Precedent

In 2004, two legal scholars called up an interesting idea. Disturbed by an increasingly polarized Supreme Court confirmation process that they believed damaged the Court's legitimacy and produced mediocre nominees, they proposed a tournament to identify the "best" sitting circuit court judges, whom presidents would elevate to the High Court when a vacancy arose (Choi and Gulati 2004*b*). The tournament would identify the best circuit judges by evaluating the quality of their opinions. To measure the quality of opinions, these scholars analyzed how often other judges cited them. "Presumably," they argued, "the best opinions will be cited more often" by other judges (Choi and Gulati 2004*b*, 306). For them, opinion citation reflected opinion quality, and opinion quality part of judicial excellence.

Others have set their sights on opinion quality for more political reasons. Politicians often target opinion quality to excuse their noncompliance with judicial decisions. They also focus on opinion quality to vilify courts—sometimes wrongly, sometimes rightly. For example, after the Supreme Court claimed the power of judicial review in *Marbury v. Madison* (1803), President Jefferson complained to anyone who would listen that the opinion was poorly constructed, something his congressional trucklers used to attack it (Hall and Deardorff 2006, 24).[1] Abraham Lincoln responded to the Court's *Dred Scott* decision thusly: "we think the *Dred Scott* decision is erroneous. We know the court that made it, has often over-ruled its own decisions; and we shall do what we can to have it to over-rule this" (White 2010, 238). And of course, President Franklin Roosevelt expressed his criticism of the quality of Supreme Court opinions that went against him. (We devote more attention to that episode in Chapter 10.) When external actors perceive judicial opinions to be low quality, they use that weakness to circumvent them.

Still others have examined opinion quality for teaching purposes. Some have examined opinion quality simply to identify what makes for a good opinion. Popkin (2007) examined the imagery of Judge Posner's writings. Balkin (2008) and others periodically release rankings of the best and worst opinions. Scholars believe that if they know what makes a high quality opinion, they can teach it to judges, lawyers, and law students and improve the state of American law.

In this chapter, we examine opinion quality and cognitive aging. If our previous chapters have anything to say on the matter, it is that aging will influence the quality of opinions judges write. As judges age and some of their cognitive capacities decline,

[1] Yes, we know that *Marbury* was not the first time the Supreme Court engaged in judicial review. See, e.g., *Hylton v. United States*, 3 U.S. 171 (1796). It was, however, the first case in which the Court used it to strike an Act of Congress.

Cognitive Aging and the Federal Circuit Courts: How Senescence Influences the Law and Judges.
Ryan C. Black, Ryan J. Owens, Patrick C. Wohlfarth, Oxford University Press. © Ryan C. Black, Ryan J. Owens, Patrick C. Wohlfarth 2024. DOI: 10.1093/oso/9780197747025.003.0007

their opinions may decline in quality. Simply put, as a judge ages, she is likely to write lower quality opinions which, in turn, other judges will cite less often.

7.1 The Broader Importance of Opinion Quality

As we alluded to above, opinion quality matters for a host of reasons. For starters, opinion quality is important to those who must live with the consequences of judicial rulings. The effects of court decisions fall, at least in large part, on the parties who win and lose. The outcome matters to the parties, but so too does the opinion the court writes. Knowing why they won or lost, what they ought to have done (but did not), or why their behaviors were (il)legal are all useful information for parties. The quality of the opinion also matters to secondary populations (Johnson and Canon 1984). Judicial opinions make policy as much as they make law. Or, perhaps we should say judicial opinions have significant legal and policy *consequences*. A high quality opinion can go a long way toward explaining a rationale and channeling future behaviors among the broader public. Knowing *why* a person can or cannot do something is often just as important as knowing *whether* the person can.

Not surprisingly, opinion quality is also tied to judicial legitimacy. High-quality opinions can enhance a court's legitimacy (Zink, Spriggs, and Scott 2009). In the face of strong countermajoritarian headwinds, federal judges lean in to their courts' legitimacy. This institutional legitimacy grows and shrinks as a function of opinion quality. And legitimacy fuels the judiciary's power. Therefore, opinion quality can influence judicial power (Tyler and Rasinski 1991). And, because aging influences opinion quality, aging can influence judicial power.

Imagine the best-case scenario: a federal appellate court composed of judges with the acumen to analyze every perspective of a legal debate and the capacity to write wise opinions. That court would earn trust, win legitimacy, and amass power. Even people who opposed the court's rulings would (perhaps begrudgingly) concede its perspicacity. Now imagine the worst-case scenario: a court of blockheads—simpletons who concern themselves only with case winners and losers and whose opinions exhibit little more reasoning than grunts on a page. Even the most committed ideologues who supported the court's rulings would blush (if only in private) at their "gains" (but see Armaly 2021). Simply put, high-quality opinions enhance judicial power and legitimacy; low-quality opinions manifest the opposite.

Opinion quality is important to understand as well because it is tied to compliance with judicial decisions.[2] Lower courts (Black, Owens, Wedeking, and Wohlfarth 2016) and federal agencies (Spriggs 1996) are more likely to comply with higher quality Supreme Court opinions. When judges invest the effort to write a high-quality opinion, the opinion leaves less ambiguity for lower court judges to manipulate and insert their own policy preferences (Peltason 1971). Examining criminal procedure cases, Romans (1974, 39) argued that after the Supreme Court decided *Escobedo v. Illinois* (1963), "state courts could more readily express their own views... than

[2] Compliance, of course, is also tied to judicial legitimacy, with legal and political actors less likely to comply with less legitimate courts.

would have been possible if the decision had been more clearly expressed and unequivocal." But even those who seek to apply upper court precedent faithfully can benefit from higher quality opinions. If aging reduces opinion quality, it may reduce compliance with court precedent.

Opinion quality also matters in terms of judicial promotion and retention. We already mentioned the tournament proposal by Choi and Gulati (2004*b*).[3] But opinion quality actually is tied to some appointments already. The American Bar Association's Standing Committee on the Federal Judiciary evaluates nominees to federal judgeships based on three components: their integrity, their judicial temperament, and their professional competence; professional competence turns in part on a nominee's writing abilities (Smelcer, Steigerwalt, and Vining 2013). Opinion quality influences the Committee's evaluation which, in turn, can influence whether lower court judges climb to higher courts. Relatedly, many states have created Judicial Performance Evaluations (JPEs) to identify whether sitting judges write satisfactory opinions and, therefore, should be retained in state judicial retention elections.[4]

All this is to say that, normatively, the quality of judicial opinions matters. It matters to the litigants and broader populations who must pattern their behavior pursuant to them. It matters in terms of the courts' legitimacy. It matters to those who must implement decisions. And, it matters to those who evaluate judges. Consequently, if aging leads to decreased opinion quality, scholars ought to know. Decreased opinion quality could have serious downstream consequences.

Empirically, however, scholars know little about cognitive aging and the quality of judicial decisions.[5] There is some work on opinion quality broadly. For example, Klein (2002) sought to analyze whether judges cite other judges' opinions based on the authoring judge's reputation. Klein analyzed U.S. Courts of Appeals decisions between 1983 and 1995 in the areas of antitrust, search and seizure, and environmental law. He began with cases that announced new legal rules and then focused his attention on subsequent cases in other circuits that involved the same legal issues. He examined the conditions under which judges in those other circuits adopted the first court's ruling. It turns out that judges adopted or refused to adopt new rules based (in part) on the original author's prestige and expertise. In other words, a judge with a good reputation observed greater influence in other circuits than a judge with a poor reputation (see also Klein and Morrisroe 1999).

Hinkle (2015) undertook a similar, but more extensive, analysis of every circuit court's search and seizure cases decided between 1990 and 2010. Her underlying goal was slightly different than Klein's. She sought to determine whether legal precedent constrains circuit court judges. She examined this question by comparing judges' citation and treatment of *persuasive* precedent (opinions decided by other circuits) versus judges' citation and treatment of *binding* precedent (opinions decided within

[3] For another study that examines how circuit court judges can angle for elevation, see Black and Owens (2016).

[4] JPEs generally consist of evaluations by a committee of attorneys and non-attorneys who examine whether a judge manages his or her cases efficiently, decides cases based on applicable facts and law, maintains proper courtroom decorum, and, most important for our purposes, explains his or her decisions clearly (Kourlis and Singer 2007, 201).

[5] In an unpublished study, Madden (2023) finds that older judges write increasingly readable opinions.

one's own circuit). That is, Hinkle leveraged the fact that circuit precedents are controlling within their own circuits but are only persuasive in other circuits.[6] She discovered that judges are more likely to treat an ideologically distant precedent negatively when it comes from outside the circuit than when it comes from inside the circuit. These results suggested that binding precedent is, in fact, constraining—at least as it relates to the negative treatment of precedent. (For the curious, her results did not suggest that judges are any more likely to treat binding precedent more positively than persuasive precedent.)

As we stated earlier in this book, the only systematic effort to determine whether cognitive aging influences the quality of opinions comes from Judge Richard Posner. Posner (1995*a*) spends a chapter in his book, *Aging and Old Age*, analyzing when judges cite other judges' opinions. He lumps judges together into 5-year cohorts (years in which they were appointed) and then examines how often other cohorts cite them. His results showed that during 1985–1989, judges were more likely to cite opinions written by younger cohorts of judges—those appointed after 1964—than opinions written by older cohorts. In other words, there was some age-related decline in judging, but it largely occurred at advanced ages (Posner 1995*a*, 185).

In short, there is an aged-judge-sized gap in our knowledge of opinion quality. Do aging judges write lower quality opinions than younger judges? To answer, we pick up where Posner, Hinkle, and Klein left off. We examine how judges cite judicial opinions. We expect that as a judge ages, she will write opinions that receive fewer citations from others. The judiciary will simply ignore older judges' opinions. We also expect that, when cited, those aging judges' opinions will receive more negative and fewer positive treatments.

7.2 Data and Measures

We employ Hinkle's (2015) data on the citation and treatment of circuit court precedents in the area of Fourth Amendment search and seizure law. Hinkle selected these data because they provided "a discrete set of legal issues that are routinely raised in litigation . . . where it is possible to incorporate almost the entire body of circuit precedent . . ." (2015, 725–726). In other words, the issue area allowed her (and us) to examine the universe of relevant search and seizure cases. The data are organized at the dyad level, specifically the precedent–treatment dyad. Hinkle collected her *precedential opinions* from published merits opinions decided from 1953 to 2010 that cited the Fourth Amendment to the U.S. Constitution and contained either the word "search" or "seizure." This population consists of 13,345 opinions. Her *treating opinions* are the subset of such decided cases from 1990 to 2010 ($N \approx 7,000$) that cited and treated one of those cases. To identify what precedential opinions *could* have been cited by the treating opinions—surely not *every* other search and seizure precedent was on point—she looked to the subset of precedential opinions decided prior to the treating opinion that were in the top half of textual similarity to the eventual treating

[6] For example, if a judge in the Seventh Circuit faces a Seventh Circuit precedent, she is bound by it. But any other circuit's decision is only persuasive in the Seventh Circuit.

opinion. This leads to the identification of more than 35 million treating opinion-precedential pairings, with citation occurring in 44,456 of them, which works out to approximately 0.13% (i.e., just over one-tenth of one percent).[7]

We mirror Hinkle's approach. Our first dependent variable is simply a binary measure for whether a judge cites a precedent. Our second dependent variable measures whether, conditional on citing the precedent, a judge treated the precedent negatively, neutrally, or positively. This dependent variable uses the Shepard's Citations data (available through the Lexis legal database). A decision that "followed" a precedent is a positive treatment. Brief citations or citations that "explain" or "harmonize" a precedent are coded as neutral.[8] Finally, a negative treatment includes the following Shepard's classifications: "overruled," "criticized," "questioned," "limited," "disapproved," and "distinguished."[9]

Our main covariate of interest in both models is *Precedent Author Age*, which is the original precedent author's age (in years) at the time he or she published the opinion. We include a host of controls as well. First, we control for the age of the treating judge. *Treating Author Age* is the age (in years) of the judge who interpreted and treated the original precedent. We also control for *Precedent Author Experience* and *Treating Author Experience* to account for each of those judges' experience.

The remainder of our independent variables are those also appearing on the right-hand-side of Hinkle's analysis. A few of these will be involved in additional interactions, so we devote a few sentences to Hinkle's measurement of them here. *Ideological Distance* is "the absolute value of the difference between the Judicial Common Space (JCS) score of the author of the treatment case and the author of the precedent" (Hinkle 2015, 727). Additionally, *Binding Precedent* takes on a value of 1 if the precedent comes from within the judge's home circuit; 0 otherwise. We interact the two variables to obtain *Ideological Distance* × *Binding Precedent*. These measures examine the interplay between ideology and law in legal development.

Next, *Similarity Percentile* is "the percentile of a precedent's similarity to the treatment case compared to all other possible precedents in the data set" (Hinkle 2015, 727). Hinkle used cosine similarity scores to identify cases that were similar to the case at hand and those that were so different there was no way they might be cited in the case at hand. "Just as Google uses mathematical formulas to perform an automated ranking of how similar the text of a query is to each website, [Hinkle] calculate[d] how similar each treatment case [was] to every case preceding it in the data set" (Hinkle 2015, 726).[10]

[7] The number of observations in our analysis is "only" around 30.5 million. The main reason for this is that we focus on dyads where both opinions, precedent and treatment, were issued through signed—as opposed to unsigned/per curiam—opinions. This is because we want to examine the ages of those opinions authors. We also lose a total of six precedent opinions due to incomplete case information that prevented us from identifying the authorship of these opinions.

[8] We note that this approach pools actual substantive treatment—i.e., explaining or harmonizing—with non-treatment, which is simple citation. We discuss this point in more detail when examining variation in treatments in the section starting on page 127.

[9] As Hinkle (2015, 727) states: "The (rare) Shepard's treatment 'Superseded,' while negative in character, actually signals a precedent that has been rendered irrelevant due to a subsequent statute.

[10] Hinkle examines only cases that in the top 50% of the similarity ranking.

Elite Precedent Author takes on a value of 1 if the precedent author scored in the top-25-most prestigious judges, as measured by Klein and Morrisroe (1999); 0 otherwise. *Dissent in Precedent* equals 1 if the original precedent contained a dissenting opinion; 0 otherwise. *En Banc Precedent* equals 1 if the original precedent came from an *en banc* panel of judges. *Precedent Vitality* measures the number of times the precedent was treated positively and negatively prior to the decision in the case. It measures the number of positive treatments minus the number of negative treatments. *Precedent Treatments* counts the number of times the precedent was treated positively or negatively prior to the decision. *Precedent Citations* measures the number of times the precedent was cited prior to the decision. *Precedent Age* accounts for the number of years the precedent existed at the time of the treatment. *Precedent Age-Squared* is the square of that term; it accounts for the possibility of non-linear age effects (Black and Spriggs 2013). *Precedent Length* measures the logged number of words in the precedent under consideration. *Opinion Length* is the logged number of words in the opinion that cites or treats the precedent. *Quotations in Precedent* measures the proportion of quoted text in the precedent under consideration. *Number of Binding Precedents* counts the number of in-circuit precedents available to the judge deciding the case, with the assumption that the more options she has available, the less likely she will be to cite any one particular precedent. Finally, *Treatment Caseload* is "the average number of cases terminated per active judge in the circuit and year of the treatment case" (Hinkle 2015, 728).

7.3 Methods and Results

7.3.1 Citations

Because our dependent variable in this first analysis is binary (whether or not the precedent is cited in the case under analysis), we employ a probit regression model with robust standard errors clustered on each treating case.[11] Table 7.1 presents our results. The most important finding, at least for now, is that *Precedent Author Age* is significantly and negatively related to a judge's decision to cite precedent. Both in the bivariate model and the full model, the coefficient on *Precedent Author Age* is negative and statistically significant. What this means is that all else equal, the older the precedent-writing judge was (at the time she wrote the opinion), the less likely it is for the treating judge to cite that opinion.

Figure 7.1 graphs the results for *Precedent Author Age*.[12] Our y-axis for this and the figures that follow deviates slightly from the canonical presentation of results in choice models. That is, rather than showing the probability of citation occurring conditional on the covariates, we instead present the expected number of citations

[11] The results we report here and throughout this chapter come from analyzing the full dataset. Hinkle (2015), by contrast, reports results obtained after estimating propensity scores for whether a treatment is binding. See page 133 of the chapter's appendix for additional discussion about this choice.

[12] All numerical values plotted and discussed in this section of the chapter come from stochastic simulations (King, Tomz, and Wittenberg 2000; Brambor, Clark, and Golder 2006).

Table 7.1 The Impact of Opinion Author Age on Circuit Court Judges' Citation of Precedent

	(1)	(2)
Precedent Author Age	−0.0012**	−0.0015**
	(0.0002)	(0.0003)
Treatment Author Age	−0.0018**	−0.0013**
	(0.0003)	(0.0006)
Precedent Author Experience		−0.0028**
		(0.0004)
Treatment Author Experience		0.0009
		(0.0007)
Ideological Distance		−0.0303**
		(0.0108)
Binding Precedent		1.1033**
		(0.0084)
Ideo. Dist × Binding Prec.		−0.0267*
		(0.0139)
Similarity Percentile		0.0376**
		(0.0004)
Elite Precedent Author		0.0025
		(0.0077)
Dissent in Precedent		−0.0203**
		(0.0055)
En Banc Precedent		0.0217
		(0.0346)
Precedent Vitality		0.0128**
		(0.0013)
Precedent Treatments		0.0083**
		(0.0017)
Precedent Citations		0.0176**
		(0.0005)
Precedent Age		−0.0636**
		(0.0009)
Precedent Age-Squared		0.0006**
		(0.0000)
Precedent Length		−0.0234**
		(0.0035)
Quotations in Precedent		−0.5234**
		(0.0364)
Opinion Length		0.2220**
		(0.0060)
Number of Binding Precedents		−0.1210**
		(0.0093)
Treatment Caseload		0.00004
		(0.00003)
Constant	−2.8160**	−6.7401**
	(0.0232)	(0.0946)
N	30,497,294	30,497,294
BIC	618,416	428,989

Note: Table entries are probit regression coefficients with robust standard errors (clustered on the 6,975 treating cases in the data) in parentheses. The dependent variable reflects whether a judge cites a precedent for each precedent–treatment dyad. ** and * denote $p < 0.05$ and $p < 0.10$, respectively (two-tailed).

per opinion. Recall that instances of non-citation massively outnumber instances of actual citation. There are roughly 30,500,000 non-citations (zeroes) but fewer than 41,000 citations (ones). Or, stated differently, for every citation in Hinkle's dyadic data, there are around 750 instances of non-citation. Even this ratio is a bit tricky to wrap one's head around, but imagine that instead of having your heart beat roughly once every second, it beat only once every 12 minutes.[13]

So, what we do instead is start by calculating the probability that an individual precedent was cited in a treating opinion (i.e., what one normally does). Next, we multiply this *very* small value by 4,372, which is the average number of precedents that exists for a given treatment opinion. In other words, we evaluate a hypothetical world where the entirety of a treatment author's precedent pool is populated by precedents with our specified values of the independent variables. To be clear, we do this only to avoid bombarding you with very, very low probabilities, which people have difficulty comprehending (Camerer and Kunreuther 1989). And, since we are simply multiplying by a constant, there are absolutely no shenanigans going on here. If all of this still seems too radical for you, then you can just take our numbers, divide them by 4,372, and brush up on your long division in the process.

Return to Figure 7.1. The x-axis is straightforward: it shows the age of the precedent's author, ranging from 37 (our sample minimum) to 93 (our sample maximum). The figure shows that as the precedent author's age increases, the likelihood that the treating judge cites it decreases. In fact, there is a 32% decrease in citations per opinion between our youngest author and our oldest author. Treating judges cited 0.111 opinions per case from our youngest authors but 0.077 opinions per case from our oldest authors. Even among less extreme values, age plays a noteworthy role in whether a judge cites another judge's opinion. Treating judges cited 0.102 opinions per case from a 51-year-old opinion author but 0.084 opinions per case from a 79-year-old author—roughly an 18% decrease.

While of less concern, it is worth pointing out that our controls perform largely as expected. The older a treatment judge is, the less likely she is to cite precedents in general. Also depressing the likelihood of citations are: precedent author experience, increasing distance between the judge and the precedent, a dissent in the original precedent, precedent age, the length of the precedent, quotes in the precedent, and the number of binding precedents. Contributing to a greater likelihood of citations are: whether the precedent is binding, the similarity score, the precedent's vitality, the number of treatments and citations of the precedent, the squared age of the precedent, and the length of the current opinion.

As described above, a clever aspect of Hinkle's research design is the ability to distinguish between precedentially binding cases and merely persuasive cases. Table 7.1 tells us that, all else equal, treating judges are significantly more likely to cite binding precedent than persuasive precedent. This is to be expected. But what happens when obligation, in the form of binding precedent, and quality, in the form of a precedent authored by an aged judge, face off? To answer that question, we re-estimate the previous model while interacting precedent type and our author age

[13] Even the blue whale, the mammal with the world's slowest heartbeat, has a ticker that thumps at least four times per minute (Desmond 2015).

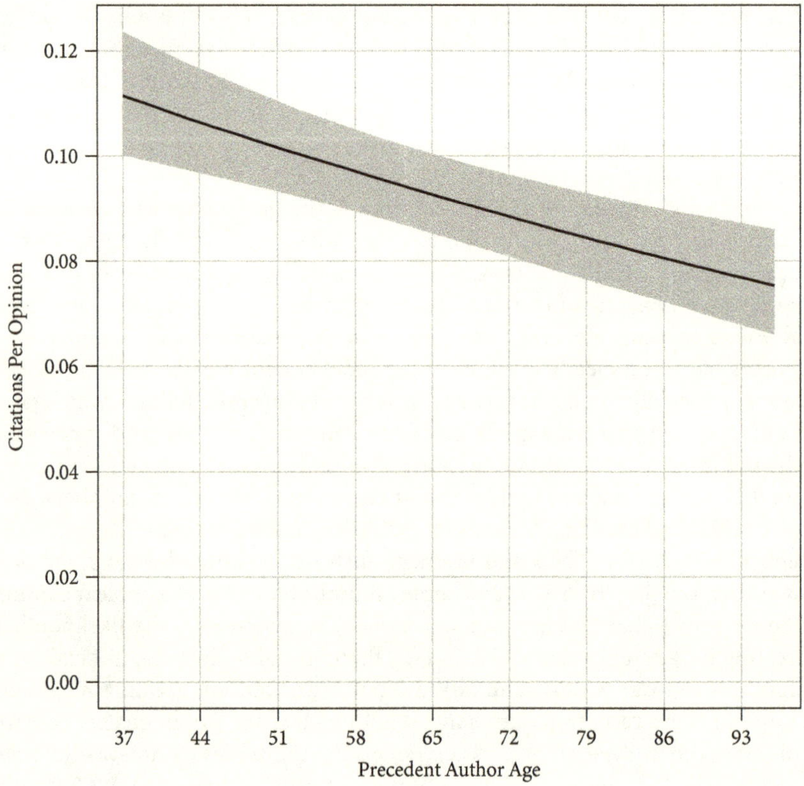

Figure 7.1 The impact of precedent author age on citations per opinion. Figure reports the predicted number of citations per opinion (with 95% confidence intervals), conditional on a given value of age (while holding all other predictors constant), using results from Model 2 in Table 7.1.

measures.[14] Interestingly, our results suggest that *Precedent Author Age* continues to play a dampening effect on the likelihood of citation in both types of precedent. That is, even when a judge is obligated to consider a decision authored by another judge within her circuit, she is more likely to ignore that precedent when it is authored by an aged judge.

We plot this interaction in the two panels of Figure 7.2, which show that the negative effect of *Precedent Author Age* contaminates both opinions that a treating judge is bound to apply as well as those that she has discretion to consider. Among binding precedents (the left panel), as *Precedent Author Age* increases, the likelihood that a judge will cite the opinion decreases. Treating judges cite 4.54 binding precedents per case from our youngest authors but 3.58 binding precedents per case from a

[14] The model includes separate interactions for both the age of the precedent author and the treatment author. Given the interactive nature of this model, Table 7.3 in the chapter appendix presents these results.

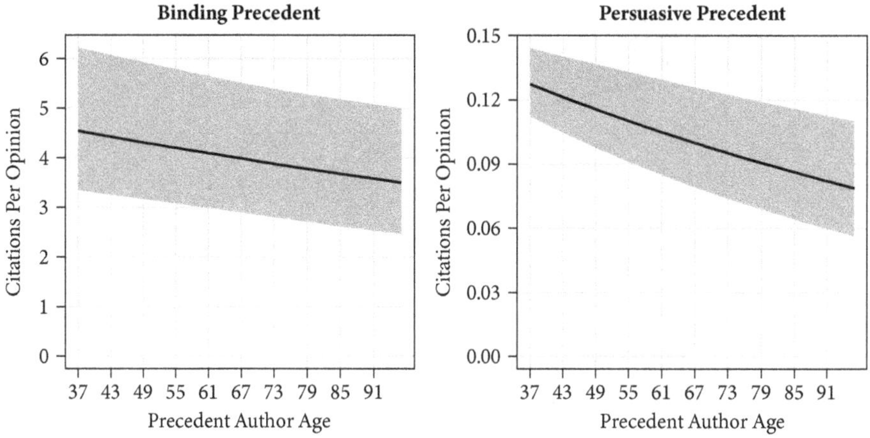

Figure 7.2 The impact of precedent author age on citations per opinion, conditional on persuasive vs. binding precedents. Figure reports the predicted number of citations per opinion (with 95% confidence intervals), conditional on a given value of age (while holding all other predictors constant) using results from Model 2 in Table 7.3.

91-year-old author. This is a 21% decrease and, again, *it comes among the precedents these judges are supposed to cite*.

The same dynamics also apply to persuasive precedents (the right panel), as well. When a treatment opinion author is considering a non-binding precedent for inclusion in her opinion, she applies an additional discount factor among those opinions authored by aged judges relative to those by younger judges. When the precedent author is young, we predict approximately 0.13 citations per opinion (or about one citation in every eight opinions). By contrast, when the opinion author is very old, the expected number of citations per opinions drops by around 38% to a value of 0.08 (or around one citation for every 12–13 opinions). It is worth noting that although the relative decrease for the persuasive precedent (i.e., −35%) is bigger than the relative decrease for binding precedent (i.e., −21%), this is due to the very small values involved for persuasive precedent (compare the values of the y-axes). If we evaluate the difference of the differences in terms of the number of citations, we find that the effect of precedent author age is significantly more harmful for binding precedent than it is for persuasive precedent ($p < 0.001$).

Moving on, we add a third layer—ideological distance—to the interplay between precedent author age and binding precedent status.[15] Hinkle found that ideological distance exerted a negative and statistically significant impact on the probability of a citation, but only for binding precedents. Figure 7.3 presents our results for evaluating whether *Precedent Author Age* further conditions this relationship. The organization

[15] This also means we have estimated a third model that interacts the age of the precedent author with both ideological distance and whether the precedent was binding as opposed to persuasive (i.e., this is a three-way interaction). In keeping with the approach used for the previous interaction, we also interact age of the treatment author with these measures, as well. Since this model is even more complicated than the one discussed just a moment ago, these results, too, are presented in Table 7.4 in the chapter appendix.

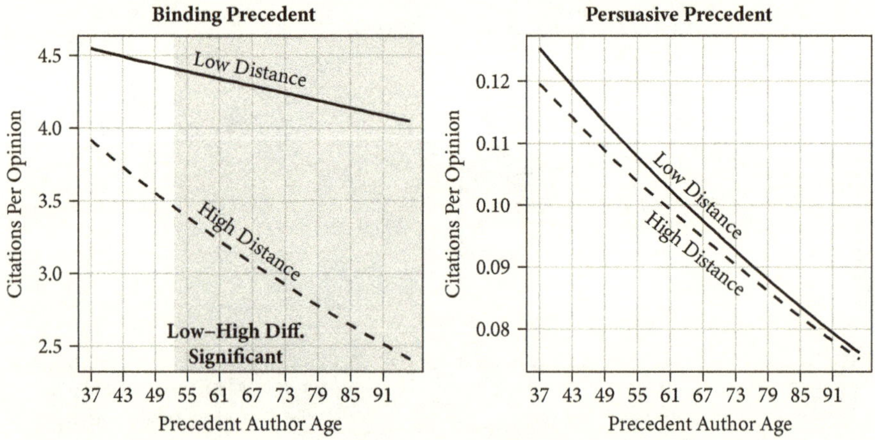

Figure 7.3 The impact of precedent author age on citations per opinion, conditional on persuasive vs. binding precedents and ideological distance. Figure reports the predicted number of citations per opinion, conditional on a given value of age (while holding all other predictors constant) using results from Model 2 in Table 7.4.

of the panels is identical to the previous figure; *Opinion Author Age* appears on the x-axis and we plot our citations per opinion outcome of interest.

The left panel presents the effect of ideology and age for binding precedents; line type shows whether the level of ideological distance was low (solid line) or high (dashed line).[16] Starting with the left panel, we see negative slopes for the two values of ideological distance, but one is clearly steeper than the other. The negative impact of *Precedent Author Age* is especially pernicious when the precedent author is also ideologically distant.

More specifically, begin with an ideologically close precedent author. There is roughly a 10% decrease in citations per opinion as one examines a very young versus a very old precedent author. Now consider an ideologically distant precedent author. The relative decrease over that same young-to-old transition is about 56%. Aging has more than five times the impact on reducing the likelihood of citation when it is paired with another undesirable attribute (i.e., ideological disagreement).

We can also evaluate these results from a slightly different perspective by examining how a treatment author penalizes a precedent that is ideologically distant versus proximate. Compare the two lines for a given value of age. The gray shaded region in the figure identifies values of age for which the gap between the low and high distance precedents is statistically significant. Our results show that, when a precedent author is young, there is no statistically significant difference in the citation likelihood when comparing ideologically close versus distant precedent authors. When the precedent author ages, however, an ideologically proximate precedent is 62% more likely to

[16] We use values of 0.03 for low distance and 0.92 for high distance. These correspond to the 5th and 95th percentile values in the sample, respectively.

be cited than an ideologically distant precedent—a difference that is significant. Ideology, in other words, only activates when accompanied by author age.

By contrast, consider the right panel, which plots the joint effect of precedent author age and ideological distance in non-binding, persuasive precedents. The slope of both lines is, again, negative, which tells us that treatment authors are decreasingly likely to cite opinions as precedent author age increases. Unlike binding precedents, however, the lines' slopes are nearly parallel and statistically indistinguishable from one another. This result indicates that ideology plays no significant role in either attenuating or exacerbating the effect of precedent author age. And the result is consistent with Hinkle's results.

To summarize, our citation analysis shows that the age of an opinion writer has both direct and indirect effects on the extent to which future judges are willing to cite a precedent. By a direct effect, we simply mean that, all else equal, opinions authored by older judges are less likely to be cited than opinions authored by younger judges (i.e., Figure 7.1). But, as we have just demonstrated, indirect effects also exist. Precedent author age combines with other opinion attributes, such as whether the precedent is binding or persuasive (i.e., Figure 7.2) or whether the ideological distance between the precedent and treatment opinion authors is low or high (i.e., Figure 7.3).

7.3.2 Positive, Neutral, and Negative Citations

The decision to cite precedent is an important and essential step of legal development, but so too is the matter of *how* one cites precedent. Does a judge treat it positively by applying its logic? Or, does a judge treat it negatively by distinguishing or somehow narrowing it? We address those questions here. For this treatment model, we again follow Hinkle (2015) and deploy a multinomial probit regression model. Our possible treatment outcomes are: positive, neutral, or negative treatment. Since this model focuses on substantive treatment, it necessarily excludes instances where a treatment opinion author elected not to cite (i.e., treat) a precedent.[17]

Table 7.2 presents parameter estimates for the Hinkle covariates while adding our author age variables. The coefficients presented are relative to a baseline of neutral treatment, which, as we mention above, is a simple citation. As Column 1 and Column 3 show, in models with only *Precedent Author Age* and *Treatment Author Age* included as regressors, the coefficients in the negative treatment equation are negative and insignificant for *Precedent Author Age* and positive and insignificant for *Treatment Author Age*. The coefficients in the positive treatment equation are positive but insignificant for *Precedent Author Age* (precedent author, $p = 0.12$) and positive and significant for *Treatment Author Age*.

[17] We note that Hinkle (2015) acknowledges the possible concern of a lack of independence between the initial decision to cite at all and the subsequent decision about what sort of treatment to apply to cited decisions (see also Black 2011). As she notes, however, the prevailing statistical approach to combat this concern, a selection model, labors under a number of assumptions and other methodological problems that counsel against its use here.

Table 7.2 The Impact of Opinion Author Age on Circuit Court Judges' Treatment of Precedent

	Negative		Positive	
	(1)	(2)	(3)	(4)
Precedent Author Age	−0.0013	−0.0041*	0.0017	−0.0022
	(0.0013)	(0.0022)	(0.0011)	(0.0018)
Treatment Author Age	0.0027	0.0001	0.0038**	0.0014
	(0.0020)	(0.0030)	(0.0017)	(0.0028)
Precedent Author Experience		0.0079**		0.0069**
		(0.0028)		(0.0023)
Treatment Author Experience		0.0048		0.0031
		(0.0036)		(0.0033)
Ideological Distance		0.3605**		0.0421
		(0.0809)		(0.0762)
Binding Precedent		−0.2222**		0.0444
		(0.0540)		(0.0473)
Ideo. Dist × Binding Prec.		−0.3136**		−0.0093
		(0.0990)		(0.0867)
Similarity Percentile		0.0253**		0.0164**
		(0.0017)		(0.0010)
Elite Precedent Author		−0.0248		−0.1300**
		(0.0506)		(0.0426)
Dissent in Precedent		0.0908**		0.0026
		(0.0374)		(0.0298)
En Banc Precedent		−0.0963		0.2366
		(0.2461)		(0.1789)
Precedent Vitality		−0.0937**		0.0602**
		(0.0100)		(0.0085)
Precedent Treatments		0.1061**		0.0525**
		(0.0109)		(0.0090)
Precedent Citations		−0.0232**		−0.0172**
		(0.0033)		(0.0026)
Precedent Age		0.0244**		0.0156**
		(0.0061)		(0.0050)
Precedent Age-Squared		−0.0004*		−0.0002
		(0.0002)		(0.0002)
Precedent Length		−0.0731**		0.0140
		(0.0258)		(0.0200)
Quotations in Precedent		0.1330		1.0261**
		(0.2531)		(0.2035)
Opinion Length		0.1856**		0.1635**
		(0.0325)		(0.0286)
Constant	−2.0250**	−5.1897**	−1.7488**	−4.6656**
	(0.1495)	(0.4064)	(0.1266)	(0.3375)
N	42,391	42,391	42,391	42,391
BIC	53,969	52,438	53,969	52,438

Note: Table entries are multinomial probit regression coefficients with robust standard errors (clustered on the 6,458 treating cases in the data) in parentheses. Estimates are relative to baseline of neutral treatment. The dependent variable reflects whether, conditional on citing the precedent, a judge treated the precedent negatively, neutrally, or positively. ** and * denote $p < 0.05$ and $p < 0.10$, respectively (two-tailed).

Moving on to the fully specified model, Column 2 reveals that *Precedent Author Age* is negative and statistically significant. Our results suggest that, relative to neutral treatment, judges are *less* likely to treat precedents negatively when they are authored by increasingly aged judges. (More on this in a second.) We fail to find a significant effect for the role of *Treatment Author Age* as exerting influence on either positive or negative treatment relative to neutral ones. Older treatment authors are no more (or less) likely to treat a precedent positively or negatively (relative to neutral treatment) as they age. At the same time, Column 4 does not suggest that the opposite is true. Relative to neutral treatment, we do *not* find that precedents authored by older judges are more likely to be treated positively.

To explicate what might be going on here, Figure 7.4 reveals predicted probabilities.[18] Along the x-axis, we present three hypothetical precedent authors: a 42-year-old, a 62-year-old, and an 84-year-old. These values correspond to the 1st, 50th, and 99th percentile values of our data. The bars within the plot show, for each of these judges, the predicted probability of negative treatment (black bar), neutral treatment (light gray bar), and positive treatment (dark gray bar).

Recall that Column 2 in Table 7.2 suggested that *Precedent Author Age* is negatively correlated with the likelihood of negative treatment. We observe an ever-so-slight decrease in the height of the black bar as one moves from left to right. We estimate a 6.9% chance of negative treatment when an opinion author was 42 years old; a 6.2% chance when she was 62 years old; and a 5.6% chance when she was 84 years old. All told, this absolute decrease of 1.3% corresponds to a 19% relative reduction in the likelihood of negative treatment. Upon first glance, this would seem to contradict our hypothesis of increased negative treatment with age. But stay with us.

We also observe a decrease in positive treatment as one moves from left to right. We estimate a 15.0% chance of positive treatment when an opinion author was 42 years old; a 14.4% chance when she was 62 years old; and a 13.8% chance when she was 84 years old. These changes, of course, are not huge. But, we can confidently say that there is a statistically significant uptick in the neutral category as precedent author age increases. We estimate a 78.1% chance of neutral treatment when an opinion author was 42 years old; a 79.3% chance when she was 62 years old; and an 80.6% chance when she was 84 years old. Given the zero-sum nature of probability, some basic math tells us that it cannot be only negative treatments moving to the neutral category. That is, our increase in neutral is 2.5% but our decrease in negative was just 1.3%.

On the margins, then, treating opinion authors are slightly less likely to engage *at all* with precedents written by aged judges beyond a perfunctory citation, which is predominately the form of "treatment" being captured by the neutral coding in the data.[19] This aligns with our earlier results, where we found that judges are less likely

[18] We generated these values using the `mgen` command as implemented in SPost13 for Stata 16.1 by Long and Freese (2014). This differs from the approached used in the citation models earlier in the chapter due to the lack of a closed-form solution to calculating probabilities from a multinomial probit model.

[19] In the parlance of Shepard's, there are actual substantive treatments that exist that are neutral. In Spriggs and Hansford's (2000) study, which was based on the prevailing Shepard's codebook at the time, those treatments were "harmonized" and "explained." Subsequent updates by Shepard's eliminated harmonized and added "cited in dissenting opinion" as well as "interpreted or construed by," noting that these "citing references with *analysis available*... contain treatment of your case that is neither positive

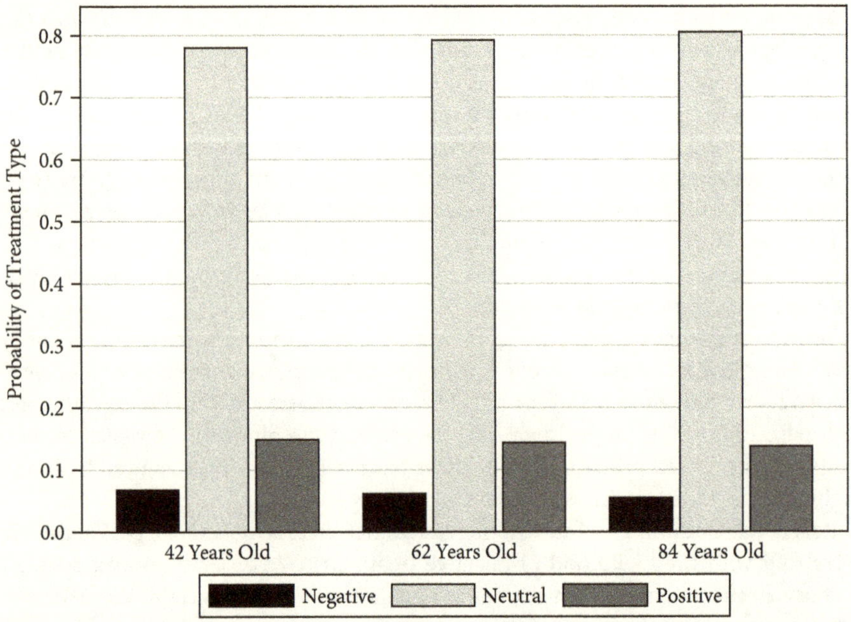

Figure 7.4 The impact of precedent author age on precedent treatment. Figure reports the predicted probability of positive vs. neutral vs. negative treatments, conditional on a given value of age (while holding all other predictors constant) using results from Models 2 and 4 in Table 7.2.

to cite opinions by judge authors as they age. In short, while older judges' opinions are not treated more negatively or less positively, as we had hypothesized, they are more likely to be ignored altogether.

We next examine interactive models. As we did with our citation analysis, we begin by looking at whether precedent author age interacts with whether a precedent is binding or persuasive. Figure 7.5 presents the results.[20] The y-axis identifies the marginal effect of moving from persuasive to binding precedent on the probability of a negative, neutral, or positive treatment. The x-axis identifies a 42-year-old, a 62-year-old, and an 84-year-old opinion author. The shaded bars show 95% confidence intervals for negative (black), neutral (light gray), and positive (dark gray) treatments. The symbols in the middle of the rectangles provide point estimates. If a rectangle crosses the solid black line at zero, then we can say no statistically significant effect exists for that scenario.

Consider, first, the effect of binding precedent on treating authors' decisions to treat precedents *negatively*. Among all judges, the fact that the precedent is binding significantly reduces the likelihood that the treating judge negatively treats the

nor negative" (emphasis added) (LexisNexis 2020). Critically, however, from Shepard's perspective, there needs to be substantive analysis. As we note above, however, these data pool substantive neutral treatments along with simple citations.

[20] See Table 7.5 in the chapter appendix for the model results.

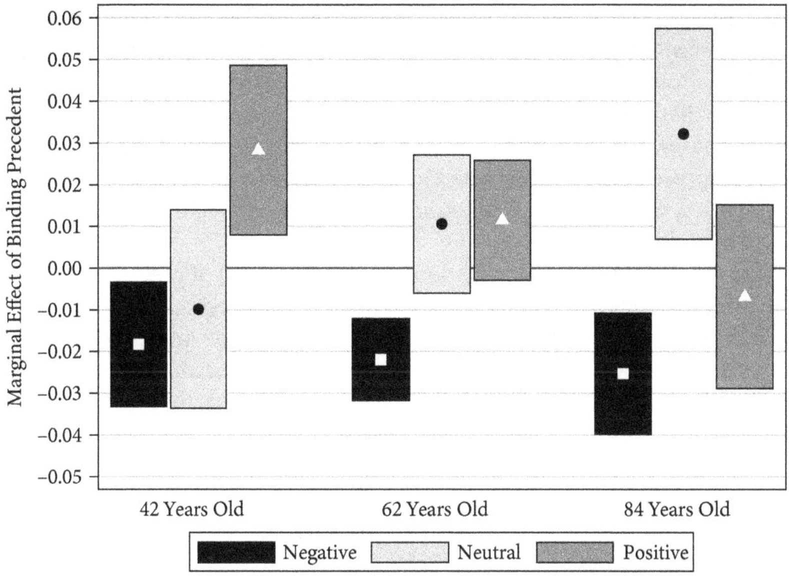

Figure 7.5 The impact of binding precedent on precedent treatment, conditional on precedent author age. Figure reports the marginal effect of binding precedent (with 95% confidence intervals), conditional on a given value of age (while holding all other predictors constant).

precedent. This is not surprising since the judge is (theoretically, at least) bound by that precedent. To be sure, some minor variation exists in the magnitude of the effects. Binding precedent triggers a 1.8% decline in negative treatment among the opinions written by the 42-year-old judge, a 2.2% decrease among the opinions written by the 62-year-old judge, and a 2.5% decrease among the opinions written by the 84-year-old judge. None of those pairwise differences are statistically significant, however. In short, judges of all ages are less likely to treat binding precedents negatively than to treat persuasive precedents negatively.

Some differences emerge when we consider *neutral* treatments. The marginal effects for the 42-year-old judge and for the 62-year-old judge are not statistically significant. (The p-values for the 42-year-old and 62-year-old judges are 0.42 and 0.22.) The confidence interval on the 84-year-old judge, however, is greater than 0, indicating a positive and significant effect. Treating judges are 3.2% more likely to treat an old judge's opinion neutrally when it is binding versus when it is merely persuasive.[21] This result is meaningful because judges are supposed to follow binding precedent.

Now consider the *positive* treatment of binding versus persuasive precedent. Figure 7.5 shows that the effect of binding precedent is statistically significant *only* for

[21] We note, and you probably do too, some overlap between the confidence intervals for neutral treatment across the three judges. Subsequent evaluation of the difference in the marginal effects shows that the 84-year-old's effect is significantly larger than both the 62-year-old's and the 42-year-old's.

the 42-year-old judge. A treating judge is 2.8% more likely to treat binding precedent (versus persuasive precedent) positively if authored by a 42-year-old judge. This is consistent with our earlier claim that other judges regard younger judges' opinions more highly than older judges' written opinions. Indeed, as the age of the precedent author increases, the magnitude of the effect shrinks considerably.[22] Recall that a judge treats precedent positively when he or she "follows" it. What this means is that judges do not appear to follow *binding precedents* (relative to non-binding precedents) authored by older judges.[23]

Finally, we complete our investigation into the treatment of precedent by examining the three-way interaction among ideological distance, precedent author age, and whether the precedent was binding versus persuasive. Of chief interest to us is whether ideological proximity between the treating judge and the precedent author conditions any of the differences we just uncovered. The short answer is that very little changes at all.[24]

7.4 Conclusion

Opinion quality matters for a host of reasons. It influences those directly effected by judicial decisions. It shapes judicial legitimacy and power. It can lead to greater or lesser compliance with court decisions and even judicial promotion. The quality of an opinion can also influence whether other judges apply its rationale more broadly. The evolution and diffusion of law turns, in part, on the quality of the opinion that creates it.

If opinion quality matters for all these reasons, scholars ought to know the factors that lead to greater opinion quality. We examined whether age-related cognitive declines influence the quality of opinions. More specifically, we explored whether judges are less likely to rely on aging judges' opinions. The results reveal that opinion quality decreases with age. As judges age, their colleagues cite their opinions with less frequency. What is more, they do so in the cases that are supposed to bind them. And while judges are not more likely to treat opinions written by older judges more negatively (or less positively), they are more likely simply to ignore them altogether.

We leave it to the reader to determine whether these results are "good" or "bad." On the one hand, it is somewhat reassuring that older judges' opinions are not being systematically hammered by their colleagues. If they were overwhelmingly treated negatively, we would have a tremendous problem in our judiciary. On the other hand, the fact that older judges' opinions are largely ignored by their colleagues does not

[22] The p-value for the 62-year-old's marginal effect is 0.12. All visual differences among pairwise comparisons in the marginal effects are statistically significant.

[23] One alternative reading of this result is that *all* opinions by older judges are simply of higher quality than those by younger judges. Thus, the lack of an additional uptick when a precedent is binding is not evidence of a lack of quality, but rather a surplus of it. Alas, the data do not support this conclusion. If we evaluate the probability of positive treatment for persuasive precedents, we find no significant increase as precedent author age increases. We do see some unignorable evidence that positive treatment of binding precedents is less likely as precedent author age increases ($p = 0.11$), which casts significant doubt upon the universally high-quality nature of older judges' opinions.

[24] We produce the results of these models in Table 7.6 in the appendix.

strike us as a good thing. An opinion that is so insignificant or unimportant as to warrant even a mention is an opinion that has not made a mark. Again, maybe that's fine. But when one considers these findings alongside the rest of this book, it is hard to believe the results are anything but troubling. Simply put, it appears that as judges age, their colleagues become less confident in the opinions they write.

7.5 Appendix

7.5.1 Pre-Processing by Matching on Binding Precedent

The results we report here and throughout this chapter come from analyzing the full dataset. Hinkle (2015), by contrast, reports results obtained after estimating propensity scores for whether a treatment is binding. This approach is analytically important given that she is interested in something that approaches a but-for question: but for a precedent being binding versus persuasive, would a judge cite and treat it? Propensity score matching allows her to estimate the probability of treatment—in her analysis, whether a precedent is binding—as a function of the full gamut of her explanatory variables. For our context, the need and feasibility of following this path is less clear. For starters, our concept of interest—an opinion author's age—is continuous as opposed to dichotomous. Additionally, although Hinkle rightly notes the plausibility that many of the controls could be confounders for whether a precedent is binding versus not, we have fewer concerns in our context. That is, one would have to believe something exists that is correlated *both* with whether a judge cites/treats a specific precedent *and* is also correlated with the age of that judge. As we have throughout this book, we continue to control for judicial experience of both the treatment and precedent authors. We also control for the age of a given precedent. Beyond these two time-based features, we see little reason to be concerned about un-modeled confounders. And, what is more, to the extent any unaccounted for confounders do exist (e.g., whether a judge has dementia), any pre-processing we do with our data will have no impact on their omission since we can only balance on features for which measures exist.

7.5.2 Ideological Distance, Precedent Author Age, and Binding Precedent

We examined the three-way interaction among ideological distance, precedent author age, and whether the precedent was binding versus persuasive. Figure 7.6 shows the same elements as Figure 7.5, but evaluates the those elements in two states of the world: one where the ideological distance between the treating judge and the precedent author is very small (left, hollow symbols) and one where the distance is very large (right, filled symbols).[25]

[25] The small value of ideological distance is equal to 0 and the large value is equal to 1. These are approximately the 5th and 98th percentiles.

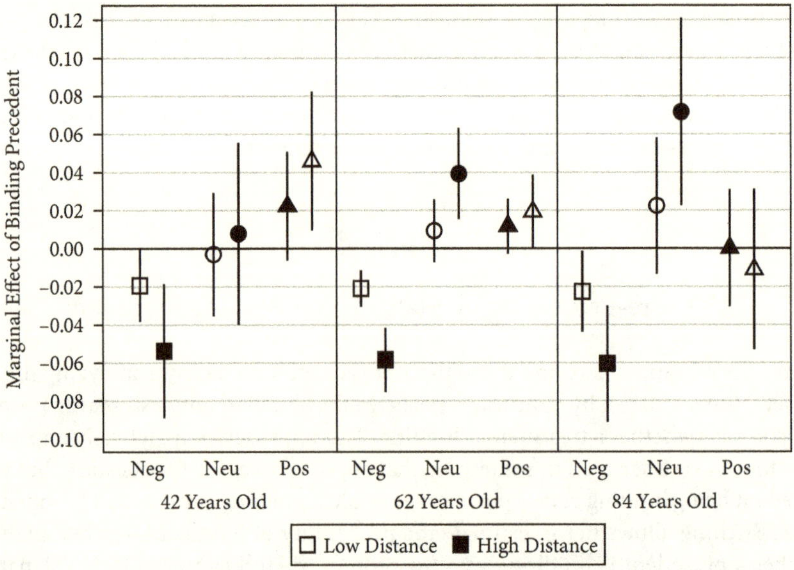

Figure 7.6 The impact of binding precedent on precedent treatment, conditional on precedent author age and ideological distance. Figure reports the marginal effect of binding precedent (with 95% confidence intervals), conditional on a given value of age and high vs. low ideological distance (while holding all other predictors constant).

Our two-way interaction found that binding precedents were, for precedent authors of all ages, less likely to be negatively treated relative to their persuasive counterparts. When we look at this effect for low versus high distance precedents, we find that, to varying degrees, the effect is stronger when the treatment author and precedent author are ideologically distant.[26] Why this might be, we are not sure, but since the relationship obtains for all three of our precedent authors, we are content to note it and move on.

Consider neutral treatments. Our previous analysis found that binding precedent status resulted, relative to persuasive precedents, in a higher likelihood of neutral treatment only for precedents authored by very old judges. We have the faintest whiff that this effect is magnified when ideological distance between the treatment author and precedent author is large ($p = 0.17$). We also find that this same dynamic seems to be in play for our 62-year-old judge, as well, with neutral treatment being more likely when the precedent is both binding and ideologically distant but not when it is binding and proximate ($p = 0.06$).

Finally, we conclude with positive treatments. Arguably our most interesting and important finding from the earlier two-way interaction was that binding precedent status seems to result in a more positive treatment only if it is a young author's precedent. That is, treatment authors give no additional positive credit to binding

[26] The p-values for the difference between low and high distances for negative treatments are 0.14 (42 years old), 0.01 (62 years old), and 0.08 (84 years old).

precedents written by older judges. Adding the element of ideological distance does nothing to alter this conclusion. The binding status of a younger author's precedent is no more (or less) likely to elicit subsequent positive treatment when it was ideologically proximate as opposed to distant ($p = 0.39$).[27]

Taken together, these findings reveal little evidence that ideological distance between the treating judge and the authoring judge conditions the effects of binding precedent on the nature of treatment. More generally, we find that precedent author age has a modest unconditional role (i.e., Figure 7.4). This role, however, is conditioned in a manner consistent with our expectations once one accounts for whether the precedent is binding (i.e., Figure 7.5).

7.5.3 Interactive Model Results

In the chapter's main text, we discuss the results of four interactive models. We provide the tables of these model results. Table 7.3 reports the results for the impact of author age (both the author of the precedent opinion and the treatment opinion) and precedent type (i.e., binding vs. persuasive) on citations (see, Figure 7.2). Table 7.4 provides the results for the three-way interaction of age, precedent type, and ideological distance (between the ideal points of the precedent vs. treatment opinion authors) on citations (see, Figure 7.3). Table 7.5 reports the impact of age and precedent type on (positive vs. neutral vs. negative) treatments (see, Figure 7.5). And Table 7.6 shows the results for the three-way interaction of age, precedent type, and ideological distance on treatments.

Table 7.3 The Conditional Impact of Opinion Author Age and Binding Precedent on Circuit Court Judges' Citation of Precedent

	(1)	(2)
Precedent Author Age	−0.0024**	−0.0019**
	(0.0003)	(0.0004)
Treatment Author Age	−0.0033**	−.0027**
	(0.0005)	(0.0007)
Binding Precedent	0.7974**	0.9199**
	(0.0439)	(0.0483)
Precedent Author Age × Binding Prec.	0.0005	0.0006
	(0.0004)	(0.0004)
Treatment Author Age × Binding Prec.	0.0021**	0.0023**
	(0.0006)	(0.0006)
Precedent Author Experience		−0.0028**
		(0.0004)

Continued

[27] The p-value for the marginal effect of binding precedent when ideological distance is low is 0.12, which is why the confidence interval whisker on the hollow triangle crosses the zero line. It would be ill advised to conclude that no effect exists here and, critically, we cannot reject the null of no difference between the two triangle points (i.e., that's the 0.39 value we reference in the text).

Table 7.3 *Continued*

	(1)	(2)
Treatment Author Experience		0.0009
		(0.0007)
Ideological Distance		−0.0298**
		(0.0108)
Ideo. Dist × Binding Prec.		−0.0280**
		(0.0139)
Similarity Percentile		0.0376**
		(0.0004)
Elite Precedent Author		0.0023
		(0.0078)
Dissent in Precedent		−0.0203**
		(0.0055)
En Banc Precedent		0.0218
		(0.0346)
Precedent Vitality		0.0128**
		(0.0013)
Precedent Treatments		0.0083**
		(0.0017)
Precedent Citations		0.0177**
		(0.0005)
Precedent Age		−0.0636**
		(0.0009)
Precedent Age-Squared		0.0006**
		(0.0000)
Precedent Length		−0.0235**
		(0.0036)
Quotations in Precedent		−0.5217**
		(0.0364)
Opinion Length		0.2219**
		(0.0060)
Number of Binding Precedents		−0.1209**
		(0.0093)
Treatment Caseload		0.00004
		(0.00003)
Constant	−2.9736**	−6.6369**
	(0.0381)	(0.0990)
N	30,497,294	30,497,294
BIC	535,605	428,985

Note: Table entries are probit regression coefficients with robust standard errors (clustered on the 6,975 treating cases in the data) in parentheses. The dependent variable reflects whether a judge cites a precedent for each precedent–treatment dyad. ** and * denote $p < 0.05$ and $p < 0.10$, respectively (two-tailed).

Table 7.4 The Conditional Impact of Opinion Author Age, Binding Precedent, and Ideological Distance on Circuit Court Judges' Citation of Precedent

	(1)	(2)
Precedent Author Age	−0.0033**	−0.0020**
	(0.0005)	(0.0006)
Treatment Author Age	−0.0040**	−.0025**
	(0.0006)	(0.0008)
Binding Precedent	0.7702**	0.8919**
	(0.0630)	(0.0672)
Ideological Distance	−0.2944**	−0.0201
	(0.0895)	(0.0946)
Ideo. Dist × Binding Prec.	0.0498	0.0457
	0.1165	(0.1212)
Precedent Author Age × Binding Prec.	0.0013**	0.0014**
	(0.0007)	(0.0007)
Precedent Author Age × Ideo. Dist	0.0024**	0.0002
	(0.0010)	(0.0010)
Precedent Author Age × Ideo. Dist × Binding Prec.	−0.0018	−0.0022
	(0.0013)	(0.0013)
Treatment Author Age × Binding Prec.	0.0019**	0.0019**
	(0.0008)	(0.0008)
Treatment Author Age × Ideo. Dist	0.0019*	−0.0003
	(0.0010)	(0.0011)
Treatment Author Age × Ideo. Dist × Binding Prec.	0.0006	0.0010
	(0.0013)	(0.0014)
Precedent Author Experience		−0.0027**
		(0.0004)
Treatment Author Experience		0.0009
		(0.0007)
Similarity Percentile		0.0376**
		(0.0004)
Elite Precedent Author		0.0020
		(0.0078)
Dissent in Precedent		−0.0203**
		(0.0055)
En Banc Precedent		0.0213
		(0.0346)
Precedent Vitality		0.0128**
		(0.0013)
Precedent Treatments		0.0083**
		(0.0017)
Precedent Citations		0.0177**
		(0.0005)
Precedent Age		−0.0636**
		(0.0009)
Precedent Age-Squared		0.0006**
		(0.0000)
Precedent Length		−0.0235**
		(0.0036)
Quotations in Precedent		−0.5225**
		(0.0364)
Opinion Length		0.2219**
		(0.0060)

Continued

Table 7.4 *Continued*

	(1)	(2)
Number of Binding Precedents		−0.1209**
		(0.0093)
Treatment Caseload		0.00004
		(0.00003)
Constant	−2.8565**	−6.6399**
	(0.0504)	(0.1052)
N	30,497,294	30,497,294
BIC	535,642	429,048

Note: Table entries are probit regression coefficients with robust standard errors (clustered on the 6,975 treating cases in the data) in parentheses. The dependent variable reflects whether a judge cites a precedent for each precedent–treatment dyad. ** and * denote $p < 0.05$ and $p < 0.10$, respectively (two-tailed).

Table 7.5 The Conditional Impact of Opinion Author Age and Binding Precedent on Circuit Court Judges' Treatment of Precedent

	Negative		Positive	
	(1)	(2)	(3)	(4)
Precedent Author Age	0.0016	−0.0014	0.0056**	−0.0018
	(0.0022)	(0.0028)	(0.0020)	(0.0024)
Treatment Author Age	0.0083**	0.0047	0.0088**	0.0054
	(0.0034)	(0.0041)	(0.0031)	(0.0038)
Binding Precedent	0.2010	0.4835	0.7099**	0.7342**
	(0.3024)	(0.3132)	(0.2576)	(0.2632)
Precedent Author Age × Binding Prec.	−0.0034	−0.0040	−0.0053**	−0.0056**
	(0.0028)	(0.0029)	(0.0024)	(0.0024)
Treatment Author Age × Binding Prec.	−0.0075*	−0.0073*	−0.0067**	−0.0056*
	(0.0038)	(0.0040)	(0.0033)	(0.0033)
Precedent Author Experience		0.0078**		0.0069**
		(0.0029)		(0.0023)
Treatment Author Experience		0.0050		0.0031
		(0.0036)		(0.0033)
Ideological Distance		0.3580**		0.0357
		(0.0811)		(0.0761)
Ideo. Dist × Binding Prec.		−0.3085**		−0.0003
		(0.0992)		(0.0865)
Similarity Percentile		0.0253**		0.0164**
		(0.0017)		(0.0010)
Elite Precedent Author		−0.0224		−0.1268**
		(0.0506)		(0.0426)
Dissent in Precedent		0.0914**		0.0032
		(0.0374)		(0.0297)
En Banc Precedent		−0.0974		0.2382
		(0.2461)		(0.1787)
Precedent Vitality		−0.0943**		0.0598**
		(0.0100)		(0.0085)

Precedent Treatments		0.1060**		0.0525**
		(0.0109)		(0.0090)
Precedent Citations		−0.0233**		−0.0174**
		(0.0033)		(0.0026)
Precedent Age		0.0248**		0.0159**
		(0.0061)		(0.0049)
Precedent Age-Squared		−0.0004*		−0.0002
		(0.0002)		(0.0002)
Precedent Length		−0.0729**		0.0142
		(0.0258)		(0.0200)
Quotations in Precedent		0.1269		1.0239**
		(0.2530)		(0.2036)
Opinion Length		0.1860**		0.1634**
		(0.0325)		(0.0286)
Constant	−2.2419**	−5.6511**	−2.2711**	−5.1610**
	(0.2599)	(0.4575)	(0.2344)	(0.3942)
N	42,391	42,391	42,391	42,391
BIC	53,695	52,465	53,695	52,465

Note: Table entries are multinomial probit regression coefficients with robust standard errors (clustered on the 6,458 treating cases in the data) in parentheses. Estimates are relative to baseline of neutral treatment. The dependent variable reflects whether, conditional on citing the precedent, a judge treated the precedent negatively, neutrally, or positively. ** and * denote $p < 0.05$ and $p < 0.10$, respectively (two-tailed).

Table 7.6 The Conditional Impact of Opinion Author Age, Binding Precedent, and Ideological Distance on Circuit Court Judges' Treatment of Precedent

	Negative		Positive	
	(1)	(2)	(3)	(4)
Precedent Author Age	0.0027	0.0001	0.0041	0.0007
	(0.0039)	(0.0042)	(0.0034)	(0.0037)
Treatment Author Age	0.0111**	0.0073	0.0011	−0.0022
	(0.0047)	(0.0051)	(0.0042)	(0.0047)
Binding Precedent	0.3202	0.5522	0.0201	0.0773
	(0.4584)	(0.4626)	(0.3861)	(0.3885)
Ideological Distance	0.9807	0.9304	−1.372**	−1.3195**
	(0.6549)	(0.6712)	(0.6398)	(0.6443)
Ideo. Dist × Binding Prec.	−0.2246	−0.3988	1.7435**	1.6460**
	(0.8102)	(0.8215)	(0.7499)	(0.7551)
Precedent Author Age × Binding Prec.	−0.0008	−0.0019	−0.0027	−0.0034
	(0.0048)	(0.0048)	(0.0040)	(0.0040)
Precedent Author Age × Ideo. Dist	−0.0035	−0.0035	0.0036	0.0029
	(0.0073)	(0.0074)	(0.0067)	(0.0067)
Precedent Author Age × Binding Prec. × Ideo. Dist	−0.0064	−0.0056	−0.0067	−0.0055
	(0.0090)	(0.0091)	(0.0079)	(0.0080)
Treatment Author Age × Binding Prec.	−0.0099*	−0.0104*	0.0017	0.0028
	(0.0055)	(0.0055)	(0.0046)	(0.0046)

Continued

Table 7.6 *Continued*

	Negative		Positive	
	(1)	(2)	(3)	(4)
Treatment Author Age × Ideo. Dist	−0.0061 (0.0074)	−0.0056 (0.0076)	0.0188** (0.0075)	0.0186** (0.0076)
Treatment Author Age × Binding Prec. × Ideo. Dist	0.0050 (0.0095)	0.0069 (0.0095)	−0.0208** (0.0087)	−0.0207** (0.0088)
Precedent Author Experience		0.0079** (0.0029)		0.0069** (0.0023)
Treatment Author Experience		0.0049 (0.0036)		0.0031 (0.0033)
Similarity Percentile		0.0253** (0.0017)		0.0164** (0.0010)
Elite Precedent Author		−0.0232 (0.0506)		−0.1269** (0.0426)
Dissent in Precedent		0.0901** (0.0374)		0.0032 (0.0298)
En Banc Precedent		−0.0977 (0.2463)		0.2383 (0.1788)
Precedent Vitality		−0.0942** (0.0100)		0.0597** (0.0085)
Precedent Treatments		0.1060** (0.0109)		0.0527** (0.0090)
Precedent Citations		−0.0233** (0.0033)		−0.0174** (0.0026)
Precedent Age		0.0246** (0.0061)		0.0161** (0.0049)
Precedent Age-Squared		−0.0004* (0.0002)		−0.0002 (0.0002)
Precedent Length		−0.0725** (0.0258)		0.0141 (0.0200)
Quotations in Preceden t		0.1236 (0.2529)		1.0286** (0.2037)
Opinion Length		0.1860** (0.0325)		0.1630** (0.0286)
Constant	−2.6435** (0.3827)	−5.9069** (0.5281)	−1.718** (0.3425)	−4.6100** (0.4594)
N	42,391	42,391	42,391	42,391
BIC	53,777	52,537	53,777	52,537

Note: Table entries are multinomial probit regression coefficients with robust standard errors (clustered on the 6,458 treating cases in the data) in parentheses. Estimates are relative to baseline of neutral treatment. The dependent variable reflects whether, conditional on citing the precedent, a judge treated the precedent negatively, neutrally, or positively. ** and * denote $p < 0.05$ and $p < 0.10$, respectively (two-tailed).

8
Cognitive Aging and Following Supreme Court Precedent

Long before his legacy bore the shame of an alleged sexual harasser,[1] Judge Stephen Reinhardt was a liberal icon who routinely clashed with the United States Supreme Court. In *Compassion in Dying v. Washington* (1996) (*en banc*), he ruled that the state of Washington could not constitutionally implement a pro-life law that prohibited doctors from performing assisted suicide. The Supreme Court reversed him in *Washington v. Glucksberg* (1997). In *Silveira v. Lockyer* (2002), he ruled that the Second Amendment's right to bear arms was a collective, not an individual right, and that the government enjoyed broad authority to regulate firearms. The Supreme Court reversed his position in a similar case in *D.C. v. Heller* (2008). In *Gonzales v. Planned Parenthood* (2006), he wrote the majority opinion that struck down the federal Partial-Birth Abortion Ban Act of 2003. The Supreme Court reversed him in *Gonzales v. Carhart* (2007).

Reinhardt disregarded and scoffed at those very Supreme Court justices who regularly reversed him. He asserted that lower court judges should not change their views "in order to please the Supreme Court" (cited in Cross 2005, 379). He impugned that "one can only contemplate with dread the answer the current [Supreme] Court would have given had it been asked to overrule *Plessy v. Ferguson*."[2] He purported to "follow the law the way it used to be, before the [conservative] Supreme Court began rolling back a lot of people's rights" (Carlsen 1996; cited in Baum 2006). For most judges, the judicial hierarchy demands obeisance to higher courts.[3] For Reinhardt, upper court review was an obstacle.

Was Reinhardt alone or do other circuit court judges react to the Supreme Court similarly? Reinhardt's example shows that circuit judges sometimes have the desire to shirk High Court precedent. In this chapter, we examine how aging circuit court judges treat Supreme Court precedent. How does cognitive aging fit into all this? Do aging judges take on the cognitively complex task of faithfully applying High Court precedent, or do they simply rely on ideological heuristics? Not surprisingly, given the findings in other chapters, we discover that as they age, judges become increasingly likely to rely on ideological shortcuts.

[1] https://www.politico.com/news/2020/02/13/ex-clerk-accuses-late-9th-circuit-judge-of-harassment-114817.

[2] https://www.aclu.org/blog/civil-liberties/exile-memory-judge-stephen-reinhardt.

[3] For an excellent discussion of whether lower courts really should or must obey superior court precedents, see Caminker (1994).

Cognitive Aging and the Federal Circuit Courts: How Senescence Influences the Law and Judges.
Ryan C. Black, Ryan J. Owens, Patrick C. Wohlfarth, Oxford University Press. DOI: 10.1093/oso/9780197747025.003.0008

8.1 Lower Court Treatment of Upper Court Precedent

Circuit court judges often have the means to dodge High Court precedent. The Supreme Court simply cannot review most circuit court decisions. As we have stated throughout this book, the circuits decide roughly 50,000 cases each year; the Supreme Court decides a mere 60–70 cases.[4] Though the High Court could decide more cases, the norms of holding oral argument and engaging in extensive briefing and opinion writing make it unlikely that it could review enough lower court decisions to be a serious auditing threat. Circuit judges enjoy significant latitude to decide cases as they see fit.

What is more, they often have different goals than Supreme Court justices. One judge remarked: "We follow [Supreme Court rulings] when we can't get around them" (Baum 1978, 212). The fact of the matter is presidents and senators choose people to be circuit court judges not for their compatibility with the High Court, but rather, for their legal and policy principles (Giles, Hettinger, and Peppers 2001).[5] Conservatives and Republicans seek to fill the circuits with legal conservatives while liberals and Democrats seek to fill them with legal liberals. The kind of acquiescence the Supreme Court wants from lower court judges does not influence the judicial selection process in any meaningful way. Consequently, at any particular time, and regardless of the High Court's composition, the judiciary is filled with judicial liberals *and* judicial conservatives whose goals do not always square up with the Court.

Lower court judges can evade Supreme Court policies numerous ways (Murphy 1959; Paulsen 1990). Assuming a High Court precedent is not directly on point, they can simply ignore the Court's decisions and cite one of their own instead (Manwaring, Reich, and Wasby 1972). They can distinguish the Court's precedents by claiming they do not apply to the case at hand. Perhaps the facts in the High Court case are "different enough" from the current case as to allow the circuits to give the Supreme Court the slip. They can simply interpret the Supreme Court decision narrowly by stating that the holding only applied to limited situations. More aggressively, they can criticize or even question the Court's opinion in an effort to weaken that decision's foundation (Tarr 1977).

To be sure, a long train of studies shows that lower courts often comply with Supreme Court doctrine (see, e.g., Johnson 1979; Gruhl 1980; Stidham and Carp 1982; Songer 1987, 1988; Songer and Sheehan 1990; Songer and Haire 1992; Songer, Segal, and Cameron 1994; Wahlbeck 1998; Benesh 2002; Benesh and Reddick 2002; Cross 2005; Hoekstra 2005; Luse et al. 2009). But then again, studies also reveal patterns to noncompliance. Four factors tend to explain lower court noncompliance with Supreme Court precedent:

- Characteristics of the Supreme Court's decision;
- Lower court resources;

[4] https://www.supremecourt.gov/opinions/slipopinion/22.

[5] To be sure, presidents and senators sometimes use a judge's reversal rate as a proxy for quality, but this is often laced more with political intent than with actual belief in reversal rates as a legitimate measure of things like judge quality.

- The clarity of the Supreme Court's opinions; and
- Ideological congruence between the lower courts and the Supreme Court.

Some scholars have argued that lower court compliance turns on the characteristics of the Supreme Court's decision. For example, Murphy (1964) argues that a Supreme Court decision which attracts only a small majority of justices signals jurisprudential weakness and thereby invites lower court noncompliance. "The greater the majority," he argues, "the greater the appearance of certainty and the more likely a decision will be accepted and followed in similar cases" (66) (cited in Johnson 1979, 793). In their study of state supreme court treatment of U.S. Supreme Court precedent, Kassow, Songer, and Fix (2012) likewise find that state supreme courts are more likely to treat Supreme Court precedents positively when large coalitions created them. Benesh and Reddick (2002) find that lower courts comply more quickly with unanimous Supreme Court precedents than with precedents created by bare majorities.

Others have suggested that lower courts are more likely to comply when they have the resources to know about and understand upper court decisions (see, e.g., Johnson and Canon 1984; Baum 1978). Judges who *want* to follow a Supreme Court precedent will be better able to do so if they have the staff to research those precedents, to understand them, and to get them in front of their judges. Simply knowing about new Supreme Court decisions can be a time consuming endeavor for an already stretched circuit court judge. With additional law clerks and professional staff attorneys, judges can stay current and comply; without such resources, they may find themselves out of touch and non-compliant.

The clarity of the Supreme Court's opinions also influences whether and how lower court judges comply with High Court decisions. Black, Owens, Wedeking, and Wohlfarth (2016) found that lower court judges were more likely to comply with highly readable Supreme Court opinions than with less readable opinions. Others have found similar results (Baum 1976, 1978; Staudt 2004). Wasby (1993) argues that "greater clarity is generally thought to produce greater compliance" (371). Corley and Wedeking (2014) find that lower courts are more likely to treat a Supreme Court precedent positively when the precedent expresses more certainty in its language. Circuit judges may interpret a precedent positively or negatively as a function of its clarity.

Most important for our purposes are the findings that lower court judges are less likely to comply with ideologically distant Supreme Court precedents (e.g., Benesh 2002; Songer, Segal, and Cameron 1994; Songer and Haire 1992; Hettinger, Lindquist and Martinek 2003*c*; Romans 1974). Kassow, Songer, and Fix (2012) find that ideological agreement with U.S. Supreme Court precedent leads state supreme courts to treat that precedent positively: "a liberal court," they find, "is more likely to positively treat precedent when such a positive treatment will lead to a liberal outcome" (379). They also find that conservative state supreme courts are more likely to treat conservative precedents positively. Comparato and McClurg (2007) show that some state supreme courts drag their feet for ideological reasons when forced to apply Supreme Court precedent. Benesh (2002) finds that while case facts influence lower federal court judges' decisions to overturn confessions, so too do their ideological predispositions. After *Brown*, many Southern judges who were ideologically opposed to the decision dug in their heels and obstructed (Peltason 1971).

Ideological differences between lower court judges and the Supreme Court may explain patterns of compliance; what remains unclear is whether the effects of ideology remain stable as judges age. Again, executive functioning and processing speed decline with age. This means that, holding all else equal, a judge's cognitive costs increase as he ages. And when cognitive costs increase, people rely on shortcuts to simplify their decisions. Ideology is an obvious shortcut for judges. As such, we believe that a judge will find it harder to overcome his ideological preferences and faithfully apply Supreme Court precedent as he ages—the cognitive costs of confronting those differences and conceding to the High Court may be too large.

8.2 Data and Measures

To examine how aging judges rely on the cognitive shortcut of ideology as they interpret and apply Supreme Court precedent, we turn to data from Black, Owens, Wedeking, and Wohlfarth (2016). They followed the approach of previous studies—e.g., Westerland et al. (2010)—and began with a random sample of over 500 Supreme Court opinions decided between the 1953 and 2000 terms. These decisions represent the set of precedents in our sample that circuit court judges could later interpret. We zeroed in on every federal circuit court case that later applied those sample precedents through 2001, which yielded roughly 9500 total treatment cases. We then identified the judges who served on each circuit panel and created an observation for each individual circuit judge's vote.

Our dependent variable—*Judge Treatment Vote*—represents *Shepard's* treatment categories and denotes whether each judge cast a vote to treat a Supreme Court precedent positively, neutrally, or negatively, to which we assign values of +1, 0, and −1. A decision that "followed" a precedent reflects a positive treatment. A decision that "explained" or "harmonized" a precedent represents a neutral treatment. (We do not include simple citations without any analysis in this category.) A decision that "overruled," "criticized," "questioned," "limited," "superseded," or "distinguished" a precedent represents a negative treatment (Hansford and Spriggs 2006; Westerland et al. 2010).

We identified the individual judges sitting on the panel in each treatment case and recorded whether they (1) voted with the majority, (2) issued a regular or special concurrence, or (3) dissented. Using these individual voting records, we coded the judges' votes that supported the majority disposition as favoring the precedent treatment outcome identified by Black, Owens, Wedeking, and Wohlfarth (2016). That is, we coded the dependent variable as a 1 for judges who voted with the majority (or concurred) in a case whose outcome reflected a positive treatment of precedent.[6]

[6] We dropped all votes from judges who dissented from the panel majority's decision due to the inability to determine the reasons for those judges' favored interpretations of a precedent. For instance, it is unclear if a dissenting judge in a case where the panel majority issued a negative interpretation necessarily favored a positive (or even neutral) interpretation of that precedent. This decision leads us to drop 869, or 3.17%,

We assigned a 0 to majority (or concurring) judge votes in cases that resulted in a neutral treatment and a −1 to votes favoring a negative treatment.

Our main covariates of interest focus on each judge's age and ideological distance from the Supreme Court precedent interpreted. *Judge Age* is the number of years between the year the judge heard the case under review and his or her birth year. To code *Judge-Precedent Ideological Distance*, we take three steps. First, to measure the ideological content of each High Court precedent, we use the Judicial Common Space score (Epstein et al. 2007) of the median justice in the Supreme Court majority coalition that enacted the precedent. Second, we rely on each lower court judge's JCS score to measure his or her ideal point.[7] Third, we compute the absolute value of the difference between the two scores. Given that we are interested in how judge age conditions the impact of ideological distance, we include an interaction term between *Judge Age* and *Ideological Distance*.

Among our control predictors, we account for each judge's experience on his or her appointed court to ensure that the results for judge age are not simply due to experience.[8] We code *Judge Experience* as the number of years the judge served on his or her commissioned court at the time of the decision. We also account for how the impact of experience may be conditional on whether the judge sits by designation from a non-circuit court. Thus, we assign a 1 to *Non-Circuit Designation* if the judge was not currently commissioned to a U.S. Court of Appeals (0 otherwise) and interact it with *Judge Experience*. Next, we follow Black, Owens, Wedeking, and Wohlfarth (2016) and include *Opinion Clarity*. To measure the opinion's clarity, we adopt Black, Owens, Wedeking, and Wohlfarth's (2016) composite measure, which represents the principal component (or, shared variance) of 28 separate textual readability indicators. Larger values represent greater readability (or, clarity) while smaller scores represent less readability.[9]

of the total judge votes recorded in the sample of precedent treatment cases. The results are substantively consistent when we retain these dissenting votes and code them as reflecting support for an outcome that is opposite of the majority—e.g., a dissenting judge favors a positive (negative) treatment in a circuit decision where the panel majority negatively (positively) interprets the precedent. The results are also consistent if we aggregate the data to the case-level, thereby using the median age and ideological distance of the circuit panel in the analysis. And, the results are consistent if we drop the 179 (0.65% of) judge votes that represent special concurrences (which favor a different legal justification for the panel majority's favored disposition).

[7] When district court judges sit by designation on a circuit panel, or when the appeal is from a three-judge district court panel, we follow Giles, Hettinger, and Peppers (2001) and use the common space scores of the home-state senators.

[8] The results are consistent if we instead code experience as the total number of years that a judge has served on the federal bench, including all commissioned courts.

[9] Because we replicate Black, Owens, Wedeking, and Wohlfarth's (2016) test of opinion readability, we also include their measure of the number of false full stops present when generating the opinion clarity indicator. As they put it (p. 51): "The readability measures look at things like the number of words per sentence, and other features contained within sentences. The readability measures often use periods to determine the stopping point of sentences. Because many legal citations include periods (e.g., the citation to volume 100, page 1 of the United States Reports is 100 U.S. 1), there is a concern the software might falsely impose sentence stops and, thereby, result in a higher count for the number of sentences for a given number of words (among other things). This might wrongly determine texts with greater numbers of citations are more readable. We wanted to be sure our readability measure did not simply pick up the amount of legal authority contained in an opinion, which is, of course, distinct from readability. Legal authority thus would

Lower court judges may interpret Supreme Court precedents based on whether they expect the current Supreme Court to view them favorably. That is, circuit courts may be less likely to apply a precedent positively as the sitting Supreme Court becomes increasingly distant ideologically from that precedent. They may anticipate the High Court's eventual rejection of that precedent (Benesh and Reddick 2002; Westerland et al. 2010). To measure *Supreme Court-Precedent Distance*, we start with the ideological content of each Supreme Court precedent using the JCS score of the median member of its majority coalition (as discussed above). Next, to measure the ideological location of the sitting Court, we follow Westerland et al. (2010) and calculate the JCS score of the median justice on the Court. We then compute the absolute value of the difference between these two scores. Larger values represent a sitting Supreme Court that is predisposed to reject or minimize a precedent, so the circuit panel should be less likely to interpret it positively.

Next, Hansford and Spriggs (2006) find that the strength of a Supreme Court precedent affects lower court judges' interpretation of it. Circuit judges are more likely to apply precedents positively that, over time, the High Court has interpreted favorably. We measure *Positive Vitality* and *Negative Vitality* as the number of previous positive and negative Supreme Court interpretations of that precedent, respectively (up to, but not including, the year in which a case was decided). We further control for multiple precedent characteristics that may influence how circuit judges vote. First, we account for the likelihood that more complex precedents will affect how lower court judges apply them. We measure *Case Complexity* using the total number of amicus brief in each precedent-setting Supreme Court case, as greater participation from external parties often signifies greater case complexity (Collins 2008*a*) and could reduce the probability of positive treatment. We obtain data on amicus participation from Collins (2008*a*), which was updated by Black, Owens, Wedeking, and Wohlfarth (2016). We also examine the size of the majority coalition as an indicator of internal (dis)agreement on the precedent-setting Court. We expect that a smaller majority coalition will generate decisions that future lower court judges are less likely to interpret positively. We code *Majority Votes* as the number of justices that joined the precedent-setting case's majority coalition.[10]

Next, we account for instances when the original precedent-setting Supreme Court opinion altered its own prior precedent, as lower court judges may be less likely to interpret such opinions positively (Benesh and Reddick 2002). We code *Precedent Alteration* as 1 if the precedent-setting Court majority formally altered an existing precedent; 0 otherwise.[11] We also include a control predictor for precedents which, themselves, struck down a federal or state law as unconstitutional. *Federal Judicial Review* takes on a value of 1 if the Court struck down an act of Congress; 0 otherwise. *State Judicial Review* takes on a value of 1 if the precedent nullified a state's law,

be a confounder. So, we treated this issue like any other possible confounder: we measure it and control for it. Thus, all our models in the remaining chapters control for what we call *False Full Stops*."

[10] We use the *majVotes* variable in the Supreme Court Database to identify the size of the majority coalition.

[11] We utilize the *precedentAlteration* variable in the Supreme Court Database to identify decisions that formally altered prior precedent.

regulation, or constitutional provision; 0 otherwise.[12] Next, we control for the age of the Supreme Court precedent under review. *Precedent Age* reflects the number of years between the Supreme Court's precedent-setting opinion and the circuit court's treatment of that precedent. Lastly, we account for differences in precedent compliance across different issue areas by including fixed effects for the primary issue area of the precedent-setting Supreme Court case.[13]

8.3 Methods and Results

Because the dependent variable is a three-category, ordered outcome, we estimate an ordered logistic regression model.[14] We employ robust standard errors clustered on the circuit court treatment case to account for the possibility of correlated errors among judges serving on the same circuit panel.[15]

Table 8.1 reports the parameter estimates of a baseline specification (including only *Judge Age*, *Ideological Distance*, and the interaction between them) and a second model with all control predictors. The results show that *Judge Age* activates the impact of *Judge-Precedent Ideological Distance* on circuit judges' interpretations of Supreme Court precedent. This effect is present in both the baseline and the full model. The greater the ideological distance between the circuit judge and the High Court precedent, the lower the probability of a positive treatment. Similarly, the greater the ideological distance between the circuit judge and the High Court precedent, the greater the probability of a negative treatment. More importantly, the magnitude of this relationship increases markedly among older judges. In fact, *Ideological Distance* exhibits no discernible impact on the youngest judges in the sample.

Consider Figures 8.1(a) and 8.1(b), which report the average marginal effects of *Ideological Distance* on the probability of a positive or negative treatment, respectively, across the observed range of *Judge Age*. Judges younger than 59 years old—roughly 38% of the total judge-vote observations in the sample—exhibit no statistically significant proclivity to treat precedents based on their ideological predispositions. Older judges, however, are significantly—and increasingly—likely to favor positive treatments of ideologically similar precedents and negative treatments of ideologically divergent precedents. Figure 8.1(c) reports the average marginal effects of *Ideological Distance* on the probability of a neutral treatment vote. These

[12] We utilize the *declarationUncon* variable in the Supreme Court Database to code these variables. *Federal Judicial Review* and *State Judicial Review* take on a value of 1 when *declarationUncon* equals 2 and 3, respectively.

[13] We use the "issueArea" indicator in the Supreme Court Database to identify the precedent's primary issue area.

[14] Several control predictors violate the parallel regression assumption, showing significantly different effects across the two ordered combinations of the dependent variable. None of our variables of interest do, however. The results for the interactive effect of *Judge Age* and *Ideological Distance* are virtually identical if we instead estimate a partial proportional odds model that estimates two separate parameters for those predictors (Williams 2006). The results are also consistent if we estimate these models using a multinomial logit model.

[15] The results for the interactive effects of *Judge Age* and *Ideological Distance* are consistent when estimating classical (i.e., non-robust) standard errors.

Table 8.1 The Conditional Impact of Judge Age and Ideological Distance on Lower Court Compliance with Supreme Court Precedent

	(1)	(2)
Judge Age	0.002	0.000
	(0.002)	(0.003)
Judge-Precedent Ideological Distance	0.350	0.687*
	(0.385)	(0.379)
Judge Age × Ideological Distance	−0.010*	−0.014**
	(0.006)	(0.006)
Judge Experience		0.009**
		(0.003)
Non-Circuit Designation		0.017
		(0.078)
Judge Experience × Designation		−0.007
		(0.005)
Opinon Clarity		0.013*
		(0.007)
Supreme Court-Precedent Distance		−1.366**
		(0.162)
Positive Vitality		0.180**
		(0.018)
Negative Vitality		−0.117**
		(0.027)
Case Complexity		0.022**
		(0.009)
Majority Votes		0.027*
		(0.017)
Precedent Alteration		−0.307**
		(0.120)
Federal Judicial Review		−1.928**
		(0.440)
State Judicial Review		−0.332**
		(0.102)
Precedent Age		−0.009**
		(0.003)
Cutpoint 1	−1.092	−1.150
	(0.155)	(0.220)
Cutpoint 2	−0.296	−0.319
	(0.155)	(0.219)
Issue Area Controls	No	Yes
N	26,586	26,586
χ^2	23.14**	413.88**
BIC	51,465	50,314

Note: Table entries are ordered logistic regression estimates with robust standard errors (clustered on the treatment case) in parentheses. The dependent variable represents each individual judge's vote in U.S. Circuit Courts of Appeals cases applying Supreme Court precedent (1 = positive treatment; 0 = neutral treatment; −1 = negative treatment). Model 2 includes, but does not display, fixed effects controls for the primary issue area of each circuit treatment case and a predictor representing false full stops. ** and * denote $p < 0.05$ and $p < 0.10$, respectively (two-tailed).

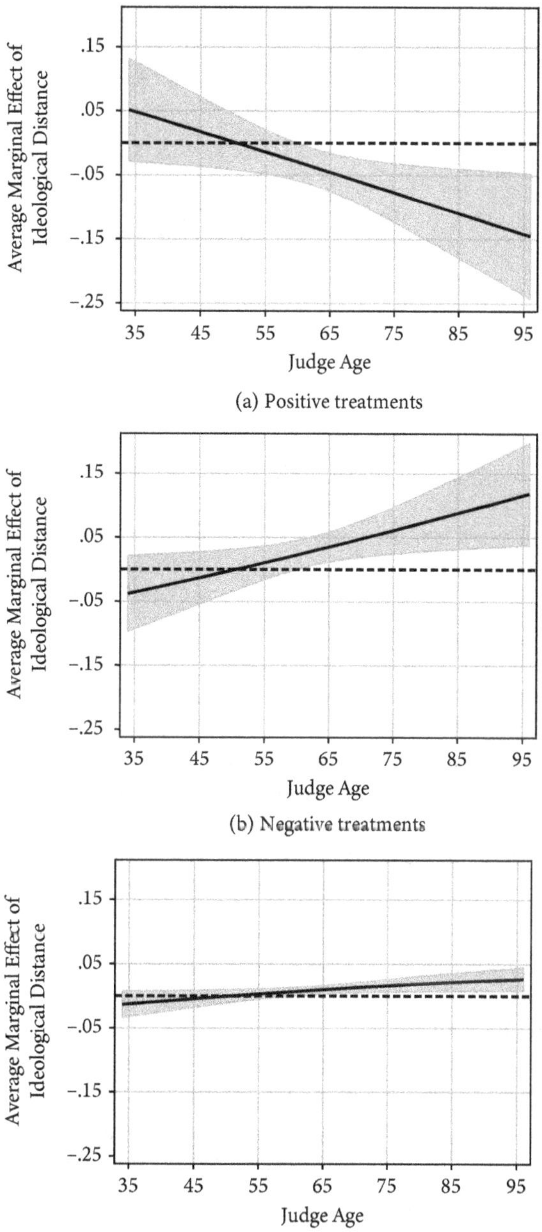

(a) Positive treatments

(b) Negative treatments

(c) Neutral treatments

Figure 8.1 The effect of ideological distance on circuit court treatments of U.S. Supreme Court precedent, conditional on judge age. Panel (a) displays the average marginal effect of *Ideological Distance* (with 95% confidence intervals) on the probability of a positive treatment across the range of *Judge Age* using results from Model 2 in Table 8.1. Panel (b) displays the results when predicting a negative treatment and Panel (c) displays the results for neutral treatments.

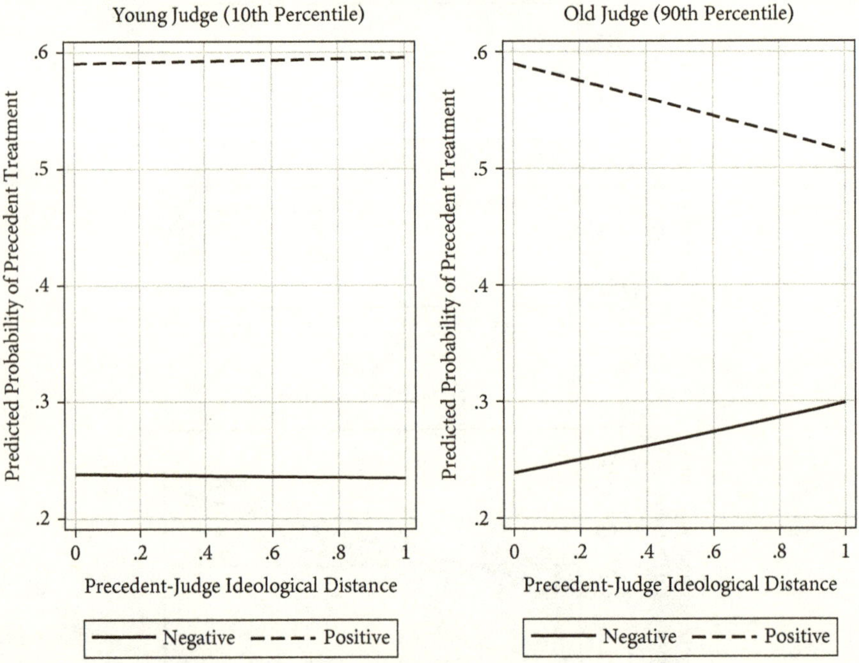

Figure 8.2 The impact of judge age and ideological distance on circuit court treatments of U.S. Supreme Court precedent. Estimates reflect the predicted probability that a judge votes to support a positive vs. negative circuit court treatment across the range of (precedent-judge) *Ideological Distance* using results from Model 2 in Table 8.1. The left panel reports the results when holding *Judge Age* constant at the 10th percentile (i.e., 49 years old) while the right panel show the results for the 90th percentile (i.e., 74 years old).

results suggest that older judges are increasingly likely to favor neutral treatments of ideologically divergent precedents, but the magnitude of this effect is modest.

Figure 8.2 better illustrates the predicted magnitude of these effects. It demonstrates the predicted probability that a judge treats a precedent positively or negatively across the range of precedent-judge *Ideological Distance.* The left panel reports the results when we examine a 49-year-old judge (i.e., holding *Judge Age* constant at the 10th percentile). The probability that this young circuit court judge treats a precedent positively or negatively is virtually constant across the range of ideological distance. In fact, the probability of a positive treatment is 0.59 at the 10th percentile of *Ideological Distance* and still 0.59 at the 90th percentile. Likewise, the probability of a negative treatment is 0.24 at the 10th percentile and 0.24 at the 90th percentile—not much change at all.

The right panel of Figure 8.2 shows the results for a 74-year-old judge (i.e., holding *Judge Age* constant at the 90th percentile). Older judges are significantly more likely to treat precedents based on their ideological predispositions. When a 74-year-old judge encounters an ideologically close precedent (10th percentile of *Ideological Distance*), there is a 0.59 probability she treats the precedent positively.

That probability decreases to 0.54, however, when the 74-year-old judge confronts an ideologically distant precedent (90th percentile).

The probability of a negative treatment follows a similar ideologically based pattern. When a 74-year-old judge faces an ideologically close precedent (10th percentile of *Ideological Distance*), there is a 0.24 probability he treats the precedent negatively. And that probability increases to 0.28 when the judge encounters an ideologically distant precedent. While the magnitude of this change may seem modest, it is nearly half the magnitude of the effect of a similar change in *Supreme Court-Precedent Distance*. Further, the magnitude of these effects are even more pronounced among judges older than 74, which has become increasingly common in the U.S. Courts of Appeals.

In short, the data suggest that age enhances a judge's propensity to interpret Supreme Court precedents based on ideology—and we believe ideology becomes more influential with age because judges use it as a shortcut to compensate for their cognitive decline.

8.4 Conclusion

We examined the behavior of circuit court judges as it relates to the treatment of Supreme Court precedent. We asked whether age influences how judges treat High Court precedent. The results show that when judges age, they become more likely to treat precedent positively when they agree with it and become more likely to treat it negatively when they disagree with it.

The implications are clear. Older judges seem to rely more than younger judges on ideology when they interpret and apply Supreme Court precedent. They appear to take shortcuts. These findings are doubly important when one considers how low the probability of upper court review really is. For the Supreme Court, this portends trouble in terms of obtaining compliance from circuit judges.

9
Cognitive Aging and Panel Composition

Sometimes, court majorities consist of odd coalitions—judges who agree with one another in unexpected ways. Such was the case in *Servo Kinetics v. Tokyo Precision Instruments* (2007). The case involved three companies. Servo Kinetics bought machine parts from Tokyo Precision Instruments up until Moog, Inc. purchased Tokyo Precision. After its purchase, Moog ended its relationship with Servo. In response, Servo sued the two companies for breach of contract and sought to "pierce the corporate veil" by suing the parent company, Moog, through Tokyo Precision. The federal district court granted summary judgment to Tokyo Precision on all counts, ending Servo's case.

An odd coalition of judges on the Sixth Circuit Court of Appeals, however, reversed. The court majority consisted of Judge Eric Clay and Judge Allen Sharp. They believed that the district court judge ought to have denied summary judgment. They believed the facts could have established Tokyo Precision's liability. Therefore, the case ought to have proceeded to a trial. Judge Jeffrey Sutton dissented. He believed the facts and law supported the district court's ruling.

What made the majority unique was that the panel consisted of a Democratic-appointed judge (Clay) and two Republican-appointed judges (Sharp and Sutton). We might, therefore, have expected a conservative outcome in the case. Instead, the "*DRR*" panel (Democratic-Republican-Republican) produced a liberal decision—it opened up the two companies to liability. Clay was able to divide the two Republican-appointed judges. How was this possible? The case was legally complex. And Sharp was a district judge sitting by designation. But something else might have explained Clay's "pickoff." The Republican-appointed Sharp was 75 years old. He passed away less than two and a half years after the court published its decision. Did cognitive dulling allow Sharp to be swayed by Clay?

We illustrated in previous chapters that aging judges require more time to complete tasks and that they increasingly rely on cognitive heuristics. This chapter considers a different decision-making dynamic. Here, we focus on panel composition. We ask: Do judges, as they age, exert less influence over their panel colleagues? Conversely, do judges become more susceptible to group-based panel composition as they age? And, does a panel of judges appointed by a president of the "other" party persuade older judges more than younger judges to change their votes?

To answer these questions, we examine *Counter-Judges* and *Twain Judges.*[1] A Counter-Judge is someone who sits with two panel colleagues appointed by a president of the "other" party (Hinkle, Nelson, and Hazelton 2020). For example, a

[1] "Twain" is an old English word for "two."

Cognitive Aging and the Federal Circuit Courts: How Senescence Influences the Law and Judges.
Ryan C. Black, Ryan J. Owens, Patrick C. Wohlfarth, Oxford University Press. DOI: 10.1093/oso/9780197747025.003.0009

Counter-Judge would be a Republican-appointed judge who sits on a panel with two Democratic-appointed judges (*R*DD), or a Democratic-appointed judge who sits with two Republican-appointed judges (*D*RR). (We bold the *R* and the *D* to highlight the particular judge we consider.) A Twain Judge, on the other hand, is a judge who shares appointment partisanship with another judge on the three-judge panel. In the previous example, the two Democratic-appointed judges or two Republican-appointed judges would be Twain Judges. Given what we know about cognitive aging, we expect that as they age, Counter-Judges will be less effective at influencing their colleagues. That is, an old Republican-appointed judge will be less effective than a young Republican-appointed judge at pulling the Democratic-appointed Twain Judges to the conservative position. (And the same in reverse for aging Democratic-appointed Counter-Judges.) We also believe that as they age, Twain Judges will be more susceptible to the influence of Counter-Judges. And, we expect that a larger number of panel colleagues appointed by a president of the other political party will increasingly influence judges as they age.

The empirical results we collect from two separate analyses—one focusing on the case level and a second examining individual judges' votes—support our overall argument. Panel composition increasingly influences judges as they age. They are less influential as Counter-Judges and are more susceptible as Twain Judges. Like the other chapters in the book, this chapter shows that cognitive aging influences federal circuit court judges.

9.1 The Effects of Panel Composition

Judges in the U.S. Courts of Appeals generally decide cases on three-judge panels. The judges who serve on those panels are randomly selected from the broader population of judges in that circuit. For example, as of November 2023, the Seventh Circuit Court of Appeals employed ten active judges. Those ten judges ranged in age from 44 years old to 85 years old. Because the circuits (usually) assign their judges randomly to sit on panels, the composition can vary. One panel on the Seventh Circuit might consist of Judge Rovner (aged 85), Judge Brennan (60), and Judge Jackson-Akiwumi (44). Another might consist of Chief Judge Sykes (66), Judge Easterbrook (75), and Judge Pyror (46).[2] When three judges sit together to resolve a dispute, they expose each other to their views. And, just as gravity can bend a ray of light, one judge can influence another judge to vote in ways she otherwise would not have voted. Scholars often refer to this phenomenon as a "panel effect."

Numerous studies reveal that panel composition can influence how judges vote. Some examine how one judge's policy preferences can constrain her colleagues' votes (Cross and Tiller 1998; Sunstein et al. 2006; Kim 2009; Kastellec 2011; Epstein, Landes, and Posner 2013; Hinkle, Nelson, and Hazelton 2020). Analyzing how a Counter-Judge can influence Twain Judges, Hinkle, Nelson, and Hazelton (2020) show that the presence of one Republican-appointed Counter-Judge can induce at

[2] In important cases, and when the full circuit votes to do so, the entire complement of judges will hear a case *en banc*.

least one Democratic-appointed Twain Judge to vote more conservatively. Other studies analyze how Twain Judges can rein in a Counter-Judge. As an example, Epstein, Landes, and Posner (2013) find that a Republican-appointed judge who votes alongside two other Republican-appointed judges (*RRR*) has a 0.66 probability of casting a conservative vote. But that same Republican-appointed judge has only a 0.52 probability of casting a conservative vote when he serves with two Democratic-appointed judges (*RDD*).[3]

Studies also reveal how a judge's sex (Farhang and Wawro 2004; Boyd, Epstein, and Martin 2010; Erikson 2022) or race (Kastellec 2013) can influence colleagues' votes. Boyd, Epstein, and Martin (2010) show that one female judge can cause a panel with two male colleagues to uphold sex discrimination complaints they otherwise would not uphold. "[T]he presence of a female on a panel," they find, "actually causes male judges to vote in a way they otherwise would not—in favor of plaintiffs" (406). Other studies find similar outcomes when they examine race. Kastellec (2013) analyzed all published U.S. Courts of Appeals decisions from 1971 to 2008 involving affirmative action. His study reveals that a non-black judge is approximately 25 percentage points more likely to support affirmative action programs when she serves on a panel with a black judge than when she serves on a panel without a black judge. Remarkably, "of the 30 cases in which at least one black judge participated, 27 (90%) resulted in a decision in favor of affirmative action. And in only one case did a black judge write a dissent" (Kastellec 2013, 178–179).[4]

Why judges change their votes as a function of panel composition is unclear, but scholars have proposed at least three explanations. One common theory involves the *norm of consensus* (see, e.g., Hinkle, Nelson, and Hazelton 2020). Circuit court judges appear eager to reach unanimous decisions. Collegial judges that look to reach consensus may defer to colleagues' views. The motivation to acquiesce is often rooted in protecting the outward appearance and legitimacy of the institution (e.g., Hettinger, Lindquist, and Martinek 2006). It may also have to do with the massive workload under which these judges toil, which makes unnecessary work and conflict gratuitous. A second theory emphasizes the role of *deliberation* among judges. This theory holds that judges may persuade their panel colleagues to depart from their views by sharing information they may not have considered (e.g., Boyd, Epstein, and Martin 2010). For example, in the Boyd, Epstein, and Martin (2010) study, female judges were able to share their experiences with their male colleagues, which led them to change their votes. Finally, a third theory explains the influence of panel composition by focusing on judges' strategic efforts *to evade upper court review*. Judges sometimes try to insulate their decisions from review. But a dissenter on a three-judge panel can gum up the works by acting as a whistleblower. A dissent can signal to upper court judges that the decision is somehow wrong. The dissenter thereby can increase the odds of upper court review and reversal (Cross and Tiller 1998). To avoid this possibility,

[3] Similarly, among Democratic-appointed judges, "the probability of a conservative vote is 37 percent when the other panel members are both [Democratic-appointed judges (*DDD*)] . . . and 52 percent when both of the others are" Republican-appointed judges (*DRR*) (Epstein, Landes, and Posner 2013, 196).

[4] Scholars have since extended evidence of panel effects beyond voting to opinion citations (e.g., Szmer, Christensen, and Grubbs 2020) and the application of precedent (e.g., Hinkle 2017).

Twain Judges bargain with Counter-Judges, particularly when the Twain Judges are ideologically distant from the reviewing court.[5]

9.2 Cognitive Aging and Panel Composition

Prior studies do not consider whether cognitive aging conditions the effects of panel composition. To be sure, some studies examine the effects of judge age as a means to test *other* theories (Kastellec 2013). For example, in their case-level analysis of panel effects, Hinkle, Nelson, and Hazelton (2020) include Counter-Judge age but only as a measure of one judge's likely future dealings with another. Panel colleagues, they argue, should be less likely to support a Counter-Judge's position when they expect fewer future interactions with that judge.[6] Other studies consider how the length of a judge's tenure may affect his or her decisions (Epstein, Landes, and Posner 2013). Yet, to our knowledge, scholarship has not considered how cognitive aging interacts with panel composition.

The practice of judging, after all, is cognitively taxing. Effective judging demands quick processing speed and solid executive functioning. Judges must be able to recall existing precedents and relate them to present case facts. They must have the mental dexterity to manage a diverse docket with cases that present decidedly different legal issues. And, they must be able to manage their time and workload effectively. Yet, as we discussed earlier, an aged judge is likely to suffer from a loss of executive functioning, memory, and attention. Executive functioning, in particular, is critical for problem solving and legal reasoning (e.g., Baltes 1993). An older judge is likely to suffer from a diminished capacity to process information and to assess how legal precedent bears on the case at hand. Cognitive health can aid in these efforts and help a judge persuade colleagues.

We believe that as they age, judges will rely more on their colleagues as decision-making shortcuts. A judge who suffers from declining processing speed and reasoning abilities will look to compensate for those deficits. As a consequence, aging judges will be increasingly likely to rely on simplifying heuristics to help them make decisions. Relying on colleagues can serve as a shortcut. For similar reasons, judges may evaluate aging judges' positions and opinions to be less trustworthy. Judges may be less deferential to, or otherwise less influenced by their older colleagues. In other words, if there is reason to question the preparation and soundness of an older colleague's views in a case, panel colleagues should be less inclined to support them.

[5] Hinkle, Nelson, and Hazelton (2020) test all of these theories. While their empirical results offer some degree of support for all three, they most strongly support the review-avoidance theory.

[6] This view of Counter-Judge age as a predictor of panel effects is certainly plausible. We believe, though, that our cognitive aging theory observes more support. This is so because we find *both* that older Counter-Judges are less successful than younger Counter-Judges at influencing Twain Judges *and* that older Twain Judges are more easily persuaded than younger Twain Judges. The time horizon argument would explain the first finding (that Twain Judges can dismiss judges with whom they do not expect to serve) but not the second. Cognitive aging explains both.

9.3 Case-Level Data and Measures

To evaluate whether panel composition increasingly effects judges as they age, we turn to data compiled by Hinkle, Nelson, and Hazelton (2020). In their study on the determinants of partisan panel effects, the authors collected the universe of published Fourth Amendment search and seizure cases in the U.S. Courts of Appeals (excluding the Federal Circuit) from 1953–2010.[7] These 57 years of cases offer an effective means to assess cognitive aging and panel composition. Our unit of analysis is the case outcome. We examine only those cases with published decisions issued by a panel of judges who were appointed by presidents with different partisan affiliations. This would be two Republican-appointed judges serving alongside one Democratic-appointed judge (RRD), or two Democratic-appointed judges with one Republican-appointed judge (DDR).[8] Our analytical focus is on the Counter-Judge's impact on the Twain Judges.

Dependent Variable. We code the dependent variable, *Counter Outcome*, as 1 if a panel with one Republican-appointed judge and two Democratic-appointed judges reaches a conservative outcome, or if a panel with one Democratic-appointed judges and two Republican-appointed judges issues a liberal decision; 0 otherwise. Table 9.1 represents our coding scheme.

Independent Variables. Two covariates assess the impact of age. *Counter-Judge Age* measures the age (in years) of the Counter-Judge at the time of the decision. We expect that as they age, Counter-Judges will influence Twain Judges less. Next, *Maximum Twain Age* is the age (in years) of the oldest Twain Judge. We alternatively measure *Average Twain Age* as the average age of the two Twain Judges. The twain measures

Table 9.1 Dependent Variable Coding—Counter Outcome

Panel Composition	Case Outcome	Dependent Variable
RDD	Liberal	0
RDD	Conservative	1
RRD	Liberal	1
RRD	Conservative	0

Note: The dependent variable follows Hinkle, Nelson, and Hazelton (2020), which identifies case outcomes that are consistent with the counter-judge's political predisposition (1 = outcome aligns with the counter-judge's predisposition; 0 = outcome does not align with the counter-judge). Panel composition represents the party of the president that appointed each judge on the panel; the counter-judge is a Republican (Democrat) that serves alongside two Democrats (Republicans).

[7] The authors used Lexis to identify these cases. They excluded decisions with two-judge panels, those that did not reach the merits, and decisions with split outcomes. As Hinkle, Nelson, and Hazelton (2020) argue, search and seizure cases offer a useful issue context because: (1) they appear frequently on appellate dockets; (2) they likely present fewer disparities in issue expertise across judges that could confound a panel effects test (in large part because judges participate in so many search and seizure cases); and (3) search and seizure precedent is much more stable compared to many other issue areas.

[8] We thus follow Hinkle, Nelson, and Hazelton (2020) and exclude cases with politically unified panels.

allow us to capture whether older Twain Judges are more susceptible to influence from Counter-Judges than are younger Twain Judges.

Because we obtained Hinkle, Nelson, and Hazelton's (2020) replication data, we are able to include as controls the full battery of predictors they employed in their analysis. This includes a control for Counter-Judges who have assumed senior status. *Senior Status* takes on a value of 1 if the Counter-Judge has taken senior status; 0 otherwise. *Pr(Future Panel)* captures the expected probability, based on circuit size, that the Counter-Judge will expect to serve on another panel with the Twain Judges.[9] Next, *Counter-Judge-Panel Same City* represents the number of Twain Judges (ranging from 0 to 2) who share chambers in the same city as the Counter-Judge.[10] Alternatively, when the Counter-Judge sits by designation from either another circuit or a district court, Twain Judges should expect fewer future interactions with the Counter-Judge and may lead them to deliberate less with her. We assign a 1 to *Counter-Judge Circuit Designation* and *Counter-Judge District Designation* if the Counter-Judge is sitting on a panel by designation from another circuit or district court, respectively; 0 otherwise. *Co-Tenure* is the total number of years the Counter-Judge served with the Twain Judges (combined) up until the case published. One might expect greater Counter-Judge influence when that judge served longer with her colleagues. *Subject Expertise* equals 1 if the Counter-Judge was a former prosecutor or public defender; 0 otherwise. *Elite Law School* takes on a value of 1 if the Counter-Judge attended a top-14 law school; 0 otherwise. *Counter-Judge-Panel Tenure Difference* is the the number of years that the Counter-Judge served minus the number of years served by the Twain Judge with the least experience.[11]

The next set of controls accounts for strategic explanations for Counter-Judge success. The three-judge panel may seek to avoid review by the circuit as a whole (*en banc* review) or review by the U.S. Supreme Court. As ideological distance between the panel and these auditors increases, so too does the likelihood of review. Yet, as Hinkle, Nelson, and Hazelton (2020) note, the impact of ideological distance will be even stronger when the Counter-Judge blows the whistle and dissents from a decision that overturns the lower court decision (e.g., George 1999; Black and Owens 2009; Black and Boyd 2012). We create two ideological distance measures and interact them with an indicator for Counter-Judge alignment with the lower court. Specifically, we measure the ideological distance between the panel median and the circuit median (*Panel-Circuit Distance*) and the ideological distance between the panel median and the U.S. Supreme Court median (*Panel-Supreme Court Distance*) using the absolute value of the difference in their respective Judicial Common Space scores (Epstein et al. 2007). We assign a 1 to *Counter-Judge-Lower Court Aligned* if the lower court

[9] Hinkle, Nelson, and Hazelton (2020, 283, fn. 8) employ the following formula: Pr(Future Panel) = $(N-2)/[(N-1)/2]$, where N equals the number of sitting (active) judges on that particular circuit court.

[10] Twain judges who share the Counter-Judge's chambers location are likely to have more future enCounters with her and that might lead them to deliberate more with the Counter-Judge.

[11] This predictor departs from the model specification in Hinkle, Nelson, and Hazelton (2020), who include two dichotomous predictors to account for when the Counter-Judge is either the longest-serving or shortest-serving judge on the panel. The results are consistent if we substitute our tenure predictor with those two dichotomous predictors. The results are also consistent if we instead measure this predictor using the non-Counter-Judge panel judge with the longest tenure.

ruling was liberal (conservative) and the Counter-Judge's predisposition is also liberal (conservative), as inferred from the party of the president that appointed the Counter-Judge; 0 otherwise. Lastly, we create two interaction terms between *Counter-Judge-Lower Court Aligned* and each ideological distance measure.

Another set of controls are dichotomous predictors that account for other case-specific factors that may affect Counter-Judge success. *Amicus Participation* accounts for those cases where external parties have filed at least one amicus brief. *Civil Case* identifies cases that involve a civil claim, as opposed to a criminal or *habeas corpus* claim. *Per Curiam* accounts for decisions that the panel decided with a *per curiam* opinion. Such cases tend to be less complex and less politically salient. *Post-1984 Case* controls for the difference in circuit court decisions before versus after six Supreme Court decisions changed search and seizure law in 1984 (Kritzer and Richards 2005). Each of these dichotomous predictors individually take on a value of 1 if a case presents the given characteristic; 0 otherwise. Lastly, we include circuit fixed effects in all but the simplest, baseline model to account for possible differences across circuits.

9.4 Case-Level Methods and Results

We estimate logistic regression models because our dependent variable is binary. We employ robust standard errors.[12] We estimate a total of six models. Models 1–3 employ *Maximum Twain Age*; models 4–6 employ *Average Twain Age*. For each of the two ways to operationalize twain age, we estimate three models: a baseline model without any controls, a second model with only circuit court fixed effects as controls, and a third model that includes the full battery of controls.

Table 9.2 reports the parameter estimates of all six models. The results support our hypotheses. First, as they age, Counter-Judges become less influential. The negative and statistically significant coefficient on *Counter-Judge Age* means that as the Counter-Judge ages, she becomes less likely to move her twain colleagues to her position. Second, the positive and statistically significant coefficient on *Maximum Twain Age* (and on *Average Twain Age*) shows that the age of the Twain Judges positively predicts Counter-Judge success. That is, as Twain Judges age, they become more susceptible to the Counter-Judge's influence. Notably, the effects are consistent across all six models.

Graphical depictions are easier to understand. Consider, first, the estimated effects of Counter-Judge age, presented in Figure 9.1. The Figure displays the predicted probability of Counter-Judge success (with 95% confidence intervals) using the results from Model 3 in Table 9.2. It illustrates the predicted probability that a decision is consistent with the Counter-Judge's presumed position across the range of *Counter-Judge Age*. The probability of Counter-Judge success is 0.51 when viewing the youngest Counter-Judge in the sample (a 38-year-old), but decreases to 0.35 for the oldest Counter-Judge (a 93-year-old). This 0.16 decrease in the probability of Counter-Judge success represents a 31% change. Even when we exclude the most

[12] The results are consistent if we instead estimate classical (non-robust) errors.

Table 9.2 The Impact of Aging on Counter-Judge Panel Effects in the U.S. Courts of Appeals

	(1)	(2)	(3)	(4)	(5)	(6)
Counter-Judge Age	−0.022**	−0.020**	−0.015**	−0.021**	−0.019**	−0.016**
	(0.002)	(0.002)	(0.004)	(0.002)	(0.002)	(0.004)
Maximum Twain Age	0.016**	0.017**	0.011**			
	(0.003)	(0.003)	(0.003)			
Average Twain Age				0.021**	0.023**	0.014**
				(0.003)	(0.003)	(0.004)
Senior Status (Counter-Judge)			0.049			0.041
			(0.083)			(0.082)
Pr(Future Panel)			−0.222			−0.221
			(0.317)			(0.317)
Counter-Judge-Panel Same City			−0.003			0.001
			(0.049)			(0.049)
Counter-Judge Circuit Designation			−0.146			−0.121
			(0.268)			(0.268)
Counter-Judge District Designation			0.029			0.047
			(0.125)			(0.126)
Counter-Judge-Panel Cotenure			0.013**			0.012**
			(0.003)			(0.003)
Counter-Judge Subject Expertise			0.078			0.087
			(0.061)			(0.061)
Counter-Judge Elite Law School			0.113**			0.115**
			(0.055)			(0.055)
Counter-Judge-Panel Tenure Difference			0.002			0.004
			(0.003)			(0.004)

Continued

Table 9.2 *Continued*

	(1)	(2)	(3)	(4)	(5)	(6)
Panel-Circuit Distance			0.304			0.307
			(0.197)			(0.197)
Panel-Supreme Court Dist.			1.033**			1.016**
			(0.254)			(0.253)
Counter-Judge-Lower Court Aligned			1.750**			1.746**
			(0.102)			(0.101)
Aligned × Circuit Dist.			0.491*			0.484*
			(0.270)			(0.270)
Aligned × SC Dist.			0.320			0.346
			(0.351)			(0.351)
Amicus Participation			−0.041			−0.047
			(0.187)			(0.187)
Civil Case			0.033			0.034
			(0.063)			(0.063)
Per Curiam			0.087			0.083
			(0.080)			(0.079)
Post-1984 Case			−0.458**			−0.457**
			(0.064)			(0.064)
Constant	−0.014	−0.164	−1.212**	−0.246	−0.461*	−1.341**
	(0.234)	(0.244)	(0.316)	(0.253)	(0.266)	(0.337)
Circuit Fixed Effects	No	Yes	Yes	No	Yes	Yes
N	8,902	8,902	8,902	8,902	8,902	8,902
BIC	12,061	12,120	10,173	12,056	12,112	10,172

Note: Table entries are logistic regression coefficients with robust standard errors in parentheses. The data come from Hinkle, Nelson, and Hazelton (2020), which includes all published search and seizure cases in the U.S. Courts of Appeals among split panels, 1953–2010. The dependent variable represents, for each case, if the panel's decision is consistent with the Counter-Judge's presumed policy preference. ** and * denote $p < 0.05$ and $p < 0.10$, respectively (two-tailed).

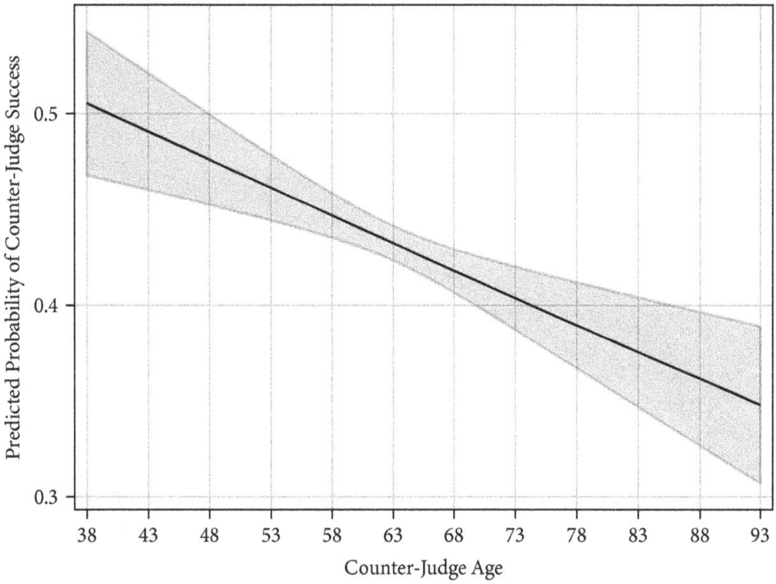

Figure 9.1 The impact of counter-judge age on case outcomes in the U.S. Courts of Appeals. Estimates reflect the predicted probability that the case outcome is consistent with the counter-judge's preference across the range of *Counter-Judge Age* using results from Model 3 in Table 9.2.

extreme values of *Counter-Judge Age* and, instead, examine the 10th to 90th percentile (i.e., comparing a 51- to 77-year-old Counter-Judge), the data reveal an expected decrease of approximately 0.08 in the probability of Counter-Judge success. In short, the results show that Counter-Judges are less successful as they age.

Now consider the effects of Counter-Judge age on the Twain Judges. We predicted that as Twain Judges age, they would be more susceptible to Counter-Judge influence. Figure 9.2 shows the predicted probability of Counter-Judge success across the range of *Maximum Twain Age*. The predicted probability of Counter-Judge success is 0.38 when the oldest of the Twain Judges is at the lowest point in the sample (41 years old). That probability increases to 0.49 when viewing the oldest Twain Judge in the sample (96 years old). Though this predicted change of 0.11 is somewhat smaller than the *Counter-Judge Age* finding, it is still substantively significant; it represents a 29% increase in the probability of Counter-Judge success. What is more, a shift from the 10th to 90th percentile (i.e., comparing a 57- to 79-year-old panel judge) still exhibits an expected increase of nearly 0.05 in the probability of Counter-Judge success.

Some of the control predictors are statistically significant. Twain judges are more likely to adopt the Counter-Judge's position when they have served together longer. Counter-Judges trained at top law schools also see more success. Counter-Judges are more successful when circuit-Supreme Court ideological distance increases, especially when a Counter-Judge dissent would highlight a reversal of the lower court's decision. The Counter-Judge is also significantly more successful as the distance between the panel and entire circuit median increases, among those instances where

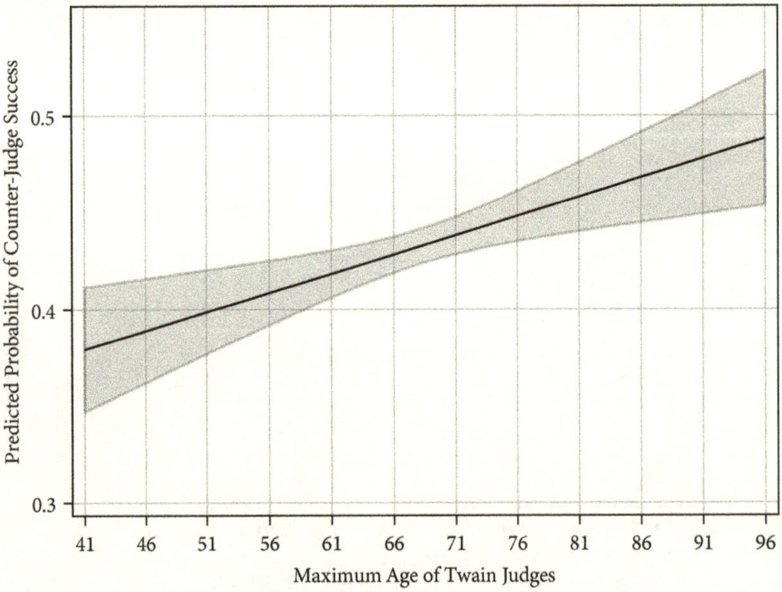

Figure 9.2 The impact of panel judge age (excluding the counter-judge) on case outcomes in the U.S. Courts of Appeals. Estimates reflect the predicted probability that the case outcome is consistent with the counter-judge's preference across the range of *Maximum Twain Age* using results from Model 3 in Table 9.2.

departing from the Counter-Judge's preference would also overturn the lower court. Lastly, the Counter-Judge wins less often in cases following the jurisprudential shift in search and seizure law.

Taken together, the results uncover that aging and panel composition matter. Counter-Judges become less influential with age. And Twain Judges become more susceptible to influence as they age.

9.5 Individual-Level Data and Measures

We now undertake a second examination of panel composition effects. Here, we employ data from a variety of cases (not just search and seizure cases) and with a unit of analysis that focuses on the individual judge vote. Instead of looking at the effects of a Counter-Judge on Twain Judges, here we consider whether a judge casts a counter-ideological vote (i.e., a Republican-appointed judge voting liberally or a Democratic-appointed judge voting conservatively) as a function of that judge's age and panel composition. For instance, if panel colleagues shape a judge's votes, we should expect a Republican-appointed judge to be less likely to cast a conservative vote if one or both of his panel colleagues are Democratic-appointed judges than if they are both Republican-appointed judges. Democratic-appointed judges, conversely, should be less likely to cast conservative votes as their panel sheds Republican-appointed judges. Table 9.3 summarizes our empirical expectations.

Table 9.3 Individual-Level Panel Effects Empirical Expectations

Judge Type & Vote	Panel Effects Expectation
Probability Republican Casts Conservative Vote:	*RRR* > *RRD* > *RDD*
Probability Democrat Casts Conservative Vote:	*DRR* > *DDR* > *DDD*

Note: The dependent variable follows Epstein, Landes, and Posner (2013), which identifies whether judges cast a conservative vote. The table lists the order of expected probabilities that a judge will issue a conservative vote as a function of panel composition (based on the party of the president that appointed each judge).

To pursue this empirical test, we turn to the data and analysis of partisan panel effects reported in Epstein, Landes, and Posner (2013). Epstein and colleagues examined data originally collected by Sunstein et al. (2006), which included all published decisions in the U.S. Courts of Appeals from 1995–2001 across 13 politically salient issue areas.[13] Epstein, Landes, and Posner (2013) expanded these data by adding age discrimination cases and by extending the sample of all cases through 2008. The updated data identify individual judge votes in nearly 5,000 total U.S. Courts of Appeals cases. The unit of analysis in this approach is the individual judge vote.[14]

Dependent Variable. The dependent variable, *Conservative Vote*, takes on a value of 1 if the judge cast a conservative vote and 0 if the judge cast a liberal vote.

Independent Variables. Our main covariates are a series of interaction terms. We use the partisan affiliation of each judge's appointing president to capture the presence of partisan panel effects. Following Epstein, Landes, and Posner (2013), we first split the sample into two separate models—one model that examines Democratic-appointed judges and a second model that examines Republican-appointed judges. We then create three dichotomous indicators to reflect the partisan composition of the other two panel judges (that are serving on the panel with the judge whose vote is the outcome for a given observation)—two Democrats (*DD Panel*), two Republicans (*RR Panel*), or one from each party (*DR Panel*). When we model the votes of Democratic judges, we examine the *DRR* Panel and *DDR* Panel indicators while omitting the *DDD* Panel as the baseline category. For Republican judges' votes, we include the *RDD* Panel and *RRD* Panel indicators (while omitting the *RRR* Panel as the baseline). If panel composition influences judges' votes, on average, we would expect to see that among Democratic-appointed judges, the likelihood of casting a conservative vote is lowest when their panel colleagues are two Democrats (*DDD*) but substantially higher when they are two Republicans (*DRR*). Alternatively, among Republican-appointed judges, the probability of a conservative vote should be highest with two Republican panel colleagues (*RRR*) and significantly lower when their panel colleagues are Democratic-appointed judges (*RDD*).

[13] These issue areas include: abortion; the Americans with Disabilities Act; affirmative action; campaign finance; capital punishment; contracts; Environmental Protection Agency; federalism; piercing the corporate veil; sex discrimination; sexual harassment; takings clause; and Title VII.

[14] The analysis of two issue areas—Americans with Disabilities Act and age discrimination—begins in 1998.

We suspect that cognitive aging conditions these effects. We code *Judge Age* as the judge's age (in years) at the time the opinion published. We then interact *Judge Age* with the panel partisanship indicators. In other words, for the Democratic-appointed judge analysis, we create two multiplicative terms: *DDR* × *Judge Age* and *DRR* × *Judge Age*. Among Republican judges, we create: *RRD* × *Judge Age* and *RDD* × *Judge Age*. If age accentuates the impact of panel composition, we should observe greater effects as judges age.

We also include as control variables all of the other predictors that Epstein, Landes, and Posner (2013) specified in their analysis. Circuits tend to affirm lower court decisions. We thus assign a 1 to *Conservative District Decision* if the district court's decision under review by the circuit court was conservative and a 0 if it was liberal. (Recall that our dependent variable is whether the judge cast a conservative vote.) We next adopt the Epstein, Landes, and Posner (2013) proxy for the political composition of the entire circuit court, as individual judges may cast votes with an eye toward the prospect of *en banc* review. *Proportion Republican Circuit* is the proportion of active judges on the circuit court whom Republican presidents appointed.[15]

Epstein, Landes, and Posner (2013) also include five predictors to control for various characteristics of the individual judges. *Former District Judge* takes on a value of 1 if the circuit judge under analysis was elevated from a district court to the circuit court; 0 otherwise. *Female Judge* and *Nonwhite Judge* equal 1 when those judges are women and Black, Hispanic, or Asian; 0 otherwise. *Judge Tenure* represents the number of years the judge served on the circuit court at the time of the decision. *Senior Judge* takes on a value of 1 for judges with senior status at the time of the decision; 0 otherwise. Lastly, we follow Epstein, Landes, and Posner (2013) and include fixed effects for issue area and the year of the decision.

9.6 Individual-Level Methods and Results

Given that our dependent variable is binary, we estimate logistic regression models with standard errors clustered on the judge.[16] We estimate a total of six models. Models 1–3 report the results for the votes of Democratic-appointed judges. Models 4–6 display the results for Republican-appointed judges. And, for both groups of judges, we estimate three models: a baseline model without any controls, a second model with only issue area and time fixed effects as controls, and a third model that includes all control predictors.

Table 9.4 reports the parameter estimates.[17] The results show some support for the argument that panel composition has an increasing effect as judges age. Figure 9.3 better illustrates the magnitude of these results. Panels (a) and (b) report

[15] The results are substantively consistent if instead of including the "Reversal Ratio" predictor from Epstein, Landes, and Posner (2013)—i.e., the proportion of votes to reverse liberal district court decisions divided by the proportion of votes to reverse conservative decisions.

[16] The results are consistent if we instead cluster the standard errors on the case citation, if we estimate general robust standard errors, or if we estimate classical (non-robust) errors.

[17] The number of observations that we report differs slightly from the results reported by Epstein, Landes, and Posner (2013).

Table 9.4 The Impact of Aging on Individual Panel Effects in the U.S. Courts of Appeals

	Democratic Judges			Republican Judges		
	(1)	(2)	(3)	(4)	(5)	(6)
Judge Age	−0.015*	−0.014*	−0.010	−0.002	−0.001	−0.004
	(0.008)	(0.008)	(0.009)	(0.006)	(0.006)	(0.008)
DD Panel				−0.197	0.016	−0.041
				(0.586)	(0.637)	(0.602)
DR Panel	−0.216	−0.147	0.031	0.095	0.106	0.281
	(0.540)	(0.542)	(0.578)	(0.377)	(0.411)	(0.412)
RR Panel	−0.768	−0.492	−0.491			
	(0.577)	(0.587)	(0.579)			
DD Panel × Judge Age				−0.006	−0.010	−0.008
				(0.009)	(0.010)	(0.009)
DR Panel × Judge Age	0.009	0.009	0.005	−0.005	−0.006	−0.008
	(0.008)	(0.008)	(0.009)	(0.006)	(0.006)	(0.006)
RR Panel × Judge Age	0.023**	0.020**	0.018**			
	(0.009)	(0.009)	(0.009)			
Conservative District Decision			1.318**			1.247**
			(0.111)			(0.075)
Proportion Republican Circuit			1.429**			0.764**
			(0.287)			(0.237)
Former District Judge			0.206**			0.030
			(0.089)			(0.077)
Female Judge			−0.111			−0.350*
			(0.089)			(0.180)
Non-white Judge			−0.012			−0.286**
			(0.083)			(0.121)
Judge Tenure			−0.002			−0.002
			(0.008)			(0.007)
Senior Judge			−0.108			0.035
			(0.166)			(0.098)
Constant	0.408	0.317	−1.279*	0.798**	0.384	−0.332
	(0.534)	(0.614)	(0.689)	(0.366)	(0.408)	(0.525)
Issue Area Fixed Effects	No	Yes	Yes	No	Yes	Yes
Decision Year Fixed Effects	No	Yes	Yes	No	Yes	Yes
N	5,441	5,441	5,421	8,532	8,532	8,503
BIC	7,478.26	7,108.39	6,787.03	11,370.28	10,409.62	9,957.24

Note: Table entries are logistic regression coefficients with standard errors (clustered on the judge) in parentheses. The data come from Epstein, Landes, and Posner (2013), which includes all published cases in the U.S. Courts of Appeals involving one of 14 issue areas, 1995–2008. The dependent variable represents whether each individual judge's vote supports a conservative (or liberal) outcome. ** and * denote $p < 0.05$ and $p < 0.10$, respectively (two-tailed).

the average marginal effects (with 95% confidence intervals) of panel composition on the likelihood that a Democratic-appointed judge will issue a conservative vote across the observed range of *Judge Age*. (We use the results from Model 3 in Table 9.4 to generate these predicted effects.) Panel (a) reports the effects while serving alongside two Republican-appointed judges (relative to the baseline category of two Democratic-appointed judges). Panel (b) displays the results for a panel with one other Democratic-appointed judge and one Republican-appointed judge.

There is no statistically significant evidence of panel effects when a Democratic-appointed judge who is younger than 48 years old serves on a panel with two Republican-appointed judges. That judge is no more likely to cast a conservative vote with two GOP-appointed colleagues than when she serves alongside two Democratic-appointed judges.[18]

Yet, as *Judge Age* increases, Democratic-appointed judges become significantly more likely to cast conservative votes when serving with two Republican-appointed judges (relative to a panel with two Democratic-appointed judges). Specifically, judges at the 90th percentile of *Judge Age* (80 years old), are 0.19 more likely to cast a conservative vote when serving with two Republican-appointed judges (relative to a panel with two Democratic-appointed judges). By contrast, Democratic-appointed judges at the 10th percentile (51 years old) are only 0.08 more likely to cast a conservative vote (again, relative to a panel with two Democratic-appointed judges). This age effect is both statistically significant and substantively important.[19]

Additional predicted probabilities reveal this dynamic (see Figure 9.4 in the appendix.). When considering a 51-year-old Democratic-appointed judge, the probability of a conservative vote when serving with two fellow Democratic-appointed judges (*DDD*) is 0.42. That probability increases somewhat to 0.48 when serving with one Republican-appointed judge (*DDR*) and 0.50 when serving with two Republican-appointed judges (*DRR*). This a total increase of 0.08. Contrast those probabilities with an 80-year-old Democratic-appointed judge. She is 0.36 likely to cast a conservative vote alongside two Democratic-appointed judges (*DDD*), 0.44 likely when serving with one Republican-appointed judge (*DDR*), and 0.55 likely when the panel includes two Republican-appointed judges (*DRR*). This is a total increase of 0.19—over twice the effect on the younger judge. In short, the impact of panel effects among Democratic-appointed judges is substantively greater as they age.

The results among Republican-appointed judges display a similar pattern. Panels (c) and (d) in Figure 9.3 report the average marginal effects (with 95% confidence intervals) among Republican-appointed judges across the observed range of *Judge Age*.[20] Panel (c) reports the effects when the panel has two Democratic-appointed judges (relative to the baseline category of two Republican-appointed judges). Panel (d) shows the results with one Democratic-appointed judge and one Republican-appointed judge. There is no discernible influence on conservative votes when a 45-year-old (or younger) Republican-appointed judge serves alongside two Democratic-appointed judges relative to two Republican-appointed judges. Aging Republican-appointed judges, however, appear somewhat less likely to cast a conservative vote when serving with two Democratic-appointed judges (relative to a panel with two Republican-appointed judges). Specifically, Republican-appointed

[18] Though, this represents less than 5% of the sample observations.

[19] The difference in the average marginal effects of *DRR* when *Judge Age* is 80 years old versus 51 years old is statistically significant ($p<0.05$; two-tailed).

[20] We use the results from Model 6 in Table 9.4 to generate these predicted effects.

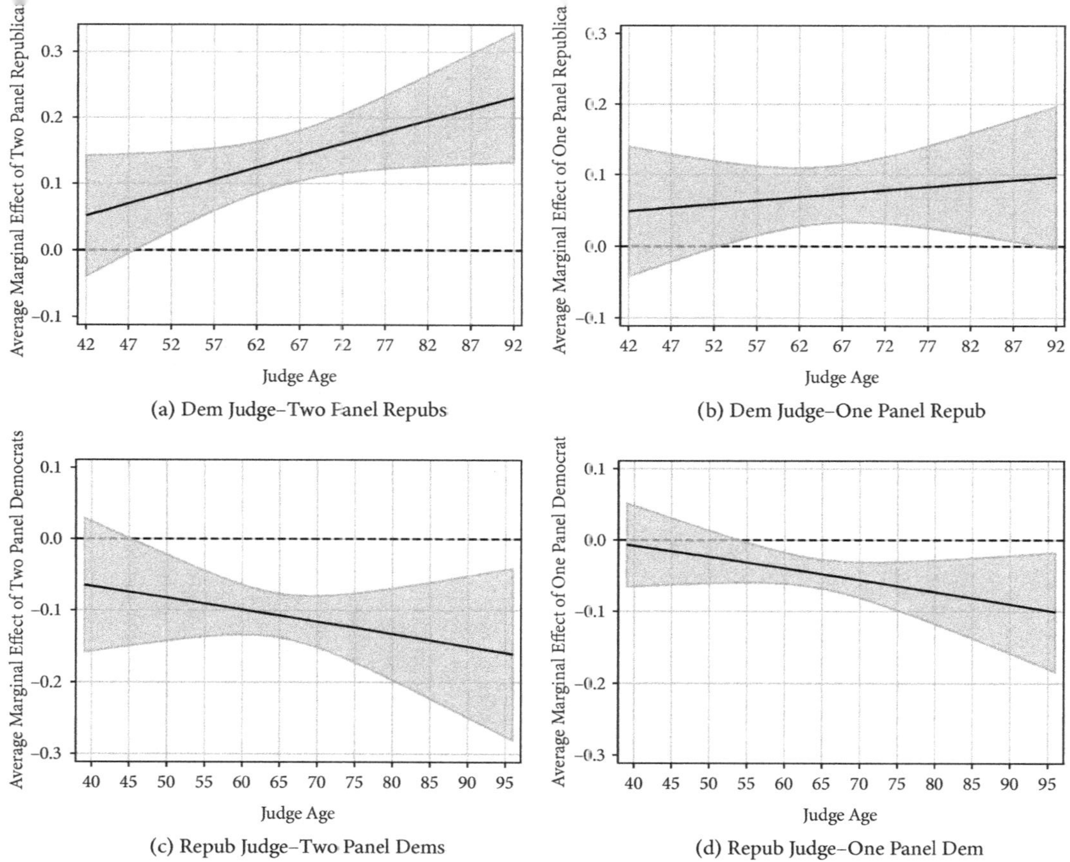

Figure 9.3 The effects of panel composition and judge age in the U.S. Courts of Appeals. Estimates reflect the average marginal effect of each panel composition indicator on the probability that the judge casts a conservative vote across the range of *Judge Age* using results from Model 3 (for subfigures (a) and (b)) and Model 6 (for subfigures (c) and (d)) in Table 9.4. The baseline category in subfigures (a) and (b) is a panel with two Democratic judges. The baseline category in subfigures (c) and (d) is a panel with two Republican judges.

judges at the 90th percentile on the age distribution (75 years old), are 0.12 less likely to cast a conservative vote when serving with two Democratic-appointed judges (relative to a panel with two Republican-appointed judges) while those at the 10th percentile (52 years old) are 0.09 less likely to do so; though, the difference between these two marginal effects is not statistically significant.

The data do suggest that age affects a Republican-appointed judge who serves alongside one Democratic-appointed judge, though the effects are much more muted. Panel (d) of Figure 9.3 shows no statistically significant decrease in the probability of a conservative vote when a 53-year-old Republican-appointed judge (or younger)—approximately 10% of the sample—serves alongside one Democratic-appointed judge compared to a panel with two Republican-appointed judges. Republican-appointed judges at the 10th percentile on *Judge Age* are 0.03 less likely to cast a conservative vote compared to roughly 0.07 less likely at the 90th percentile.[21]

Again, further probabilities can illuminate these results (see Figure 9.5 in the appendix.). A 52-year-old Republican-appointed judge has a 0.66 probability of supporting a conservative outcome when serving with two fellow Republican-appointed judges. That probability decreases to 0.63 when the panel has one Democratic-appointed judge and to 0.57 with two Democratic-appointed judges. A 75-year-old Republican-appointed judge has a 0.64 probability of voting conservatively alongside two Republican-appointed judges, 0.58 when serving with one Democratic-appointed judge, and 0.52 with two Democratic-appointed judges. Taken together, a young Republican-appointed judge is about 0.085 less likely to vote conservatively when the panel has two Democratic-appointed judges versus two fellow Republican-appointed judges; the predicted difference for an older judge is roughly 0.125. Although the magnitude of the results among Republican-appointed judges is somewhat muted (compared to the results for Democratic-appointed judges), they still exhibit a pattern of results that is broadly consistent with our argument. Aging Republican-appointed judges are increasingly likely to use their colleagues as decision-making heuristics.

Among the control predictors, Democratic- and Republican-appointed judges are significantly more likely to support conservative outcomes if the district court also ruled in a conservative fashion. Next, all judges are more likely to issue conservative votes when there is a greater proportion of Republican-appointed judges serving on the circuit as a whole. Among Democratic-appointed judges, those who previously served as a district court judge are more likely to support conservative outcomes. And Republican-appointed nonwhite judges are significantly less likely than white Republican-appointed judges to vote conservatively.

9.7 Conclusion

This chapter offers additional evidence that cognitive aging influences circuit court judges. We have shown that aging is an important dimension to the panel effects literature. Prior studies have offered extensive evidence of the interpersonal effects

[21] The two-tailed p-value when testing the equality of these two marginal effects is 0.18.

of judging and how individual judges can induce their colleagues to behave in unexpected ways. Aging affects these interpersonal interactions in a way that is consistent with our theoretical premise. As judges age, they become increasingly likely to rely on colleagues to inform their decisions, just as they become less influential.

The type of heuristic we uncover differs significantly from those we previously considered. In earlier chapters, we focused on aging judges' reliance on ideology as a shortcut. In this chapter, we showed how older judges exhibit stronger evidence of partisan panel effects—that is, how they are more likely to depart from their political predisposition and adopt the views of their colleagues. To be sure, while this result may seem inconsistent with earlier chapters, it is compatible. Scholars have demonstrated how federal judges make decisions based on a variety of goals and competing considerations across different cases and contexts (e.g., Songer and Haire 1992). These considerations include ideological goals (e.g., Hettinger, Lindquist, and Martinek 2004), legal constraints (e.g., Hinkle 2015), hierarchical dynamics (e.g., Haire, Lindquist, and Songer 2003), and other contextual factors (e.g., Songer 1987). The evidence we uncover in this chapter suggests that sometimes older judges use heuristics to pursue policy goals; other times they do so based on other competing considerations.

We next begin to examine the practical consequences of aging in the federal judiciary. In light of evidence to suggest that older judges take longer to complete essential tasks and rely more than their younger colleagues on various decision-making heuristics, to what extent does it matter? Does the average citizen view the decisions of aging judges negatively? Is there a cost to the institution when aging judges make decisions? Does an aging judiciary lead the public to support various institutional reforms that can mitigate the effects of aging? We turn to these questions in the next two chapters.

9.8 Appendix

9.8.1 Predicted Probabilities

In the chapter's main text, we discuss predicted probabilities generated from the individual-level models reported in Table 9.4. We provide figures of these probabilities below. Figure 9.4 illustrates the predicted probability that Democratic-appointed judges issue a conservative vote as a function of *Judge Age* and the partisan composition of the three-judge panel. Figure 9.5 presents the predicted probabilities among Republican-appointed judges.

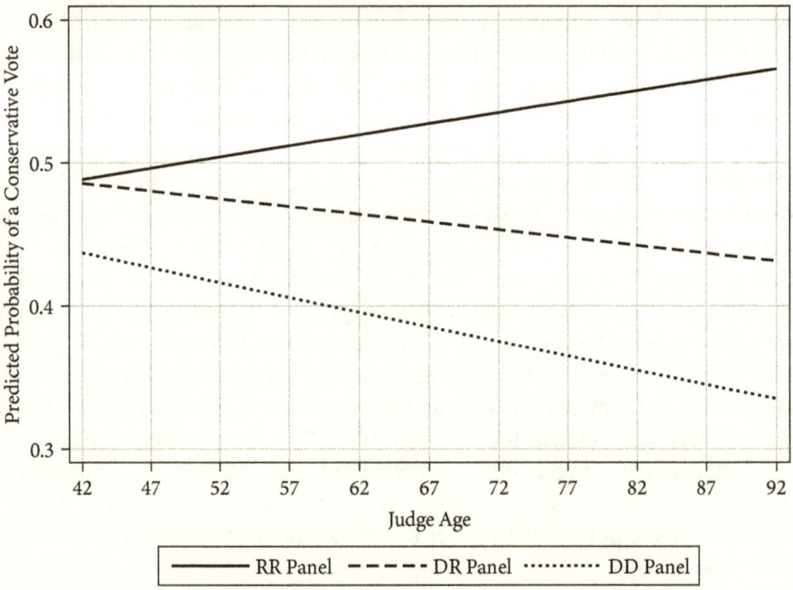

Figure 9.4 The impact of panel composition and judge age among Democratic judges in the U.S. Courts of Appeals. Estimates reflect the predicted probability that a Democratic-appointed judge casts a conservative vote across the range of *Judge Age*, for each panel composition type, using results from Model 3 in Table 9.4.

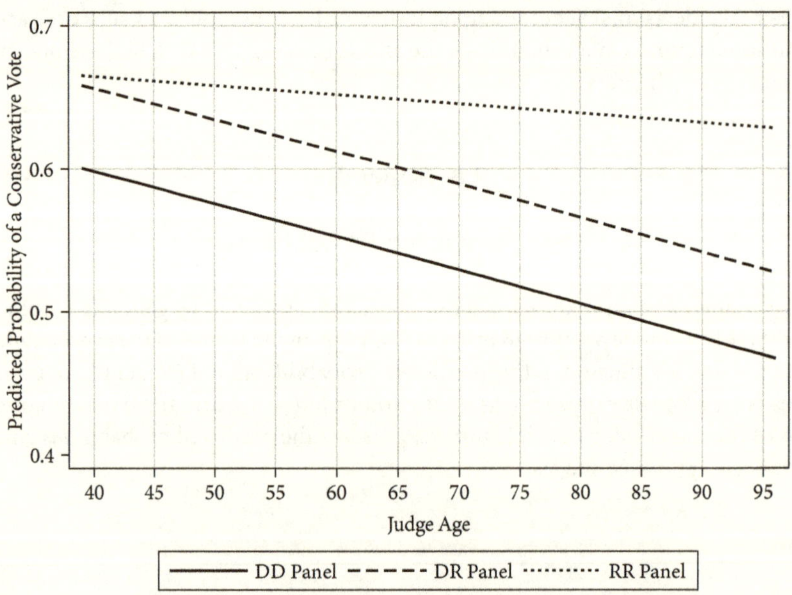

Figure 9.5 The impact of panel composition and judge age among Republican judges in the U.S. Courts of Appeals. Estimates reflect the predicted probability that a Republican-appointed judge casts a conservative vote across the range of *Judge Age*, for each panel composition type, using results from Model 6 in Table 9.4.

10
Public Attitudes toward Aged Judges

In 1937, President Franklin Roosevelt asked Congress to pass legislation that would allow him to appoint an additional justice to the Supreme Court for any current justice over the age of 70 who did not retire.[1] Chief Justice Hughes and Justices Van Devanter, McReynolds, Sutherland, Butler, and Brandeis all exceeded age 70. And, not coincidentally, all but Brandeis were conservative. Since these six sitting justices were older than 70, the law would have empowered FDR to add six new justices and increase the Court to 15 justices.

Roosevelt made two arguments to justify his plan. His first claim was that aged justices were *unable to complete their tasks timely*. He worried about justices remaining on the bench "to the very edge of the grave" (Shesol 2010, 294–295), stating: "By bringing into the judicial system a steady and continuing stream of new and younger blood, I hope, first, to make the administration of all federal justices speedier and therefore less costly" (Scigliano 1971, 45). His second claim was that the Court needed justices who held *current perspectives*. The courts needed "a constant infusion of new blood" because "little by little, new facts become blurred through old glasses fitted, as it were, for the needs of another generation; older men, assuming that the scene is the same as it was in the past, cease to explore or inquire into the present or the future" (Cushman 1994, 208–209). In short, FDR argued that older justices had lost their mental acuity and were out of step with current thinking.

Roosevelt's experience may or may not be instructive. On one hand, it shows that the public often can detect self-serving claims (Frankfurt 2005) and may reject a political party's efforts to "reform" a judiciary in its image. The public rebuffed him. Most people recognized that his plan was nothing but a cynical effort to neuter the Supreme Court. Even Senate Democrats refused to move forward with it. They rebuked FDR in a manner to which he was unaccustomed (see, e.g., Blake 2019). On the other hand, people's attitudes toward judicial tenure may have changed since FDR tried to pack the High Court. Politics and society today are different in ways that might matter. What is more, because federal courts are involved in so much more today than they were in the 1930s, people might very well tolerate the kinds of changes FDR sought. Indeed, members of both major political parties today have called for changes.

That today's federal judges are older than ever before has not escaped notice. Popular media outlets have written stories about how "no other western democracy allows" lifetime tenure as the U.S. does (Berman 2020). Members of Congress have proposed legislation to end lifetime tenure. Judges themselves have even undertaken

[1] There have been other significant reforms to the judiciary of course. Congress has added new circuits and split existing circuits post-Reconstruction (Barrow 1988; Howard 1981). And while these all had policy consequences and could be contentious, they did not rise to the same level as FDR's Court Packing plan.

Cognitive Aging and the Federal Circuit Courts: How Senescence Influences the Law and Judges.
Ryan C. Black, Ryan J. Owens, Patrick C. Wohlfarth, Oxford University Press. DOI: 10.1093/oso/9780197747025.003.0010

efforts to minimize some of the effects that can arise from cognitive aging (Goldstein 2011). But aside from some limited polling data, we know little about the *general public's* attitudes toward aged judges or toward proposed policy changes to address lifetime tenure. The question we address in this chapter is whether judicial aging influences everyday Americans' views of the courts, and how they evaluate proposed changes to lifetime tenure.

10.1 The Public and an Aging Judiciary

The judiciary's primary source of power come from its perceived legitimacy. Courts have an unusual connection to institutional legitimacy. Unlike officials in elected political institutions, who claim legitimacy by winning contested elections among free people, judges must find non-electoral ways to build and sustain institutional support. While there are numerous ways they can encourage such support, one chief approach is to decide cases fairly and objectively based on law, logic, and history (Tyler 2021). Research shows that people are more likely to support court rulings (or at least recognize the theoretical value of those rulings) when they internalize the judiciary's institutional legitimacy (e.g., Nelson and Tucker 2021; Nelson and Gibson 2020; Gibson and Nelson 2015; Caldeira and Gibson 1992). The issue before us is whether superannuated judges diminish support for courts.

Is the public more or less supportive of younger or older judges? It could well be that judge age does not matter to people. After all, many people may *expect* judges to be at least a little gray. Some people have made the argument (sometimes jokingly, but with effect) that a judge needs "wrinkles to show experience [and] gray hair to show wisdom" (Gray 2013). When people conjure an image in their minds about judges, they tend to think of older people. As one study put it, "[t]he default figure of a judge is . . . wise and fatherly" (Bandes 2007, 627). Judge Wapner in *The People's Court* is, perhaps, an archetype. But others exist as well. The judges in *My Cousin Vinny*, *Anatomy of a Murder*, *Judgment at Nuremberg*, and *A Civil Action* were all somewhat old and may have represented commonly held views of judges. These popular media presentations likely reflect what most people envision when they think of judges. As such, the public may be fine with older judges.

Yet, polling suggests the opposite is true. An April 2021 poll showed that 63% of respondents supported an age limit for judges.[2] An October 2018 poll, which asked similar questions, found that 78% of the public supported age limits.[3] A November 2004 survey found that roughly 60% of people wanted an age limit for judges, with respondents over 65 among those *most likely* to favor mandatory retirement.[4] These polls are similar to other recent polls about older people in public service more broadly. One such poll found that only 12% of the public believed that having more older people in elected office would be a good thing for the country—and 42% thought it would make things worse. The same poll showed that 73% of the

[2] https://tinyurl.com/ipsosReformPoll.

[3] https://fixthecourt.com/wp-content/uploads/2018/10/October-2018-TL-poll-results.pdf.

[4] https://www.nbcnews.com/id/wbna6602068.

public believes that there should be an age limit for elected officials.[5] A February 2024 poll found that 86% of people believed President Biden was too old to serve a second term.[6] These data suggest that the public may in fact find an aging judiciary discomfiting.

Although the surveys in the previous paragraph do not explain *why* respondents appear to favor institutional reform, it may be that people think judicial performance declines with age. As we have mentioned throughout this book, judging depends heavily on cognitive capacity. Judges must read thousands of pages, understand the material, and apply the principles they learned. They must deduce how the cases before them interact with precedent and statutes. These functions requires considerable cognitive exertion. And the effectiveness of key cognitive domains declines with age (e.g., Drag and Bieliauskas 2010; Harada, Love, and Triebel 2013; Powell 1994; Salthouse et al. 1989; Salthouse 1991). Most people who have lived with aging family members or friends have witnessed such age-related changes, particularly among the extremely old. There is reason to suspect, then, that people may wince over a graying judiciary and welcome institutional reform.

10.2 Empirical Expectations and Survey Experiment

Court reformers sometimes argue that the public is less supportive of aged courts than they are of younger courts (Calabresi and Lindgren 2006). That position, in turn, reflects common perceptions of the elderly. As one study put it, "negative perceptions towards older people and ageing [*sic*] tend to predominate in modern societies . . . older people are more often perceived as having poor physical and mental health, unattractive, [and] forgettable" (Bai 2014, 232). On television, older people often are portrayed as forgetful, rigid, or incompetent (Davis and Davis 1985; but see Miller et al. 2004). "In general, people hold more negative attitudes towards older adults" than younger adults (Kite et al. 2005, cited in Bai 2014). When creating an "Image of Aging Scale," Levy, Kasl, and Gill (2004) sent over 750 people, aged 70 years or older, a survey which asked: "when you think of an old person, what are the first five words or phrases that come to mind?" Roughly 60% of the response words were negative; a mere 17% were positive. If the argument is correct, respondents exposed to an old judge's decision (compared to a young judge's decision) will:

- exhibit lower support for that decision and judicial authority (e.g., the proposition that the court's decision should be the final word on the matter);
- express more negative views of the judge (i.e., confidence, trust in decision-making fairness, the belief that the judge follows the Constitution, perceptions of conscientiousness);
- confer less legitimacy toward the judiciary as a whole; and
- exhibit greater support for institutional reforms targeted at the judiciary (i.e., an 18-year term limit and a mandatory retirement age).

[5] https://www.cbsnews.com/news/elected-officials-maximum-age-limits-opinion-poll-2022-09-08/.
[6] https://www.npr.org/2023/05/23/1177617666/more-than-6-in-10-say-bidens-mental-fitness-to-be-president-is-a-concern-poll-fi.

What is more, we might expect that a *picture* of the judge's face or an *explicit suggestion* that he has suffered from a loss of mental acuity will exacerbate these effects. Hummert et al. (1994) found that young, middle-aged, and older adults all associated photos of older people with negative stereotypes. Seeing a picture of an old judge might enhance underlying skepticisms. Similarly, we expect that respondents who are told that an older judge shows signs of cognitive decline may be more inclined to question the soundness of the judge's decision. All this we address with a survey experiment.

We examine the public's views on aging judges by designing and implementing a novel survey experiment. We presented respondents with a vignette of a hypothetical affirmative action decision and investigated how exposure to written and visual cues about a judge's age influenced support for the judge's decision, support for institutional reforms, and the institutional authority of federal courts. We chose to treat respondents with an affirmative action decision because it offered a policy context that was prominent in political discourse at the time. It also was an issue about whose outcome respondents likely had preferences. We recognize that one tradeoff of this choice is that the results may not generalize to other policy contexts, especially those that are less politically salient.

We implemented our survey experiment in late December 2022 using Lucid Theorem, which "fills surveys with nationally representative audiences."[7] Though a convenience sample, Lucid improves upon earlier platforms like Amazon's Mechanical Turk by using respondent quotas to achieve a census-balanced sample. Lucid samples provide demographic and experimental results that track well with U.S. national benchmarks (Coppock and McClellan 2019) and are increasingly common in experimental studies like ours (see, e.g., Black et al. 2023). A total of 1,005 respondents completed our survey.[8]

Our experimental design features a number of key elements. First, we manipulated whether the respondent agreed or disagreed with the court's decision. We did so by asking respondents (prior to their exposure to the treatments), "How much of a factor should an applicant's race or ethnicity be when a college or university decides whether to admit the applicant as a student?" Response options were: not a factor, minor factor, or major factor.

[7] https://lucidtheorem.com/faq.

[8] We included one attention check question before a respondent was assigned to an experimental condition and one comprehension check question after exposure to the experimental materials. Failure to answer either question correctly resulted in the termination of the survey for that respondent. A total of 2,478 respondents began the survey; 1,192 successfully passed the initial attention check question (i.e., roughly 48%). This means that around 84% passed the post-treatment question (1,005/1,192). There is no significant relationship between the condition to which a respondent was randomly assigned and whether he or she correctly answered the post-treatment attention question ($p = 0.26$). There are systematic patterns with respect to who failed the initial attention check question, however. In particular, we find an increased likelihood of failure among respondents who are young, female, non-white, less educated, and less wealthy. Political independents were more likely to fail than either Republicans or Democrats, but there was no differences between Republicans and Democrats.

Figure 10.1 Vignette Photographs for Courtroom (left), Old Judge (middle), and Young Judge (right) Conditions. The young judge photo was de-aged using neural filters in Adobe Photoshop. The image for the old judge comes from Minear and Park (2004) and is the "JWmale85neutral" image. The bench image comes from the Wisconsin Supreme Court.

We did so because a person's desire to "win" a policy victory may condition how he or she responds to the judge's age. Just as "winning" can moot a person's concerns over procedural unfairness (Armaly 2021), benefitting from an aged judge's decision could dull the abstract desire—if one exists—for younger judges. Respondents who agree with the decision may overlook the judge's age or cognitive condition. And those who disagree with the decision may show greater sensitivity to age-related concerns.[9] In other words, sensitivity to aged judges might be lowest among respondents who agree with the decision and greatest among those who disagree with it. We must—and we do—account for that possibility.

Second, we manipulated the age and cognitive capacity of our fictional judge, whom we named "William Tyler." Respondents observed one of three conditions. In the first two conditions, we told respondents that "During oral argument in the case, [59-year-old/79-year-old] Judge William Tyler asked several straightforward questions that showed his familiarity with the case." Respondents in the third condition were told "During oral argument in the case, 79-year-old Judge William Tyler asked several awkward questions that raised concerns about his mental health." We added this additional element only to the 79-year-old judge condition. We based the example on press reports about an aging Justice Thurgood Marshall when he showed cognitive decline (Garrow 2000).

Third, we manipulated whether the respondents saw a picture of the judge in front of a courtroom or just the courtroom itself. Importantly, as Figure 10.1 shows, we used the same judge image for both pictures. We began with an image of a 79-year-old man for the 79-year-old judge, and then used Adobe Photoshop's "neural filters" option to make the judge look 59.

All told, then, our experiment was a 2 × 3 × 2 design. After exposure to one vignette (see the chapter's appendix for examples of these complete vignettes), we asked respondents to answer several questions. Focusing on their attitudes toward the

[9] Indeed, scholarship on court support and judicial legitimacy suggests that people's views toward courts and judges are shaped, in large part, on their agreement with judicial decisions (Christenson and Glick 2019). People who believe the Supreme Court is ideologically close to it support it more than those who believe the Court is ideologically distant from them (Bartels and Johnston 2013; Christenson and Glick 2015).

decision, we asked respondents: "Do you agree or disagree with the court's decision?" They could respond that they: strongly (dis)agreed, somewhat (dis)agreed, or neither disagreed nor agreed, which we refer to as a 5-point agreement scale.

We next asked respondents four questions that focused on their attitudes toward Judge Tyler. First, we asked respondents: "How much confidence do you have in the ability of Judge William Tyler to do his job?" Response options were: no confidence at all, not much confidence, some confidence, or complete confidence. Second, we asked: "Do you agree or disagree that Judge William Tyler follows the Constitution when making decisions?" (5-point agreement scale); third, we asked: "Do you agree or disagree that Judge William Tyler can be trusted to set aside his personal interests and judge fairly?" (5-point agreement scale). Fourth, we asked: "Do you agree or disagree that Judge William Tyler behaves responsibly, is organized and hard-working, and follows norms and rules in his job as a judge?" (5-point agreement scale).

We also asked two questions that tapped into respondents' views of the court's authority in the American political system and compliance with the decision (Bartels and Johnston 2020). One question asked: "How much authority do you think this court's decision should have over colleges, universities, and the American people?" Respondents could answer: complete authority, some authority, not much authority, and no authority at all. The second question asked: "Do you believe that the court's ruling should be accepted as the final word on this issue?" The available answer options on the 5-point response scale were: Definitely No (Yes), Probably No (Yes), and Not Sure.

Additionally, we measured the change in the level of legitimacy—comparing pre-treatment versus post-treatment survey responses—that respondents ascribed to the federal courts using the battery of items commonly employed in previous research (see, e.g., Gibson and Nelson 2015). We estimated a latent trait score from a graded response model using seven items (asked both before and after the treatment vignette), each followed by a five-point response scale: strongly agree, agree, neither agree nor disagree, disagree, strongly disagree. Given that our object of interest was the federal courts in general—as opposed to the Supreme Court specifically—we modified the items accordingly. The specific statements we presented to our respondents were as follows:

- It is inevitable that federal courts get mixed up in politics; therefore, we ought to have stronger means of controlling the actions of those courts.
- The federal courts ought to be made less independent so that they listen a lot more to what the people want.
- Judges on the federal courts who consistently make decisions at odds with what a majority of the people want should be removed from their position as judges.
- Federal judges are just like any other politicians; we cannot trust them to decide court cases in a way that is in the best interests of our country.
- If the federal courts started making a lot of decisions that most people disagree with, it might be better to do away with those courts altogether.
- The federal courts get too mixed up in politics.
- The right of the federal courts to decide certain types of controversial issues should be reduced.

Our final response items asked respondents to indicate (both pre-treatment and post-treatment) their level of support for an 18-year term limit and a 75-year old mandatory retirement age. The term limit question read:

> Once federal judges take office, the Constitution allows them to serve for the rest of their lives. This means they have no term limit or mandatory retirement age. Recently, Congress has suggested creating an 18-year term limit for federal judges. This means that when a judge has served on the bench for 18 years, he or she would have to retire and allow a new judge to be selected. Do you support or oppose this proposal?

The retirement age question then read:

> What about a proposal to establish a mandatory retirement age of 75 years old for federal judges? This means that when a judge turns 75 years old, he or she would have to retire and allow for a new judge to be selected.

The survey responses took on one of five options: strongly oppose (favor), somewhat oppose (favor), and neither favor nor oppose.

Aside from the key survey vignette and response items, we asked a series of questions at the beginning of the survey i.e., prior to exposure to treatment to account for attributes that might affect respondents' level of support for institutional reform. First, to help establish that our sample is a good representation of the American public, we asked a general presidential approval question, modeled after the traditional Gallup survey item: "Do you approve or disapprove of the way Joe Biden is handling his job as president?" Respondents could: approve, disapprove, or express no opinion.

We also accounted for the likelihood that the respondent's perceived ideological compatibility with the case outcome may affect his or her responses (e.g., Bartels and Johnston 2013). In particular, those who hold views that are closer to their perception of the Supreme Court's ideological orientation may be less likely to support institutional reform. We asked respondents the following two questions, attached numerical values to each answer, and then determined the absolute value of the distance between the two: "In politics today, would you describe your views as..." and "Thinking about the United States Supreme Court in Washington and the decisions it has been making lately, would you say that the Supreme Court is...." The response choices for both of these questions were very liberal, liberal, moderate, conservative, or very conservative.

Likewise, we measured respondents' trust in government. We asked: "Generally speaking, how much do you trust the federal government as a whole to operate in the best interests of the American people?" Respondents could reply with the following answers: a great deal, a fair amount, not too much, and none at all.

To account for the possibility that knowledge of the courts might influence how people perceive them, we assessed respondents' knowledge of the federal judiciary. We also asked three multiple choice questions (correct answers appear in bold):

1. "How are federal judges put in their jobs?"
   - Appointed by the House Judiciary Committee
   - Authorized by the American Bar Association
   - Elected by the people
   - **Nominated by the President and confirmed by the Senate**
   - None of the above
2. "Which level of courts in the federal judiciary conducts trials?"
   - **District Courts**
   - Court of Appeals
   - Court of Inquiry
   - Supreme Court
   - None of the above
3. "How long are federal judges allowed to serve in their jobs?"
   - Two years
   - Six years
   - Ten years
   - Fifteen years
   - **None of the above**

Following the general approach of Gibson and Nelson (2015), we also accounted for respondents' perceptions of the rule of law. We implemented the following battery of statements, asking respondents to indicate their agreement (disagreement) on a 5-point agreement scale. The rule-of-law items included:

- Sometimes it might be better to ignore the law and solve problems immediately rather than wait for a legal solution.
- The government should have some ability to bend the law in order to solve pressing social and political problems.
- When it comes right down to it, the law is not all that important; what's important is that our government solve society's problems and make us all better off.

Lastly, we utilized several standard demographic responses that Lucid always collects from survey respondents. These included questions on respondents' age, sex, race, education, income, and partisan identification.

10.3 Methods and Results

We employ five dependent variables: *Case Attitudes*, *Judge Attitudes*, *Legitimacy Attitudes*, *Retirement Age Support*, and *Term Limits Support*. We rescale each variable to range from 0 to 1, where 0 indicates minimum support and 1 represents maximum support. Using these dependent variables, we estimate a series of fractional logistic regression models.[10]

[10] See the chapter's appendix for a table with parameter estimates for these models.

Case Attitudes is a latent trait score that we estimated from a graded response model using the three items reflecting a respondent's attitudes toward the case result, as described in the vignette text to which they were assigned. These questions measured respondents' agreement with the case outcome, the amount of authority they believe the decision should have, and the extent to which they think the decision should be the final word on the issue.

Judge Attitudes is a latent trait score that we estimated from a graded response model using the four items tapping into a respondent's attitudes toward Judge Tyler. These questions measured respondents' confidence in Tyler's ability to do his job, their belief that Tyler follows the Constitution, their trust in Tyler's ability to be fair, and their (dis)agreement with the claim that Tyler behaves in a conscientious manner.

Legitimacy Attitudes measures the difference, for each respondent, in their pre-treatment and post-treatment legitimacy attitudes. Each of these come from separate graded response models that we estimated using responses to the battery of seven legitimacy items identified earlier (e.g., "it is inevitable that federal courts get mixed up in politics. . . .").

Retirement Age Support measures the difference between each respondent's pre-treatment and post-treatment support for a 75-year-old mandatory retirement age proposal.

Term Limits Support measures the difference between each respondent's pre-treatment and post-treatment support for an 18-year judicial term limit.

Our key covariates of interest are categorical variables for each of our three experimental manipulations—judge age, photo content, and policy winner status—as well as the interaction among those terms.[11] We also include a litany of control variables for each of our models, including each survey respondent's age, sex, race, education, income, rule-of-law attitudes, court knowledge, and perceived ideological distance from the Supreme Court.

10.3.1 Judge Age Results

We first tested the argument that people are less supportive of older judges.[12] Figure 10.2 provides mixed findings but, overall, shows only some support for the idea that the public recoils at aged judges. Consider respondents' views at the case level. We asked them about their agreement with the case outcome, the amount of authority they believe the decision should have, and the extent to which they think the judge's decision should be the final word on the issue. There is no significant difference

[11] Recall that our pre-treatment measure of support for affirmative action in higher education allowed for three values—not a factor, minor factor, and major factor—whereas the case outcome vignette was simply dichotomous—allowed or prohibited. We had intended to generate a three-level winner status variable to allow for nuance among those different categories. As only 5% of our sample opted for the major factor response, however, we had insufficient variation in our data to implement this approach.

[12] As noted above, we asked each of our respondents—prior to exposure to treatment—whether they approved, disapproved, or had no opinion of the way Joe Biden is handling his job as president. Our survey respondents report 46% approval, 48% disapprove, and 7% have no opinion. FiveThirtyEight estimated President Biden's approval to be 43% and his disapproval to be 51% during the time when our data were being collected (December 23–31, 2022). Our sample, then, appears to be a bit more supportive of Biden than the population, but not excessively so.

in views between respondents exposed to a 59-year-old judge and respondents exposed to a 79-year-old judge. On the other hand, there is a significant difference ($p = 0.06$) in views between respondents exposed to a 59-year-old judge (0.52) and respondents exposed to a 79-year-old judge with cognitive concerns (0.49)—though the substantive magnitude of this difference is modest. Interestingly, the results reveal no significant difference ($p = 0.19$) between respondents who observed a healthy 79-year-old judge and those who observed a 79-year-old judge with cognitive concerns. Perhaps these limited results exist because our treatment was so subtle. Rather than simply noting that the judge asked several awkward questions that raised concerns about his mental health, we could have made a larger and more bombastic issue of those cognitive concerns. Such an approach may have produced stronger results.

Moving on to judge attributes, we see clearer results. Recall that judge attributes touch on respondents' confidence in the judge's ability to do his job, their belief that the judge follows the Constitution, their trust in the judge's ability to be fair, and their (dis)agreement with the claim that the judge behaves in a conscientious manner. Once again, we observe no significant difference in views between respondents exposed to a 59-year-old judge and those exposed to a healthy 79-year-old judge ($p = 0.73$). Yet, when exposed to the 79-year-old judge who displayed cognitive concerns, the results shifted markedly. Respondents were significantly less supportive ($p = 0.00$) of the 79-year-old judge who displayed cognitive concerns (0.48) than the 59-year-old judge (0.58) and the healthy 79-year-old judge (0.58). These results, in particular, portend at least some trouble for an aging judiciary. If judges display clear signs of cognitive decline, people will hold less confidence in the judges' abilities to do their jobs. For an institution that relies on public acceptance of its authority, such an outcome would be devastating.

Looking, next, at legitimacy attitudes, we see muted effects. There is a statistically significant ($p = 0.05$), though slight, difference in views between respondents exposed to a 59-year-old judge versus those exposed to a healthy 79-year-old judge. Those exposed to a 59-year-old judge had a score of 0.60 while those exposed to a healthy 79-year-old judge had a score of 0.59. And there also is a statistically significant, slight difference ($p = 0.02$) in views between respondents exposed to a 59-year-old judge (0.60) and those exposed to a 79-year-old judge with cognitive concerns (0.58). Again, there were no significant differences between respondents who observed a healthy 79-year-old judge and those who observed a 79-year-old judge with cognitive concerns.

Somewhat surprisingly, respondents did not meaningfully change their support for a retirement age or mandatory term limit after any of the judge-age vignettes. Support for a retirement age hovers around 0.50 regardless of judge age condition. Similarly, support for term limits runs between a low of 0.501 for those exposed to the 79-year-old judge with cognitive concerns to a high of 0.514 for those exposed to a 59-year-old judge, but this difference is not statistically significant ($p = 0.23$).

Taken together, these results indicate mild changes after respondents read a vignette about a 79-year-old judge with cognitive concerns, but not much else.[13]

[13] One possible explanation for these muted results is that respondents failed to perceive our manipulation of the judge's age within our vignettes. However, results from our experiment suggest this is not the case. Individuals assigned to the young judge recalled him being significantly younger than those assigned to either of the 79-year-old judge conditions. See the chapter's appendix for additional details and discussion.

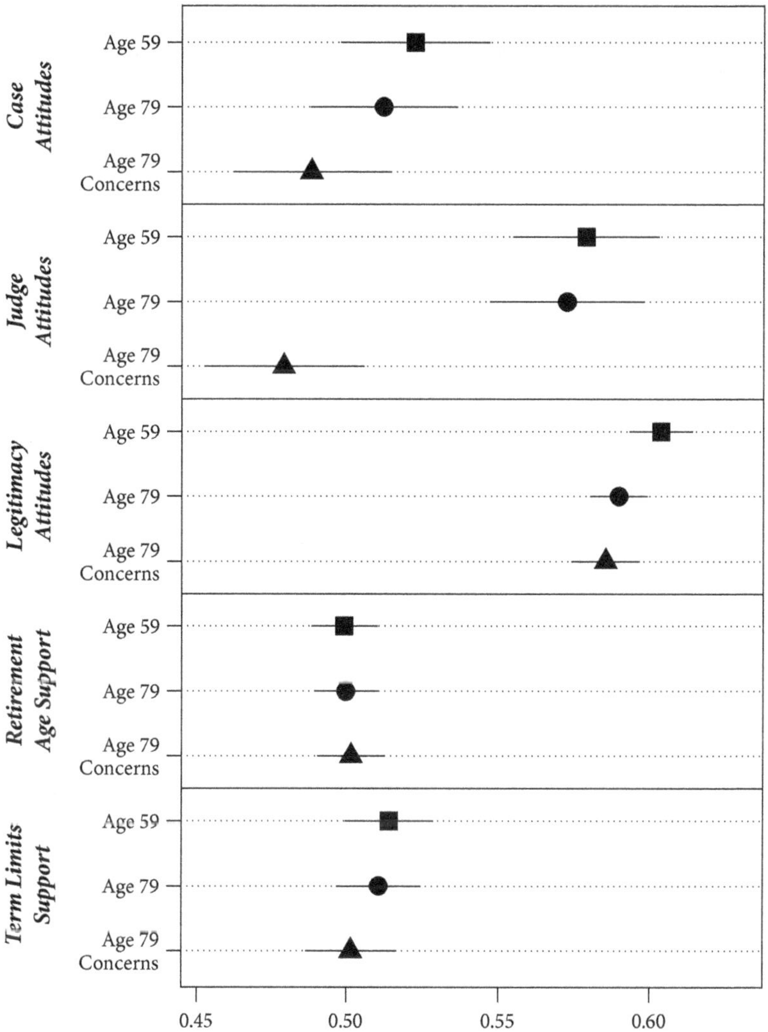

Figure 10.2 Average treatment effects of judge age on attitudes toward the judiciary. Estimates represent the average predicted support (with 95% confidence intervals) for each treatment condition of the judge's age (59, 79, or 79 while expressing cognitive concerns).

Respondents held slightly more negative views at the case level when they read about the 79-year-old judge with cognitive concerns (versus a 59-year-old). Views of the judge were 10 points more negative when reading about a 79-year-old judge with cognitive concerns than when reading about a 59-year-old judge. And, views of judicial legitimacy decreased only slightly when people read about a 79-year-old judge with cognitive concerns (versus a 59-year-old). Of course, while these results are somewhat modest, we remind the reader that our treatment was modest as well. Perhaps had we explained Judge Pauline Newman's alleged behavior (as described in the book's introduction) or something similar, the results may have been more marked. Indeed, the fact that we retrieved any results with a subtle treatment suggests to us that there is much more here that can be studied.

10.3.2 Photographic Accentuation Results

We next examine the importance of visual cues to respondents when they saw pictures. Figure 10.3 plots the average treatment effects for the six unique configurations of our judge age and photo content treatments and does so for each of the five dependent variables we examined. There are two ways a reader can work through these results. One way is to hold the age of the judge constant and examine whether the images matter. Applying that approach to Figure 10.3, one would identify a specific *shape*—square, circle, or triangle—and then compare the white version of that point with the solid black version of that point.

Another way is to hold a specific type of photographic treatment constant and examine whether there are significant differences when moving from the 59-year-old judge to the 79-year-old judge to the 79-year-old judge with mental health concerns. Applying that approach to Figure 10.3, one would focus on the *color* (either the hollow white or solid black shapes) and then analyze changes across age. There's quite a bit to consider here, so we had better get started.

Case Attitudes. We start with the case attitudes. Holding constant the age of the judge to which a respondent was assigned, we find no significant evidence that observing a picture of that judge significantly changes respondents' case attitudes relative to when they see a photo of a courtroom bench alone. That is, support for the case outcome is not appreciably higher for respondents in the 59-year-old judge photo condition (black square) versus the 59-year-old bench photo condition (white square). The same is true for the 79-year-old judge condition (the black and white circles are not appreciably different) and the 79-year-old cognitive concerns judge condition (the black and white triangles are not appreciably different).

We now hold the images constant and examine age effects. Consider respondents who saw a photo of the bench (the white shapes). Although there is a gradual decrease as one moves from the white square (59-year-old, bench image) to the white circle (79-year-old, bench image) to the white triangle (79-year-old with cognitive concerns), none of these three pairwise differences are statistically significant.

The story is slightly different when respondents saw a photo of the judge. There is no significant difference between the 59-year-old judge (black square) and 79-year-old judge (black circle) ($p = 0.59$). There is, though, some evidence of a difference ($p = 0.11$) between the 59-year-old judge (black square = 0.53) and the 79-year-old judge with cognitive concerns (black triangle = 0.49). There is no significant difference ($p = 0.29$) between the 79-year-old judge (black circle) and the 79-year-old judge with cognitive concerns (black triangle).

Judge Attitudes. Moving down the plot, we next consider respondents' judge attitudes. Once again, we begin by holding constant the age of the judge to which a respondent was assigned and asking whether images matter. Consider the 59-year-old judge. Observing a picture of that judge significantly changed

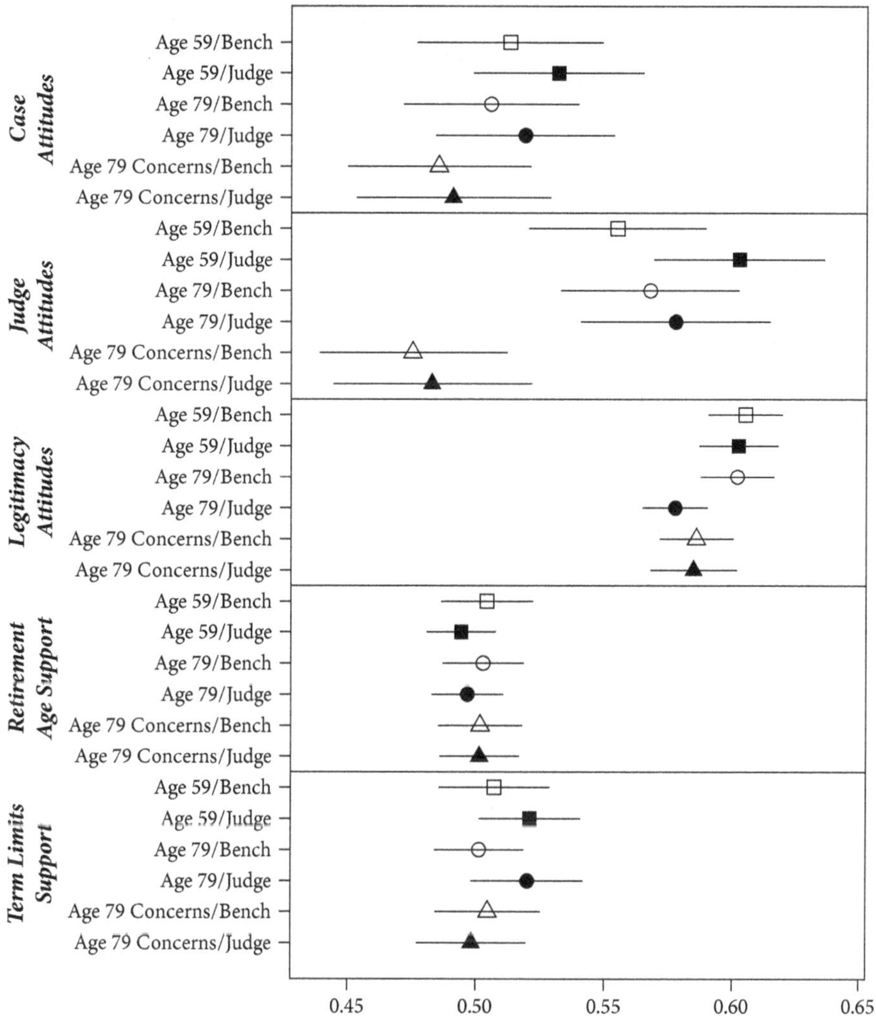

Figure 10.3 Average treatment effects of judge age and visual cues on attitudes toward the judiciary. Estimates represent the average predicted support (with 95% confidence intervals) for each treatment combination of the judge's age (59, 79, or 79 while expressing cognitive concerns) and visual cue (headshot picture of the judge or a generic courtroom "bench").

respondents' case attitudes relative to when they saw a photo of a courtroom bench alone. Respondents who saw a generic courtroom bench photo had an average support score of 0.55. But those who saw a photo of the 59-year-old judge revealed a support score of 0.60 ($p = 0.05$). For the 79-year-old judge, the difference in a bench image versus a human image was not significant ($p = 0.69$); neither was the difference in scores for the 79-year-old judge with cognitive concerns ($p = 0.78$).

Seeing an image of the judge versus the bench only mattered when examining young judges, where a judge picture boosted support.

Now hold the images constant and examine age effects. Consider respondents who saw a photo of the bench (the white shapes). Respondents continue to show no difference in support for a judge when comparing a 59-year-old judge with a 79-year-old judge ($p = 0.61$). But they showed significant differences in judge support when comparing a 59-year-old judge with the 79-year-old judge with cognitive concerns. They also showed significant differences when comparing the 79-year-old judge with the 79-year-old judge with cognitive concerns.

The story is roughly the same when respondents saw a photo of the judge. Respondents revealed no difference in support for a judge when comparing a 59-year-old judge with a 79-year-old judge ($p = 0.33$). But they revealed significant differences when comparing both the 59-year-old judge and the 79-year-old judge to the 79-year-old judge with cognitive concerns. Respondents showed a score of 0.60 for a 59-year-old judge but a favorability score of 0.48 for a 79-year-old judge with cognitive concerns. This 0.12 difference is strong evidence of an aged judge effect. It appears that respondents, when viewing an image of judges, were concerned with the cognitively declining judge.

Legitimacy Attitudes. The middle panel of Figure 10.3 plots the differences in respondent's pre-treatment and post-treatment legitimacy scores. Respondents exposed to the 59-year-old reacted no differently to a picture of the bench (white square) versus a picture of the judge (black square). Among those assigned to the healthy 79-year-old judge, respondents who saw merely the bench itself reported slightly higher legitimacy scores (0.60) relative to those who saw a photo of the judge (0.58). Respondents exposed to the 79-year-old judge with cognitive concerns reacted no differently to a picture of the bench than to a picture of the judge. The image did not matter much.

We next evaluate the effect of age while holding the photo content constant. We begin again with respondents who saw images of the bench. Respondents reported slightly higher legitimacy attitudes when the judge was 59-years-old versus 79-years-old with cognitive concerns. The difference between the two judges is 0.019 ($p = 0.06$). We also find a slight legitimacy disadvantage for the 79-year-old judge with cognitive concerns relative to his healthy 79-year-old counterpart. The difference is 0.016 with a p-value of 0.12. There were no differences between the 59-year-old judge and the healthy 79-year-old judge ($p = 0.76$).

Similar results obtain when we examine photos of the judge. Again, respondents reported slightly higher (0.018, $p = 0.14$) legitimacy attitudes when the judge was 59-years-old versus 79-years-old with cognitive concerns. There are no differences between the healthy 79-year-old judge and the 79-year-old judge with cognitive concerns ($p = 0.50$). Respondents who saw a photo of the 79-year-old healthy judge showed significantly lower legitimacy attitudes relative to the 59-year-old judge ($p = 0.01$).

Retirement Age Support. No treatments revealed any significant differences in support for a mandatory retirement age. Seeing a photo of the judge versus the courtroom bench had no significant difference for any of the three judge ages. The p-values for the photo differences (bench versus judge) are 0.38 (59-year-old), 0.56

(79-year-old), and 0.98 (79-year-old with cognitive concerns). Similarly, there were no significant changes across judge age when holding the bench photo constant. The p-values for the age differences in the courtroom bench condition are: 0.90 (59-years-old versus 79-years-old), 0.83 (79-years-old with cognitive concerns versus 59-years-old), and 0.92 (79-years-old with cognitive concerns versus 79-years-old). Nor were there any effects across age while holding the judge photo constant. The p-values for the judge photo condition are: 0.80 (59-years-old versus 79-years-old), 0.49 (79-years-old with cognitive concerns versus 59-years-old), and 0.65 (79-years-old with cognitive concerns versus 79-years-old).

Term Limits Support. As with the retirement age results, we fail to find any noteworthy evidence of a within-judge photo content effect for any of the three judge treatments. Respondents reported no different support for term limits when they saw a 59-year-old judge versus a bench photo. The same is true of those who saw a 79-year-old judge or a 79-year-old with cognitive concerns. The bench versus judge photo distinction was no distinction at all.

Holding the courtroom photo constant reveals no differences across judge age. (The white shapes are not different from each other.) But holding the judge photo constant reveals minor differences. Respondents who saw the 79-year-old with cognitive concerns displayed lower levels of support for term limits than respondents who saw either the 59-year-old judge ($p = 0.01$) or the 79-year-old judge ($p = 0.16$). This result runs counter to what we would expect to find, but is consistent with the earlier finding in Figure 10.2, which showed a slight (yet insignificant) decrease in support for term limits among those in the 79-year-old with cognitive concerns condition.[14]

10.3.3 Policy Agreement Results

Finally, we examine whether winning influences respondents' evaluations. Again, we define "winning" as whether a respondent was predisposed to agree with the case outcome. Here, we examine the effect of winning within a specific value of judge age, and also the effect of judge age while holding constant whether someone was a policy winner versus a policy loser. Figure 10.4 provides the results.

Case Attitudes. We begin by holding age constant and examining the effects of winning versus losing. Winning clearly influences case attitudes. The black solid points in the top panel of Figure 10.4 are greater than their white hollow counterparts. These differences range from a low of 0.15 for a 79-year-old judge with cognitive concerns to a high of 0.19 for a 59-year-old judge. For every judge age and cognitive condition, winning generated more favorable outcomes than losing.

Potentially more interesting, however, are comparison within the policy loser treatments. Losing respondents reported that exposure to a policy defeat was equally troubling regardless of the judge. The average case support was 0.431 for a

[14] There is mixed evidence that the photographs caused respondents to take greater notice of the judge's age. Among respondents assigned to a 79-year-old judge, seeing a photograph of him resulted in a significantly higher assessment of his age relative to those saw the courtroom bench. We found no similar difference among those assigned to the 59-year-old judge ($p = 0.56$).

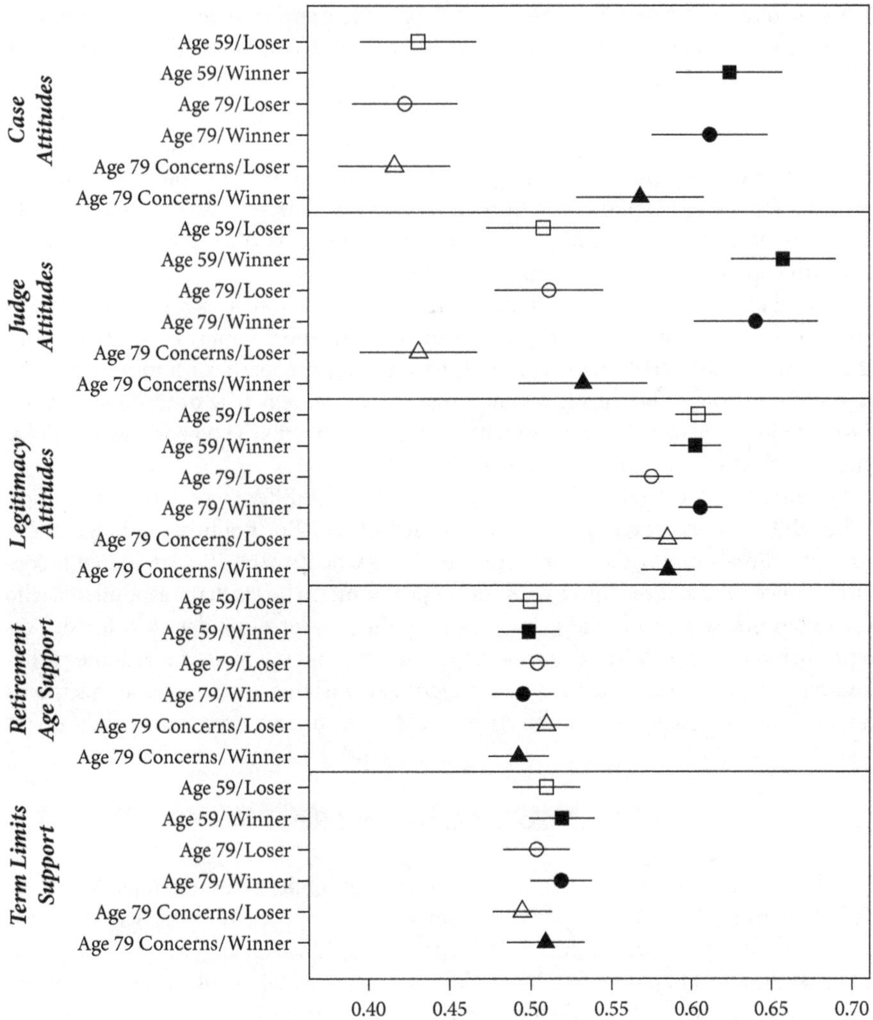

Figure 10.4 Average treatment effects of judge age and policy winners on attitudes toward the judiciary. Estimates represent the average predicted support (with 95% confidence intervals) for each treatment combination of the judge's age (59, 79, or 79 while expressing cognitive concerns) and policy winners/losers (whether the respondent was predisposed to agree with the decision).

59-year-old judge's opinion, 0.423 for a 79-year-old judge's opinion, and 0.416 for an opinion by a 79-year-old judge with cognitive concerns. None of these pairwise differences are statistically significant. The p-values for the age differences in the policy loser condition are: 0.73 (59-year-old versus 79-year-old), 0.56 (79-year-old judge with cognitive concerns versus 59-year-old), and 0.79 (79-year-old judge with cognitive concerns versus 79-year-old).

Surprisingly, however, the data reveal that not all policy wins are created equal. Winning respondents who observed a 59-year-old judge had an average case support value of 0.62. Winners assigned to a 79-year-old judge had an average value of 0.61. And, winners who observed a 79-year-old judge with cognitive concerns had an average score of 0.57. The difference between the 59-year-old judge and the healthy 79-year-old judge is not statistically significant. But, the difference between the 79-year-old judge with cognitive concerns and the 59-year-old judge is statistically significant ($p = 0.03$). So too is the difference between the 79-year-old judge with cognitive concerns and the healthy 79-year-old judge ($p = 0.11$). This result runs contrary to what we – and the literature – would expect and potentially hints at limitations to the "baggage" a policy winner might be willing to accept as a condition of this victory.

Judge Attitudes. Holding judge age constant, we find once again that for all three judge treatments, respondents assigned to the policy winner condition had significantly more positive attitudes toward the judge than respondents assigned to the policy loser condition. That's perhaps not a surprise.

We find some differences when looking at the effect of judge age while holding constant whether a respondent was a policy loser or winner. Unlike before, however, these differences exist for both policy outcomes. Consider policy losers. Losing respondents who observed a 59-year-old judge had average judge attitude score of 0.508. Losing respondents who observed a 79-year-old judge averaged a score of 0.511. And, losing respondents who observed the 79-year-old judge with cognitive concerns averaged a score of 0.431. Although the difference between the 59-year-old judge and the healthy 79-year-old judge was not statistically significant, the difference between the 79-year-old judge with cognitive concerns and the other two judges is significantly less.

Now consider policy winners. Judge attitudes toward the 59-year-old judge, the healthy 79-year-old judge, and the 79-year-old judge with cognitive concerns were 0.658, 0.641, and 0.533, respectively. And, just as with the policy loser treatment, the 79-year-old judge with cognitive concerns was significantly less than either the 59-year-old judge or the healthy 79-year-old judge. There was no significant difference, however, between the 59-year-old judge and the healthy 79-year-old judge ($p = 0.51$). In short, although being a policy winner enhanced a respondent's view of the judge (as did a judge's age on its own), there were no meaningful interactions between winner status and our age manipulations.

Legitimacy Attitudes. Moving to the middle panel of the figure, we notice a pronounced narrowing in the gaps among our plotted points. Whereas receiving a favorable policy outcome produced significant differences in how a respondent felt about both the case and the judge in that case, we see much less evidence when we instead ask about more enduring attitudes toward the judiciary as a whole. In that sense, our results accord with work by Gibson and others who argue that diffuse support for the U.S. Supreme Court is not substantially tied directly to case outcomes (Gibson and Nelson 2015; Gibson and Caldeira 2011; Gibson, Caldeira, and Spence 2003).

Holding age constant, we search for the effects of winning versus losing. We find a single significant within-judge difference for our 79-year-old judge. Respondents who observed the 79-year-old judge displayed average legitimacy attitudes of 0.605 when they won but 0.575 when they lost ($p = 0.001$). No equivalent differences exist for either the 59-year-old judge ($p = 0.86$) or the 79-year-old judge with cognitive concerns ($p = 0.99$).

Holding losing status constant reveals similarly muddled effects. Among losing respondents, legitimacy attitudes averaged 0.604 when the loss was handed to them by a 59-year-old judge, 0.575 when delivered by a 79-year-old judge, and 0.585 when from a 79-year-old judge with cognitive concerns. The difference between the 59-year-old judge and the 79-year-old judge is significant ($p = 0.003$) as is the difference between the 59-year-old judge and the 79-year-old judge with cognitive concerns ($p = 0.07$). The difference between the 79-year-old judge and the 79-year-old judge with cognitive concerns is not ($p = 0.33$).

Holding winning status constant reveals that among winning respondents, there is no significant difference between the 79-year-old judge and the 59-year-old judge ($p = 0.77$). There is a slight difference between the 79-year-old judge with cognitive concerns and the 59-year-old judge ($p = 0.14$). And there is a significant difference between the 79-year-old judge and the 79-year-old judge with cognitive concerns ($p = 0.06$), with the judge with cognitive concerns triggering lower scores.

Retirement Age Support. Adding the policy winner dimension to the mix does little to clarify our results concerning support for a mandatory retirement age. Holding age constant, we see that winners are no more or less likely than losers to support a mandatory retirement age when the judge in the case was 59-years-old ($p = 0.92$) or a healthy 79-years-old ($p = 0.42$). Winning may have mattered to respondents who observed a 79-year-old judge with cognitive concerns, however ($p = 0.14$). We fail to find any significant or suggestively significant differences when assessing the differential impact of judge age while holding constant policy winner or policy loser status.

Term Limits Support. In terms of support for term limits, we (again) find no significant differences here. Winning versus loses yields no significant change while holding constant the age of the judge who rendered the decision. Similarly, when focusing on individual in the same policy winner (or loser) condition, movement within that category from one judge age to another reveals no significant differences.

Our discussion to this point has focused on our treatments. Our models also included a host of demographic and substantive controls. In general, these variables perform mostly as expected. In the interest of efficiency, we limit ourselves to summarize noteworthy results (see the chapter appendix for a table of results and, more usefully, figures for each control).

Independents score slightly lower than Republicans and Democrats in Case Attitudes and Judge Attitudes. Respondents aged 30 score lower (0.53) than respondents age 64 (0.56) on Judge Attitudes. They are also more supportive (0.51) than respondents age 64 (0.49) of a retirement age. Respondents with a high school degree or less scored lower (0.58) on judicial legitimacy than respondents with a graduate degree (0.60). Female respondents scored lower (0.59) on judicial legitimacy than males (0.60). Non-white respondents had a higher legitimacy score (0.60) than white respondents (0.58). People who scored higher on the rule of law questions had a slightly larger legitimacy score (0.60) than those who scored lower on the rule of law questions (0.59). Ideological distance between the respondent and Supreme Court mattered as well. Respondents who perceived themselves as highly distant from the Court scored 0.42 on the Case Attitude measure while those who perceived themselves as ideologically close to the Court scored a value of 0.56. The results were similar for the Judge Attitude measure, with ideologically distant respondents scoring 0.46 and close respondents scoring 0.60. Somewhat surprisingly, ideologically distant respondents were slightly less supportive (0.48) of a retirement age than ideologically close respondents (0.51).

10.4 Conclusion

Some have suggested that as federal judges become older, the public's support for courts may decrease. But there has been little empirical work on the effects of judge aging on court support. This chapter examined whether court support changes as a function of judge age and perceived cognitive capacity. The results were mixed. The only result that approached consistency was the finding that cognitive concerns dampens support for judges. But the results were limited.

More work needs to be done on this topic. For starters, we showed respondents only one case. It could be that respondents exposed iteratively to older judges—and especially, older cognitively diminished judges—might react differently. What is more, it is unclear whether other cases might generate different results. At least in the affirmative action context, aging does not seem to matter much. But perhaps in technically complex cases (e.g., digital privacy) we would find something else. And, of course, we should note again that our treatments were fairly modest in nature. We noted simply that an aging judge displayed some cognitive concerns. Had we pushed age-related decline harder, we may have observed more stronger results.

Surprisingly, neither age nor cognitive impairment moved the dial much in terms of support for term limits or a retirement age. This suggests that reform advocates might have a harder time supporting such reforms by focusing on age *per se* and an easier time supporting reforms by focusing on things like accountability or representation. We certainly take no position on the merit of such reforms but can see how groups might make their arguments. And that takes us to our next chapter.

10.5 Appendix

10.5.1 Experimental Materials

Figure 10.5 provides two sample vignettes used in the survey experiment. The left panel displays the vignette with a young judge in a case where affirmative action was permitted by the judge. The right panel displays the vignette expressing mental health concerns about an old judge in a case where affirmative action was ruled unconstitutional by the judge.

A federal court recently ruled that the U.S. Constitution allows the use of affirmative action in higher education admissions. When deciding whether to admit new students, colleges and universities had been considering the applicants' race in efforts to enhance student-body diversity. During oral argument in the case, 59-year-old Judge William Tyler (pictured above) asked several straightforward questions that showed his familiarity with the case. Later, writing for the court, Judge Tyler concluded that the use of race in this context satisfies the Constitution's guarantee of equal treatment under law. Such practices, his opinion said, "are completely consistent with the 14th Amendment and our constitutional history."

A federal court recently ruled that the U.S. Constitution prohibits the use of affirmative action in higher education admissions. When deciding whether to admit new students, colleges and universities had been considering the applicants' race in efforts to enhance student-body diversity. During oral argument in the case, 79-year-old Judge William Tyler (pictured above) asked several awkward questions that raised concerns about his mental health. Later, writing for the court, Judge Tyler concluded that the use of race in this context violates the Constitution's guarantee of equal treatment under law. Such practices, his opinion said, "are completely inconsistent with the 14th Amendment and our constitutional history."

Figure 10.5 Experimental vignettes for young judge in affirmative action allowed (left) and old judge with mental health concerns in affirmative action not allowed (right) conditions.

10.5.2 Model Parameter Estimates

Table 10.1 reports the full parameter estimates of the fractional logistic regression models and results that we discuss in the chapter's main text. The five dependent variables (all ranging from 0 to 1) include: *Case Attitudes*, *Judge Attitudes*, *Legitimacy Attitudes*, *Retirement Age Support*, and *Term Limits Support*.

10.5.3 Judge Age Manipulation Checks

The final question on our survey for all respondents asked them to provide the approximate age of the judge in the case from five multiple-choice options: 40 years old, 50 years old, 60 years old, 70 years old, and 80 years old. We put the question at the very end of the survey—as opposed to immediately after the vignette—since we specifically told respondents how old the judge was. We thus captured, to the fullest extent possible, whether a respondent remembered a key aspect of our experimental manipulation.

Analyzing these responses as continuous, the average response for those assigned to the 59-year-old judge was 61.2 years old. The analogous values for the 79-year-old judge and the 79-year-old judge with concerns were 70.4 and 71.8 years old, respectively. All three of these pairwise differences are statistically significant.

Keeping the responses as they were naturally coded does not change our conclusion that the manipulation was successful. A plurality of respondents—46%—assigned to the 59-year-old judge said he was 60 years old. 31% said he was 70 years old and 18% said he was 50 years old. Only 3% each said he was very young (i.e., 40) or very old (i.e., 80). For the 79-year-old judge, 58% said he was 70, 25% said he was 80, and 14% said he was 60. Only 2% said he was 50 and less than 1% said he was 40 years old. The analogous percentages for the 79-year-old judge with concerns are 52% said 70, 37% said 80, 5% said 60, 2% said 50, and 3% said 40.

Table 10.1 Parameter Estimates for Fractional Logistic Regression Model

	Case Attitudes	Judge Attitudes	Legitimacy Attitudes	Retirement Age Support	Term Limits Support
Old Judge	0.06	0.12	−0.06	0.01	0.03
	(0.09)	(0.09)	(0.04)	(0.03)	(0.05)
Old Judge Concerns	−0.05	−0.13	−0.05	0.02	0.02
	(0.09)	(0.09)	(0.03)	(0.03)	(0.05)
Policy Winner	0.51**	0.38**	−0.01	−0.00	0.09*
	(0.09)	(0.09)	(0.04)	(0.05)	(0.06)
Old Judge × Policy Winner	−0.17	−0.18	0.11**	−0.03	−0.10
	(0.13)	(0.13)	(0.05)	(0.06)	(0.07)
Old Judge Concerns × Policy Winner	−0.04	−0.15	0.01	−0.06	−0.06
	(0.13)	(0.13)	(0.05)	(0.06)	(0.08)
Photo of Judge	0.07	0.12	−0.01	−0.02	0.10*
	(0.09)	(0.09)	(0.04)	(0.03)	(0.05)
Old Judge × Photo of Judge	−0.16	−0.22*	−0.03	0.00	−0.10
	(0.12)	(0.12)	(0.05)	(0.04)	(0.07)
Old Judge Concerns × Photo of Judge	0.03	−0.12	0.01	0.01	−0.12*
	(0.13)	(0.13)	(0.05)	(0.05)	(0.07)
Policy Winner × Photo of Judge	−0.04	0.01	0.00	−0.00	−0.14*
	(0.13)	(0.13)	(0.06)	(0.06)	(0.08)
Old Judge × Policy Winner × Photo of Judge	0.32*	0.26	−0.05	0.02	0.24**
	(0.18)	(0.19)	(0.07)	(0.08)	(0.10)
Old Judge Concerns × Policy Winner × Photo of Judge	−0.14	0.03	−0.00	0.03	0.14
	(0.19)	(0.19)	(0.08)	(0.08)	(0.11)
Respondent Independent	−0.12**	−0.14**	0.00	−0.02	0.02
	(0.05)	(0.06)	(0.02)	(0.02)	(0.03)
Respondent Republican	−0.04	−0.02	0.00	0.01	−0.02
	(0.05)	(0.05)	(0.02)	(0.02)	(0.03)
Age of Respondent	0.00	0.00**	0.00	−0.00*	−0.00
	(0.00)	(0.00)	(0.00)	(0.00)	(0.00)
Female Respondent	−0.03	−0.04	0.03*	−0.00	−0.02
	(0.04)	(0.04)	(0.02)	(0.02)	(0.02)
Non-White Respondent	0.06	0.07	−0.04**	−0.02	−0.03
	(0.05)	(0.05)	(0.02)	(0.02)	(0.03)
Education Level of Respondent	−0.01	0.01	0.01*	−0.00	−0.01
	(0.02)	(0.02)	(0.01)	(0.01)	(0.01)
Income Level of Respondent	−0.02	−0.02	−0.01	−0.01	−0.00
	(0.02)	(0.02)	(0.01)	(0.01)	(0.01)
Support for Rule of Law Score	0.01	−0.01	−0.02*	0.00	−0.01
	(0.03)	(0.03)	(0.01)	(0.01)	(0.02)
Knowledge Score	0.02	0.02	0.01	0.02	−0.01
	(0.03)	(0.03)	(0.01)	(0.01)	(0.02)
Ideological Distance from Supreme Court	−0.09**	−0.09**	0.00	−0.02**	0.00
	(0.02)	(0.02)	(0.01)	(0.01)	(0.01)
Constant	−0.03	0.05	0.25**	0.12**	0.07
	(0.11)	(0.11)	(0.04)	(0.05)	(0.06)
N	982	982	982	967	969

Note: Table entries are fractional logistic regression coefficients with standard errors in parentheses. ** $p<0.05$ and * $p<0.10$ (two-tailed). See chapter text for details about the measurement of these dependent variables. The number of observations is below the 1,005 who completed the survey and is different across some of the models due to missing values in responses.

10.5.4 Control Variable Results

The following figures present the results for the predicted impacts of the control variables: party identification (Figure 10.6); age (Figure 10.7); education (Figure 10.8); sex (Figure 10.9); ideological distance (Figure 10.10); income (Figure 10.11); knowledge (Figure 10.12); race (Figure 10.13); and rule-of-law perceptions (Figure 10.14).

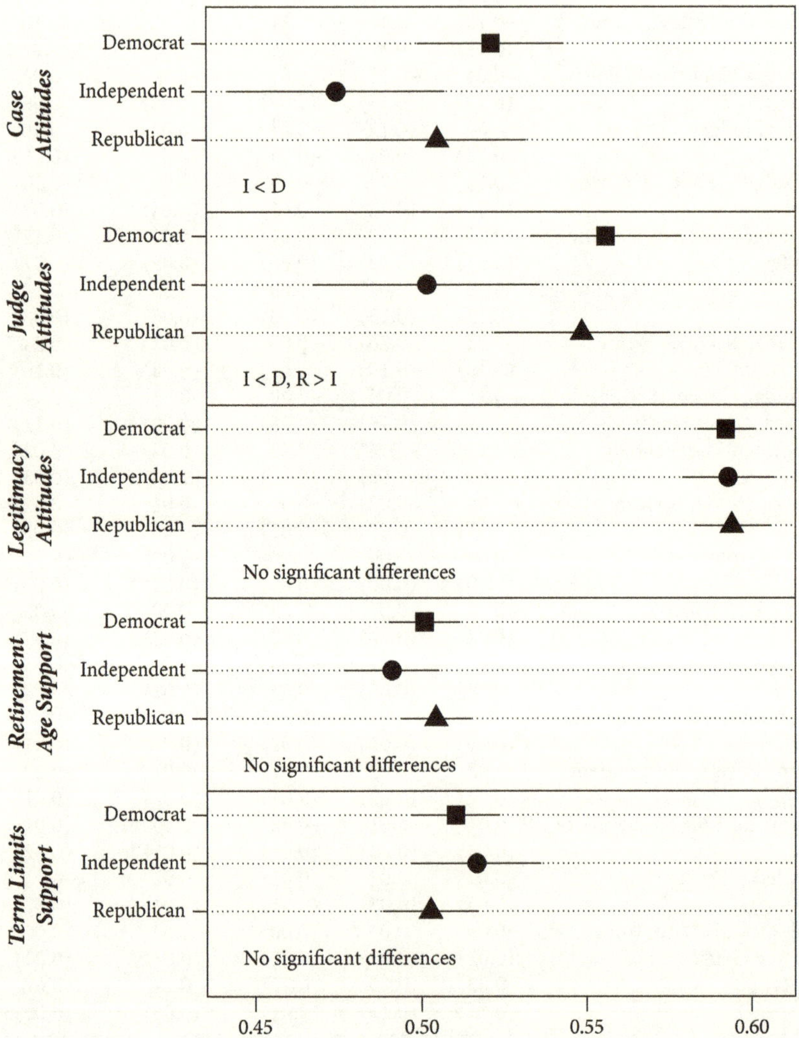

Figure 10.6 Average treatment effects of party identification on attitudes toward the judiciary. Annotations within the various panels of the plot identify pairwise differences that are statistically significant ($p < 0.10$); I = Independent, D = Democrat, and R = Republican.

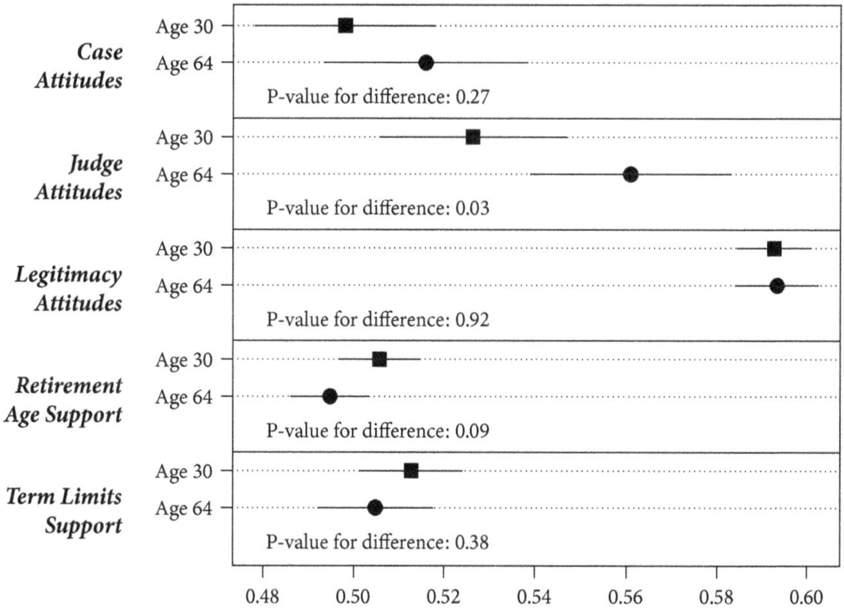

Figure 10.7 Average treatment effects of age on attitudes toward the judiciary.

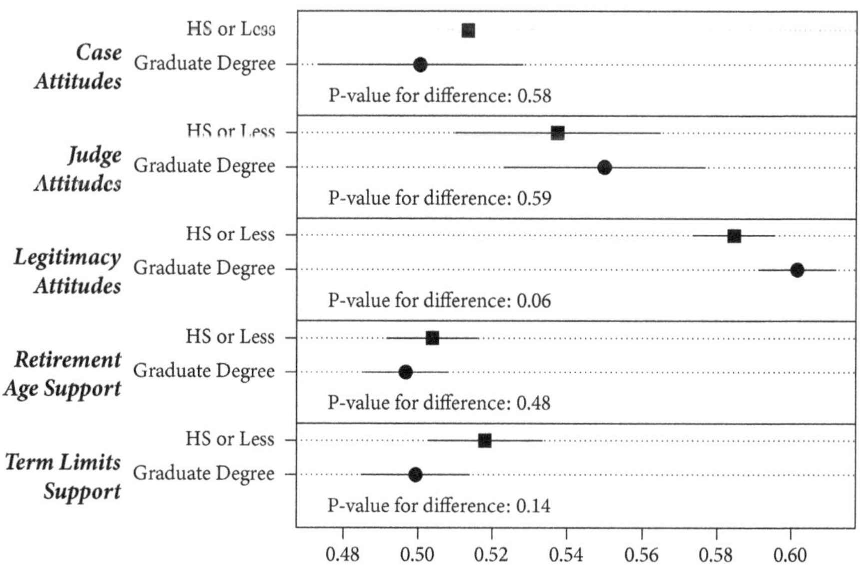

Figure 10.8 Average treatment effects of education on attitudes toward the judiciary.

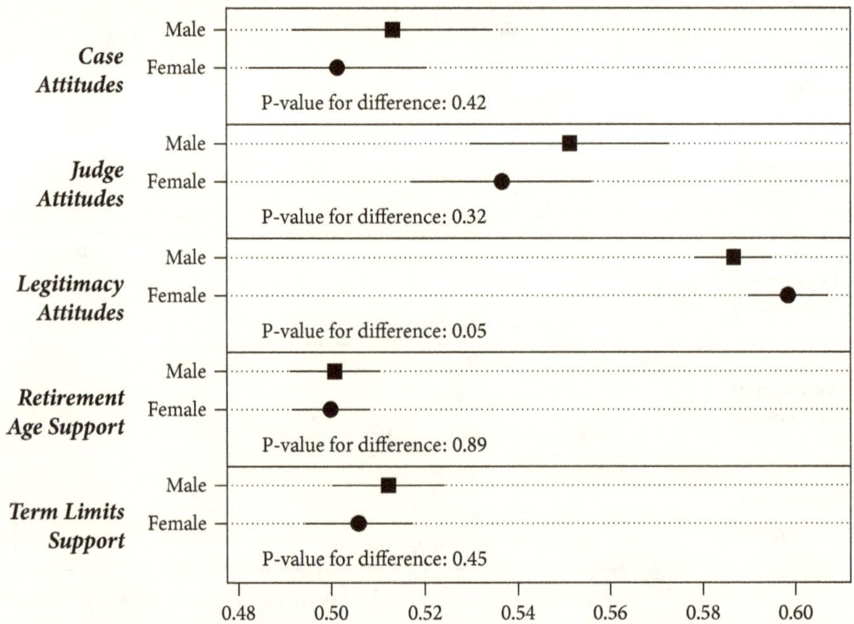

Figure 10.9 Average treatment effects of sex on attitudes toward the judiciary.

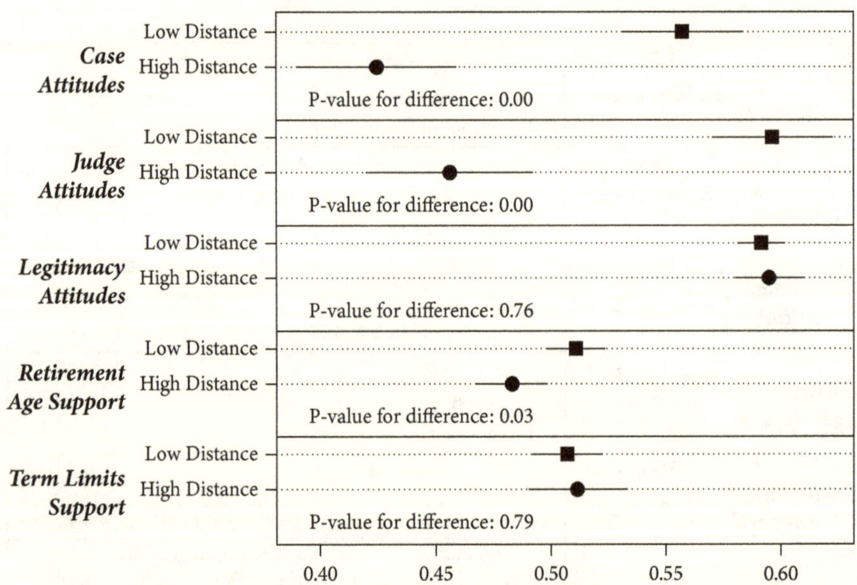

Figure 10.10 Average treatment effects of ideological distance from the court on attitudes toward the judiciary.

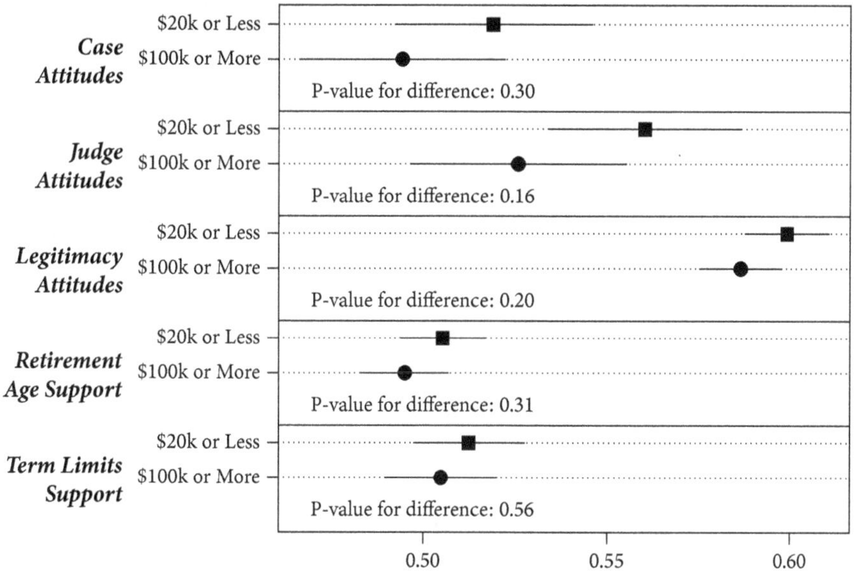

Figure 10.11 Average treatment effects of income on attitudes toward the judiciary.

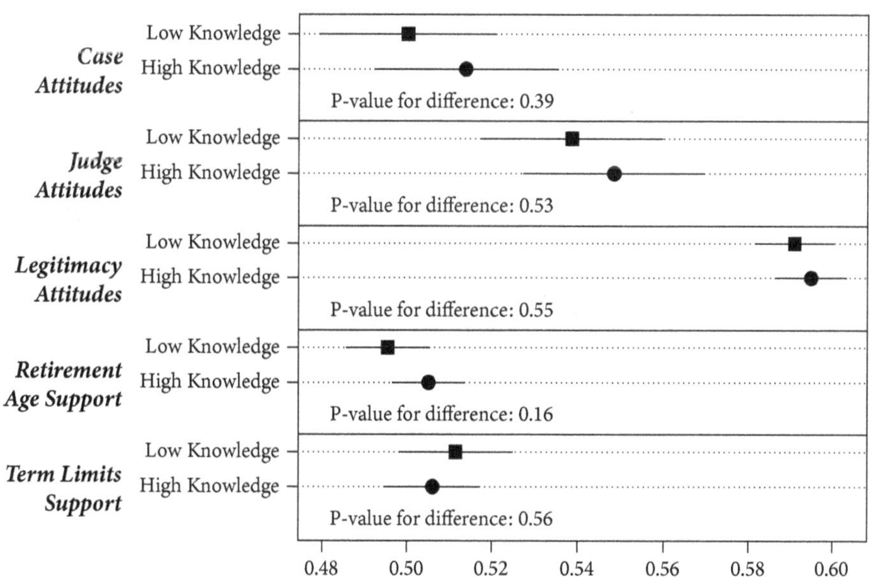

Figure 10.12 Average treatment effects of knowledge on attitudes toward the judiciary.

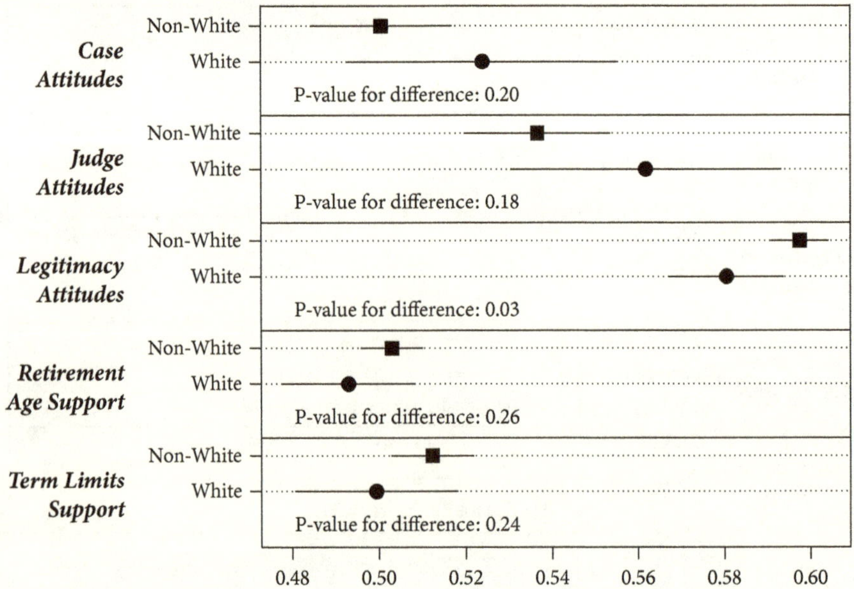

Figure 10.13 Average treatment effects of race on attitudes toward the judiciary.

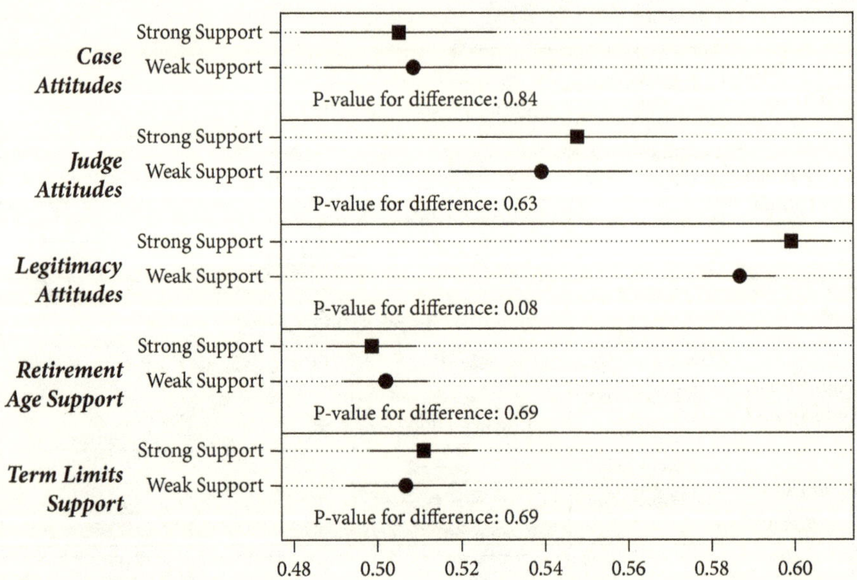

Figure 10.14 Average treatment effects of views on the rule of law on attitudes toward the judiciary.

11
Public Support for Judicial Reforms

On August 2, 2022, Senator Sheldon Whitehouse (D-CT) and four Senate Democrats introduced a bill to end lifetime tenure for Supreme Court justices. While it is easy to believe the bill was nothing but a partisan temper tantrum—politicians sometimes challenge courts that decide cases in ways they dislike—the truth is that people across the ideological spectrum increasingly have called for significant modifications to the federal judiciary. Senator Ron Johnson (R-WI) indicated he is open to revising lifetime tenure. So too have Senators John Kennedy (R-LA), Marco Rubio (R-FL), and Ted Cruz (R-TX).[1] The general concept of structural judicial reform appears to enjoy bipartisan support.

As we mentioned in the previous chapter, two particular reforms have picked up steam: a mandatory retirement age and a term limit for federal judges. To read the polls, one might believe Americans strongly support such reforms. But the polls have serious weaknesses in terms of their real world validity. They tend not to present respondents with the major arguments for and against the reforms. Those arguments surely would reach people under real world conditions. Nor do polling questions generally explain who, politically, introduced the reforms. Under our polarized polity, Democrats may reject Republican-backed reforms; Republicans may deny Democratic-backed reforms. Just as important, the polls tend not to discuss any of the accompanying costs associated with pursuing a reform. They fail to gauge the intensity of people's support for those reforms. In short, despite the massive consequences and normative issues surrounding judicial reforms, we know alarmingly little about the public's views on them.

In this chapter, we employ a unique design that tests people's support for reforms based on the proposers' identity, the costs they would be willing to bear to achieve the reforms, and a series of supporting or opposing arguments related to the reforms. The results show that Democrats and those who perceive the Supreme Court to be ideologically distant from them are most enthusiastic for these changes. Surprisingly, though, even a majority of Republicans appear willing to support these reforms. People are most supportive when co-partisans propose reforms, but majorities support them even when proposed by opposite partisans. Having said that, when we inform respondents of the costs associated with pursuing these reforms, support dampens significantly. The overall support for term limits and mandatory retirement may not be as strong as the initial indicators suggest. In terms of the rhetoric for and against the reforms, claims that the reforms would remove mentally unfit judges and bring the courts closer to public opinion appear to be most persuasive.

[1] See https://fixthecourt.com/2022/08/senatorsonscotustermlimits/.

Cognitive Aging and the Federal Circuit Courts: How Senescence Influences the Law and Judges.
Ryan C. Black, Ryan J. Owens, Patrick C. Wohlfarth, Oxford University Press. DOI: 10.1093/oso/9780197747025.003.0011

11.1 The Survey Experiment

We seek to investigate who supports age and term limits and whether their support changes when exposed to arguments for, and against, those reforms.[2] We fielded our survey experiment in late August 2022 and obtained 1,143 respondents.[3] As in our previous chapter, we used Lucid Theorem, which "fills surveys with nationally representative audiences."[4] Our experimental design features three key elements. First, we manipulated two reforms as experimental treatments—a mandatory retirement age and an 18-year term limit—and randomly assigned respondents to one of these two conditions. We chose to use these reforms because they are two of the most prominent proposals that appear in political discourse today.[5] The manipulation of two different reform proposals allows us to consider whether respondents' support for reform is more malleable when confronted by one particular reform versus another.

Second, for each of the two reform conditions, we randomly assigned respondents to one of three partisan frames that identified who initiated the proposed reform: a Republican coalition in Congress, a Democratic coalition in Congress, or a bipartisan coalition. Thus, there are six total reform conditions:

- Retirement Age proposed by a bipartisan coalition;
- Retirement Age proposed by Democrats;
- Retirement Age proposed by Republicans;
- Term Limit proposed by a bipartisan coalition;
- Term Limit proposed by Democrats; and
- Term Limit proposed by Republicans.

Randomly varying the partisan frame in this manner allows us to account for the possibility that a respondent may be more likely to support reform when his or her political preference matches that of the coalition proposing it. After we exposed respondents to one of these six (randomized) partisan reform conditions, we measured—on a 7-point scale—their support for the particular reform. Specifically, the survey asked:

[2] We pre-registered our survey experiment with the "AsPredicted" platform at the University of Pennsylvania's Wharton Credibility Lab (see *Mandatory Retirement Age and Term Limits*, registration #105578).

[3] We included one attention check question before a respondent was assigned to an experimental condition and one comprehension check question after exposure to the experimental materials. Failure to correctly answer either question resulted in the termination of the survey for that respondent. A total of 2,707 respondents began the survey; 1,441 of them successfully passed the initial attention check question (i.e., roughly 53%). Approximately 82% of the remaining individuals correctly answered the post-treatment comprehension check question. Failure rates were higher for respondents assigned to the term limits reform (22%) relative to the retirement age reform (13%), but there are no significant differences in failure rate among the reform proposer partisanship ($p = 0.38$). There are systematic differences with respect to who failed the initial attention check question. In particular, we find an increased likelihood of failure among respondents who are young, male, non-white, less educated, and less wealthy. Republicans were least likely to fail (0.34 probability), followed by Democrats (0.50 probability), and then Independents, who were the most likely (0.56 probability).

[4] https://lucidtheorem.com/faq.

[5] See, e.g., https://www.reuters.com/legal/government/prominent-us-appeals-court-judge-calls-supreme-court-term-limits-intriguing-2022-08-25/

> Once federal judges take office, the Constitution allows them to serve for the rest of their lives. This means they have no term limit or mandatory retirement age. Recently, [Republican Leaders/Democratic Leaders/A bipartisan group of both Republican and Democratic leaders] in Congress proposed [the mandatory retirement age of 75/creating a term limit of 18 years] for federal judges. Do you favor or oppose this proposal?

Respondents could answer that they strongly opposed the reform, opposed it, somewhat opposed it, neither favored nor opposed it, somewhat favored it, favored it, or strongly favored it.

Among respondents who expressed either support for or indifference to the reform, we then assessed the intensity of their attitudes. Following the support versus opposition question, we highlighted the fact that it would require a constitutional amendment to achieve the reforms, which would take time and resources. Our goal, of course, was to determine whether these expected costs dampened their enthusiasm. We asked:

> Establishing [a mandatory retirement age/an 18-year term limit] might require changing the U.S. Constitution. This process would be politically time consuming and could make it harder for elected officials to address other issues. How important is it to you that the United States government implement [a mandatory retirement age/an 18-year term limit] for federal judges?

Respondents could answer that they thought the proposal was not at all important, slightly important, somewhat important, very important, or extremely important.

The third element of the experiment sought to assess how arguments for and against the particular reforms influenced respondents' support. We included three arguments for each reform and three arguments against each reform. That is, each respondent received nine total questions (presented in random order) with a different configuration of a single argument for, and a single argument against, the reform (the order in which the arguments appeared was also randomized for each of the nine questions). Table 11.1 shows these six arguments.

After respondents received each of the nine supporting versus opposing argument pairings, we asked them to evaluate which side they believed had the stronger argument. Specifically, we asked: "Which of these two arguments do you think is stronger, the supporters' argument or the opponents' argument?" Respondents could reply on a 5-point scale: much stronger (weaker), somewhat stronger (weaker), or about the same. After respondents observed the battery of nine argument pairings, we repeated the two questions that asked them to indicate their level of support for the particular reform proposal and the intensity with which they held that attitude (as noted above).

In addition, we asked respondents a series of questions at the beginning of the survey to account for attributes that might generally affect their support for reform. We asked respondents to report their age. Given the connection between aging judges and arguments for institutional reform, older and younger respondents may have

Table 11.1 Supporting and Opposing Arguments Manipulated in the Survey Experiment

Mandatory Retirement Age Arguments	
Supporting	**Opposing**
Remove mentally unfit judges who might otherwise continue to decide cases.	Remove experienced judges from important jobs.
Open up seats to new judges more often, which will bring the federal judiciary closer to the beliefs and ideas of people today.	Remove mentally capable judges who can still do their jobs.
Reduce backlogs and speed up the judicial process because younger judges write judicial opinions more quickly than older judges.	Open up seats to new judges more often, which would increase political conflict in the judicial appointment process.

Term Limits Arguments	
Supporting	**Opposing**
Reduce political conflict over judicial appointments because openings would be predictable and balanced across presidents over time.	Remove capable judges who can still do their jobs.
Open up seats to new judges more often, which would bring the federal judiciary closer to the beliefs and ideas of people today.	Make it more likely that judges would decide cases in a biased manner because they have to worry about getting their next job.
Reduce political influence in a judge's decision when to retire.	Increase turnover among judges, which might create more instability in the law.

Note: Respondents were exposed to each of the nine unique pairwise combinations of the supporting and opposing arguments. The order in which those nine combinations was presented was randomized, as was whether the supporting or opposing argument was presented first within each pairing.

different views. Next, to help establish that our sample is a good representation of the American public, we asked a general presidential approval question, modeled after the traditional Gallup survey item. We asked: "Do you approve or disapprove of the way Joe Biden is handling his job as president?" Respondents could answer saying: approve, disapprove, or no opinion.

Next, we accounted for the likelihood that perceived ideological compatibility with the Supreme Court may affect a respondent's attitudes toward reform (e.g., Bartels and Johnston 2013). Those who hold views that are closer to their perception of the Court's ideological orientation may be less likely to support reform. We first asked respondents to characterize their own views as being very liberal, liberal, moderate, conservative, or very conservative.[6] We then asked them to make the same ideological characterization about the Supreme Court.[7] To generate our ideological distance

[6] The specific question wording was: "In politics today, would you describe your views as . . . ."

[7] The full text of this question was "Thinking about the United States Supreme Court in Washington and the decisions it has been making lately, would you say that the Supreme Court is . . . ."

measure, we attached numerical values to these two questions' values, and then determined the absolute value of the difference between them.

Following Gibson and Nelson (2015), we accounted for respondents' support for the rule of law. People who express greater support for the rule of law may be less likely to support these reforms. We implemented the following battery of statements, asking respondents to indicate their agreement (disagreement) on a 5-point agreement scale. We then estimated a graded item response model to generate a *Support for Rule of Law Score*, which we use in the models presented in the pages ahead. The rule-of-law items were:

- It is not necessary to obey a law you consider unjust;
- Sometimes it might be better to ignore the law and solve problems immediately rather than wait for a legal solution;
- The government should have some ability to bend the law in order to solve pressing social and political problems;
- It is not necessary to obey the laws of a government I did not vote for; and
- When it comes right down to it, the law is not all that important; what's important is that our government solve society's problems and make us all better off.

Next, we assessed respondents' knowledge of the federal judiciary because support for institutional reform may be different among those with less or greater knowledge of it. We assessed respondents' knowledge of the federal judiciary by asking three multiple choice questions, which we then used as inputs to estimate an item response model to generate a *Knowledge Score*, which we use in the models that follow (answers in bold are correct):[8]

- How long are federal judges allowed to serve in their jobs?
  –Two years
  –Six years
  –Ten years
  –**None of the above**
- About how old is the average federal judge today?
  –40 years old
  –50 years old
  –60 years old
  –**70 years old**
  –80 years old

[8] We note, with the benefit of hindsight, that the average judge age question is probably not a great indicator of the latent quantity of interest—i.e., how much basic knowledge an individual has about the judiciary. Since our ultimate use of it is through a measurement model—as opposed to an additive index—if the question has not especially useful empirical properties (i.e., it poorly discriminates among those with high versus low knowledge), then the model will capture that in a way that the more basic additive approach cannot (Badas 2019).

- How are federal judges put in their jobs?
  –Appointed by the House Judiciary Committee
  –Authorized by the American Bar Association
  –Elected by the people
  –Nominated by the President and confirmed by the Senate
  –None of the above

Lastly, we utilized several standard demographic responses that Lucid collects from survey respondents. These included questions on sex, race, education, income, and partisan identification.

11.2 Methods and Results

Before we present the results, we confirm that our sample fairly represents the American public. Gallup fielded a poll on President Biden's approval on September 1, 2022, which is just two days after we launched our survey experiment (i.e., August 30). Their sample shows 56% disapproved of Biden, 42% approved, and 2% had no opinion.[9] Our sample was similar: 56% disapproved, 37% approved, and 7% had no opinion.

11.2.1 Partisan Cues and Initial Support for Reform

We begin by presenting simple plots derived from cross-tabulations in Figure 11.1. Each plot corresponds to one of the six experimental states of the world to which we assigned a respondent. That is, the results examine a combination of a particular reform (retirement age versus term limits) and who proposed the reform (Bipartisan Group, Democratic leaders, or Republican leaders). Within each plot, we show how the respondents viewed each proposal. The top row of the figure focuses on the retirement age proposal. The bottom row focuses on the term limit proposal. The leftmost column represents a bipartisan proposal. The middle column represents a Democratic proposal. And, the rightmost column represents a Republican proposal.

The first and most obvious result is that a significant proportion of respondents appear to support these major structural reforms to the Court (more on this below). At least a majority of respondents appeared to support both reforms. This suggests, at least at first glance, that much of the soil has been tilled for reform. To be sure, the degree of support changes based on who supports the proposal, but there is considerable support for both reforms, with retirement age receiving slightly more support than term limits. Overall, Republican respondents tend to be less supportive than Democrats, as they likely see these proposals as efforts to challenge a jurisprudentially conservative federal judiciary. In some conditions, independents are even more skeptical of proposals than Republicans. But overall, there is more support than we anticipated.

[9] The Gallup poll was in the field from September 1–16. Ours was active August 30–September 2. https://news.gallup.com/poll/329384/presidential-approval-ratings-joe-biden.aspx.

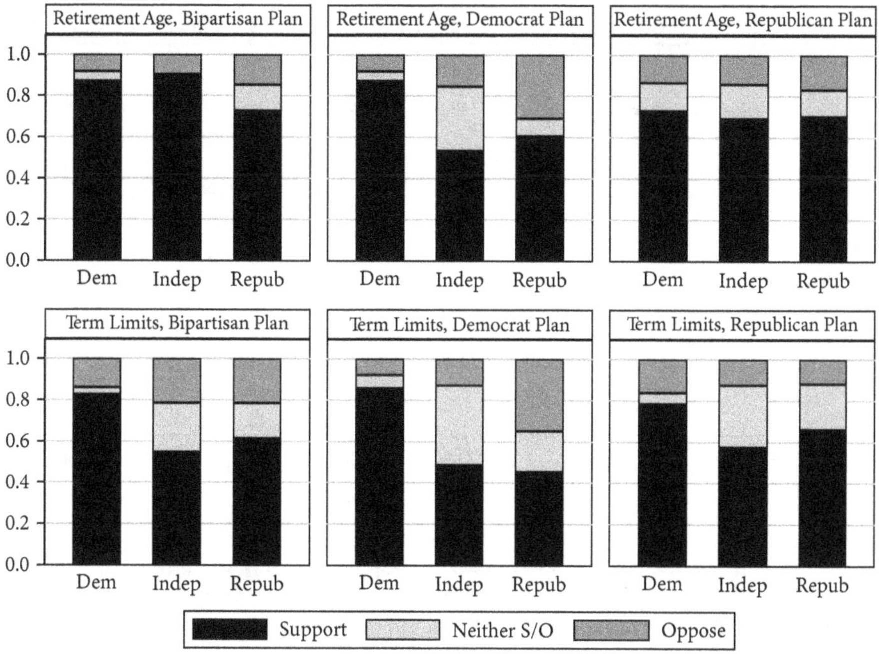

Figure 11.1 Initial Support for Reform by Reform Identity, Proposer of the Reform, and Partisan Identification of the Respondent. The six panel titles correspond to a combination of a specific reform—mandatory retirement age or term limits—and the identity of the congressional leaders who proposed it (Bipartisan Plan, Democrat Plan, or Republican Plan). Within each plot, we show the respondent's partisan identification along the x-axis—Dem(ocrat), Indep(endent), or Repub(lican).

To dig deeper into the results, we modeled them statistically. Our dependent variable measures each respondent's *Support For The Reform*. Though the responses fall on a 7-point scale, ranging from strongly oppose to strongly favor the proposal, we employ a three-category dependent variable: oppose in some form, neither support nor oppose, or support in some form. We take this approach as our initial substantive interest here is in simply understanding the determinants of basic support, opposition, or indifference among our respondents.[10] Our main interest is a three-way categorical interaction that includes *Respondent Partisanship* (Democrat, Independent, Republican), *Proposer Identity* (Democrat, Bipartisan, Republican) and *Reform Type* (Age Limit, Term Limit). We also control for demographics (age, sex, race, education, income) as well as support for the rule of law, knowledge about the federal judiciary, and perceived ideological distance from the Supreme Court.[11]

[10] We measured it on the finer-grained scale because it allows us to incorporate that potentially important variation in some of the additional analyses that follow below (e.g., assessing the importance of implementing the reform in a world of policy trade-offs). See Black, Owens, and Wohlfarth (2023) for an analysis of the term limits respondents that utilizes the finer-grain measure.

[11] Table 11.4, found in the chapter's appendix, displays the parameter estimates for the ordered logistic regression model.

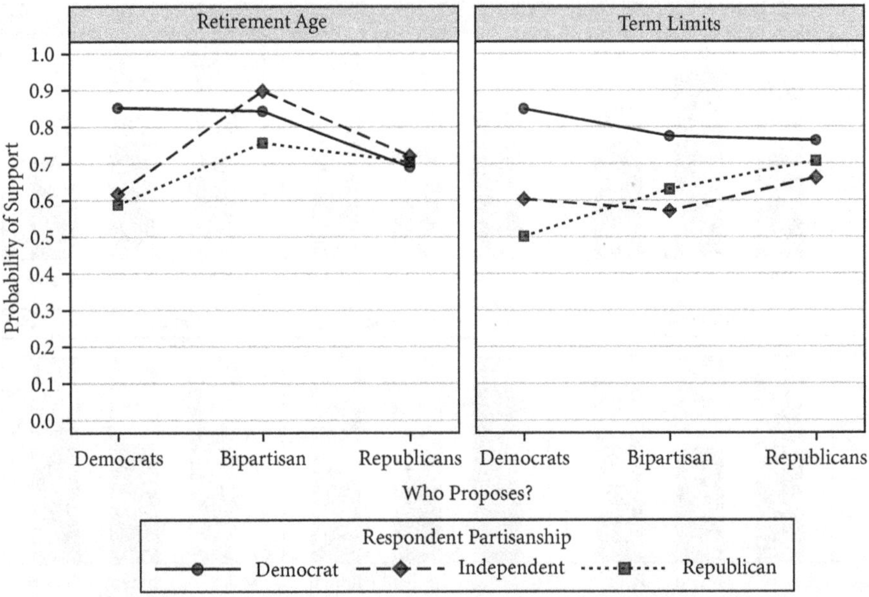

Figure 11.2 Probability of Reform Support Based on Respondent Partisanship and Partisanship of Proposer.

Figure 11.2 provides a graphical portrayal of the results. We focus on each of the two reforms separately, with the retirement age proposal on the left and the term limit proposal on the right. The x-axis for each plot indicates who proposed the reform. Within each panel, we plot the predicted probability a respondent supports the proposal as a function of whether he or she was a Democrat (circles), an Independent (diamonds), or a Republican (squares). To make the representation cleaner, we have removed the confidence intervals (see, i.e., Austin and Hux 2002), and describe only the statistically significant differences between any two points. We also offer Table 11.2 and Table 11.3, which provide a textual representation of these figures along with specific numerical values to help ease substantive interpretation.

Just as the raw data showed, all of the predicted probabilities reach or exceed 0.50. No matter the proposal or the proposer, the predicted values always suggest that a respondent is more likely than not to support a reform. Having said that, we now consider each reform and how partisans react to them.

Democratic Respondents–Retirement Age. Consider the Democratic respondents' reactions to the retirement age proposal. When Republicans propose a retirement age, Democratic respondents have a 0.69 probability of supporting it. But when a bipartisan coalition proposes it, Democratic respondents have a 0.84 probability of support. This difference is statistically significant ($p = 0.02$). Democrats are no more (or less) supportive of a bipartisan proposal than they are one offered by fellow Democrats.

Independent Respondents–Retirement Age. Next, consider the Independents' reactions to the retirement age proposal. They have strong preferences for bipartisan

Table 11.2 Respondents' support for retirement age proposal as a function of respondent partisanship and partisanship of proposer. Support scores connected by line are significantly different from each other.

Retirement Age Proposal		
Respondent	**Proposer**	**Support**
Democrat	Republican	0.69
Democrat	Bipartisan	0.84
Democrat	Democrat	0.85
Independent	Republican	0.72
Independent	Bipartisan	0.90
Independent	Democrat	0.62
Republican	Republican	0.70
Republican	Bipartisan	0.76
Republican	Democrat	0.59

Table 11.3 Respondents' support for term limit proposal as a function of respondent partisanship and partisanship of proposer. Support scores connected by line are significantly different from each other.

Term Limit Proposal		
Respondent	**Proposer**	**Support**
Democrat	Republican	0.78
Democrat	Bipartisan	0.79
Democrat	Democrat	0.85
Independent	Republican	0.66
Independent	Bipartisan	0.57
Independent	Democrat	0.60
Republican	Republican	0.71
Republican	Bipartisan	0.63
Republican	Democrat	0.50

proposers. An independent has a 0.62 probability of supporting a Democratic-proposed retirement age, a 0.90 probability of supporting a bipartisan proposal, and a 0.72 probability of supporting a Republican proposal. Both the Democratic-Bipartisan and Bipartisan-Republican differences are significant ($p < 0.05$), but the Democrat-Republican difference is not ($p = 0.21$).

Republican Respondents–Retirement Age. Now, consider the Republican respondents' reactions to the age limit proposal. Like their Democratic counterparts, they tend to prefer proposals from co-partisans. We estimate that a Republican respondent has a 0.59 probability of supporting a Democratic-proposed retirement age, a 0.76 probability of supporting a bipartisan retirement age proposal, and a 0.70 probability of supporting a Republican proposal. In terms of significant differences, the Democrat-Bipartisan frame difference is statistically significant ($p = 0.03$), the

Bipartisan-Republican is not ($p = 0.46$), and the Democrat-Republican is insignificant ($p = 0.13$).

Democratic Respondents–Term Limit. Democratic respondents in the term limits condition (the right panel of Figure 11.2) show some preference for co-partisan proposers, but none of the pairwise differences are statistically significant ($p > 0.20$).

Independent Respondents–Term Limit. Among independents assigned to the term limits group, the likelihood of support is (surprisingly) lowest if the proposal is Bipartisan (0.57), a bit higher if Democratic (0.60), and highest if Republican (0.66). None of these differences in point estimates are statistically significant, however ($p > 0.20$).

Republican Respondents–Term Limit. Republican responses to the term limit proposal are driven more by partisan differences. A Republican respondent has a 0.50 probability of supporting a term limit proposal offered by Democrats, a 0.63 probability of supporting a bipartisan term limit proposal ($p = 0.11$), and a 0.71 probability of supporting a Republican-proposed term limit ($p = 0.29$ compared with Bipartisan; $p = 0.01$ when compared to Democrats).

The only statistically significant relationship among our controls is that respondents who are increasingly distant ideologically from the Supreme Court are generally more supportive of reforms. Figure 11.3 shows the effect of the distance between a respondent's self-reported ideology and his or her subjective assessment of the the Supreme Court's ideology. We measured both of these variables on a 5-point scale, so a value of zero means that the respondent reported his or her ideology to be the same as the Supreme Court's ideology. Conversely, a value of four indicates maximum separation (e.g., the respondent reported that she was very liberal but assessed the Supreme Court as being very conservative). The greater that distance, the more a respondent supports these reforms. When a respondent is minimally distant from the Court, her probability of support is 0.64 (still a fairly high number). When, however, the respondent is maximally distant, that probability increases to 0.84. This 0.20 gain is a relative increase of approximately 31%.[12] These findings accord with recent studies that show a connection between Supreme Court legitimacy and things like partisan or ideological agreement with decisions (see, e.g., Bartels and Kramon 2022; Bartels and Johnston 2020; Zilis 2018; Armaly 2018; Christenson and Glick 2015; Nicholson and Hansford 2014; Bartels and Johnston 2013).

Taken together, these initial results suggest that respondents largely supported both proposals. Those findings accord with other, non-experimental polls fielded near the time of our study and their resultant headlines.[13] Respondents revealed a slightly stronger preference for the age limit proposal than for term limits. Moreover, they tended to support reforms more when co-partisans led the way than when opposite partisans took the lead, but these differences are not nearly as stark as one might have expected.

[12] Does ideological distance matter more (or less) for one proposal versus another? Not according to our analysis. We evaluated this possibility by estimating a model that interacted the reform with our distance measure. The marginal effect of a one-unit increase in ideological distance on support is an identical 0.05 for both proposals.

[13] For example, the subheading for the AP/NORC poll on the Supreme Court in late July 2022 said: "Most Americans favor constitutional reforms to the Supreme Court to impose term limits and age limits for justices."

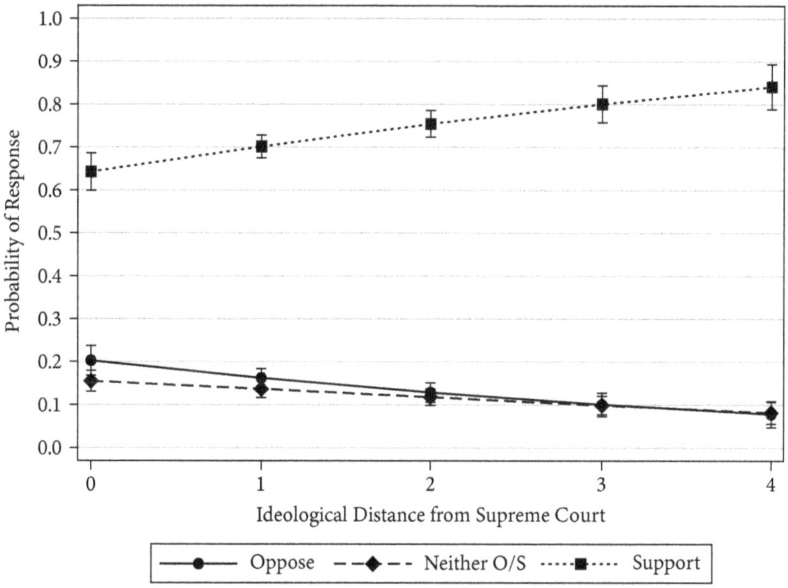

Figure 11.3 Ideological Disagreement and Attitudes Toward Reform. Predicted probability that a respondent opposes, neither opposes nor supports, or supports a reform (y axis) conditional on her ideological distance from the Supreme Court (x-axis). Vertical whiskers around points denote 95% confidence intervals. Results come from the ordered logistic regression model presented in Table 11.4 and were generated using the margins command in Stata 16.1.

11.2.2 Strength of Support

How intense are these respondents' preferences? Do they *really* care about such reforms or do their answers reflect only abstract interests? We followed up with those respondents who indicated that they would support (or were indifferent to) a reform and asked them whether they would be *willing to bear costs* to achieve the reforms. Specifically, we asked:

> Establishing [a mandatory retirement age/an 18-year term limit] might require changing the U.S. Constitution. This process would be politically time consuming and could make it harder for elected officials to address other issues. How important is it to you that the United States government implement [a mandatory retirement age/an 18-year term limit] for federal judges?

Figure 11.4 presents the descriptive results for this question. Looking at the retirement age proposal, 13% of respondents who originally supported a retirement age conceded that the issue—when it came with policy tradeoffs—was not at all important to them. Similarly, 23% said the issue was only slightly important. And, 29% said it was somewhat important. Only 36% said the issue was either very important

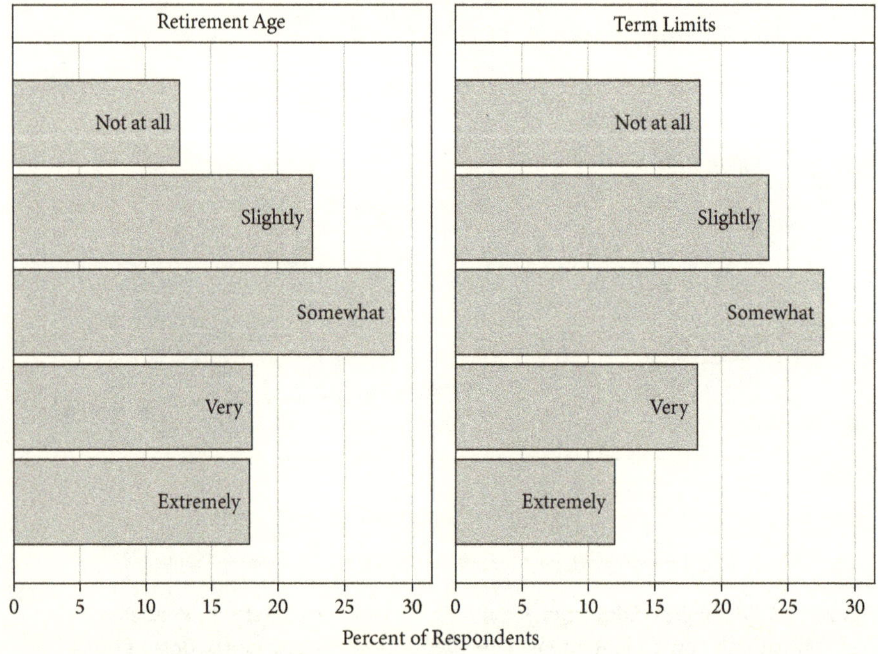

Figure 11.4 Importance of Reform Among those Not Opposed. Bars within each panel report percent of respondents attaching a particular level of importance to implementing a mandatory retirement age (left) or term limits (right) after being told that such a change might requiring changing the U.S. Constitution. This question was only asked to those who expressed either support or a lack of opposition to a given reform (i.e., it was not asked of those who initially opposed reform).

(18%) or extremely important (18%). The results for the term limits proposal are similar; 19% of respondents who originally expressed support for term limits now claimed that the issue—when it came with policy tradeoffs—was not at all important to them. About 24% said the issue was only slightly important, 28% said it was somewhat important, and only 30% said the issue was either very important (18%) or extremely important (12%).

To evaluate the conditions under which a respondent would hold these beliefs about importance, we statistically modeled the relationship. Our dependent variable is the five-category importance measure: not at all important; slightly important; somewhat important; very important; and extremely important. Our covariates are the same as our Partisanship and Support for Reform model, with controls for initial level of support for the reform (three categories), the respondent's party ID, what reform the respondent was exposed to, which party proposed the reform, the same demographic information as the first model, rule of law attitudes, knowledge about judiciary, and the respondent's perceived ideological distance from the Supreme Court.

Unsurprisingly, a respondent's initial support for a reform correlates closely with his or her later importance response. Consider a respondent who said she neither supports nor opposes a potential reform. The model predicts that such an individual has a 0.80 probability of indicating that reform was either "not at all important" (0.46) or only "slightly important" (0.34). By contrast, a respondent who strongly favored a reform has a 0.64 probability of answering that the reform is either "very important" (0.32) or "extremely important" (0.32). There is only a 0.10 probability that this strong supporter says the issue is of minimal importance (i.e., the two lowest categories).[14]

Since our initial support variable was measured post-treatment, it incorporates the salient aspects of our experimental manipulation—namely, which reform is proposed as well as the proposer's partisanship. Still, we continue to find that a respondent's own partisanship correlates with her appetite for seeing the reform pursued. A Democratic respondent has a 0.31 probability of expressing a lower level of importance; a Republican or Independent respondent, by contrast, has probabilities of 0.43 and 0.40, respectively. Individuals in all three groups are nearly identical in terms of their likelihood of expressing a middling level of support (i.e., somewhat important) for reform, with a probability estimate of around 0.28. At the upper end of support, however, we again see partisan differences. Democrats have a 0.40 probability of expressing one of the two higher levels of support when a Democrat proposes the reform compared to analogous probabilities of 0.29 for Republicans and 0.32 for Independents.[15]

Among the controls, a respondent's sex exerts a small but statistically significant effect on reform importance. Females see reform as less important than males. A female respondent has a 0.40 probability of indicating low importance for reform; a male respondent has a 0.35 probability. This 5-point difference persists when we examine higher levels of support for reform. Males have a 0.37 probability of being in the top two values whereas females have a 0.32 probability. This effect is not conditioned by the specific identity of the reform proposed. We also find a negative association between a respondent's support for the rule of law and his or her interest in seeing a reform implemented. Someone at the 10th percentile of our *Rule of Law Score* has a 0.38 probability of saying reforming is either very or extremely important. By contrast, someone in the 90th percentile has around a 0.31 probability of replying in this manner. This effect is also not conditioned by whether the reform is term limits or retirement age.

[14] We find no evidence that of an interactive effect between initial support and which reform a respondent was asked about and her level of stated importance on the issue. That is, the marginal effect of a one-unit increase in initial support does not yield a larger (or smaller) effect on the predicted importance when comparing term limits versus the retirement age respondents.

[15] There is some evidence that the specific identity of the proposed reform has a differential impact among respondents of different parties. We find no significant differences within Democrats for term limits versus retirement age. For Republican respondents, however, when the proposed reform is retirement age, they express a significantly higher level of importance as compared to when the reform is term limits. We estimate a 0.13 probability that a Republican respondent indicates reform is extremely important if the issue is retirement age but a 0.09 probability if the issue is term limits. This difference is statistically significant ($p = 0.02$). Consistent with the general pattern of results we've seen so far, Independents tend to behave more like Republicans than Democrats. They show some evidence of assigning greater importance to retirement age versus term limits, but the statistical strength of those differences is weaker (e.g., 0.15 [retirement age] vs. 0.10 [term limits] probabilities for very important, $p = 0.09$).

11.2.3 Comparing Arguments For and Against Reform

Recall that we exposed each respondent to three arguments for and three arguments against the proposal to which they were randomly assigned. They told us which argument they thought was stronger. Because our quantity of interest is a respondent's assessment of an argument, we reshape our data such that the unit of analysis is each of the nine evaluations we have for all of our respondents. For example, for our age limit condition, we have around 600 subjects, which provides roughly 5400 [600 × 9] argument assessments. To estimate the effect of each argument supporting or opposing on the subsequent rating, we simply employ indicator variables for each argument (i.e., three for support, three for opposing). This allows us to estimate the effect of a supporting (or opposing) argument having controlled for the other arguments it was paired against. A positive and significant difference for a supporting argument, for example, tells us that this argument generates greater support relative to the other two supporting arguments across the spectrum of opposing arguments against which it was paired.[16]

We control for respondent pre-argument support for the reform, whether the reform was retirement age or term limits, their partisan identification, the partisan identity of who proposed the reform, demographic controls, each respondent's knowledge about the judiciary, and his or her support for the rule of law. Since the support and oppose argument pairings varied by reform, we split the data and estimate separate models for each (see Table 11.6 in the Appendix).

We start with our results for a mandatory retirement age, which we portray graphically in Figure 11.5. The two arguments that seem to persuade people to support a mandatory retirement age are those that claim it would "open up seats to new judges more often, which will bring the federal judiciary closer to the beliefs and ideas of people today" (support = 0.51) and that a retirement age would "remove mentally unfit judges who might otherwise continue to decide cases" (support = 0.50). The argument that a mandatory retirement age would "reduce backlogs and speed up the judicial process because younger judges write judicial opinions more quickly than older judges" was less persuasive (support = 0.37).

Looking at the arguments against a mandatory retirement age, the most persuasive appears to be that it would "remove experienced judges from important jobs" (oppose = 0.27). But close on its heels are the other two arguments. The claim that a mandatory retirement age would "remove mentally capable judges who can still do their jobs" (oppose = 0.26) is nearly as strong, as is the argument that it would "open up seats to new judges more often, which would increase political conflict in the judicial appointment process" (oppose = 0.25).

We next consider the results for a term limit, which we portray in Figure 11.6. Once again, we see much stronger support for the reform than opposition to it. All three supportive arguments worked reasonably well. The claim that term limits would

[16] An alternative approach would be to include separate indicator variables for each of the nine argument pairings. This would be most appropriate if we had not exposed all respondents to all nine of the unique pairwise comparisons. Since our experimental design did present all nine comparisons, however, this more statistically costly approach is not needed.

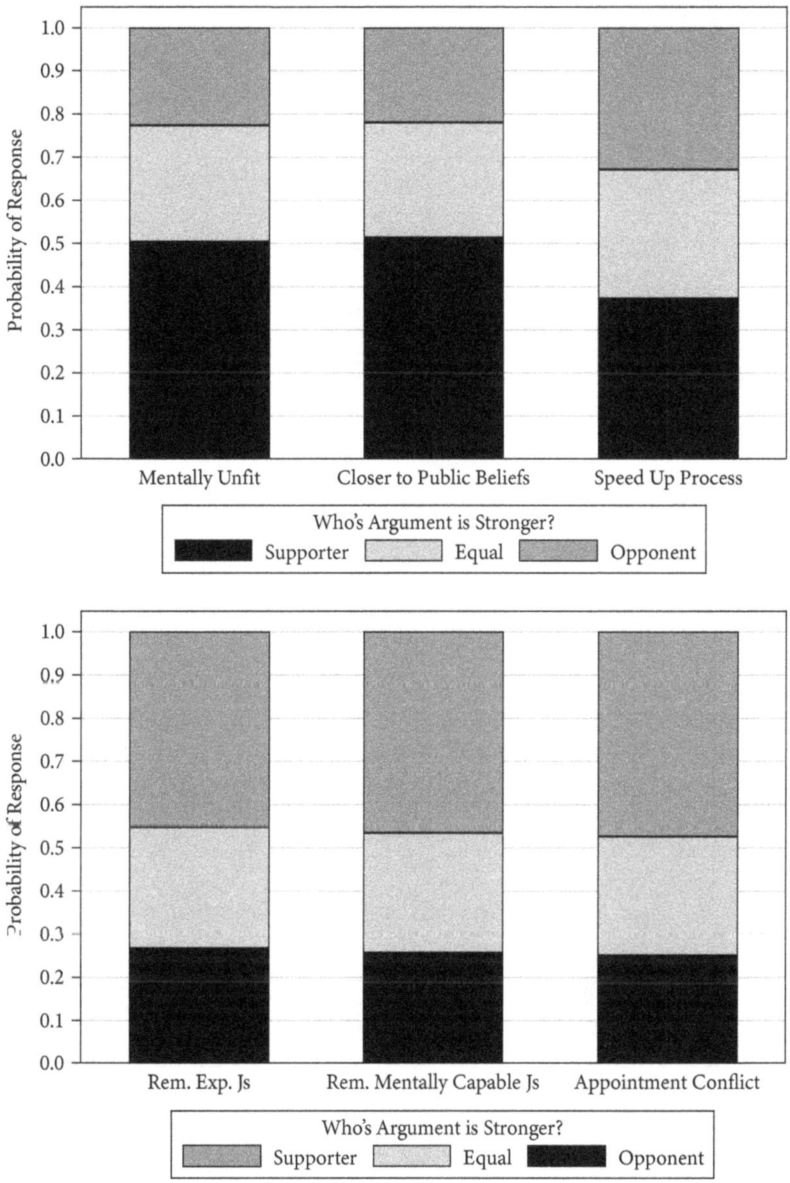

Figure 11.5 Responses to Arguments For and Against Mandatory Retirement. The top panel shows arguments in favor of a mandatory retirement age. The bottom panel shows arguments against a mandatory retirement age. Plotted values are predicted probabilities that come from the ordinal logistic regression model reported in Table 11.6.

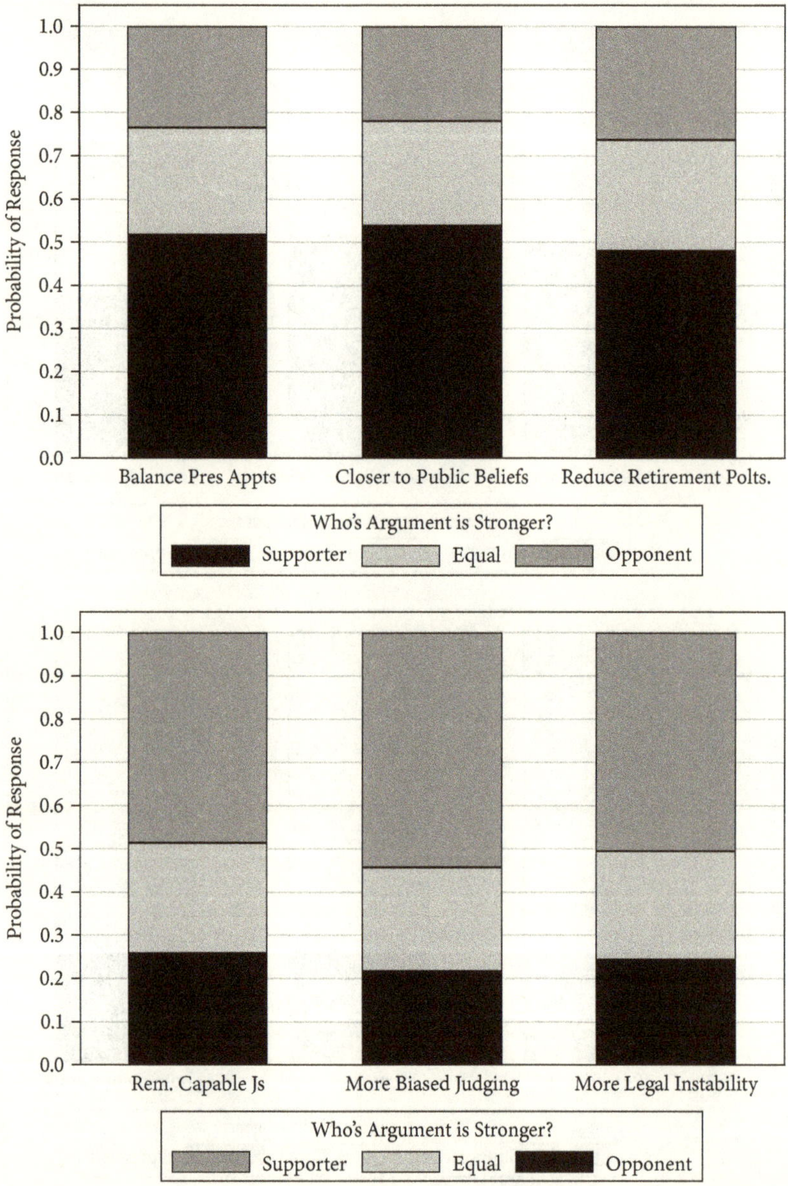

Figure 11.6 Responses to Arguments For and Against Term Limits. The top panel shows arguments in favor of a term limits. The bottom panel shows arguments against term limits. Plotted values are predicted probabilities that come from the ordinal logistic regression model reported in Table 11.6.

"open up seats to new judges more often, which would bring the federal judiciary closer to the beliefs and ideas of people today" (support = 0.54) was strongest. Next in terms of strength was the argument that term limits would "reduce political conflict over judicial appointments because openings would be predicted and balanced across presidents over time" (support = 0.52). Finally, and still somewhat strong, was the argument that term limits would "reduce political influence in a judge's decision when to retire" (support = 0.48).

As to the arguments in opposition, the strongest argument was that term limits could "remove capable judges who can still do their jobs" (oppose = 0.26). Second was the argument that term limits would "increase turnover among judges, which might create more instability in the law" (oppose = 0.24). And a close third was the claim that term limits would "make it more likely that judges would decide cases in a biased manner because they have to worry about getting their next job" (oppose = 0.22).

11.2.4 Malleability of Reform Attitudes

Can people be persuaded in their views? It's a question that reform advocates and opponents are sure to have. The evidence is mixed. Figure 11.7 below shows a visual cross-tabulation (spine plot) of our pre- and post-argument support measure. Each panel corresponds to a specific proposed reform. The x-axis identifies how a respondent initially responded and the y-axis shows where he or she ended up after exposure to the battery of supporting and opposing arguments. The size of each box is proportional to the number of respondents in that combination of pre- and post-arguments attitudes.

The results reveal significant consistency. For both retirement age and term limits, the upper right square in both panels show that most people supported the same policies after exposure to the battery of arguments as they did prior to exposure. Fully 87% of respondents in the mandatory retirement age group and 84% of the term limit group who initially supported the reforms clung to those initial views. Likewise, those who initially opposed reform generally continued to hold those attitudes even after exposure to the arguments (the bottom left boxes). Among those initially opposed to either a retirement age or term limits, 79% continued to oppose it.

We see more movement among respondents who initially were indifferent about the proposed reforms. 40% of respondents who were neither in favor of nor opposed to a retirement age remained as such. After exposure to the battery of arguments, however, 40% opposed a retirement age compared to just 21% whose views changed to support such a proposal. Among respondents in the term limit group, a near majority (49%) continue to be "neither nors," 35% switched to oppose term limits, and 16% switched to support them.

Although a strong majority of respondents show attitudinal consistency across the two times we asked about their support, around 21% of respondents changed attitudes in a meaningful manner. By meaningful, we mean not simply upgrading from "somewhat support" to "support," but rather switching from support to oppose, oppose to support, or from a fence-sitting position to one of actual support or

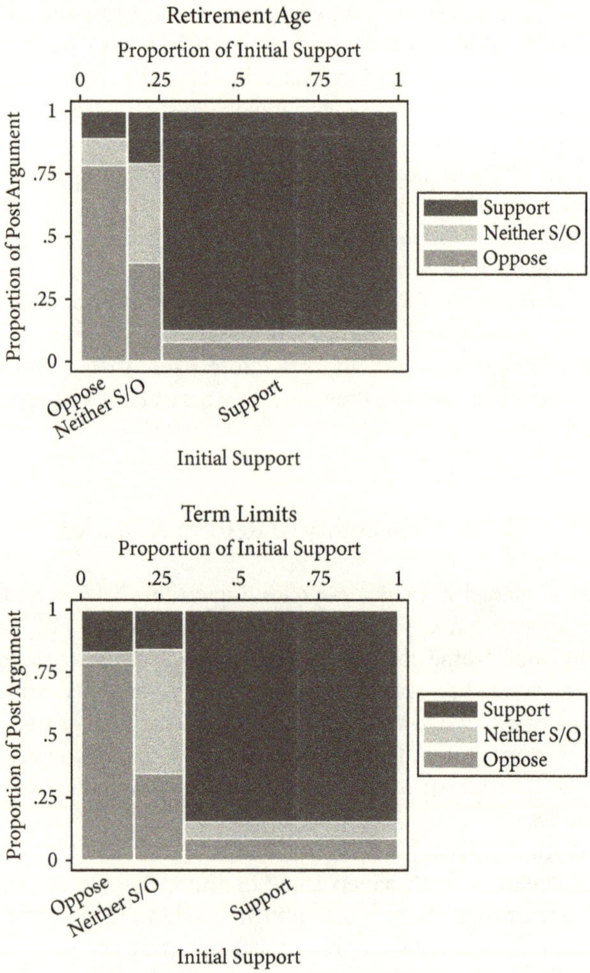

Figure 11.7 Cross-tabulation (spine plot) of our pre- and post-argument support measure. Size of each box is proportional to the number of respondents in that combination of pre- and post-arguments attitudes.

opposition. Were these changes random or did any arguments appear to influence their decisions?

To assess this question, we generated two additional dependent variables that focus on those "significant shifters." *Respondent Becomes Opposer* examines the 961 individuals who initially either supported the reform to which they were assigned or who said they neither supported nor opposed it. (We include the fence-sitters because we are interested in learning about what factors might sway their decision to move from neutrality to taking a specific side.) *Respondent Becomes Opposer* equals 1 if, after exposure to the battery of supporting and opposing arguments described in the previous section, the respondent indicated their opposition to the reform.

Conversely, if the respondent remained unchanged, the variable takes on the value of 0. Approximately 13% of the respondents made such a switch.

Respondent Becomes Supporter, takes an analogous approach among the individuals in our data whose initial responses showed opposition (or indifference) to the reform to which they were assigned. There were 332 individuals in our data who initially opposed or were indifferent to the reform. *Respondent Becomes Supporter* equals 1 if the respondent shifted views and indicated their support for the reform after exposure to the battery of supporting and opposing arguments; 0 if the respondent remained unchanged. 16% of the respondents made this switch.

Our independent variables start with those from the strength of initial support model discussed earlier in the chapter. In particular, we account for the respondent's initial support, his or her partisanship, the partisanship of who proposed the reform, the specific reform itself, the respondent's support for the rule of law, level of knowledge, and distance from the Supreme Court. We also control for demographic features such as the respondent's age, sex, race, education, and income.

We also include *Net Pro-Support Responses*, which we calculate by measuring the number of times a respondent said the supporting argument for reform was stronger than the opposing argument, and then subtracting from that value the number of times the respondent said the opposing side was stronger. Large positive values, then, indicate the respondent overwhelmingly favored the supporting side; large negative values indicate the opposite. Our intuition here is straightforward. Those who express more initial support for a reform will be less likely to oppose it after the arguments (i.e., the first dependent variable) and more likely to support it.

Because our dependent variables are dichotomous, we turn to a logistic regression model. (See Table 11.7 in the chapter's appendix for model parameter estimates.) Of particular interest is the sign and significance of *Net Pro-Support Responses*. It performs as we hypothesized and is statistically significant in both models.[17] Individuals who found the pro-reform arguments more compelling were significantly less likely to become opposers. That also means, of course that those who sided with the opposing arguments for a given reform were more likely to jump ship and become opposers. And, in the context of the switching from opposition to support, the opposite of these statements is true. Finding the pro arguments more compelling is associated with a higher probability of switching from opposition (or neutrality) to supporting a reform.

But, just how meaningful are these effects? The y-axis on Figure 11.8 shows the probability that a respondent switches from support to oppose (left panel) and oppose to support (right panel). The x-axis identifies each respondent's *Net Pro-Support Responses*. Consider the left panel—the respondent who initially supported or was neutral toward a reform. If that respondent went on to indicate that all nine of the opposing arguments were stronger than than supporting arguments (i.e., Net

[17] Recall that respondents who said they neither supported nor opposed a given reform are included as possible "converts" in each model. We do so because it is substantively important to know if exposure to arguments might sway these individuals. Our results, however, are robust to either excluding them altogether or, alternatively, including a separate dummy variable for whether someone was initially a "neither nor" respondent.

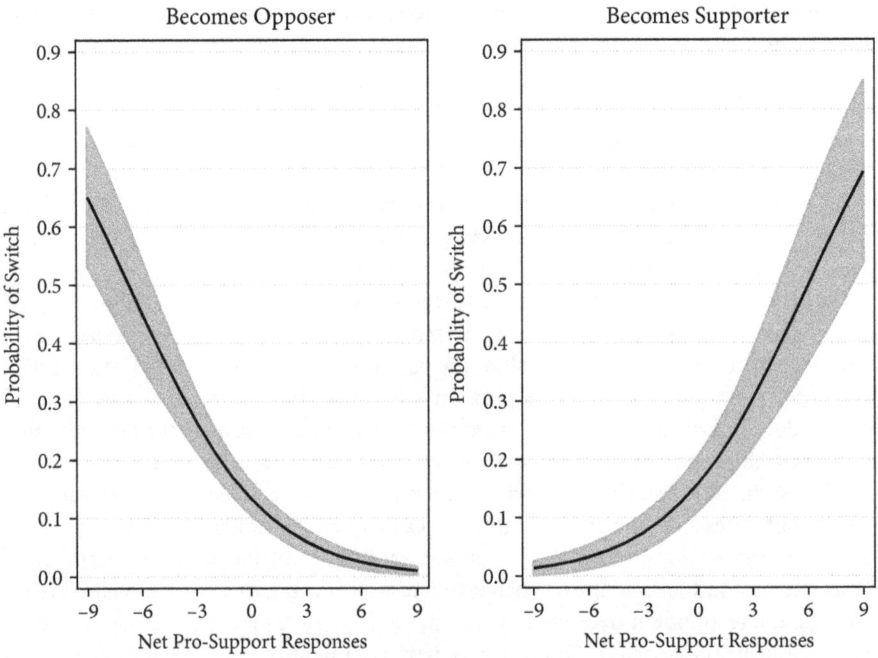

Figure 11.8 Effect of Argument Responses on Switching Reform Attitudes. The left panel shows the effect of the *Net Pro-Support Responses* on the likelihood a respondent who was either supportive or neutral toward reform switches to opposing the reform. The right panel shows this effect among those who initially opposed or was neutral. The shaded gray region in both panel shows the 95% confidence interval around the estimate. We generated these predicted values using the `mgen` command, as implemented by Long and Freese (2014) in Stata 16.1.

Pro-Support Responses = −9), there is a 0.65 probability that she will change her views toward the reform. As the balance of responses becomes increasingly positive, the individual is, unsurprisingly, less likely to jump off the pro-reform ship. When an individual shows indifference across the arguments (i.e., 0 on the x-axis), we estimate just a 0.13 probability that she becomes opposed to the reform. This is not surprising, of course, since we are looking exclusively at those who initially supported (or were indifferent toward) the proposal.

The right panel tells a nearly identical story. As a respondent indicates that the supporting arguments are more compelling than the opposing arguments, she is significantly more likely to switch from opposition (or indifference) to support. It takes favoring quite a few supporting arguments, however, before she switches to support. If the respondent supports six of the nine supporting statements over their opposing statements, we estimate approximately a coin flip chance that she will subsequently support the reform. These results seem to suggest that respondent attitudes can change; still, it bears mentioning that even uniformly preferring the pro-reform arguments generates a probability of attitudinal change of 0.69. Our best guess is that the individual would change her view, but there is still nearly a one-in-three chance that she will not.

A few of our control variables are associated with whether a respondent switches from support to opposition. Respondents who initially were more supportive of a reform are, unsurprisingly, less likely to switch to opposition. Respondents with greater support for the rule of law were, after exposure to the argument battery, more likely to switch from support to opposition. Ideological compatibility with the current Supreme Court is negatively associated with switching from support to opposition. And, finally, wealthier individuals appear less likely to switch to opposition.

By contrast, this same set of predictors fails to produce significant relationships when looking at those who switch from opposition to support. Only *Net Pro-Support Responses* achieves significance at the level of 0.10 or better. Even the level of initial support a respondent expressed for the reform does not matter (i.e., $p = 0.66$).[18] We suspect that at least some of this is due to the smaller number of observations—roughly one-third of the other model—and the relative rarity with which individuals changed their views—only about 16% of the time.

11.3 Conclusion

Federal courts have come under increasing scrutiny. Much of this scrutiny is a function of disagreement with judicial decisions. It tracks the increased political polarization we have seen in the last few decades. Arguments that once were dismissed as radical and unthinkable are now mainstream. Scholars, elected officials, and journalists are now clamoring for age limits and term limits for federal judges. But it has remained unclear just how deep and wide that support is and which arguments will drive support for and against the reforms.

We examined respondents' views on a mandatory retirement age and a required term limit for federal judges. The results show that Democrats and those who perceive the Supreme Court to be ideologically distant from them are most enthusiastic for these changes. Still, over a majority of Republicans are willing to support them. Overall, support appears greatest when proposed by a bipartisan group of leaders. Partisans are most likely to support the reforms when co-partisans propose the changes. But majorities will support them even when proposed by opposite partisans. When we inform respondents that there might be significant costs to bear to effectuate these reforms, support dampens, suggesting that the overall support is not nearly as

[18] Only one variable—*Proposal is Bipartisan* shows even "no man's land" or "gray zone" evidence of significance. Recall this measure is an indicator variable for the party a respondent was told had proposed the reform. Our results suggest that bipartisan reforms are least likely to generate a switch to support (probability = 0.11); the probability for Democrat ones is 0.17 and for Republicans the probability is 0.20. The p-values for the pairwise differences are: Bipartisan vs. Democrats (0.12), Bipartisan vs. Republicans (0.04), and Democrats vs. Republicans (0.53).

strong as the first round indicators suggest. Yet even there, we see fairly strong support for the reforms, particularly among Democrats and those with low Rule of Law scores.

In terms of the rhetoric for and against the reforms, the arguments in favor of reform tend to be strong while the arguments against are less so. The claims that the reforms would bring the courts closer to the public's beliefs and remove mentally unfit judges appear to be strongest.

Taken together, these results indicate that pro-reform advocates have perhaps the easier frame. If they focus on removing mentally unfit judges and making the courts more responsive, they may achieve gains. On the other hand, opponents of these reforms must focus on the opportunity costs involved, the fact that the reforms would require a constitutional amendment, and that it could lead to legal instability.

We have addressed only a portion of this important argument. But the results we discover in this chapter suggest that the conversation—and policy debates—over judicial reform are just beginning.

11.4 Appendix

We report the full parameter estimates of the ordered logistic regression models and results that we discuss in the chapter's main text. Table 11.4 displays the results when estimating respondents' initial support for institutional reform. Table 11.5 reports the results when predicting the intensity of respondents' initial support for institutional reform. Table 11.6 shows the results when respondents' were presented with arguments for and against institutional reform. And, Table 11.7 reports the results when estimating the change in respondents' support for institutional reform following exposure to arguments for and against reform.

Table 11.4 Parameter Estimates for Initial Support for Reform

	Coef.	S.E.
Respondent Independent	−1.305**	0.434
Respondent Republican	−1.433**	0.445
Term Limits Reform	−0.023	0.503
Respondent Independent × Term Limits Reform	−0.038	0.613
Respondent Republican × Term Limits Reform	−0.338	0.615
Bipartisan Plan	−0.073	0.488
Republican Plan	−0.970**	0.433
Respondent Independent × Bipartisan Plan	1.804**	0.780
Respondent Independent × Republican Plan	1.454**	0.588
Respondent Republican × Bipartisan Plan	0.876	0.611
Respondent Republican × Republican Plan	1.502**	0.560
Term Limits Reform × Bipartisan Plan	−0.431	0.681
Term Limits Reform × Republican Plan	0.398	0.640
Respondent Independent × Term Limits Reform × Bipartisan Plan	−1.440	0.988
Respondent Independent × Term Limits Reform × Republican Plan	−0.624	0.844
Respondent Republican × Term Limits Reform × Bipartisan Plan	0.175	0.842
Respondent Republican × Term Limits Reform × Republican Plan	−0.025	0.807
Age of Respondent	0.002	0.005
Female Respondent	0.100	0.138
Non-White Respondent	0.140	0.175
Education Level of Respondent	0.065	0.051
Income Level of Respondent	0.072	0.058
Support for Rule of Law Score	0.065	0.084
Knowledge Score	−0.071	0.109
Ideological Distance from Supreme Court	0.285**	0.068
κ_1	−1.523**	0.561
κ_2	−0.687	0.554
N	1,143	
Pseudo R^2	0.063	

Note: Results are maximum likelihood estimates of Coef(ficient) and S(tandard) E(rror) from an ordered logistic regression model with our three-category reform support dependent variable (1 = Oppose, 2 = Neither Support Nor Oppose, 3 = Support). ** $p < 0.05$ and * $p < 0.10$ (two-tailed).

Table 11.5 Parameter Estimates for Strength of Initial Support for Reform

	Coef.	S.E.
Initial Support for Reform	1.259**	0.077
Respondent Independent	−0.477**	0.176
Respondent Republican	−0.647**	0.147
Term Limits Reform	−0.223*	0.120
Bipartisan Plan	−0.149	0.144
Republican Plan	−0.175	0.149
Age of Respondent	0.004	0.004
Female Respondent	−0.318**	0.122
Non-White Respondent	−0.178	0.156
Education Level of Respondent	−0.013	0.046
Income Level of Respondent	−0.121**	0.048
Support for Rule of Law Score	−0.192**	0.082
Knowledge Score	0.016	0.099
Ideological Distance from Supreme Court	0.056	0.057
κ_1	3.964**	0.566
κ_2	5.616**	0.587
κ_3	7.289**	0.612
κ_4	8.695**	0.630
N	959	
Pseudo R^2	0.158	

Note: Results are maximum likelihood estimates of Coef(ficient) and S(tandard) E(rror) from an ordered logistic regression model with our five-category reform importance dependent variable (1 = not at all important, 2 = slightly important, 3 = somewhat important, 4 = very important, 5 = extremely important), which was measured only for individuals who expressed no opposition to the reform to which they were exposed. ** $p < 0.05$ and * $p < 0.10$ (two-tailed).

Table 11.6 Parameter Estimates for Evaluation of Reform Arguments

	Retirement	Term Limits
Closer to Public Beliefs (+)	0.05 (0.06)	
Speed Up Process (+)	−0.61** (0.07)	
Remove Mentally Capable (−)	0.06 (0.04)	
Appointments Conflict (−)	0.10** (0.05)	
Closer to Public Beliefs (+)		0.11** (0.05)
Reduce Retirement Politics (+)		−0.18** (0.06)
More Bias Next Job (−)		0.28** (0.07)
More Legal Instability (−)		0.09 (0.06)
Respondent Independent	−0.33** (0.15)	−0.76** (0.16)
Respondent Republican	−0.57** (0.15)	−1.00** (0.16)
Initial Support for Reform	1.02** (0.08)	0.94** (0.09)
Bipartisan Plan	−0.16 (0.14)	−0.05 (0.15)
Republican Plan	−0.06 (0.13)	−0.02 (0.15)
Support for Rule of Law Score	−0.08 (0.07)	−0.22** (0.08)
Knowledge Score	−0.14 (0.09)	0.00 (0.10)
Ideo. Dist. from Supreme Court	0.10* (0.05)	0.14** (0.06)
Age of Respondent	−0.01** (0.00)	−0.00 (0.00)
Female Respondent	0.00 (0.12)	−0.05 (0.12)
Non-White Respondent	−0.30** (0.15)	0.01 (0.16)
Education Level of Respondent	−0.12** (0.05)	−0.05 (0.05)
Income Level of Respondent	−0.01 (0.05)	0.05 (0.05)
κ_1	0.19 (0.33)	0.58 (0.39)
κ_2	1.63** (0.34)	1.95** (0.40)
N	5,390	4,880
Pseudo R^2	0.094	0.116

Note: Results are maximum likelihood coefficients with parentheses showing standard errors (clustered on each of the unique respondents in the data; 600 for Retirement Age and 543 for Term Limits). The underlying model is an ordered logistic regression model with our three-category argument evaluation variable (1 = opponent stronger, 2 = both equally strong, 3 = support stronger). ** $p < 0.05$ and * $p < 0.10$ (two-tailed).

Table 11.7 Respondent Change in Reform Attitudes after Argument Exposure

	Respondent Becomes	
	Opposer	**Supporter**
Net Pro-Support Responses	−0.31**	0.30**
	(0.03)	(0.04)
Term Limits Reform	0.23	−0.07
	(0.25)	(0.40)
Initial Reform Support	−0.54**	−0.08
	(0.13)	(0.17)
Respondent Independent	−0.44	0.50
	(0.37)	(0.52)
Respondent Republican	0.08	0.53
	(0.32)	(0.53)
Proposal is Bipartisan	−0.35	−0.69
	(0.29)	(0.46)
Proposal is Republican	−0.22	0.27
	(0.29)	(0.43)
Support for Rule of Law Score	0.29**	0.05
	(0.14)	(0.23)
Knowledge Score	−0.15	0.13
	(0.19)	(0.31)
Ideological Distance from Supreme Court	−0.23*	0.21
	(0.12)	(0.17)
Age	−0.01	−0.02
	(0.01)	(0.02)
Female	−0.16	0.28
	(0.24)	(0.39)
Non-White	−0.20	−0.09
	(0.30)	(0.44)
Education Level	0.04	−0.14
	(0.09)	(0.15)
Income Level	−0.17*	0.19
	(0.10)	(0.16)
Constant	2.47**	−1.39
	(0.98)	(1.01)
N	961	332
Pseudo R^2	0.358	0.281

Note: Table entries are logistic regression coefficients with robust standard errors in parentheses. ** $p < 0.05$ and * $p < 0.10$ (two-tailed). The left column examines whether a respondent who was indifferent or an opposer switched views to become a supporter. The right column examines analogous switches from indifference/support to opposition.

12
Conclusion

We discovered a lot in this book. And what we discovered points in one direction. We found that judges require more time to craft their opinions as they age, and that they tend to rely more on cognitive shortcuts when they bargain over opinion content (Chapter 4). We found that judges' written opinions become shorter and less cognitively complex as they age (Chapter 5), that aging judges increasingly rely on their law clerks to write their opinions and increasingly borrow language from party briefs (Chapter 6). Their judicial colleagues across the circuits are less likely to cite judges' opinions as they age (Chapter 7). Likewise, we learned that aging judges, in an effort to compensate for increased cognitive demands, apply Supreme Court precedent an increasingly ideological manner (Chapter 8). We determined that with age, legal influence on panels wanes while susceptibility to persuasion increases (Chapter 9). We observed some (though limited) evidence that public support for judges declines when people witness judges with cognitive concerns (Chapter 10). And, we discovered that Republicans and Democrats appear at least somewhat poised to accept changes to judicial tenure (Chapter 11). Table 12.1 summarizes these results.

It is worth reiterating that we obtained the findings in our book even in the presence of senior status as an accommodation for aging. In other words, the effects of cognitive aging on judges *would be even greater* than we discovered if senior status was not an option. On average, elderly judges labor to fulfill their tasks.

To be sure, our findings are not without their limitations. We were unable directly to measure cognitive aging among judges. Since we could not put them in functional MRIs or perform similar tests on them, we were forced to rely on inference. (Indeed, even the federal judiciary was unable to force Judge Newman to take neurological tests!) Taking the evidence together, we have inferred that cognitive aging influences judges. In this endeavor, then, we are like most social scientists who collect data, hypothesize, and then subject those hypotheses to tests.

Further, as we indicated earlier in the book, cognitive aging does not effect everyone at the same age or in the same way. Aging effects some people at earlier ages than others. And it effects some cognitive domains in some people and different cognitive domains in others. But what is clear is that the average effects of cognitive aging are largely negative. Scholars have shown that declines tend to begin in a person's 30s and continue with age. We return to our theme: Cognitive aging effects all people. Judges are people. And so cognitive aging effects judges.

At this point, readers likely want to know what reforms, if any, policymakers or the judiciary *should* adopt. Before we address that important question, we must set some

Cognitive Aging and the Federal Circuit Courts: How Senescence Influences the Law and Judges.
Ryan C. Black, Ryan J. Owens, Patrick C. Wohlfarth, Oxford University Press. DOI: 10.1093/oso/9780197747025.003.0012

Table 12.1 Summary of Findings for Each Chapter and Substantive Analysis

Topic	Primary Findings
(4) Opinion Writing	Age ↑ time to write opinion draft Age ↑ Pr(threats) among ideologically distant judges Age ↑ effects of ideological distance on Pr(reject) change
(5) Opinion Content	Age ↓ opinion cognitive complexity Age ↓ opinion length Age ↑ sentence length Age ↑ language inconsistency
(6) Opinions, Clerks, Briefs	Age ↑ reliance on clerks Age ↑ opinion similarity with briefs Age ↑ opinion copying from briefs
(7) Opinion Quality	Age ↓ Pr(later cite) Age ↓ Pr(later cite) among binding precedents Age ↓ Pr(later cite) among binding, distant precedents
(8) Follow Sup. Ct. Precedent	Age × Distance ↓ Pr(positive treatment) Age × Distance ↑ Pr(negative treatment)
(9) Panel Composition	Age ↓ Counter-Judge success Age ↑ influence by others
(10) Attitudes Toward Judges	Some opposition to aged judge with cognitive concerns Image of healthy young judge ↑ support
(11) Support for Reforms	Support high regardless of proposer Support ↑ with distance from Court Support ↑ when courts will become closer to public Support ↑ when remove mentally unfit judges

boundaries for *acceptable* change. To do that, we first must address the core principles undergirding *why* the Constitution protects judicial independence and grants federal judges lifetime tenure. Any reform, we argue, must remain consistent with those core principles. We proceed, then, by examining the purposes of judicial independence, what Congress has done in the past to address the concerns of cognitively aging judges, and then what reforms might be possible today.

12.1 The Purposes of Judicial Independence and Lifetime Tenure

We begin by examining judicial independence. Judicial independence exists when judges "are free from the direct influence of the coordinate branches of government and the vagaries of public passions and opinions" (Peabody 2011, 1). Its purpose is to allow judges to decide cases without fear for their lives or for their jobs. Judicial independence permits judges to decide cases as they believe the law dictates, and not on how some other person or group wants them to decide. Blackstone's *Commentaries* call judicial independence "one of the main preservative[s] of the public liberty" (Paley 2016, 1:259–260). Judicial independence protects liberty. It is what permits judges to stand athwart history, yelling "Stop!" when the masses blindly seek unconstitutionally to carry on.[1] Justice Joseph Story once remarked: "if the tenure of office of the judges is not permanent, they will soon be rendered odious, not because they do wrong; but *because they refuse to do wrong*" (Story 1873, §1606)(emphasis added).

In this way, lifetime tenure is a form of credible commitment—a long-term investment in legal doctrine and (relatively) stable judicial behavior. A credible commitment is an institutional decision to protect decision makers from pursuing their short-term interests at the expense of long-term interests. As North and Weingast (1989, 804) note, "a ruler can establish [a credible] commitment in two ways. One is by setting a precedent of 'responsible behavior,' appearing to be committed to a set of rules that he or she will consistently enforce. The second is by being constrained to obey a set of rules that do not permit leeway for violating commitments." A judge with lifetime tenure has the power to consider the law—and long-term legal goals—rather than short-term political interests that might subvert important legal, social, or institutional considerations.

Throughout history, states and nations adopted various methods to obtain judicial independence. One foundational method is to ensure that judges are not physically harmed for their decisions (Helmke and Rosenbluth 2009). Unfortunately, in many countries, reprobates threaten and attack judges for their decisions. For example, Mexican drug cartels have killed judges who ruled against them.[2] Guatemalan judges have expressed fears of "terrorism" from organized crime (Bowen 2013, 838). In 1989 and 1990, Columbia saw 39 homicides or attempted homicides against its judges and public ministry employees (Pardo 1992, 28). Domestic terrorists have even threatened U.S. Supreme Court justices. Justices Kavanaugh (Turley 2022) and Alito (Taranto and Rivkin 2023) both faced serious death threats from unhinged opponents of their votes in *Dobbs v. Jackson Women's Health Organization* (2023). Under such threatening conditions, judicial independence cannot endure.

Judicial independence also requires that the law protect judicial tenure in office and judges' financial livelihoods. Without such protections, most judges would hedge their decisions. They would vote not as the law or as their jurisprudential principles dictated but, rather, as those who controlled their salaries or their careers wanted them to vote. For, to hold power over a judge's livelihood "amounts to a power over his will" (Federalist 79).[3]

Consider El Salvador. In 2021, the president and his legislative supporters removed all five judges from the Supreme Court's Constitutional Chamber and replaced them

[1] This is a paraphrase of William Buckley's assertion that conservatism "stands athwart history, yelling Stop, at a time when no one is inclined to do so, or to have much patience with those who so urge it" (Buckley 1955, 5).

[2] https://www.americanbar.org/news/abanews/publications/youraba/2020/youraba-september-2020/assault-on-judicial-independence/.

[3] Independence is not only focused on the removal side; it also can be addressed through selection mechanisms. Some governmental units have sought to enhance judicial independence via their selection processes. For example, some U.S. states and foreign countries use (putatively) nonpartisan commissions to select judges (Owens et al. 2015). Others require judges to pass written exams to hold office. The declared purpose of these efforts is to select (and retain) the kind of judges who will decide cases objectively and independently of political or ideological bias. The judges selected through this process are presumed to be unafraid to follow the law—even in the face of public backlash.

with judicial cronies (Freeman and Beltran 2021). Surely, electoral minorities became more vulnerable to abuse as a consequence. Speaking of which, in Venezula, Hugo Chavez "dissolved the Supreme Court *en masse* in 1997, suspended about 300 lower level judges, and appointed 101 new judges to the bench" in an effort to obtain a more compliant judiciary (Helmke 2005, 1). It worked. Similar efforts occurred in Ecuador, Paraguay, and Argentina (Helmke 2005). Lest one think only Latin America suffers these problems, policymakers in Turkey (Kenyon 2023), Israel (Debre and Federman 2023), and even the United States (Birle 2023) have sought to weaken their judiciaries to consolidate political power. Wherever judicial independence exists, political strongmen will seek to diminish it in an effort to amass unchecked power.

Thankfully, Anglo-American law has long protected judicial tenure—but nothing lasts forever. In 1641, King Charles I determined that British judges would hold commissions *quam diu se bene gesserint* (as long as they shall behave themselves well). Of course, Charles II and James II later ignored that promise and made judicial appointments by pleasure. But after the Glorious Revolution and James II's forced abdication, England adopted the Act of Settlement, which provided that "upon the accession of the House of Hanover judicial commissions were to be issued *quam diu se bene gesserint*" (Smith 1976, 1110). To be sure, Parliament could remove those judicial commissions; and the commissions themselves expired upon the King's death (Story 1873, §1602). Nevertheless, the Act was a strong first step toward greater judicial independence. In 1761, King George III fortified judicial independence when he declared that judges would hold office during good behavior *even after the King died*: "I look upon the independency and uprightness of the Judges of the land as essential to the impartial administration of justice, as one of the best securities to the rights and liberties of my loving subjects, and as most conducive to the honour of the crown" (Smith 1976, 1110).

Yet, "Farmer George" did not extend that right to the American colonists, which led (in part) to the Revolution. The King made colonial judges dependent on his grace for their continued commissions. In fact, one of the Declaration of Independence's complaints against the King was that "He has made Judges dependent on his Will alone, for the tenure of their offices, and the amount and payment of their salaries."[4] To violate judicial independence was to violate the colonists' rights as Englishmen.

And so when it came time to form a stronger national government in 1787, the Framers of the Constitution adopted the good behavior standard and lifetime tenure to protect judicial independence. Article III § 1 of the Constitution states: "The judges, both of the supreme and inferior courts, shall hold their offices during good behaviour. . . ." Policymakers historically have interpreted this provision to mean that federal judges continue in office until death takes them, until they retire, or until Congress impeaches and removes them for treason, bribery, or other high crimes and misdemeanors (Whittington 1999; Tassel 1993). Alexander Hamilton offered strong support for judicial independence when he argued that legislatures could not be trusted to hold firm against the vicissitudes of short-term political desires. The people needed independent federal judges so as "to guard the Constitution and the

[4] See https://www.archives.gov/founding-docs/declaration-transcript.

rights of individuals from the effects of those ill humours, which the arts of designing men... sometimes disseminate among the people..." (Hamilton 78). Our forebears experienced the failures of a judiciary that relied solely on public support or support from a crown or legislature; they designed institutions to alleviate those failures. Judicial independence is intentionally anti-majoritarian so as to protect people from majoritarian tyranny.

Accordingly, any reforms designed to rectify cognitive aging must protect judicial independence. It is to those possible reforms that we now turn.

12.2 Previous Reforms to Address Aging Judges

Congress has passed legislation to address the concerns of cognitively aging judges. In 1869, it allowed federal judges who were 70 years or older and had served at least ten years on the bench, to retire and receive their full salaries for life. The law sought to incentivize aged judges to retire. Up until the law's passage, many judges remained in office until they died to keep receiving salaries. Without any pension, their primary (and often only) way to obtain income was to remain on the court. They remained, many withered, and some were catastrophically disabled (e.g., Garrow 2000). The 1869 pension incentivized elderly judges to retire and allowed mentally fit judges to succeed them. Not surprisingly, elderly judges took advantage. As Yoon (2005) shows, the median years of active service among all judges decreased from 18 before the pension reform to 10 after it. Further, the median years of active service among judges over 70 years old dropped from 7 before the law to 2 after it. Pension reform led aged judges to retire.

In 1919, Congress created the position of the senior judge. As we discussed earlier in the book, senior status allows older judges to hear a reduced load of cases yet still receive their full salaries. The judge can take on a reduced docket load and continue to receive a full salary, and the president can then nominate an additional judge. (When that senior judge later retires, no new vacancy occurs.) Judges who take senior status must simply perform the work an active judge would have performed over three months of a year. Judges can choose to meet these obligations by hearing cases or by undertaking administrative obligations alone.

In 1939, Congress passed the Administrative Office Act, which created Judicial Councils in each circuit. It empowered each Council to "make all necessary orders for the effective and expeditious administration of the business of the courts within its circuit" (Burbank 1982; Re 1981). Some argued that the Act allowed Judicial Councils to replace or remove mentally unfit judges.[5] But the Councils never undertook such action and its constitutionality remained (and remains) unclear.

[5] In *Chandler v. Judicial Council of the Tenth Circuit of the United States* (1970), Chief Justice Burger stated: "There can, of course, be no disagreement among us as to the imperative need for total and absolute independence of judges.... But it is quite another matter to say that each judge in a complex system shall be the absolute ruler of his manner of conducting judicial business." Justice Douglas took the opposite view, declaring: "neither one [judge] alone nor any number banded together can act as censor and place sanctions on [another judge]. Under the Constitution, the only leverage that can be asserted against him is impeachment." *See Chandler* (Douglas, J., Dissenting).

In 1948, Congress continued to address the issue, legislating that:

> Whenever any circuit or district judge eligible to resign or retire under this section does neither, and *the President* finds that such judge is unable to discharge efficiently all the duties of his office by reason of permanent mental or physical disability and that the appointment of an additional judge is necessary for the efficient dispatch of business, the President may make such appointment by and with the advice and consent of the Senate. If such additional judge is appointed, the vacancy subsequently caused by the death, resignation, or retirement of the disabled judge shall not be filled.[6]

The law did not specify the conditions under which the president could find that a judge was unable to discharge his duties. No matter. No president exercised such power (Abelite, Michalos, and Rogue 2021). And the constitutionality of the law was doubtful in any case. In 1954, Congress revised the legislation again to make clear who had the authority to determine whether a judge was disabled. It stated: "*A circuit or district judge*, desiring to retire under this section, shall furnish to the President a certificate of disability signed by the chief judge of his circuit."[7] This revised provision seemed to indicate that a judge would be responsible for determining his own disability. Then, in 1957, Congress again tinkered with the language, this time suggesting that a judge's *colleagues* could sign a certificate of disability that would open up a new position on the court:

> Whenever any judge of the United States appointed to hold office during good behavior who is eligible to retire under this section does not do so and a certificate of his disability *signed by a majority of the members of the Judicial Council of his circuit* in the case of a circuit or district judge . . . is presented to the President and the President finds that such judge is unable to discharge efficiently all the duties of his office by reason of permanent mental or physical disability and that the appointment of an additional judge is necessary for the efficient dispatch of business, the President may make such appointment by and with the advice and consent of the Senate. Whenever any such additional judge is appointed, the vacancy subsequently caused by the death, resignation, or retirement of the disabled judge shall not be filled.[8]

In 1980, Congress again returned to the issue when it passed the Judicial Councils Reform and Judicial Conduct and Disability Act. The law expanded the group of people who could seek the removal of unfit judges. It declared that any person who believed a judge "is unable to discharge all the duties of office by reason of mental or physical disability" could file a complaint with the court clerk to that effect (Baker 1985; Burbank 1982).[9] Since 1990, chief judges have been able to initiate that review

[6] See 28 U.S.C. §372(b); June 25, 1948, c. 646, 62 Stat. 903 (emphasis added).
[7] Feb. 10, 1954, c. 6, §4(a), 68 Stat. 12.
[8] Pub.L. 85–261, Sept. 2, 1957, 71 Stat. 586.
[9] See 28 U.S.C. §351(a); 94 Stat. 2036–2037.

process even if no one has filed a complaint (Breyer 1996, 993). The chief judge of the circuit would review the complaint. He or she could dismiss it if it did not meet statutory requirements, if it related to the merits of a decision (rather than to the judge's mental or physical state), or if the accused judge resolved the issue (e.g., retired or agreed to take corrective action). But if the complaint survived that threshold examination, the chief judge had to appoint a committee "to investigate the complaint and file with the council a report containing its findings and recommendations" (Burbank 1982, 286). The council, in turn, was authorized "to take such action" as would be appropriate to "assure the effective and expeditious administration of the business of the courts" (Burbank 1982, 286). If the Council were to find the judge is, in fact, disabled, it could order a number of actions: it could temporarily suspend the judge from hearing cases until the disability was cured. It also could certify that the judge was disabled and notify the president pursuant to the procedures we identified above in 28 U.S.C. §372(b).

As our findings throughout this book reveal, this legislation has not been enough to prevent the effects of cognitive aging among circuit court judges. One can count on one hand the number of judges who have been sanctioned for failing to discharge their duties for reason of mental disability. As far as we can tell, that very short list includes only Judge Pauline Newman, whom we discussed in the book's introduction.

An analysis of the disability complaints people have filed against judges—and the responses thereto—reveal the current law's impotence. Figure 12.1 shows the number of disability-related complaints about federal circuit court judges from 1997 to 2022. Across this 25-year time period, people filed nearly 1000 complaints. The average number of complaints each year was 38. People filed such complaints across all of the circuits. But aside from Judge Newman's debacle, the Councils do not appear to have formally conceded a single judge suffered a mental disability.

12.3 Possible Future Reforms

Scholars and court watchers have offered a few possible reforms to address cognitive aging. We address those, and some of our own, in order of increasing difficulty. Each of these reforms are broadly consistent with judicial independence, though some more than others.

Greater Transparency. One possible reform would be to increase public awareness of aging judges' backlogs. As we mentioned in Chapter 3, in one circuit, "the circuit executive brought the names of judges who appeared to have backlog problems to the attention of the chief judge. Together they would send a constructive letter, offering assistance to address the backlog" (Barr and Willging 1993, 140). A different chief judge created a "60-day" list which contained the names of cases—and their opinion authors—that lingered beyond 60 days. At monthly meetings, that chief judge would require lagging judges to explain their delays (Barr and Willging 1993).

The judiciary could adopt similar policies across all circuits and *make those data public.* It would be a fairly easy reform since many circuits already undertake the practice privately. By getting out in front of the issue, the circuits might be able to stave off other (i.e., congressional) reforms that could be more intrusive. But if the judiciary

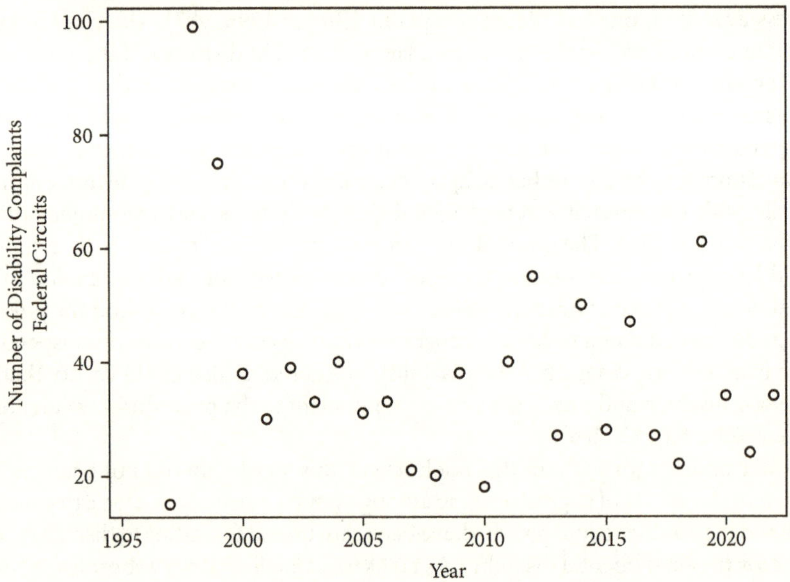

Figure 12.1 Number of disability-related complaints about federal circuit court judges, 1997–2022. Data compiled by the US Courts: https://www.uscourts.gov/statistics-reports/caseload-statistics-data-tables. This figure excludes the specialized circuit courts.

fails to move, Congress could legislatively require them to do so. Courts would note how long—after cases are concluded—each judge required to write his or her opinion. This reform would respect the core of judicial independence. It would not bias judges in any case nor threaten them for any particular decisions. Instead, it would simply alert the public to judges who operate more slowly than others. The knowledge that one's colleagues and the general public can observe delays might suffice to nudge slower judges to retire or change their practices.

One limitation, of course, is that such a reform would simply spotlight slower judges and would not *remove* unfit judges. Such backlog data may not influence a judge who is unaware of her cognitive decline to resign. This is particularly true if his or her colleagues have already taken steps, such as assigning her easier cases, to mitigate the negative effects of cognitive aging. Another limitation of this reform is that it might incentivize judges to spend less time on each case, with the quality of judging potentially decreasing as a result. To meet deadlines, judges might begin to rely more on their clerks or staff, which could generate its own problems. Still, the transparency that would arise from public dissemination of these data may be enough to incentivize at least some judges to resign, with few unintended consequences.

Pension Reform. Another reform would be to improve the positive incentives for judges to retire. Each time Congress has enhanced judicial retirement packages, judges retired (Yoon 2005; Spriggs and Wahlbeck 1995). Yoon (2005, 170) finds that "judges are 38% more likely to vacate their seats [by taking senior status, retiring, or otherwise leaving the bench] in the exact year in which they qualify for their pension than they are for all years before qualifying." Perhaps Congress could ease the Rule of 80 such that older judges could retire with fewer years of service or at an earlier age. Currently, the law declares that judges can take senior status or retire when their age (assuming it is at least 65) plus their years of service sum to at least 80.[10] Removing the age floor of 65 might help. Perhaps a Rule of 70 (minimum age of 60 plus 10 years of service) would work. Alternatively, as Yoon (2005, 176) suggests, "Congress could also experiment with partial vesting, where judges could begin partial vesting at an earlier age, and then allow full vesting" after other service. Such changes might incentivize judges to reduce their workloads or even retire at earlier ages, before decline becomes more severe.

Yet, this reform, like the previous, would not address specific judges with severe cognitive decline. It would do nothing to remove judges who suffer from cognitive decline and refuse to retire. Some judges might leave active service before cognitive aging leads to serious problems, but others will not. And even taking senior status is not enough: our data show negative results from cognitive aging even among judges having taken senior status. An additional limitation, and no small one at that, the reform would add a significant cost to the budget at a time when the federal government already spends far more than it takes in from revenue.[11] Still, the reform would be consistent with judicial independence and has already been shown to be constitutional. An incremental change such as this might address a significant number of cognitively aging judges with few unintended consequences.

Greater Resources to the Judiciary. Another possible reform—or set of reforms—would be to increase the resources that older judges enjoy. A reduced workload from senior status may be helping older judges right now. (Our results throughout the book might have been *even larger* if senior status did not exist.) Increased resources might be necessary. Congress could provide additional funding for older judges to hire more law clerks. Under current law, senior judges are awarded clerks as a function of the caseload they elect to carry. Perhaps Congress could increase funding so that senior judges could operate with a fuller complement of law clerks. Similarly, Congress might provide additional funding to hire more staff attorneys to help aging judges.

But this approach, too, would fail to address specific instances of judges with cognitive decline. Like the previous two reforms, it would do nothing to remove judges who suffer from noticeable cognitive decline. What is more, it could run the risk of law clerks or staff lawyers—none of whom are subject to the advice and consent of the Senate—becoming more influential than the judge. For example, there are stories that Supreme Court Justice Frank Murphy relied so heavily on his law clerk, Eugene Gressman, that others at the Court referred to Gressman as "Mr. Justice Gressman" (Ward and Weiden 2006, 204). Since older judges appear to be more susceptible to influence (Chapter 9), an increased number and role for staff may cause troubling effects. What is more, the approach would be costly as it require federal outlays to cover the cost of additional clerks or staff attorneys. Nevertheless, modest additional

[10] See 28 U.S.C. §371.

[11] One estimate from the mid-1990s put the annual recurring cost of a single circuit judge at approximately $760,000, which is equivalent to $1.6 million as of June 2024 (Levin and Kunz 1994, 1632).

resources, packaged with the other incremental reforms above, might be sufficient to address a majority of the problems from cognitively aging judges.

Constitutional Amendment for Term or Age Limits. The most difficult reforms—but perhaps the easiest to administer—would be those that require constitutional amendments. The proposals being floated most regularly (as of this writing) are those to impose a term limit or an age limit on federal judges. One proposal is to create an 18-year term limit (Calabresi and Lindgren 2006). Another would be an age limit set at 75 or thereabouts.

Consider the 18-year term limit. Calabresi and Lindgren (2006) propose staggered 18-year judicial term limits, at least for Supreme Court justices. As they put it: "The [Supreme] Court's membership would be constitutionally fixed at nine Justices, whose terms would be staggered such that a vacancy would occur on the Court every two years at the end of the term in every odd-numbered calendar year. Every one-term President would thus get to appoint two Justices and every two-term President would get to appoint four" (772). Staggering the vacancies every two years would relieve the pressure of each vacancy on political coalitions. If partisans lose one opportunity, they know they will enjoy another in two years. The appointees will be more in line with dominant political coalitions than a haphazard appointment system in which certain presidents get more and others fewer appointments. And, of course, there is the argument that an 18-year term will, by its overall sweep, remove judges who are aging and losing cognitive capacity (Calabresi and Lindgren 2006).

Now consider the age limit. Levinson (2008) argues that age limits may be "the only practical way to prevent judges from narcissistically remaining on the bench even after they have begun to lose a step (if not two or three) in the performance of their duties" (138–139). Many states impose age limits on their state supreme court justices. One report by the National Center for State Courts writes: "Overall, 32 states plus the District of Columbia have a retirement age for appellate or general-jurisdiction court judges; most use 70 as the threshold, and the remaining states use either 72, 74, 75 . . ." (Raftery 2016, 1). A similar requirement for federal judges would not be out of line.

There are definite strengths to these proposals. For starters, portions of this book examine these two options and find significant public support for them. The public already seems willing at least to discuss these reforms. Moreover, they would be fairly clear and easy to implement. Everyone would know when they are required to step down. Additionally, the reforms would not cost the taxpayers much money. Instead of paying for additional resources for aging judges, they would simply pay a judicial salary. Finally, the reforms are consistent with judicial independence. Judges would not come under the boot of Congress or the president, nor have their decisions upended. No outside pressure would influence their decisions any more than they do today. A lengthy tenure, either from an age limit or a term limit, still would allow the country to benefit from a judge's experience.

But that does not mean the reforms are without downsides. It is arduous to amend the Constitution. And our survey respondents showed us that when they must face political opportunity costs to amend it, they pull back their support. What is more, imposing an 18 year term limit on federal circuit court judges is unlike imposing one on Supreme Court justices. It is much easier to manage a rotation of offices among 9 justices than the nearly 200 circuit court judges. Further, like some of the statutory reforms we described above, this proposal would do nothing to address specific instances of cognitive decline. What would happen to a judge, scheduled to serve another five years, who suffers from acute cognitive decline? A judge with five years left to serve on a court would be in no meaningfully different position than he is in today. He could serve for another five years and there would be no mechanism to remove him.

During the ratification debates, Robert Yates (writing as Brutus) declared that lifetime tenure came at the cost of allowing mentally unfit judges to serve in office (Levinson 2008; Garrow 2000). He argued: "A man may... manifest that he is incompetent to the discharge of the duties of a judge, and yet give no evidence of corruption or want of integrity," and therefore not be impeached (Brutus 1788). He warned that federal judges "cannot be removed from office or suffer a diminution of salary for any error of judgment or *want of capacity*" (Brutus 1788, emphasis supplied). The threat of impeachment would not haunt the cognitively compromised, who could remain on the bench, oblivious to their decline.

Alexander Hamilton felt forced to address the argument. He claimed that leaders would be unable *objectively* to measure a judge's mental capacity. And because no objective standards existed, partisanship and jealousies would corrupt the determination. He argued:

> The mensuration of the faculties of the mind has, I believe, no place in the catalogue of *known* arts. An attempt to fix the boundary between the regions of ability and inability would much oftener give scope to personal and party attachments and enmities than advance the interests of justice or the public good. The result, except in the case of insanity, must for the most part be arbitrary.... (Hamilton 1788)(emphasis supplied)

He continued that to impose an age limit on judges would equally wrongheaded because it would remove too many qualified judges. The cost of losing good judges through an age limit outweighed the "imaginary danger of a superannuated bench" (Hamilton 1788).

The dangers are no longer "imaginary," nor are they beyond the catalogue of known arts. And so the debate continues. We are part of that debate. You, the reader, are part of that debate. Whether any reforms are necessary at this point, we leave to you and others to determine. But in all things, one must remember to proceed cautiously and carefully, always adhering to crucial first principles. As Edmund Burke once wrote: "It is with infinite caution that any man ought to venture upon pulling down an edifice which has answered in any tolerable degree or on building it up again without having models and patterns of approved utility before his eyes" (Burke 1790, 52). There is no utopian or perfect cure for the problem of cognitively aging judges. But by employing incremental changes that remain loyal to judicial independence, we might alleviate some of the most pernicious consequences.

Bibliography

Abelite, Isabella, Evelyn Michalos, and John Rogue. 2021. "Protecting the Supreme Court: Why Safeguarding the Judiciary's Independence Is Crucial to Maintaining its Legitimacy." Democracy and the Constitution Clinic Fordham University School of Law. URL: https://ir.lawnet.fordham.edu/faculty_scholarship/1112/

Aldisert, Ruggero J. 2013. "A Nonagenarian Discusses Life as a Senior Circuit Judge." *Journal of Appellate Practice and Process* 14(2): 183–213.

Alito, Samuel. 2008. "The Inaugural William French Smith Memorial Lecture: A Look at Supreme Court Advocacy with Justice Samuel Alito." *Pepperdine Law Review* 35: 465–492.

Anderson, Nicole D., Fergus I. M. Craik, and Moshe Naveh-Benjamin. 1998. "The Attentional Demands of Encoding and Retrieval in Younger and Older Adults: Evidence from Divided Attention Costs." *Psychology and Aging* 13(3): 405–423.

Armaly, Miles T. 2018. "Extra-Judicial Actor Induced Change in Supreme Court Legitimacy." *Political Research Quarterly* 71(3): 600–613.

Armaly, Miles T. 2021. "Loyalty over Fairness: Acceptance of Unfair Supreme Court Procedures." *Political Research Quarterly* 74(4): 927–940.

Austin, Peter C., and Janet E. Hux. 2002. "A Brief Note on Overlapping Confidence Intervals." *Journal of Vascular Surgery* 36(1): 194–195.

Backes-Gellner, Uschi, Martin R. Schneider, and Stephan Veen. 2011. "Effect of Workforce Age on Quantitative and Qualitative Organizational Performance: Conceptual Framework and Case Study Evidence." *Organization Studies* 32(8): 1103–1121.

Badas, Alex. 2019. "The Applied Legitimacy Index: A New Approach to Measuring Judicial Legitimacy." *Social Science Quarterly* 100(5): 1848–1861.

Bai, Xue. 2014. "Images of Ageing in Society: A Literature Review." *Journal of Population Ageing* 7(3): 231–253.

Baker, Lynn A. 1985. "Unnecessary and Improper: The Judicial Councils Reform and Judicial Conduct and Disability Act of 1980." *Yale Law Journal* 94(5): 1117–1143.

Balkin, Jack M. 2008. "The Five Worst Supreme Court Decisions of the Past Fifty Years." **URL:** *http://balkin.blogspot.com/2008/10/five-worst-supreme-court-decisions-of.html*

Baltes, Paul B. 1993. "The Aging Mind: Potential and Limits." *Gerontologist* 33(5): 580–594.

Bandes, Susan. 2007. "We Lost It at the Movies: The Rule of Law Goes from Washington to Hollywood and Back Again." *Loyola of Los Angeles Law Review* 40: 621–652.

Banich, Marie T., and Rebecca J. Compton. 2018. *Cognitive Neuroscience*. 4th ed. Cambridge University Press.

Banks, Christopher P., and David M. O'Brien. 2020. *The Judicial Process: Law, Courts, and Judicial Politics*. Online ed. CQ Press.

Barr, Jeffrey N., and Thomas E. Willging. 1993. "Decentralized Self-Regulation, Accountability, and Judicial Independence under the Federal Judicial Conduct and Disability Act of 1980." *University of Pennsylvania Law Review* 142(1): 25–207.

Barrow, Deborah J. 1988. *A Court Divided: The Fifth Circuit Court of Appeals and the Politics of Judicial Reform*. Yale University Press.

Bartels, Brandon L., and Christopher D. Johnston. 2013. "On the Ideological Foundations of Supreme Court Legitimacy in the American Public." *American Journal of Political Science* 57(1): 184–199.

Bartels, Brandon L., and Christopher D. Johnston. 2020. *Curbing the Court: Why the Public Constrains Judicial Independence*. Cambridge University Press.

Bartels, Brandon L., and Eric Kramon. 2022. "All the President's Justices? The Impact of Presidential Copartisanship on Supreme Court Job Approval." *American Journal of Political Science* 66(1): 171–186.

Baum, Lawrence. 1976. "Implementation of Judicial Decisions: An Organizational Analysis." *American Politics Quarterly* 4(1): 86–114.

Baum, Lawrence. 1978. "Lower Court Response to Supreme Court Decisions: Reconsidering a Negative Picture." *Justice System Journal* 3: 208–219.

Baum, Lawrence. 2006. *Judges and Their Audiences: A Perspective on Judicial Behavior.* Princeton University Press.

Beck, Paul Allen. 1997. *Party Politics in America.* Longman.

Benesh, Sara C. 2002. *The U.S. Courts of Appeals and the Law of Confessions: Perspectives on the Hierarchy of Justice.* LFB Scholarly Publishing.

Benesh, Sara C. 2006. "The Contribution of Extra Judges." *Arizona Law Review* 48: 301–315.

Benesh, Sara C., and Malia Reddick. 2002. "Overruled: An Event History Analysis of Lower Court Reaction to Supreme Court Alteration of Precedent." *Journal of Politics* 64(2): 534–550.

Bennett, Ilana, and David Madden. 2014. "Disconnected Aging: Cerebral White Matter Integrity and Age-Related Differences in Cognition." *Neuroscience* 276: 187–205.

Benson, Robert W., and Joan B. Kessler. 1987. "Legalese v. Plain Langauge: An Empirical Study of Persuasion and Credibility in Appellate Brief Writing." *Loyola of Los Angeles Law Review* 20: 301–322.

Berman, Russell. 2020. "No Other Western Democracy Allows This." *The Atlantic*, September 25. **URL:** *https://www.theatlantic.com/politics/archive/2020/09/supreme-court-retirement-age/616458/*

Bhattacharya, Mita, and Russell Smyth. 2001. "The Determinants of Judicial Prestige and Influence: Some Empirical Evidence from the High Court of Australia." *Journal of Legal Studies* 30: 223–252.

Birle, Jack. 2023. "Democrats Reintroduce Plan to Expand Supreme Court." Online. **URL:** *https://www.washingtonexaminer.com/news/senate/democrats-reintroduce-plan-to-expand-the-supreme-court*

Black, Ryan C. 2011. "Legal Development and Citation Practices on the U.S. Courts of Appeals." Paper presented at the 2011 annual meetings of the Midwest Political Science Association.

Black, Ryan C., and Christina L. Boyd. 2012. "US Supreme Court Agenda Setting and the Role of Litigant Status." *Journal of Law, Economics, & Organization* 28(1): 286–312.

Black, Ryan C., and James F. Spriggs. 2013. "The Citation and Depreciation of U.S. Supreme Court Precedent." *Journal of Empirical Legal Studies* 10(2): 325–358.

Black, Ryan C., Matthew E. K. Hall, Ryan J. Owens, and Eve Ringsmuth. 2016. "The Role of Emotional Language in Briefs Before the U.S. Supreme Court." *Journal of Law and Courts* 4(2): 377–407.

Black, Ryan C., and Ryan J. Owens. 2009. "Agenda-Setting in the Supreme Court: The Collision of Policy and Jurisprudence." *Journal of Politics* 71(3): 1062–1075.

Black, Ryan C., and Ryan J. Owens. 2011. "Solicitor General Influence and Agenda Setting on the U.S. Supreme Court." *Political Research Quarterly* 64(4): 765–778.

Black, Ryan C., and Ryan J. Owens. 2012. *The Solicitor General and the United States Supreme Court: Executive Influence and Judicial Decisions.* Cambridge University Press.

Black, Ryan C., and Ryan J. Owens. 2013. "Bargaining and Legal Development in the United States Courts of Appeals." *American Politics Research* 41(6): 1071–1101.

Black, Ryan C., and Ryan J. Owens. 2016. "Courting the President: How Circuit Court Judges Alter Their Behavior for Promotion to the Supreme Court." *American Journal of Political Science* 60(1): 30–43.

Black, Ryan C., Ryan J. Owens, and Jennifer L. Brookhart. 2016. "We Are the World: The U.S. Supreme Court's Use of Foreign Sources of Law." *British Journal of Political Science* 46(4): 891–913.

Black, Ryan C., Ryan J. Owens, Justin Wedeking, and Patrick C. Wohlfarth. 2020. *The Conscientious Justice: How Supreme Court Justices' Personalities Influence the Law, the High Court, and the Constitution.* Cambridge University Press.

Black, Ryan C., Ryan J. Owens, Justin Wedeking, and Patrick C. Wohlfarth. 2016. *U.S. Supreme Court Opinions and Their Audiences.* Cambridge University Press.

Black, Ryan C., Ryan J. Owens, and Patrick C. Wohlfarth. 2023. "Considering Constitutional Change: Survey Evidence on Public Attitudes towards Term Limits for Federal Judges." *New Political Science* 45(2): 335–358.

Black, Ryan C., Timothy R. Johnson, Ryan J. Owens, and Justin Wedeking. 2023. "Televised Oral Arguments and Judicial Legitimacy: An Initial Assessment." *Political Behavior* https://doi.org/10.1007/s11109-022-09848-5.

Blake, William D. 2019. "The Law 'Justice under the Constitution, Not Over It': Public Perceptions of FDR's Court-Packing Plan." *Presidential Studies Quarterly* 49(1): 204–218.

Blazer, Dan G., Kristine Yaffe, and Catharyn T. Liverman. 2015. *Cognitive Aging: Progress in Understanding and Opportunities for Action.* National Academies Press.

Block, Frederic. 2007. "Senior Status: An Active Senior Judge Corrects Some Common Misunderstandings." *Cornell Law Review* 92(3): 533–548.

Bloomfield, Louis A. 2016. "WCopyfind (Version 4.1.5)." Windows computer program available for download at http://www.plagiarism.phys.virginia.edu/Wsoftware.html (last accessed December 18, 2010).

Bodwin, Kelly, Jeffrey S. Rosenthal, and Albert H. Yoon. 2013*a*. "Opinion Writing and Authorship on the Supreme Court of Canada." *University of Toronto Law Journal* 63(2): 159–192.

Bodwin, Kelly, Jeffrey S. Rosenthal, and Albert H. Yoon. 2013*b*. "A Statistical Approach to Judicial Authorship: A Case Study of Judge Easterbrook." *Advances and Applications in Statistics* 37(2): 123–148.

Bowen, Rachel E. 2013. "Judicial Autonomy in Central America: A Typological Approach." *Political Research Quarterly* 66(4): 831–842.

Boyd, Christina L. 2015. "Federal District Court Judge Ideology Data." Available at http://cLboyd.net (last accessed January 8, 2024).

Boyd, Christina L., Lee Epstein, and Andrew D. Martin. 2010. "Untangling the Causal Effects of Sex on Judging." *American Journal of Political Science* 54(2): 389–411.

Boyd, Ryan L., Ashwini Ashokkumar, Sarah Seraj, and James W. Pennebaker. 2022. "The Development and Psychometric Properties of LIWC-22." Available at https://www.liwc.app/static/documents/LIWC-22 (last accessed February 3, 2024).

Brambor, Thomas, William Roberts Clark, and Matt Golder. 2006. "Understanding Interaction Models: Improving Empirical Analysis." *Political Analysis* 14(1): 63–82.

Breyer, Stephen. 1990. "Administering Justice in the First Circuit." *Suffolk University Law Review* 24: 29–48.

Breyer, Stephen G. 1996. "Judicial Independence in the United States." *Saint Louis University Law Journal* 40(4): 989–996.

Breyer, Stephen G., Sarah Evans Barker, Pasco M. Bowman, D. Brock Hornby, Sally M. Rider, and J. Harvie Wilkinson III. 2006. Implementation of the Judicial Conduct and Disability Act of 1980: A Report to the Chief Justice. Technical report. The Judicial Conduct and Disability Act Study Committee. **URL:** *www.supremecourtus.gov/publicinfo/breyercommitteereport.pdf*

Brittain, Blake, and Nate Raymond. 2023. "Suspended US Appeals Judge Warns her Treatment Could Erode Confidence in Judiciary." *Reuters*, September 21.

Brudney, James J., and Corey Ditslear. 2001. "Designated Diffidence: District Court Judges on the Courts of Appeals." *Law and Society Review* 35(3): 565–606.

Brutus. 1788. "Anti-Federalist Papers: Brutus 15." **URL:** *http://www.constitution.org/afp/brutus15.htm*

Buckley, William F. 1955. "Publisher's Statement." *National Review* 1(5).

Budziak, Jeffrey, and Daniel Lempert. 2023. "Aesthetic Preferences and Policy Preferences as Determinants of US Supreme Court Writing Style." *Journal of Law and Courts* 11(1): 45–66.

Budziak, Jeffrey, Matthew P. Hitt, and Daniel Lempert. 2018. "Determinants of Writing Style on the United States Circuit Courts of Appeals." *Journal of Law and Courts* 7(1): 1–28.

Buecker, Susanne, Maike Luhmann, Peter Haehner, Janina Larissa Buhler, Laura C. Dapp, Eva C. Luciano, and Ulrich Orth. 2023. "The Development of Subjective Well-Being across the Life Span: A Meta-Analytic Review of Longitudinal Studies." *Psychological Bulletin* 149(7–8): 418–446.

Burbank, Stephen B. 1982. "An Interdisciplinary Perspective on the Tenure of Supreme Court Justices." In *Reforming the Court: Term Limits for Supreme Court Justices*, ed. Roger C. Cranton and Paul D. Carrington. Carolina Academic Press, pp. 317–342.

Burbank, Stephen B., S. Jay Plager, and Gregory Ablavsky. 2012. "Leaving the Bench, 1970–2009: The Choices Federal Judges Make, What Influences Those Choices, and Their Consequences." *University of Pennsylvania Law Review* 161(1): 1–102.

Burke, Deborah M., Donald G. MacKay, Joanna S. Worthley, and Elizabth Wade. 1991. "On the Tip of the Tongue: What Causes Word Finding Failures in Young and Older Adults?" *Journal of Memory and Language* 30: 542–579.

Burke, Edmund. 1790. *Reflections on the Revolution in France.* Vol. 2008. Yale University Press.

Butler, Daniel M., and Eleanor Neff Powell. 2014. "Understanding the Party Brand: Experimental Evidence on the Role of Valence." *Journal of Politics* 76(2): 492–505.

Cabeza, Roberto. 2002. "Hemispheric Asymmetry Reduction in Older Adults: The HAROLD Model." *Psychology and Aging* 17(1): 85–100.

Cabeza, Roberto, Lars Nyberg, and Denise C. Park, eds. 2017. *The Aging Hippocampus: Linking Animal and Human Research.* Oxford University Press.

Calabresi, Stephen G., and James Lindgren. 2006. "Term Limits for the Supreme Court: Life Tenure Reconsidered." *Harvard Journal of Law and Public Policy* 29: 770–877.

Caldeira, Gregory A., and James L. Gibson. 1992. "The Etiology of Public Support for the Supreme Court." *American Journal of Political Science* 36(3): 635–664.

Camerer, Colin F., and Howard Kunreuther. 1989. "Decision Processes for Low Probability Events: Policy Implications." *Journal of Policy Analysis and Management* 8(4): 565–592.

Caminker, Evan H. 1994. "Why Must Inferior Courts Obey Superior Court Precedents?" *Stanford Law Review* 46(4): 817–873.

Carlsen, William. 1996. "Frontier Justice." *San Francisco Chronicle,* October 6: 1, 5.

Carlson, Keith, Michael A. Livermore, and Daniel Rockmore. 2015. "A Quantitative Analysis of Writing Style on the Us Supreme Court." *Washington University Law Review* 93: 1461–1510.

Carriere, Jonathan S. A., J. Allan Cheyne, Grayden J. F. Solman, and Daniel Smilek. 2010. "Age Trends for Failures of Sustained Attention." *Psychology and Aging* 25(3): 569–574.

Carstensen, Laura. 2011. *A Long Bright Future.* Public Affairs.

Carter, Rita. 2019. *The Human Brain Book.* 3rd ed. DK Penguin Random House.

Castel, Alan D., and Fergus I. M. Craik. 2003. "The Effect of Aging and Divide Attention on Memory for Item and Associative Formation." *Psychology and Aging* 18(4): 873–885.

Chen, Daniel L., Tobias J. Moskowitz, and Kelly Shue. 2016. "Decision Making under the Gambler's Fallacy: Evidence from Asylum Judges, Loan Officers, and Baseball Umpires." *Quarterly Journal of Economics* 131(3): 1181–1242.

Choi, Stephan, and Mitu Gulati. 2004*a*. "A Tournament of Judges." *California Law Review* 92(1): 299–322.

Choi, Stephen J., and G. Mitu Gulati. 2004*b*. "Chosing the Next Supreme Court Justice: An Empirical Ranking of Judge Performance." *Southern California Law Review* 78: 23–118.

Choi, Stephen J., and G. Mitu Gulati. 2005. "Which Judges Write Their Opinions (and Should We Care)?" *Florida State University Law Review* 32: 1077–1122.

Christenson, Dino P., and David M. Glick. 2015. "Chief Justice Roberts's Health Care Decision Disrobed: The Microfoundations of the Supreme Court's Legitimacy." *American Journal of Political Science* 59(2): 403–418.

Christenson, Dino P., and David M. Glick. 2019. "Reassessing the Supreme Court: How Decisions and Negativity Bias Affect Legitimacy." *Political Research Quarterly* 72(3): 637–652.

Coffin, Frank M. 1994. *On Appeal: Courts, Lawyering, and Judging.* W. W. Norton and Company.

Cohen, Jonathan Matthew. 2002. *Inside Appellate Courts: The Impact of Court Organization on Judicial Decision Making in the United States Courts of Appeals.* University Of Michigan Press.

Collins, Jr. Paul M. 2008*a*. "Amici Curiae and Dissensus on the U.S. Supreme Court." *Journal of Empirical Legal Studies* 5(1): 143–170.

Collins, Jr. Paul M. 2008*b*. *Friends of the Court: Interest Groups and Judicial Decision Making.* New York: Oxford University Press.

Collins, Jr. Paul M., Pamela C. Corley, and Jesse Hamner. 2015. "The Influence of Amicus Curiae Briefs on US Supreme Court Opinion Content." *Law and Society Review* 49(4): 917–944.

Collins, Paul M., Pamela C. Corley, and Jesse Hamner. 2014. "Me Too: An Investigation of Repetition in U.S. Supreme Court Amicus Curiae Briefs." *Judicature* 97(5): 228–234.

Comparato, Scott A., and Scott D. McClurg. 2007. "A Neo-Institutional Explanation of State Supreme Court Responses in Search and Seizure Cases." *American Politics Research* 35(5): 726–754.
Coppock, Alexander, and Oliver A. McClellan. 2019. "Validating the Demographic, Political, Psychological, and Experimental Results Obtained from a New Source of Online Survey Respondents." *Research and Politics* 6(1): 1–14.
Corley, Pamela C. 2008. "The Supreme Court and Opinion Content: The Influence of Parties' Briefs." *Political Research Quarterly* 61(3): 468–478.
Corley, Pamela C. 2009. "Uncertain Precedent: Circuit Court Responses to Supreme Court Plurality Opinions." *American Politics Research* 37(1): 30–49.
Corley, Pamela C., and Justin Wedeking. 2014. "The (Dis)Advatnage of Certainty: The Importance of Certainty in Language." *Law and Society Review* 48(1): 35–62.
Corley, Pamela C., Robert M. Howard, and David C. Nixon. 2005. "The Supreme Court and Opinion Content: The Use of the Federalist Papers." *Political Research Quarterly* 58(2): 329–340.
Cox, Gary W., and Mathew D. McCubbins. 2005. *Setting the Agenda: Responsible Party Government in the U.S. House of Representatives.* Cambridge University Press.
Cross, Frank. 2005. "Appellate Adherence to Precedent." *Journal of Empirical Legal Studies* 2(2): 369–405.
Cross, Frank B. 2007. *Decision Making in the U.S. Courts of Appeals.* Stanford University Press.
Cross, Frank B., and Emerson H. Tiller. 1998. "Judicial Partisanship and Obedience to Legal Doctrine: Whistleblowing on the Federal Courts of Appeals." *Yale Law Journal* 107(7): 2155–2176.
Cushman, Barry. 1994. "Rethinking the New Deal Court." *Virginia Law Review* 80(1): 201–261.
Dahlberg, Stefan, and Eelco Harteveld. 2016. "Left–Right Ideology as an Inferential Device in Multiparty Systems: Can Citizens Overcome Low Information by Imputing Parties' Policy Positions?" *Electoral Studies* 42: 175–187.
Dancey, Logan, and Geoffrey Sheagley. 2013. "Heuristics Behaving Badly." *American Journal of Political Science* 57(2): 312–325.
Daneman, M., and P. A. Carpenter. 1980. "Individual Differences in Working Memory and Reading." *Journal of Verbal Learning and Verbal Behavior* 19:450–466.
Dang, Linh C., Jaime J. Castrellon, Scott F. Perkins, Nam T. Le, Ronald L. Cowan, David H. Zald, and Gregory R. Samanez-Larkin. 2017. "Reduced Effects of Age on Dopamine D2 Receptor Levels in Physically Active Adults." *NeuroImage* 148(1): 123–129.
Davis, Richard H., and James A. Davis. 1985. *TV's Image of the Elderly.* Lexington Books.
Debre, Isabel, and Josef Federman. 2023. "Israel's New Government Unveils Plan to Weaken Supreme Court." Online. **URL:** *https://abcnews.go.com/International/wireStory/top-israeli-legal-official-opposes-con-minister-96186011*
Desjardins, Richard, and Arne Jonas Wamke. 2012. "Ageing and Skills: A Review and Analysis of Skill Gain and Skill Loss over the Lifespan and over Time." OECD Education Working Papers, No. 72.
Desmond, Jenni. 2015. *The Blue Whale.* Enchanted Lion Books.
Dorsen, David M. 2012. *Henry Friendly: Greatest Judge of His Era.* Belknap Press.
Downs, Anthony. 1957. *An Economic Theory of Democracy.* Harper.
Drag, Lauren L., and Linas A. Bieliauskas. 2010. "Contemporary Review 2009: Cognitive Aging." *Journal of Geriatric Psychiatry* 23(2): 75–93.
Engel, Christoph, and Keren Weinshall. 2020. "Manna from Heaven for Judges: Judges' Reaction to a Quasi-Random Reduction in Caseload." *Journal of Empirical Legal Studies* 17(4): 722–751.
Epstein, Lee, Andrew D. Martin, Jeffrey A. Segal, and Chad Westerland. 2007. "The Judicial Common Space." *Journal of Law, Economics, & Organization* 23(2): 303–325.
Epstein, Lee, Jeffrey A. Segal, and Jennifer Nicoll Victor. 2002. "Dynamic Agenda Setting on the U.S. Supreme Court: An Empirical Assessment." *Harvard Journal on Legislation* 39(2): 395–433.
Epstein, Lee, and Joseph F. Kobylka. 1992. *The Supreme Court and Legal Change: Abortion and the Death Penalty.* University of North Carolina Press.
Epstein, Lee, William M. Landes, and The Honorable Richard A. Posner. 2013. *The Behavior of Federal Judges: A Theoretical and Empirical Study of Rational Choice.* Harvard University Press.
Erikson, Robert S. 2022. "Appellate Court Assignments as a Natural Experiment: Gender Panel Effects in Sex Discrimination Cases." *Journal of Empirical Legal Studies* 19(2): 423–446.

Evans, Michael, Wayne McIntosh, Jimmy Lin, and Cynthia Cates. 2007. "Recounting the Courts? Applying Automated Content Analysis to Enhance Empirical Research." *Journal of Empirical Legal Studies* 4(4): 1007–1039.

Farhang, Sean, and Gregory Wawro. 2004. "Institutional Dynamics on the U.S. Court of Appeals: Minority Representation under Panel Decision Making." *Journal of Law, Economics, and Organization* 20: 299–330.

Feldman, Adam. 2017*a*. "A Brief Assessment of Supreme Court Opinion Language." *Mississippi Law Journal* 86(1): 106–150.

Feldman, Adam. 2017*b*. "Opinion Construction in the Roberts Court." *Law and Policy* 39(2): 192–209.

Frankfurt, Harry G. 2005. *On Bullshit.* Princeton University Press.

Freeman, Will, and Adriana Beltran. 2021. "In Central America, Rule of Law Is under Attack. El Salvador Is the Latest Victim." *Foreign Policy*, May 12. **URL:** *https://foreignpolicy.com/2021/05/12/central-america-rule-of-law-under-attack-el-salvador-nicaragua-guatemala-honduras/*

Friendly, Henry J. 1962. "How a Judge of the United States Court of Appeals Works." *Institute of Judicial Administration.*

Garrow, David J. 2000. "Mental Decrepitude on the U.S. Supreme Court: The Historical Case for a 28th Amendment." *University of Chicago Law Review* 67(4): 995–1087.

Gazzaniga, Michael S., Richard B. Ivry, and George R. Mangun. 1998. *Cognitive Neuroscience: The Biology of the Mind.* W. W. Norton & Company.

George, Tracey E. 1999. "The Dynamics and Determinants of the Decision to Grant En Banc Review." *Washington Law Review* 74: 213–274.

Gewirtz, Paul. 1987. "A Lawyer's Death." *Harvard Law Review* 100(8): 2053–2056.

Gibson, James L., and Gregory A. Caldeira. 2011. "Has Legal Realism Damaged the Legitimacy of the U.S. Supreme Court?" *Law and Society Review* 45(1): 195–219.

Gibson, James L., Gregory A. Caldeira, and Lester Kenyatta Spence. 2003. "The Supreme Court and the U.S. Presidential Election of 2000: Wounds, Self-Inflicted or Otherwise?" *British Journal of Political Science* 33(4): 535–556.

Gibson, James L., and Michael J. Nelson. 2015. "Is the U.S. Supreme Court's Legitimacy Grounded in Performance Satisfaction and Ideology?" *American Journal of Political Science* 59(1): 162–174.

Giles, Michael W., Virginia A. Hettinger, and Todd Peppers. 2001. "Picking Federal Judges: A Note on Policy and Partisan Selection Agendas." *Political Research Quarterly* 54(3): 623–641.

Goelzhauser, Greg, and Damon M. Cann. 2014. "Judicial Independence and Opinion Clarity on State Supreme Courts." *State Politics and Policy Quarterly* 14(2): 123–141.

Goldman, Sheldon. 1966. "Voting Behavior on the United States Court of Appeals, 1961–1964." *American Political Science Review* 60(2): 374–383.

Goldstein, Joseph. 2011. "Life Tenure for Federal Judges Raises Issues of Senility, Dementia." *ProPublica*, January 18.

Gorbach, T., S. Pudas, A. Lindquist, G. Oradd, M. Joseffsson, A. Salami, and L. Nyberg. 2017. "Longitudinal Association between Hippocampus Atrophy and Episodic-Memory Decline." *Neurobiology of Aging* 51: 167–176.

Gray, James P. 2013. "It's a Gray Area: What's it Like to be a Judge?" *Los Angeles Times*, August 16.

Greene, Jenna. 2022. "After Posner Retired from 7Th Circuit, a Grim Diagnosis and a Brewing Battle." *Reuters*, March 22.

Gruenfeld, Deborah H. 1995. "Status, Ideology, and Integrative Complexity on the U.S. Supreme Court: Rethinking the Politics of Political Decision Making." *Journal of Personality and Social Psychology* 68: 5–20.

Gruhl, John. 1980. "The Supreme Court's Impact on the Law of Libel: Compliance by Lower Federal Courts." *Western Political Quarterly* 33(4): 502–519.

Gunning-Dixon, Faith M., and Naftali Raz. 2000. "The Cognitive Correlates of White Matter Abnormalities in Normal Aging: A Quantitative Review." *Neuropsychology* 14(2): 224–232.

Gutchess, Angela. 2019. *Cognitive and Social Neuroscience of Aging.* Cambridge University Press.

Guthrie, Chris, Jeffrey J. Rachlinski, and Andrew J. Wistrich. 2001. "Inside the Judicial Mind." *Cornell Law Review* 86(4): 777–830.

Guthrie, Chris, Jeffrey J. Rachlinski, and Andrew J. Wistrich. 2007. "Blinking on the Bench: How Judges Decide Cases." *Cornell Law Review* 93: 1–44.
Haire, Susan, Stefanie A. Lindquist, and Donald Songer. 2003. "Appellate Court Supervision in the Federal Judiciary: A Hierarchical Perspective." *Law and Society Review* 37(1): 143–168.
Hall, Matthew. 2009. "Experimental Justice: Random Judicial Assignment and the Partisan Process of Supreme Court Review." *American Politics Research* 37(2): 195–226.
Hall, Richard L., and Alan V. Deardorff. 2006. "Lobbying as Legislative Subsidy." *American Political Science Review* 100(1): 69–84.
Hamilton, Alexander. 1788. "Federalist Number 78."
Hansford, Thomas G., and James F. Spriggs, II. 2006. *The Politics of Precedent on the U.S. Supreme Court.* Princeton University Press.
Harada, Caroline N., Marissa C. Natelson Love, and Kristen L. Triebel. 2013. "Normal Cognitive Aging." *Clinics in Geriatric Medicine* 29(4): 737–752.
Hazelton, Morgan L. W., and Rachael K. Hinkle. 2022. *Persuading the Supreme Court: The Significance of Briefs in Judicial Decision-Making.* University of Kansas Press.
Hazelton, Morgan L. W., Rachael K. Hinkle, and James F. Spriggs. 2019. "The Influence of Unique Information in Briefs on Supreme Court Decisionmaking." *Justice System Journal* 40(2): 126–157.
Helmke, Gretchen. 2005. *Courts under Constraints.* Cambridge University Press.
Helmke, Gretchen, and Frances Rosenbluth. 2009. "Regimes and the Rule of Law: Judicial Independence in Comparative Perspective." *Annual Review of Political Science* 12: 345–366.
Hertzog, Christopher, Arthur F. Kramer, Robert S. Wilson, and Ulman Lindenberger. 2009. "Enrichment Effects on Adult Cognitive Development." *Psychological Science in the Public Interest* 9(1): 1–65.
Hettinger, Virginia A., Stefanie A. Lindquist, and Wendy L. Martinek. 2003*a*. "Acclimation Effects and Separate Opinion Writing in the United States Courts of Appeals." *Social Science Quarterly* 84(4): 792–810.
Hettinger, Virginia A., Stefanie A. Lindquist, and Wendy L. Martinek. 2003*b*. "The Role and Impact of Chief Judges on the United State Courts of Appeals." *Justice System Journal* 24: 91–117.
Hettinger, Virginia A., Stefanie A. Lindquist, and Wendy L. Martinek. 2003*c*. "Separate Opinion Writing on the United States Courts of Appeals." *American Politics Research* 31(3): 215–250.
Hettinger, Virginia A., Stefanie A. Lindquist, and Wendy L. Martinek. 2004. "Comparing Attitudinal and Strategic Accounts of Dissenting Behavior on the U.S. Courts of Appeals." *American Journal of Political Science* 48(1): 123–137.
Hettinger, Virginia A., Stefanie A. Lindquist, and Wendy L. Martinek. 2006. *Judging on a Collegial Court: Influences on Federal Appellate Decision-Making.* University of Virginia Press.
Hinkle, Rachael K. 2015. "Legal Constraint in the US Courts of Appeals." *Journal of Politics* 77(3): 721–735.
Hinkle, Rachael K. 2017. "Panel Effects and Opinion Crafting in the US Courts of Appeals." *Journal of Law and Courts* 5(2): 313–336.
Hinkle, Rachael K., Michael J. Nelson, and Morgan L. W. Hazelton. 2020. "Deferring, Deliberating, or Dodging Review: Explaining Counterjudge Success in the US Courts of Appeals." *Journal of Law and Courts* 8(2): 277–300.
Hoekstra, Valerie. 2005. "Competing Constraints: State Court Responses to Supreme Court Decisions and Legislation on Wages and Hours." *Political Research Quarterly* 58(2): 317–328.
Holvast, Nina L. 2014. "Considering the Consequences of Increased Reliance on Judicial Assistants: A Study on Dutch Courts." *International Journal of the Legal Profession* 21(1): 39–59.
Horowitz, Jeremy D. 2011. "Legitimacy, Ideology, and the Use of Precedent on the U.S. Supreme Court." Paper Delivered at the Sixth Annual Conference on Empirical Legal Studies, Northwestern University Law School.
Howard, Jr., J. Woodford. 1981. *Courts of Appeals in the Federal Judicial System: A Study of the Second, Fifth, and District of Columbia Circuits.* Princeton University Press.
Hoyer, William J. 2015. *International Encyclopedia of the Social and Behavioral Sciences.* Vol. 2. 2 ed. Elsevier.
Hummert, Mary Lee, Teri A. Garstka, Jaye L. Atkinson, and Sharon Strahm. 1994. "StereoTypes of the Elderly Held by Young, Middle-Aged and Elderly Adults." *Journal of Gerontology* 49(5): 240–249.

Johnson, Charles A. 1979. "Lower Court Reactions to Supreme Court Decisions: A Quantitative Analysis." *American Journal of Political Science* 23(4): 792–8004.

Johnson, Charles A., and Bradley C. Canon. 1984. *Judicial Policies: Implementation and Impact*. CQ Press.

Johnson, Kirk. 1986. "A Solemn Tribute to Henry Friendly, A Quiet Giant of the Appeals Bench." *New York Times*, June 10.

Johnson, Timothy R. 2003. "The Supreme Court, the Solicitor General, and the Separation of Powers." *American Politics Research* 31(4): 426–451.

Jones, H. E., and H. S. Conrad. 1933. "The Growth and Decline of Intelligence: A Study of a Homogeneous Group between the Ages of Ten and Sixty." *Genetic Psychology Monographs* 13: 223–298.

Kaheny, Erin B., Susan Brodie Haire, and Sara C. Benesh. 2008. "Change over Tenure: Voting, Variance, and Decision Making on the U.S. Courts of Appeals." *American Journal of Political Science* 52(3): 490–503.

Kahneman, Daniel. 2011. *Thinking, Fast and Slow*. Farrar, Strauss, and Giroux.

Kassow, Benjamin J., Donald R. Songer, and Michael P. Fix. 2012. "The Influence of Precedent on State Supreme Courts." *Political Research Quarterly* 65(2): 372–384.

Kastellec, Jonathan P. 2011. "Panel Composition and Voting on the U.S. Courts of Appeals over Time." *Political Research Quarterly* 64(2): 377–391.

Kastellec, Jonathan P. 2013. "Racial Diversity and Judicial Influence on Appellate Courts." *American Journal of Political Science* 57(1): 167–183.

Kelly, P. H., L. Bondolfi, D. Hunziker, H. P. Schlecht, K. Carver, E. Maguire, D. Abramowski, K. H. Wiederhold, C. Sturchler-Pierrat, M. Jucker, and R. Bergmann. 2003. "Progressive Age-Related Impairment of Cognitive Behavior in App23 Transgenic Mice." *Neurobiology of Aging* 24(2): 365–378.

Kennedy, Kristen M., Karen M. Rodrigue, Gerard N. Bischof, Andrew C. Hebrank, Patricia A. Reuter-Lorenz, and Denise C. Park. 2015. "Age Trajectories of Functional Activation under Conditions of Low and High Processing Demands: An Adult Lifespan fMRI Study of the Aging Brain." *NeuroImage* 104: 21–34.

Kenyon, Peter. 2023. "Turkey Election Threatens President Erdogan's 20-Year Rule." Online. **URL:** *https://www.npr.org/2023/05/14/1176086570/turkey-election-threatens-president-erdogans-20-year-rule*

Kim, Pauline T. 2009. "Deliberation and Strategy on the United States Courts of Appeals: An Empirical Exploration of Panel Effects." *University of Pennsylvania Law Review* 157: 1319–1381.

King, Gary, Michael Tomz, and Jason Wittenberg. 2000. "Making the Most of Statistical Analyses: Improving Interpretation and Presentation." *American Journal of Political Science* 44(2): 347–361.

Kite, Mary E., Gary D. Stockdale, Bernard E. Whitley, Jr., and Blair T. Johnson. 2005. "Attitudes toward Older and Younger Adults: An Updated Meta-Analysis." *Journal of Social Issues* 61(2): 241–266.

Klein, David, and Darby Morrisroe. 1999. "The Prestige and Influence of Individual Judges on the U.S. Courts of Appeals." *Journal of Legal Studies* 19(4): 371–391.

Klein, David E. 2002. *Making Law in the United States Courts of Appeals*. Cambridge: Cambridge University Press.

Klingseisen, Anna, and David A. Lyons. 2018. "Axonal Regulation of Central Nervous System Myelination: Structure and Function." *The Neuroscientist* 24(1): 7–21.

Kosma, Montgomery N. 1998. "Measuring the Influence of Supreme Court Justices." *Journal of Legal Studies* 27: 333–372.

Kourlis, Rebecca Love, and Jordan M. Singer. 2007. "Using Judicial Performance Evalutions to Promote Judicial Accountability." *Judicature* 90(5): 200–207.

Kramer, A. F., S. Hahn, and D. Gopher. 1999. "Task Coordination and Aging: Explorations of Executive Processing in the Task Switching Paradigm." *Acta Psychologica* 101: 339–378.

Kravitz, Mark R. 2009. "Written and Oral Persuasion in the United States Courts: A District Judge's Perspective on Their History, Function, and Future." *Journal of Appellate Practice and Process* 10(2): 247–272.

Kritzer, Herbert M., and Mark J. Richards. 2005. "The Role of Law in the Supreme Court's Search and Seizure Jurisprudence." *American Politics Research* 33: 33–55.

Kropko, Jonathan, and Jeffrey J. Harden. 2019. "coxed: An R Package for Computing Duration-Based Quantities from the Cox Proportional Hazards Model." *R Journal* 11(2): 38–45.

Kropko, Jonathan, and Jeffrey J. Harden. 2020. "Beyond the Hazard Ratio: Generating Expected Durations from the Cox Proportional Hazards Model." *British Journal of Political Science* 50(1): 303–320.

Larson, Richard C., and Mauricio Gomez Diaz. 2012. "Nonfixed Retirement Age for University Professors: Modeling Its Effects on New Faculty Hires." *Service Science* 4(1): 69–78.

Levin, A. Leo, and Michael E. Kunz. 1994. "Thinking about Judgeships." *American University Law Review* 44: 1627–1654.

Levinson, Sanford. 2008. *Our Undemocratic Constitution: Where the Constitution Goes Wrong (And How We the People Can Correct It)*. Oxford University Press.

Levy, Becca R., Stanislav V. Kasl, and Thomas M. Gill. 2004. "Image of Aging Scale." *Perceptual and Motor Skills* 99(1): 208–210.

Levy, Marin K. 2021. "The Promise of Senior Judges." *Northwestern University Law Review* 115(4): 1227–1260.

LexisNexis. 2020. "Shepard's Signal Indicators and Treatments." Available at https://www.lexisnexis.com/pdf/lexis-advance/Shepards-Signal-Indicators-and-analysis-phrases-Final.pdf (last accessed January 31, 2024).

Li, William, Pablo Azar, David Larochelle, Phil Hill, James Cox, Robert C. Berwick, and Andrew W. Lo. 2013. "Using Algorithmic Attribution Techniques to Determine Authorship in Unsigned Judicial Opinions." *Stanford Technology Law Review* 16(3): 503–534.

Long, J. Scott, and Jeremy Freese. 2014. *Regression Models for Categorical Dependent Variables Using Stata*. 3rd ed. College Station, TX: Stata Press.

Lu, Ming-Teh, James B. Preston, and Peter L. Strick. 1994. "Interconnection between the Prefrontal Cortex and the Premotor Areas in the Frontal Lobe." *Journal of Comparative Neurology* 341(3): 375–392.

Luong, Gloria, Susan T. Charles, and Karen L. Fingerman. 2011. "Better with Age: Social Relationships across Adulthood." *Journal of Social and Personal Relationships* 28(1): 9–23.

Luse, Jennifer K., Geoffrey McGovern, Wendy L. Martinek, and Sara C. Benesh. 2009. "'Such Inferior Courts…': Compliance by Circuits with Jurisprudential Regimes." *American Politics Research* 37(1): 75–106.

Lyons, David M., Chou Yang, Stephan Eliez, Allan L. Reiss, and Alan F. Schatzberg. 2004. "Cognitive Correlates of White Matter Growth and Stress Hormones in Female Squirrel Monkey Adults." *Journal of Neuroscience* 24(14): 3655–3662.

Madden, Mike. 2023. "Judging Readability: A Study of Opinions Written by Apex Court Judges from Australia, Canada, South Africa, the United Kingdom, and the United States." Available at https://papers.ssrn.com/sol3/papers.cfm?abstract_id=4160956.

Manwaring, David Roger, Donald R. Reich, and Stephen L. Wasby. 1972. *The Supreme Court as Policy-maker: Three Studies on the Impact of Judicial Decisions*. Public Affairs Research Bureau, Southern Illinois University at Carbondale.

Martineau, Robert J., Kent Sinclaie, Michael E. Solomine, and Randy J. Holland. 2005. *Appellate Practice and Procedure*. Thomson.

McCormick, Peter. 1996. "The Supreme Court Cites the Supreme Court: Follow-up Citation on the Supreme Court of Canada, 1989–1993." *Osgoode Hall Law Journal* 33:453–486.

McDowd, Joan M., and Fergus I. M. Craik. 1988. "Effects of Aging and Task Difficulty on Divided Attention Performance." *Journal of Experimental Psychology: Human Perception and Performance* 14(2): 267–280.

Mears, Bill. 2012. "Biography Tells of Greatest Judge You Never Knew." *CNN.com*, April 18. **URL:** *https://www.cnn.com/2012/04/17/politics/friendly-judge-biography/index.html*

Michel, Paul R. 1998. "Effective Appellate Advocacy." *Litigation* 24(4): 19–23.

Mikva, Abner. 1995. "Maintaining Control of the Judiciary." *The Long Term View* 3(1): 9–13.

Milgram, N. W., E. Head, E. Weiner, and E. Thomas. 1994. "Cognitive Functions and Aging in the Dog: Acquisition of Nonspatial Visual Tasks." *Behavioral Neuroscience* 108(1): 57–68.

Miller, Darryl W., Teresita S. Leyell, and Juliann Mazcheck. 2004. "Stereotypes of the Elderly in U.S. Television Commercials from the 1950s to the 1990s." *International Journal of Aging and Human Development* 58(4): 315–340.

Minear, Meredith, and Denise C. Park. 2004. "A Lifespan Database of Adult Facial Stimuli." *Behavior Research Methods, Instruments, and Computers* 36: 630–633.

Mosteller, Frederick, and David L. Wallace. 1963. "Inference in an Authorship Problem." *Journal of the American Statistical Association* 58(302): 275–309.

Moyer, Laura P., John Szmer, Susan Haire, and Robert K. Christensen. 2021. "'All Eyes Are on You': Gender, Race, and Opinion Writing on the US Courts of Appeals." *Law and Society Review* 55: 452–472.

Mukaka, M. M. 2012. "A Guide to Appropriate Use of Correlation Coeffficient in Medical Research." *Journal of the Medical Association of Malawi* 24(3): 69–71.

Murman, Daniel L. 2015. "The Impact of Age on Cognition." *Seminars in Hearing* 36(3): 111–121.

Murphy, Walter F. 1959. "Lower Court Checks on Supreme Court Power." *American Political Science Review* 53(4): 1017–1031.

Murphy, Walter F. 1964. *Elements of Judicial Strategy*. Chicago: University of Chicago Press.

Neisser, Ulric. 1967. *Cognitive Psychology*. Prentice Hall.

Nelson, Michael J., and James L. Gibson. 2020. "Measuring Subjective Ideological Disagreement with the US Supreme Court." *Journal of Law and Courts* 8(1): 75–94.

Nelson, Michael J., and Patrick D. Tucker. 2021. "The Stability and Durability of the US Supreme Court's Legitimacy." *Journal of Politics* 83(2): 767–771.

Nicholson, Stephen P., and Thomas G. Hansford. 2014. "Partisans in Robes: Party Cues and Public Acceptance of Supreme Court Decisions." *American Journal Of Political Science* 58(3): 620–636.

Norman, S., S. Kemper, D. Kynette, H. Cheung, and C. Anagnopoulos. 1991. "Syntactic Complexity and Adults' Running Memory Span." *Journal of Gerontology: Psychological Sciences* 46: 346–351.

North, Douglas, and Barry Weingast. 1989. "Constitutions and Commitment: The Evolution of Institutions Governing Public Choice in Seventeenth-Century England." *Journal of Economic History* 49: 803–832.

O'Brien, Keith, and Adam Harris. 2014. "Two Is Company, Three Is a Crowd: Party Labels and Number of Candidates as Determinants of 'Incorrect' Vote Choice." *Proceedings of the Annual Meeting of the Cognitive Science Society* 36(36): 2705–2710.

Oldfather, Chad M., Joseph P. Brockhorst, and Brian P. Dimmer. 2012. "Triangulating Judicial Responsiveness: Automated Content Analysis, Judicial Opinions, and the Methodology of Legal Scholarship." *Florida Law Review* 64: 1189–1242.

Opeskin, Brian. 2015. "Models of Judicial Tenure: Reconsidering Life Limits, Age Limits and Term Limits for Judges." *Oxford Journal of Legal Studies* 35(4): 627–663.

Owens, Ryan J. 2023. "Order Effects and Oral Argument at the US Supreme Court." *Social Science Quarterly*. 104(6): 1222–1236

Owens, Ryan J., Alexander M. Tahk, Patrick C. Wohlfarth, and Amanda C. Bryan. 2015. "Nominating Commissions, Judicial Retention, and Forward-Looking Behavior on State Supreme Courts: An Empirical Examination of Selection and Retention Methods." *State Politics and Policy Quarterly* 15(2): 211–238.

Owens, Ryan J., and Justin P. Wedeking. 2011. "Justices and Legal Clarity: Analyzing the Complexity of Supreme Court Opinions." *Law and Society Review* 45(4): 1027–1061.

Owens, Ryan J., Justin P. Wedeking, and Patrick C. Wohlfarth. 2013. "How the Supreme Court Alters Opinion Language to Evade Congressional Review." *Journal of Law and Courts* 1(1): 35–59.

Owens, Ryan J., and Patrick C. Wohlfarth. 2019. "The Influence of Home State Reputation on Native Born Federal Circuit Court Judges." *Journal of Law and Courts* 7(2): 187–214.

Paley, Ruth, ed. 2016. *The Oxford Edition of Blackstone's Commentaries on the Laws of England*. 1st ed. Oxford University Press.

Paraskevoudi, Nadia, Fuat Balcı, and Argiro Vatakis. 2018. "'walking' Through The Sensory, Cognitive, and Temporal Degradations of Healthy Aging." *Annals of the New York Academy of Sciences* 1426(1): 72–92.

Pardo, Guido Bonilla. 1992. "Justice for Justice: Violence against Judges and Lawyers in Colombia: 1979–1991." **URL:** *https://www.icj.org/justice-for-justice-violence-against-judges-and-lawyers-in-colombia-1979-1991/*

Park, Denise C. 2000. *Cognitive Aging: A Primer.* Psychology Press.

Park, Denise C., Anderson D. Smith, Gary Lautenschlager, Julie L. Earles, David Frieske, Melissa Zwahr, and Christine L. Gaines. 1996. "Mediators of Long-Term Memory Performance across the Life Span." *Psychology and Aging* 11(4): 621–637.

Park, Denise C., Gary Lautenschlager, Trey Hedden, Natalie S. Davidson, Anderson D. Smith, and Pamela K. Smith. 2002. "Models of Visuospatial and Verbal Memory across the Adult Life Span." *Psychology and Aging* 17(2): 299–320.

Paulsen, Michael Stokes. 1990. "Accusing Justice: Some Variations on the Themes of Robert M. Cover's Justice Accused." *Journal of Law and Religion* 7: 33–97.

Peabody, Bruce. 2011. *The Politics of Judicial Independence.* Johns Hopkins University Press.

Peltason, J. W. 1971. *Fifty-Eight Lonely Men.* University of Illinois Press.

Peppers, Todd C. 2006. *Courtiers of the Marble Palace: The Rise and Influence of the Supreme Court Law Clerk.* Stanford University Press.

Persson, J., S. Pudas, J. Lind, K. Kauppi, L.-G. Nilsson, and L. Nyberg. 2012. "Longitudinal Structure-Function Correlates in Elderly Reveal MTL Dysfunction with Cognitive Decline." *Cerebral Cortex* 22(10): 2297–2304.

Popkin, Samuel L. 1994. *The Reasoning Voter: Communication and Persuasion in Presidential Campaigns.* 2nd ed. University of Chicago Press.

Popkin, William D. 2007. *Evolution of the Judicial Opinion.* New York University Press.

Posner, Richard. 1995*a*. *Aging and Old Age.* University of Chicago Press.

Posner, Richard A. 1995*b*. "Judges' Writing Styles (And Do They Matter?)." *University of Chicago Law Review* 62(4): 1421–1449.

Posner, Richard A. 2008. *How Judges Think.* Harvard University Press.

Posner, Richard A. 2016. *Divergent Paths: The Academy and the Judiciary.* Harvard University Press.

Posner, Richard A. 2017. *The Federal Judiciary: Strengths and Weaknesses.* Harvard University Press.

Powell, Douglas H. 1994. *Profiles in Cognitive Aging.* Harvard University Press.

Rachlinski, Jeffrey J., and Andrew J. Wistrich. 2017. "Judging the Judiciary by the Numbers: Empirical Research on Judges." *Annual Review of Law and Social Science* 13: 203–229.

Raftery, William E. 2016. "Increasing or Repealing Mandatory Judicial Retirement Ages." Report on trends in state courts National Center for State Courts. **URL:** *https://ncsc.contentdm.oclc.org/digital/collection/judicial/id/440/rec/1*

Raz, Naftali, Faith Gunning-Dixon, Denise Head, Karen M. Rodrigue, Adrienne Williamson, and James D Acker. 2004. "Aging, Sexual Dimorphism, and Hemispheric Asymmetry of the Cerebral Cortex: Replicability of Regional Differences in Volume." *Neurobiology of Aging* 25(3): 377–396.

Raz, Naftali, Ulman Lindenberger, Paolo Ghisletta, Karen M. Rodrigue, Kristen M. Kennedy, and James D. Acker. 2007. "Neuroanatomical Correlates of Fluid Intelligence in Healthy Adults and Persons with Vascular Risk Factors." *Cerebral Cortex* 18(3): 718–726. **URL:** *https://doi.org/10.1093/cercor/bhm108*

Re, Edward D. 1981. "Judicial Independence and Accountability: The Judicial Councils Reform and Judicial Conduct and Disability Act of 1980." *Northern Kentucky Law Review* 8(2): 221–258.

Rehnquist, William H. 1999. "From Webster to Word Processing: The Ascendance of the Appellate Brief." *Journal of Appellate Practice and Process* 1: 1–6.

Reuter-Lorenz, Patricia A., and Denise C. Park. 2010. "Human Neuroscience and the Aging Mind: A New Look at Old Problems." *Journal of Gerontology* 65B(4): 405–415.

Reuter-Lorenz, Patricia A., and Denise C. Park. 2014. "How Does It STAC Up? Revisiting the Scaffolding Theory of Aging and Cognitiion." *Neuropsychological Review* 24: 355–370.

Romans, Neil T. 1974. "The Role of State Supreme Courts in Judicical Policy Making: Escobedo, Miranda and the Use of Judicial Impact Analysis." *Western Political Quarterly* 27(1): 38–59.

Rosenthal, Jeffrey S., and Albert H. Yoon. 2011*a*. "Detecting Multiple Authorship of United States Supreme Court Legal Decisions Using Function Words." *Annals of Applied Statistics* 5(1): 283–308.

Rosenthal, Jeffrey S., and Albert H. Yoon. 2011*b*. "Judicial Ghostwriting: Authorship on the Supreme Court." *Cornell Law Review* 96(6): 1307–1344.
Rubin, Alvin B. 1976. "Views from the Lower Court." *UCLA Law Review* 23: 448–464.
Ryan, Joseph J., Jerome M. Sattler, and Shane L. Lopez. 2000. "Age Effects on Wechsler Adult Intelligence Scale-III Subtests." *Archives of Clinical Neuropsychology* 15(4): 311–317.
Salthouse, Timothy A. 1991. *Theoretical Perspectives on Cognitve Aging*. Erlbaum.
Salthouse, Timothy A. 1996. "The Processing-Speed Theory of Adult Age Differences in Cognitiion." *Psychological Review* 103: 403–428.
Salthouse, Timothy A. 2004. "What and When of Cognitive Aging." *Current Directions in Psychological Science* 13(4): 140–144.
Salthouse, Timothy A. 2010*a*. *Major Issues in Cognitive Aging*. Oxford University Press.
Salthouse, Timothy A. 2010*b*. "Selective Review of Cognitive Aging." *Journal of the International Neuropsychological Society* 16(5): 754–760.
Salthouse, Timothy A., Debora R. Mitchell, Eric Skovronek, and Renee L. Babcock. 1989. "Effects of Adult Age and Working Memory on Reasoning and Spatial Abilities." *Journal of Experimental Psychology: Learning, Memory, and Cognition* 15(3): 507–516.
Samaha, Adam M., Michael Heise, and Gregory C. Sisk. 2020. "Inputs and Outputs on Appeal: An Empirical Study of Briefs, Big Law, and Case Complexity." *Journal of Empirical Legal Studies* 17(3): 519–555.
Samson, Rachel D., and Carol A. Barnes. 2013. "Impact of Aging Brain Circuits on Cognition." *European Journal of Neuroscience* 37(12): 1903–1915.
Scalia, Antonin, and Bryan A. Garner. 2008. *Making Your Case: The Art of Persuading Judges*. Thomson.
Schaie, Klaus Warner. 1989. "Perceptual Speed in Adulthood: Cross-sectional and Longitudinal Analyses." *Psychology and Aging* 4: 443–453.
Schaie, Klaus Warner. 1994. "The Course of Adult Intellectual Development." *American Psychologist* 49(4): 304–313.
Schaie, Klaus Warner. 2005. *Developmental Influences on Adult Intelligence: The Seattle Longitudinal Study*. Oxford University Press.
Schanzenbach, Max, and Emerson H. Tiller. 2006. "Strategic Judging under the U.S. Sentencing Guidelines: Positive Political Theory and Evidence." *Journal of Law, Economics, and Organization* 23(1): 24–56.
Scheibe, Susanne, and Laura L. Carstensen. 2010. "Emotional Aging: Recent Findings and Future Trends." *Journals of Gerontology Series B: Psychological Sciences and Social Sciences* 65B(2): 135–144.
Scheufele, Dietram A., and Bruce V. Lewenstein. 2005. "The Public and Nanotechnology: How Citizens Make Sense of Emerging Technologies." *Journal of Nanoparticle Research* 7: 659–667.
Schmitz, T. W., F. H. Cheng, and E. De Rosa. 2010. "Failing to Ignore: Paradoxical Neural Effects of Perceptual Load on Early Attentional Selection in Normal Aging." *Journal of Neuroscience* 30(44): 14750–14758.
Scigliano, Robert. 1971. *The Supreme Court and the Presidency*. Free Press.
Serioussi, Yanir, Russell Smyth, and Ingrid Zukerman. 2011. "Ghosts from the High Court's Past: Evidence from Computational Linguistics for Dixon Ghosting for McTiernan and Rich." *UNSWLJ* 34:984.
Shafto, Meredith A., and Lorraine K. Tyler. 2014. "Language in the Aging Brain: The Network Dynamics of Cognitive Decline and Preservation." *Science* 346(6209): 583–587.
Shapiro, Fred R. 2021. "The Most-Cited Legal Scholars Revisited." *University of Chicago Law Review* 88(7): 1595–1618.
Shesol, Jeff. 2010. *Supreme Court: Franklin Roosevelt v. the Supreme Court*. W. W. Norton & Company.
Sisk, Gregory C., and Michael Heise. 2015. "'Too Many Notes'?': An Empirical Study of Advocacy in Federal Appeals." *Journal of Empirical Legal Studies* 12(3): 578–600.
Smelcer, Susan Navarro, Amy Steigerwalt, and Richard L. Vining. 2013. "Bias and the Bar: Evaluating the ABA Ratings of Federal Judicial Nominees." *Political Research Quarterly* 66(4): 827–840.
Smith, George Rose. 1973. "A Primer of Opinion Writing for Law Clerks." *Vanderbilt Law Review* 26: 1203–1210.

Smith, Joseph H. 1976. "An Independent Judiciary: The Colonial Background." *University of Pennsylvania Law Review* 124: 1104–1156.

Smith, Joseph L., and Emerson H. Tiller. 2002. "The Strategy of Judging: Evidence from Administrative Law." *The Journal of Legal Studies* 31(1): 61–82.

Solomon, Paul R., and MaryEllen Groccia-Ellison. 1996. "Classic Conditioning in Aged Rabbits: Delay, Trace, and Long-Delay Conditioning." *Behavioral Neuroscience* 110(3): 427–435.

Songer, Donald R. 1987. "The Impact of the Supreme Court on Trends in Economic Policy Making in the United States Courts of Appeals." *Journal of Politics* 49(3): 830–841.

Songer, Donald R. 1988. "Case Selection in Judicial Impact Research." *Western Political Quarterly* 41(3): 569–582.

Songer, Donald R., Jeffrey A. Segal, and Charles M. Cameron. 1994. "The Hierarchy of Justice: Testing a Principal-Agent Model of Supreme Court-Circuit Court Interactions." *American Journal of Political Science* 38(3): 673–696.

Songer, Donald R., and Reginald S. Sheehan. 1990. "Supreme Court Impact on Compliance and Outcomes: Miranda and New York Times in the United States Courts of Appeals." *Western Political Quarterly* 43(2): 297–316.

Songer, Donald R., Reginald S. Sheehan, and Susan B. Haire. 2000. *Continuity and Change on the United States Courts of Appeals.* University of Michigan Press.

Songer, Donald R., and Susan Haire. 1992. "Integrating Alternative Approaches to the Study of Judicial Voting: Obscenity Cases in the U.S. Courts of Appeals." *American Journal of Political Science* 36(4): 963–982.

Spriggs, II, James F. 1996. "The Supreme Court and Federal Administrative Agencies: A Resource-Based Theory and Analysis of Judicial Impact." *American Journal of Political Science* 40(4): 1122–1151.

Spriggs, II, James F., and Paul J. Wahlbeck. 1995. "Calling It Quits: Strategic Retirement on the Federal Courts of Appeals." *Political Research Quarterly* 48(3): 573–597.

Spriggs, II, James F., and Paul J. Wahlbeck. 1997. "Amicus Curiae and the Role of Information at the Supreme Court." *Political Research Quarterly* 50(2): 365–386.

Spriggs, II, James F., and Thomas G. Hansford. 2000. "Measuring Legal Change: The Reliability and Validity of Shepard's Citations." *Political Research Quarterly* 53(2): 327–341.

Stark, Shuana M., and Craig E. L. Stark. 2017. *Cognitive Neuroscience of Aging: Linking Cognitive and Cerebral Aging.* Oxford University Press.

Staton, Jeffrey K., and Georg Vanberg. 2008. "The Value of Vagueness, Delegation, Defiance, and Judicial Opinions." *American Journal of Political Science* 52(3): 504–519.

Staudt, Nancy C. 2004. "Agenda Setting in Supreme Court Tax Cases: Lessons from the Blackmun Papers." *Buffalo Law Review* 52(3): 889–922.

Stidham, Ronald, and Robert A. Carp. 1982. "Trial Courts' Responses to Supreme Court Policy Changes: Three Case Studies." *Law and Policy* 4(2): 215–234.

Story, Joseph. 1873. *Commentaries on the Constitution of the United States: With a Preliminary Review of the Constitutional History of the Colonies and States before the Adoption of the Constitution.* 4th ed. Little, Brown, and Company.

Sulfaro, Valerie A. 1996. "The Role of Ideology and Political Sophistication in the Structure of Foreign Policy Attitudes." *American Politics Quarterly* 24(3): 303–337.

Sunstein, Cass R., David Schadke, Lisa Michelle Ellman, and Andres Sawicki. 2006. *Are Judges Political? An Empirical Analysis of the Federal Judiciary.* Brookings.

Szmer, John, Robert K. Christensen, and Samuel Grubbs. 2020. "What Influences the Influence of U.S. Courts of Appeals Decisions?" *European Journal of Law and Economics* 49(1): 55–81.

Taranto, James, and David B. Rivkin. 2023. "Justice Samuel Alito: 'This Made Us Targets of Assassination.' " *Wall Street Journal.*

Tarr, George Alan. 1977. *Judicial Impact and State Supreme Courts.* Lexington Books.

Tassel, Emily Field Van. 1993. "Resignations and Removals: A History of Federal Judicial Service—and Disservice—1789–1992." *University of Pennsylvania Law Review* 142: 333.

Teitelbaum, Joshua C. 2006. "Age and Tenure of the Justices and Productivity of the U.S. Supreme Court: Are Term Limits Necessary?" *Florida State University Law Review* 34: 161–182.

Tetlock, Philip E., Jane Bernzweig, and Jack L. Gallant. 1985. "Supreme Court Decision Making: Cognitive Style as a Predictor of Ideological Consistency of Voting." *Journal of Personality and Social Psychology* 48: 1227–1239.

Thaler, Richard H., and Cass R. Sunstein. 2009. *Nudge: Improving Decisions about Health, Wealth, and Happiness.* Penguin Books.

Time. 1956. "The Supreme Court: An Echo Fades." **URL:** *https://content.time.com/time/subscriber/article/0,33009,893533,00.html*

Turley, Jonathan. 2022. "Arrest outside Justice Kavanaugh's Home Is Shocking. But, Sadly, Not Surprising." *USA.* June 9, 2022.

Turner, Gary R., and R. Nathan Spreng. 2011. "Executive Functions and Neurocognitive Aging: Dissociable Patterns of Brain Activity." *Neurobiology of Aging* 33:826.e.1–826.e.13.

Tversky, Amos, and Daniel Kahneman. 1974. "Judging under Uncertainty: Heuristics and Biases." *Science* 185(4157): 1124–1131.

Tyler, Lorraine K., Meredith A. Shafto, Billi Randall, Paul Wright, William D. Marslen-Wilson, and Emmanuel A. Stamatakis. 2010. "Preserving Syntactic Processing across the Adult Life Span: The Modulation of the Frontotemporal Language System in the Context of Age-Related Atrophy." *Cerebral Cortex* 20(2): 352–364.

Tyler, Tom R. 2021. *Why People Obey the Law.* Princeton University Press.

Tyler, Tom R., and Kenneth Rasinski. 1991. "Procedural Justice, Institutional Legitimacy, and the Acceptance of Unpopular US Supreme Court Decisions: A Reply to Gibson." *Law and Society review* 25(3): 621–630.

Van Asselen, M., and K. R. Ridderinkhof. 2000. "Shift costs of predictable and unexpected set shiftingin young and older adults." *Psychologica Belgica* 40: 259–273.

Verhaeghen, Paul. 2013. *The Elements of Cognitive Aging : Meta-Analyses of Age-Related Differences in Processing Speed and Their Consequences.* Oxford University Press.

Vickrey, William C., Douglas G. Denton, and Wallace B. Jefferson. 2012. "Opinions as the Voice of the Court: How State Supreme Courts Can Communicate Effectively and Promote Procedural Fairness." *Court Review: The Journal of the American Judges Association* 48(3): 74–85.

Wahlbeck, Paul J. 1998. "The Development of a Legal Rule: The Federal Common Law of Public Nuisance." *Law & Society Review* 32(3): 613–637.

Wahlbeck, Paul J., James F. Spriggs, II, and Lee Sigelman. 2002. "Ghostwriters on the Court? A Stylistic Analysis of U.S. Supreme Court Draft Opinions." *American Politics Research* 30(2): 166–192.

Wald, Patricia M. 1985. "Thoughts on Decision Making." *West Virginia Law Review* 87: 1–12.

Wald, Patricia M. 1992. "Some Real-Life Observations about Judging." *Indiana Law Review* 26(1): 173–186.

Ward, Artemus, and David L. Weiden. 2006. *Sorcerers' Apprentices: 100 Years of Law Clerks at the United States Supreme Court.* New York University Press.

Wasby, Stephan. 1993. *The Supreme Court in the Federal System.* Nelson-Hall Publishers.

Wasby, Stephen L. 2003. "Work of a Circuit's Chief Judge." *Justice System Journal* 24(1): 63–90.

Wecker, Nancy S., Joel H. Kramer, Bradley J. Hallam, and Dean C. Delis. 2005. "Mental Flexibility: Age Effects on Switching." *Neuropsychology* 19(3): 345–352.

Wedeking, Justin P. 2010. "Supreme Court Litigants and Strategic Framing." *American Journal of Political Science* 54(3): 617–631.

Weinberg, Richard A. 1989. "Intelligence and IQ: Landmark Issues and Great Debates." *American Psychologist* 44(2): 98–104.

Westerland, Chad, Jeffrey A. Segal, Lee Epstein, Charles Cameron, and Scott Comparato. 2010. "Strategic Defiance and Compliance in the U.S. Courts of Appeals." *American Journal of Political Science* 54(4): 891–905.

White, Ronald C. 2010. *A. Lincoln.* Random House.

Whiteman, Andrew S., Daniel E. Young, Andrew E. Budson, Chantal E. Stern, and Karin Schon. 2016. "Entorhinal volume, aerobic fitness, and recognition memory in healthy young adults: A voxel-based morphometry study." *NeuroImage* 126:229–238. **URL:** *https://www.sciencedirect.com/science/article/pii/S105381191501071X*

Whittington, Keith. 1999. *Constitutional Construction: Divided Powers and Constitutional Meaning*. Harvard University Press.
Williams, Richard. 2006. "Generalized Ordered Logit-Partial Proportional Odds Models for Ordinal Dependent Variables." *Stata Journal* 6: 58–82.
Wilson, Robert S., D. A. Bennett, J. L. Bienias, C. F. Mendes de Leon, M. C. Morris, and D. A. Evans. 2003. "Activity and Cognitive Decline in a Biracial Community Population." *Neurology* 61(6): 812–816.
Wingfield, Arthur. 2000. *Cognitive Aging: A Primer*. Psychology Press.
Wingfield, Arthur, and Murray Grossman. 2006. "Language and the Aging Brain: Patterns of Neural Compensation Revealed by Functional Brain Imaging." *Journal of Neurophysiology* 96(6): 2830–2839.
Wohlfarth, Patrick C. 2009. "The Tenth Justice? Consequences of Politicization in the Solicitor General's Office." *Journal of Politics* 70(1): 224–237.
Wright, Eugene A. 1973. "Observations of an Appellate Judge: The Use of Law Clerks." *Vanderbilt Law Review* 26: 1179–1196.
Yaffe, Kristine, Deborah Barnes, Michael Nevitt, Li-Yung Lui, and Kenneth Covinsky. 2001. "A Prospective Study of Physical Activity and Cognitive Decline in Elderly Women: Women Who Walk." *Archives of Internal Medicine* 161(14): 1703–1708.
Yoon, Albert. 2005. "Senior Federal Judges and the Political Economy of Judicial Tenure." *Journal of Empirical Legal Studies* 2(3): 495–549.
Yoon, Albert. 2006. "Pension, Politics, and Judicial Tenure: An Empirical Study of Federal Judges, 1869–2002." *American Law and Economics Review* 8(1): 143–180.
Zilis, Michael A. 2018. "Minority Groups and Judicial Legitimacy: Group Affect and the Incentives for Judicial Responsiveness." *Political Research Quarterly* 71(2): 270–283.
Zink, James R., James F. Spriggs, II, and John T. Scott. 2009. "Courting the Public: The Influence of Decision Attributes on Individuals' Views of Court Opinions." *Journal of Politics* 71(3): 909–925.

Index

www.ingramcontent.com/pod-product-compliance
Lightning Source LLC
Chambersburg PA
CBHW052152020126
37647CB00001B/74
* 9 7 8 0 1 9 7 7 4 7 0 2 5 *